Autism and Creativity

Michael Fitzgerald presents his stimulating study of male creativity and autism (autism being far more common in males than females), arguing that a major genetic endowment is a prerequisite of genius, and that cultural and environmental factors are less significant than has often been claimed. He illuminates his argument with studies of historical figures who showed enormous capacity for creative activity, yet had immature personalities and deficits in empathy and social interaction skills.

Chapters on the diagnosis and psychology of autism set the scene for a detailed examination of a number of important historical figures. In the Indian mathematician, Ramanujan, the classic traits of Asperger's syndrome are shown to have coexisted with an extraordinary level of creativity. More unexpectedly, from the fields of philosophy, politics and literature, scrutiny of Ludwig Wittgenstein, Sir Keith Joseph, Eamon de Valera, Lewis Carroll and William Butler Yeats reveals classic autistic features.

Autism and Creativity broadens our understanding of high-functioning autism/Asperger's syndrome, and considerably widens the diagnoses. It will prove fascinating reading, not only for professionals and students in the field of autism and Asperger's syndrome, but for anyone wanting to know how individuals presenting autistic features have on many occasions changed the way we understand society.

Michael Fitzgerald is the Henry Marsh Professor of Child and Adolescent Psychiatry, Trinity College Dublin, and Clinical and Research Consultant to the Irish Society for Autism. He is a fellow of the Royal College of Psychiatrists, a member of the Royal College of Surgeons in England, and an associate member of the British Psychoanalytical Society.

Autism and Creativity

Is there a link between autism in men and exceptional ability?

Michael Fitzgerald

Brunner-Routledge
Taylor & Francis Group

HOVE AND NEW YORK

First published 2004
by Brunner-Routledge
27 Church Road, Hove, East Sussex BN3 2FA

Simultaneously published in the USA and Canada
by Brunner-Routledge
29 West 35th Street, New York NY 10001

Reprinted 2004

Brunner-Routledge is an imprint of the Taylor & Francis Group

Copyright © 2004 Michael Fitzgerald

Typeset in Times by Mayhew Typesetting, Rhayader, Powys
Printed and bound in Great Britain by MPG Books Ltd, Bodmin,
Cornwall
Cover design by Amanda Barragry

This publication has been produced with paper manufactured to strict
environmental standards and with pulp derived from sustainable
forests.

British Library Cataloguing in Publication Data
A catalogue record for this book is available from the British Library

Library of Congress Cataloging-in-Publication Data
Fitzgerald, Michael, Dr.
   Autism and creativity : is there a link between autism in men and
exceptional ability? / Michael Fitzgerald.
        p. ; cm.
Includes bibliographical references.
   ISBN 1-58391-213-4 (hbk.)
   1. Autism. 2. Creative ability. 3. Genius and mental illness. 4.
Savant syndrome.
   [DNLM: 1. Asperger's Syndrome—psychology. 2. Autistic
Disorder—psychology. 3. Creativeness. 4. Famous Persons. WM 203.5
F554a 2004] I. Title.

   RC553.A88F55 2004
   616.89'82—dc21

                                              2003011509

ISBN 1-58391-213-4 (hbk)

Contents

Tables

Acknowledgements

I would like to thank Ms Antoinette Walker for her editorial work on the manuscript. Mr Brendan O'Brien carried out editorial work in relation to diagnostic issues and psychology of autism and proofread the manuscript. Ms Ellen Cranley was extremely patient and helpful (as always) in typing repeated drafts. Professor David Berman conducted discussions with the author for the past 12 years on Wittgenstein and read a final draft of the Wittgenstein chapter. Dr Jean Quigley read the chapter on Psychology of Autism and the Wittgenstein chapter. Dr John Hayes read the chapter on Wittgenstein. Dr Viktoria Lyons read the entire book in its final stages. I am grateful to Mr Pat Matthews, President of the World Autism Association, the Irish Society for Autism, and many parents of children with autism who have educated me for the past 30 years. The librarians at Trinity College Dublin, Ms Virginia McLoughlin and Ms Thelma Pope, were unfailingly helpful. I have also been helped by Carol Creaven of the Library of the Royal College of Surgeons in Ireland as well as Beatrice Doran and her staff. I would also like to thank Dr Paul McCarthy who has given me major support throughout my career, Ms Frances Brennan and staff at the Ballyfermot Child and Family Centre, and Mr Michael Walsh of the Northern Area Health Board. At Brunner-Routledge I would like to thank Ms Kate Hawes for commissioning the book; Ms Joanne Forshaw, editor and Ms Helen Pritt. I have had helpful discussions with Professor Michael Gill, Dr Louise Gallagher, Dr Aiveen Kirley, Ms V. Foley and Dr Aiden Corvin at Trinity College Dublin. I would like to thank my wife Frances and three sons Owen, Mark and Robert for their support during the writing of this book and for giving me the time to write it.

Chapter 1

Introduction

Genius, creativity and talent

From time immemorial humankind has searched for the roots of creativity. In antiquity those with creative powers were usually revered and deified. Certainly the most basic tasks we take for granted today, such as lighting a fire or using a wheel, were wondrous discoveries at the time. Rossman has noted how the ancients thoroughly understood the great importance of inventions and discoveries, honouring their inventors by making them gods: 'the Egyptian God Osiris taught the art of farming and the use of the plough. Prometheus, according to Greek mythology, taught the use of fire.'[1]

Over the centuries the paradigm of genius altered, shifting from one associated with place or person to one of inherent ability, according to R.C. Atkinson. He claims that in antiquity, the 'Romans spoke of the genius of a person or *place*. But by the sixteenth century this idea had been metaphorically extended to describe the innate capacity of a person.'[2] None the less, the mystery associated with genius endured. Atkinson notes that the phenomenon of genius has provoked thinkers for many centuries, most likely because it presents itself as 'inexplicable'.

Throughout history there have been many attempts to account for the phenomenon of genius, with various cultures putting forward differing explanations. Roy Porter has observed that 'Graeco-Roman antiquity had at least three major doctrines competing for attention, the "divine fire" or "God's touch" idea, the notion that creativity was the product of the melancholy humour, and of course the Muses'.[3]

The etymology of genius points to the innate or spiritual dimension of the individual. According to the *Oxford Companion to the Mind*, the word 'genius' itself comes from the Latin word *genius*, i.e. the male spirit of a household existing, during his lifetime, in the head of the family and subsequently in the divine or spiritual part of each individual.[4] In discussing genius Howe acknowledges its roots in the Latin word *genius* which, he says, 'stems from *gens*, meaning family but also from the Latin *ingenium*, denoting natural disposition or innate ability'.[5] Clearly the notion of inherent power linked to individual achievement is one that persists over time. Indeed, Mark Twain knew about innate differences when he declared that 'individual differences are what make horse races'.[6] The durability of genius is also linked with the individual. Howe points out that for Immanuel Kant, genius was an 'incommunicable gift that cannot be taught or handed on, but is mysteriously imparted to certain artists by nature, and dies with the person'.[7] This is certainly true. Similarly, the *Oxford English Dictionary* defines genius as:

> native intellectual power of an exalted type, such as is attributed to those who are esteemed greatest in any department of art, speculation or practice; instinctive and extraordinary capacity for imaginative creation, original thought, inventions, or discovery. Often contrasted with talent.[8]

Therefore in assuming that genius is innate, it is consequently implied that it cannot be acquired. On this point *Webster's New World Dictionary* states that 'talent implies an apparently native ability for a specific pursuit and connotes either that it is or that it can be cultivated by the one possessing it'.

Undoubtedly, the capacity for higher order thinking is one that distinguishes the person with genius. In his understanding of genius, Ezra Pound noted that it 'is the capacity to see ten things where the ordinary man sees one, and where the man of talent sees two or three, plus the ability to register multiple perception in the material of his art'.[9] This ability to 'see' things and effect change is ground breaking and therein lies the kernel of creativity and invention. Clearly, the creative acts of genius must be original, novel and bring about change in our understanding of a subject.

Negative connotations of genius have persisted also. Certainly, the notion of the individual rebelling against received wisdom with arrogance and narcissism has gathered currency. In this respect, Bernard Berenson's definition of genius as 'the capacity for productive reaction against one's training' is germane.[10] Arguably, the advent of change that creativity inevitably produces is not always welcomed by society, often making the genius unpopular. Indeed, Samuel Butler believed genius was 'immoral' because it disturbed the world.[11] Similarly, Jonathan Swift tells us how to recognise a true genius: 'you may know him by this sign, that the dunces are all in confederacy against him'.[12]

Creativity and autism

Many features of high-functioning autism/Asperger's syndrome (HFA/ASP) enhance creativity.[13] Certainly, the ability to focus intensely on a topic and to take endless pains to produce a creative work is a characteristic feature of this syndrome. People with HFA/ASP have an extraordinary capacity to focus on a topic for very long periods (days on end – without interruption even for meals. They do not give up when obstacles to their creativity are encountered. For this reason they can be termed workaholics and show a remarkable capacity for persistence. As inventors, they have high levels of energy and motivation, and tremendous capacities for observation. Many, such as Einstein, show an extraordinary capacity for visual imagination. Consequently, there are many inventors in the areas of engineering and mathematics with HFA/ASP. An enormous capacity for curiosity and a compulsion to understand and make sense of the world are evident too. People with HFA/ASP do not accept current scientific or other views of the world, often rejecting received wisdom and experts in their domains. In this respect they often come across as being childlike and having immature personalities.

Autism and Asperger's syndrome

Ever since the term 'autism' entered the public mind, its perception has not been linked with genius and creativity. Rather, in the minds of many people, autism is associated with a very significant learning disability, and with intelligence levels significantly below the average range. Some of these people, particularly those called autistic savants, can have special abilities, for example they are well known as calculating prodigies.

A genius is a person with high ability, with or without autism, who produces work that changes our view of a subject. This book deals with people with HFA/ASP and genius. According to Grossman,[14] a savant is 'a person of low intelligence who possesses an unusually high skill in some mental task like mental arithmetic, remembering dates or numbers or in performing other rote tasks at a remarkably high level', and savants are found more frequently among people with autism than among the general population.

Gillberg[15] gives a definition of savant skills which is relevant to the people discussed in this book, and which is different from Beta Hermelin's definition of savantism in low-functioning autism. Gillberg states that the term savant skills 'is now used for special talents at a very high level of functioning, much above what would be expected on the basis of a person's IQ'. This might refer to some of the people discussed in this book, but probably not to all.

In terms of creativity, HFA/ASP is quite different from low-functioning autism. In making the distinction between HFA/ASP and low-functioning autism, it is critically important that people with low-functioning autism are not capable of the kind of creativity described in this book. This point is very well made by Beta Hermelin, who points out that 'another requirement for true creative ability, which is certainly missing in savants, is the search for new forms of expression that characterise the history of Western art'.[16] She goes on to point out that:

> of course, the mental impairments from which savants suffer set boundaries to the development of their talents. There are no savant geniuses about. None of them will discover a new mathematical theorem, or initiate a novel stylistic movement in the visual arts or in music. Neither will a savant pianist give a novel, revealing interpretation of a Beethoven piano sonata. Their mental limitations disallow and preclude an awareness of innovative developments in the areas of their special abilities.[17]

Clearly Hermelin is describing people with 'more disabling forms of autism'. These are certainly not the people I am discussing in this book, indeed, quite the opposite. A proportion of people with the more disabling forms of autism with learning disabilities can have special abilities in remembering dates or in mathematical calculations, but they are different from the people described in this book. Hermelin points out that:

> a savant is a rare phenomenon. Between two and three percent of the population suffer from some degree of mental handicap . . . only 0.06% of these had initially been estimated to possess an unusually high level of specific ability that is far above that of the average normal person . . . savant ability is much more frequently found in those who suffer from some form of autism. An early estimate was that in every 100 autistic individuals 10 showed some high-level specific skill. However, it is more realistically held that at most 1 or 2 in 200 of those within the Autism Spectrum Disorder can justifiably be regarded as having a genuine talent.[18]

The lack of any association between autism and creativity is apparent not only among the general public but also among academics. Oliver Sacks, in his study of perhaps one of the best-known people with autism, Temple Grandin, claimed that for many people autism represented 'a child mute, rocking, screaming, inaccessible, cut off from human contact'.[19] Moreover, he points out that many people with autism are 'so lacking in subjectivity and inwardness that major creativity is beyond them'.[20] However, Sacks does concede that the possibility of a creative capacity has been suggested by Christopher Gillberg, one of the finest clinical observers of autism. Gillberg feels that 'autistic people of the Asperger type, in contrast, may be capable of major creativity'.[21] This is precisely what I plan to demonstrate in this book.

The other image of autism in the public mind is from the Hollywood film *Rainman* (1988). Undoubtedly this film gives a better background understanding to the people described in this book with HFA/ASP. However, what it does not indicate is the enormous capacity for creativity shown by these people. The capacity to hold strong beliefs and feelings, often seen to be necessary to produce a work of creativity, is perceived to be lacking in those with autism. Certainly, clinical opinion has changed on this issue and now reflects a more complex theory of mind. On this point, Ami Klin and colleagues quote a person in a support group for people with autism, who rejects the notion that a theory of mind is absent in those with autism:

> you, the neurotypicals, believe that autistic people have no feelings, no beliefs, not even sexual thoughts. Who are the ones without a theory of mind? Because we don't talk as much about these things, you assume that your beliefs about us are true. Well, this is a false belief, if I am allowed to make a little pun, another thing I am not supposed to be able to do because I am autistic.[22]

The authors point out that these remarks reflect 'his ability to think about other people's beliefs and to make deliberately sarcastic and humorous statements'. Furthermore, they also note that no researcher:

> working within the framework of theory of mind holds the notion that individuals with autism have no beliefs or feelings: rather the current theory of mind hypothesis of autism suggests that the ability to think about thinking, to have beliefs about other people's beliefs, etc. is greatly reduced, delayed, or inflexible, may be reflecting an unusual or atypical developmental acquisition of these skills.[23]

This is precisely what this book is attempting to illustrate. Moreover, it highlights this statement in a very profound way. People with HFA/ASP have beliefs, feelings and certainly show a capacity for thinking but these skills are often delayed in development. It is not an all-or-none situation. To suggest that theory of mind is absent in HFA/ASP is simplistic. Rather, the notion that varying problems in the theory of mind area exist is closer to what one will find in the people with HFA/ASP discussed in this book.

Autistic intelligence

This book is very much about 'autistic intelligence'. Hans Asperger wrote about 'autistic intelligence' and saw it as a sort of intelligence hardly touched by tradition and culture – 'unconventional, unorthodox, strangely "pure" and original, akin to the intelligence of true creativity'.[24] Such pure intelligence can be found in the descriptions of many of the people studied in this book. Certainly, Bertrand Russell used the word to describe Ludwig Wittgenstein's philosophical ability. None the less, autistic intelligence is unconventional and unorthodox. Indeed, Temple Grandin has stated that 'it is likely that genius is an abnormality'.[25] However, Grandin believes that autistic intelligence is necessary in order to add diversity and creativity in the world: 'It is possible that persons with bits of these traits are more creative, are possibly even geniuses . . . If science eliminated these genes, maybe the whole world would be taken over by accountants.'[26] In recent years tests conducted on people with autism reveal autistic intelligence to be linguistic, spatial, musical and logical in character. Moreover, these individuals are fascinated by abstraction and logic.[27]

Grandin also describes another feature that is typically found in geniuses with autism, namely, a desire for immortality:

> I have read that libraries are where immortality lies . . . I don't want my thoughts to die with me . . . I want to have done something . . . I am not interested in power, or piles of money. I want to leave something behind. I want to make a positive contribution – know that my life has meaning. Right now, I am talking about things that are at the very core of my existence.[28]

The notion of immortality and the belief that their work is of the highest possible significance has helped many geniuses with HFA/ASP to maintain their course, often in turbulent times.

Gregory has studied the nature of originality and highlighted the fact that geniuses have often made poor students:

> [I]t has been found, time and again, that those who display great originality as adults were often like Charles Darwin only mediocre as students. British scientists who became Fellows of the Royal Society show roughly the same distribution of good, mediocre, and poor degree results as to those who go into research but achieve little. The same holds for intelligence-test scores: above a surprisingly low level, there is little or no relationship between IQ and achievement in any sphere of adult endeavour yet studied. As a result, we would expect future Nobel Prize winners to show roughly the same distribution of IQ scores as their fellow students at university. In the American context, the budding scientist of high renown seems typically to be a B+ student: one who works hard when a topic captures his (or her) imagination, but otherwise does the bare minimum. Science springs to life for such individuals when they discover that instead of assimilating knowledge created by others, they can create knowledge for themselves – and are hooked from that moment onwards.[29]

Gregory also notes how mathematicians stress the process of incubation where the 'solution comes to them quite unexpectedly, in a flash' after having struggled with the problem. Usually the switch from a phase of intense concentration to one where there is no conscious control makes the brain more efficient. The tension helps to explain a remark once attributed to Einstein. He suggested that the creative scientists were the ones with 'access to their dreams'. Liam Hudson analyses how dreams can aid the creative process:

> Occasionally, a dream will actually provide the solution to a problem – as in the case of the chemist August Kekulé and his dream of the snake swallowing its own tail, the clue to the nature of the benzene ring. The implication of Einstein's remark is that, in order to innovate, the scientist, like anyone else, must break the grip on his imagination that our powers of logical-seeming storytelling impose. We must be willing to subvert the conventional wisdom on which our everyday competence lies. It is here that the research done by the advocates of creativity in the 1960s now seems most relevant. Rather than straining to see whether tests of creativity can be devised, to stand side by side with IQ tests, we can concentrate on an issue that Francis Galton identified over a century ago: the extent to which each individual can retrieve apparently irrational ideas, sift them, and put them to some constructive use. We know that individuals differ in their ability to free associate, to fantasize, and to recall their dreams. We also know that these differences have a bearing on the kinds of work people find it comfortable to do: among the intelligent, it is those who are relatively good at free associating (the divergers) who are attracted towards the arts, while those who are relatively weak in this (the convergers) are drawn towards science and technology.[30]

Certainly one could say that those with HFA/ASP are largely convergers. However, throughout history from antiquity to modern times, famous individuals have demonstrated features of HFA/ASP in widely varied disciplines.[31] Specific groups that are discussed in this book are politicians, writers, philosophers, mathematicians and scientists.

Autism, eccentricity and creativity

This book demonstrates the close relationship between HFA/ASP and eccentricity. However, the public perception of eccentricity is such that it has frequently been linked to either madness or deviancy. Weekes and Ward quote one eccentric who coins a new Beatitude alluding to the powers of those considered mad 'Blessed are the cracked, for they shall let in the light'.[32] Another work with an unfortunate title, *The Deviants' Advantage*, conveys the same idea.[33] Nevertheless, 'letting in the light' can be interpreted as the actual achievement of geniuses. Through the creative acts of genius, work can be produced that is original, novel and indeed a rejection of inherited wisdoms in favour of new knowledge. In short, acts of pure enlightenment can occur.

Weekes and Ward also quote John Stuart Mill's essay 'On Liberty', where it is implied that the role of the eccentric is essential for the benefit and furtherance of society: 'the development of society and eccentricity are interdependent . . . the wayward individual has an integral part to play in the shaping of society'.[34] Again, the notion of the genius bringing benefits to society is central to the people with HFA/ASP discussed in this book, whether it comes in the shape of technological, mathematical, philosophical, musical, or political advancement. Certainly, the link between HFA/ASP, eccentricity and creativity ought not to be underestimated in society. In this respect, the study of eccentricity and creativity needs a wider platform, as Weekes and Ward suggest:

> If eccentricity is positively associated with the ability to conceive startlingly original, artistic and technological breakthroughs, it behoves psychologists to attempt to understand the factors that may stimulate and inhibit not only the lateral thinking itself, but also the conditions in which it may freely flourish.[35]

In the rush to standardise and homogenise human behaviour by imposing rigorous scientific methods, psychology has failed to take account of behaviour that is not amenable to scientific scrutiny, or what is outside its paradigms and models. The authors point out that psychology has turned its back on the 'excitement of guesswork', on the 'intellectual search process', and the 'wonderment of speculation', which is essential to the scientific activity of people in the everyday world:

> although human psychologists, in the age of standardisation and homogenisation, may react suspiciously or adversely to overly peculiar ideas and idiosyncratic people, they should also recognise the rebellious fun in those who march to a different drummer.[36]

Moreover, the authors argue that human evolution needs 'human eccentricity' too. There is little doubt that the individuals in this book have marched to 'a different drummer', mostly to enormous positive effect. Furthermore, it is true to say that psychologists have neglected this particular type of creativity.

Genes and genius

It is generally accepted that high-ability parents may pass on high abilities genetically and create enriched environments simply because they themselves have high ability. However, the issue of the genetic transmission of talent and creativity is a complex one, though it can generally be said that all forms of creativity have some biological basis. The brain basis of creativity or giftedness has been explored by Gardner in *Extraordinary Minds*:

> Some traits that do not run in families may still be genetically trans-mitted according to a principle called emergenesis by which traits are passed on by package of genes, but only if the entire package is transmitted. Part of the package does not result in part of the trait. The claim runs counter to standard models of behavioural genetics, accord-ing to which genetic traits must by definition run in families. According to the standard model, the concordance rate in non-identical pairs should be half that of identical pairs. However, some traits do not fit this model.[37]

Gardner claims that the question in evolutionary psychology is no longer whether genetic or environmental factors determine behaviour, but 'how they interact'. He believes it extremely unlikely that there is such as thing as a 'poetry gene or a music gene' since complex human behaviours typically have a 'polygenic basis'. Without doubt, HFA/ASP has a polygenic basis. Genetic factors are likely to contribute not only to specific abilities, but also to traits such as persistence, the capacity for concentration for extended periods, and curiosity about certain types of stimulation. These properties may, in turn, affect the individual's response to educational stimulation and tuition. The result is a complex interplay between inherited traits and environmental factors, in which genetics may underpin exposure to nur-turing social and physical appearance.

The view that geniuses began their lives made from the same basic material as the rest of us, as propounded by Howe,[38] is false. The major reason why they are geniuses is that they began with different basic materials to the rest of us. Indeed, the configuration of their genes was different from the rest of us. In effect, inborn capabilities are the key to understanding geniuses from Einstein to Mozart.

The behaviour of a person with HFA/ASP could be seen as being on a slightly different position on the evolutionary scale. In one way, it could be said that HFA/ASP is governed by pre-programmed patterns. People, therefore, respond poorly to environmental change because of these pre-programmed patterns and cannot easily adapt to changing circumstances. Perhaps the most compelling reason to adapt is one arising from man's 'discontent', according to Storr. Discontent may therefore be considered adaptive because it encourages the use of the imagination. Storr claims that man's extraordinary success as a species 'springs from his discontent, which compels him to employ his imagination'.[39] Hence the use of fantasy to bridge the gap between the inner world of the imagination and the external real world becomes possible. It is possible that Newton's autistic imagination was one of the factors that helped him discover the laws of gravity. Storr notes how Einstein's special theory of relativity 'depended upon his being able to imagine how the universe might appear to an observer travelling at near the speed of light'.[40]

The autistic imagination is biologically determined. According to the *Oxford Companion to the Mind*, Einstein emphasised the importance of the creative person having access to their dreams, which in Freudian terms would be primary process thinking. However, in order for the scientist to innovate, he must 'break the grip on his imagination that our powers of logical-seeming storytelling impose'.[41] Creative people with HFA/ASP are obsessed with fundamental, bedrock discoveries. They have no interest in being merely replicative. Hence they have little regard for their contemporaries and do not conform to the values of society. They have a peculiar ability to become lost in the present, in the here-and-now, which appears to be a *sine qua non* for creativity of an HFA/ASP kind. Indeed, the HFA/ASP might facilitate this disconnectedness from the world so that creativity of pure genius can take place.

The link between genius and mathematics, particularly on the frequency of mathematical geniuses, has been explored by Dehaene, who notes that evolution is a slow, gradual process. Our genes, he argues, are 'condemned to a slow and minute evolution', where they are dependent on chance mutations. It takes thousands of 'aborted attempts before a favourable mutation, one worthy of being passed on to coming generations, emerges from the noise', for example, in the case of Newton.[42] It is therefore not difficult to understand why, over time, geniuses such as Newton and Einstein[43] are thrown up only rarely.[44]

Dehaene also claims there is little evidence to suggest that great mathematicians and calculating prodigies have been endowed with 'an exceptional neurobiological structure'.[45] I disagree completely with this view, and indeed would hold precisely the opposite one. Dehaene argues that what is special about these mathematicians is their 'disproportionate and relentless passion for numbers and mathematics', which is often sustained by their 'inability to entertain normal relations with other fellow human beings'. However, I do agree with his explanation in respect of the mathematician discussed in this book, namely Ramanujan, except that I believe that autism is a developmental disorder rather than a disease. Dehaene refers to a 'cerebral disease called autism'.[46] I would call it HFA/ASP, a developmental disorder.

Genius and madness

Genius and madness is a topic with a lengthy history. Indeed, there has been almost equal interest in the relationship between genius and madness, and between genius and creativity. Arguably, much of this has stemmed from literary movements. It is with Romanticism, writes Porter, that the 'indissoluble link between madness and artistic genius comes into its own as an autobiographical experience'.[47]

However, from antiquity to modernity the image of the tormented genius has persisted. When asked why there is no tradition of happy genius in Western culture, Professor Klibansky replied with a rhetorical 'Could a happy man have written Hamlet?'[48] Moreover, Steptoe has noted how Plato emphasised the role of inspiration from the gods, where he argued that poetic composition occurs in a 'frenzy of divine madness'.[49] Similarly, Broad points out that both Plato and Aristotle suggested 'a relationship between artistic creation and madness'.[50] In Roman times, Seneca declared that 'no great genius has ever existed without some touch of madness'.[51] Shakespeare, too, stated that 'the lunatic, the lover, and the poet – Are of imagination all compact'. The metaphysical poet, Dryden, expressed similar views on the alignment of madness and greatness 'Great Wits are sure to Madness near ally'd – And thin Partitions do their Bounds divide'.[52]

Perhaps the man who first forged a theoretical link between genius and madness was the Italian psychiatrist and criminologist, Cesare Lombroso (1836 1909). He was rather fanatical on the subject and wrote numerous books that were translated and circulated widely. In *The Man of Genius*, which was first published in 1890, he declared that he had 'discovered genius', and with it the 'various characteristics of degeneration' that formed the basis of practically all forms of congenital mental abnormality.[53] In his work, he also provided descriptions of the perceived physical and social characteristics of geniuses. Geniuses were, he stated, 'short, emaciated, sterile, microcephalic, stupid, and ugly . . . lacking in tact, in moderation, in the sense of practical life, in the virtues useful in social affairs'.[54] Indeed, he was wrong in the physical characteristics but correct in terms of the social characteristics.

Moreover, the question that arises most in terms of genius and madness is whether or not madness is an inevitable consequence of genius. On this issue, Simonton asks whether psychopathology is the cost of greatness.[55] However, the notion of cost is relative. The cost to the individual may be great, but society benefits enormously from creative people even when greatness and psychopathology are evident.

As psychiatry developed from the late nineteenth century onwards, the prevalence of mental illness among geniuses received more scrutiny. Freud observed that an artist is 'an introvert, not far removed from neurosis'.[56] Havelock Ellis in 1904 found that only 4.2 per cent of geniuses had a mental disorder and concluded that it was rare.[57] Indeed, it may not be that the activity of genius drives them mad, but conversely that they continue their creative activities in order to remain sane. According to Gregory in the *Oxford Companion to the Mind*:

> It is necessary to reconsider the idea that genius and madness are closely allied. It is not true, of course, that great poets, painters, scientists, and mathematicians are mad; far from it. On the other hand, it may well be that they work as intensely and imaginatively as they do in order to remain sane; but they have access to aspects of the mind's functioning from which those who live more staid and conventional lives are excluded, and that it is this access which gives their work both its flair and its sense of risk.[58]

In fact, people with HFA/ASP are far more likely to become suicidally depressed when they experience mental blocks in creativity. In the past many people with autism/Asperger's syndrome would have been described incorrectly as having a mental illness.

The male brain

During the research of this book, it occurred to the author that what was emerging was a description of the 'male brain', albeit a narrow version of that. Certainly, Simonton has pointed out that in the annals of science 'fewer than 1% of all notables are female'.[59] Indeed, Hans Asperger noticed this previously in 1944 in his original description of autistic psychopathy (now called Asperger's syndrome), and S. Baron-Cohen and J. Hammer commented on it in 1997.[60] Furthermore, Baron-Cohen has described the gender differences in autistic psychopathy, with the existence of 'female superiority in folk psychology and male superiority in folk physics'.[61] The style of thinking called 'strength' in folk physics is generally the focus of this book.

This book also explores the relationship between one form of psychopathology of a developmental type – autism – and creativity. It is largely about male creativity, as autism is undeniably a far more common disorder in males than in females. The diagnosis of HFA/ASP is discussed in Chapter 2. High-functioning autism and Asperger's syndrome are pervasive developmental disorders and therefore different from mental disorders such as schizophrenia and manic-depressive psychosis. The differentiation between high-functioning autism and Asperger's syndrome has never been achieved scientifically, so I have retained the term HFA/ASP. The term, while cumbersome, does describe the scientific situation today. Indeed, Asperger's syndrome is often used as a synonym for high-functioning autism.

It is possible to speculate that humankind would still be at the stage of development before the wheel was invented had it not been for the type of creativity that people with HFA/ASP developed. There is no doubt that HFA/ASP can also occur in females, and therefore a similar type of creativity should be (and is) possible. Nevertheless, to date there is no female equivalent of Newton, or no female equivalent in the mathematical/physical science domain.

Psychohistory and biography

There is nothing new in the practice of writing about gifted people from a disease-state point of view. Indeed, the term 'pathography' was coined by the Leipzig neurologist, Paul Moebius, when writing about gifted people such as Goethe and Schumann. Moebius maintained that these accounts were extensive case histories that sought evidence to support 'disease states that might be related to their creative behaviour'.[62] Certainly this style is adopted here, except with the focus on HFA/ASP as a developmental disorder.

Without a doubt this book could be described as psychohistory, as it tries to explicate what Simonton calls the 'inner workings of some important incident or influential person'.[63] However, is the historico-clinical approach a legitimate enterprise? Is the correlation between genius and HFA/ASP illusory? The style of this book is in the tradition of major international academic figures in psychiatry/psychology who have written using this methodology and in this manner. The style was particularly influenced by the international autism researcher Uta Frith, and her book with Houston called *Autism in History*. Some of the most respected scientific researchers in the field of autism have used this approach: Sula Wolff in *Loners: the Life Path of Unusual Children*, and Christopher Gillberg and Mary Coleman, commenting on historical figures in *The Biological Basis of Autism*.[64]

Examining individuals, whether alive or dead, for signs of autism will always be relative to the information available. None the less, in assessing information on a historical person, Frith and Houston claim that it is possible to come to the conclusion that a person has autism or not 'by examining . . . evidence with the hindsight of current knowledge'.[65] They also point out that 'truth itself is contingent', resulting in biographical material being assessed relatively.

As a consequence of judgements being based on biographical details, the reliability of the biographies studied could be a matter of grave concern. It is probably true that no biography is 100 per cent accurate. Moreover, it can reflect the biases and prejudices of the biographer. Certainly the biographies used here are ones that had received favourable reviews in professional journals and recognised publications such as the *Times Literary Supplement*. After all, one must choose a reference point; indeed, if one took Henry Ford's view that all 'history is more or less bunk',[66] there could be no discussion and no case histories.

In practice one can only accept biographical facts that are generally accepted by professional historians and other related experts. Clearly, if a number of independent sources agree, this increases the reliability of the facts. Nevertheless, the difficulty of an accurate description of events in a person's life is well illustrated in *Wittgenstein's Poker* by Edmonds and Eidinow. In that work a conclusion was based on the balance of probabilities. The authors point out that 'it has been said that a good diagnostician relies as much on experience and intuition as on textbook knowledge'.[67] I agree with this view, having diagnosed in excess of 800 people with Autism Spectrum Disorder since 1973. Nevertheless, these people have to meet internationally accepted criteria, for example the *Diagnostic and Statistical Manual of Mental Disorders* (DSM-IV).[68] In this book the historical record is examined to see if the individuals discussed meet either the DSM-IV criteria for autism or Gillberg's criteria.[69] It certainly shows how this form of study can increase our understanding of HFA/ASP where the correlations are not, in the author's view, illusory.

A book of this nature can also help to show how autism can foster success in political leadership (for better or worse) and enhance creativity, particularly in the mathematical and scientific domains, as well as, surprisingly, in a very specific kind of literature, e.g. *Alice in Wonderland* by Lewis Carroll. Whether an accurate assessment of Hitler's psychopathy in the early 1930s would have made any difference to the voting behaviour of the German people is hard to say, given the complexity of the issue.

In endeavouring to show the relationship between genius and autism, the advice of Frith and Houston was heeded to present certain gifted individuals as having HFA/ASP. These authors note that it is worth exploring literary accounts of autism in autobiographical form as 'they show an inner world of sensations, perceptions and emotions unique to each author'.[70] Such accounts are useful and revealing, and purposefully demonstrated in this book. Another important factor is that these literary accounts were not written for the purpose for which they are now being used. The *ad hominem* argument does not apply here because the author does not attack the person of the writer, politician, etc. but attempts to increase our understanding of these individuals by explaining their psychopathology.

Many will argue that you cannot diagnose someone you have not met, regardless of how much data you possess. I disagree. Others unfamiliar with HFA/ASP will probably make an entirely different diagnosis, e.g. narcissistic personality disorder or borderline personality disorder. None the less, I believe the psychohistorical approach shows that the diagnoses are not fanciful or speculative. Readers should see the diagnostic studies carried out on various individuals in this book as hypotheses. This then gives them the opportunity to judge whether or not the hypothesis stands up to scrutiny.

A notable shortcoming in the psychohistorical approach is that the actions and work of the individual are made to fit the paradigm imposed by the psychiatrist. One might accuse a psychiatrist of writing a book such as this as a warning 'of what may happen when people are privileged by virtue of their psychiatric training and identification to decide what is sound and scientific': a point cogently made in the scientific journal *Nature* by E. Eloma.[71] However, this book does not question the validity of the works of genius discussed here in the light of psychiatry and psychology. Indeed, Sacks has warned of the inherent risks of this activity, where we may go to extremes in 'medicalising our predecessors, reducing their complexity to expressions of neurological or psychiatric disorder'.[72] I have been well aware of this problem in the book, but in clinical settings psychologists or psychiatrists are often helpful to people in understanding their cognitive deficits or assets. People are not labelled, but their cognitive profiles are labelled in a helpful way.

Similarly, Rakitzis in *Nature* asked the following relevant question 'Should scientific, philosophical and literary texts, as well as people, be subject to medical certification? Should we question the validity of the kinetic theory of matter because one of its originators, Ludwig Boltzmann, took his own life?'[73] The answer is, of course, no.

Biographies are generally written about those who achieve greatness in a particular field. The value of such work, however, is not recognised by all. Stephen Spender responded to Monk with the words that 'all biography is fiction'.[74] I tend to disagree with this view. If all biography were fiction, then the analysis of biography would be equally fictional. I certainly do not think this to be the case. I agree with Monk, however, when he states that the point of biography 'is to understand its subject . . . and you are trying to fit the whole into a comprehensive picture, looking for themes, images, ideas that provide a key to the whole'.[75] This is precisely what this book is striving to achieve, using the concept of HFA/ASP to increase our understanding of the people discussed and their work.

The value of biography as a record of facts, as a historical document, as an analysis of the subject comes into question. On this point Monk states that 'a biography does not explain anything – it describes'. Certainly, this reference to 'describing' rather than 'explaining' has resonance with Wittgenstein's own philosophical outlook, and is indeed something he could have said. However, I disagree that biography only describes. Biography does not offer ultimate explanations for a person's actions and behaviour (if such a thing exists – I don't believe so), but it can give the best explanation given the current state of knowledge. Undoubtedly, some of the explanations I have put forward in this book will be replaced by alternative ones in the years to come. This is the nature of knowledge advancement.

In disorders such as HFA/ASP, the everyday behaviour of the person provides clues to the diagnosis of the disorder. Hence biography, with its descriptions of how the person lived, is extremely useful. Indeed, the fascination for the finer details of people's lives is one of the main attractions of biographies, as Kuehn notes:

> I do not really know what makes biographies so fascinating to so many readers. Is it simply curiosity about how the 'famous' have lived? Is it voyeurism, an unsavoury desire to glimpse the dirty little secrets of the 'great'? Is it escapism, an attempt at vicarious living, a kind of romance for the more intellectually inclined?[76]

Indeed, it's all those and more. However, attempting to make sense of an individual's life frequently can prove challenging. How individuals achieve greatness can hinge on many, often inexplicable, factors – hence the fascination. Certainly those that show creative genius can be widely eccentric with puzzling personalities, which may prove difficult for the biographer. This point has been raised by Virginia Wolff and quoted by Kuehn. She declares that 'biographies are difficult, if not impossible to write, because people are all over the place'.[77] Describing such people as 'all over the place' is in fact shorthand for being enigmatic, which is certainly part of the creativity and eccentricity of HFA/ASP. In this book the diagnosis of HFA/ASP attempts to reduce this chaos.

According to Monk, Benjamin Disraeli considered the value of biography as presenting 'life without theory'.[78] Disraeli is wrong in his assumption here, because it is impossible to produce a biography without theory. It is not possible to present facts impartially because they are inevitably filtered through the biographer's own mind-set. In discussing the personalities of a certain number of individuals and their biographies here, theory is crucial. This book deals with what Wittgenstein could call 'the kind of understanding that consists in seeing connections',[79] i.e. between people with HFA/ASP and creativity in this case. Indeed, the traits of HFA/ASP that these individuals possess are likened to the 'family resemblances' of Wittgenstein's work.

This book also runs counter to the literary criticism of the 1970s, which proclaimed 'the death of the author' and insisted on turning books into 'texts', to be read without any reference to the writer's intentions. On this point, Hughes-Hallet claims there were many 'different theoretical underpinnings, but the point was that the text became a kind of field force, a shifting example of the different social and intellectual pressures that had produced it, rather than the brainchild of one particular man or woman'.[80] This is clearly absurd and places undue significance on the interpretations of literary theorists and readers alike.

The question of whether a full explanation of creative genius can be achieved is open to debate. David Ellis asks the question many readers will ask – how can we 'enter another person's mind' and reconstitute his 'internal soliloquy'?[81] The answer is that we never can – at least not completely. The best we can hope for has been expressed by Hermione Lee, who claims that 'we can do it partly and attempt it every day of the week with the people we meet in an attempt to understand them'.[82]

Alper points out that Freud in his famous study of Leonardo da Vinci, having set careful limits on his own methodology, warned that in such an investigation the most psychoanalysts could hope to achieve was an 'understanding of the underlying psychopathology and never an explanation of the creative act of genius'.[83] Certainly in the history of psychoanalysis, too great an importance has been placed on eventism and reductionism at the expense of creativity. In psychoanalysis, according to Steptoe, there has been 'an over-emphasis on the significance of particular occurrences (eventism), reductionism in explaining behaviour in terms of internal psychological factors without taking the social and cultural context into account, the trivialisation of creativity as a product of early psychosexual experience or neurosis'.[84]

The genetic fallacy: the created work and the creator

This book aims to show how personality might shape a genius's work, or indeed give the reader a greater understanding of the genius's personality so that their work can be appreciated in a wider context. However, throughout the ages people have been more predisposed to view the work of the creator as independent of his/her personality. Certainly this climaxed in the twentieth century with the 'death of the author' theory. Jerry Fodor argues that civilised people try their best to avoid the genetic fallacy: 'they think the work is one thing and the worker is another'.[85]

Undoubtedly, the genetic fallacy continues to gain momentum. In recent times Wittgenstein's biographer Ray Monk has debated with Martin Amis and others in *The Times* magazine the issue of the personality and the created work. Monk considers that the idea that knowledge of a writer's life will somehow explain his/her work is 'simply crass'.[86] But that is not entirely true. Whether a person decides to be a physicist or a fiction writer, it is partly determined by their personality. Furthermore, the topic that a writer decides to write about will also be partly determined by his/her personality. While great caution is necessary in making linkages between the personality of people with genius and their work, it is an effort both necessary and important.

It is in philosophy that a rejection of the genetic fallacy is viewed as an attempt to undermine the discipline. The notion that philosophy is independent of the person producing it is a fundamental concept in philosophy.[87] However, the undeniable fact remains that philosophy is produced by human beings. The assertion by some philosophers that if philosophy fell off a tree it would still be of interest to them – though extreme – shows that they cannot choose to ignore the real relationship between phenomena and this world.

Over the past few hundred years there has been an excessive focus on the work of geniuses as purely rational acts independent of their personality. Certainly, the view of the philosopher Rush Rhees (one of Wittgenstein's disciples) needs to be rejected. According to Levi, Rhees denies that anything can be learnt about a writer or artist through their work, and that his life will help us 'understand his work'.[88] It is clear that the personality must be taken into account when assessing the value of a great work. It is not possible to separate the personality of the individual from his work, despite Christopher Gehrke's assertion that:

> I believe it is of the utmost importance to be able to separate the character of a thinker, from the work that the thinker has produced. The question of whether or not Heidegger believed what he wrote, is not only unanswerable, but unimportant to philosophy. Suppose Heidegger did not believe a single word he wrote; would that change any of his writings? No. They would still be the same words, and the same ideas. We must not disqualify a philosopher, or at least his works, because of his shortcomings as a person. Heidegger was a coward and a Nazi. Augustine was a womaniser, Sartre was a pretentious ass. None of these personal remarks bear upon the works of philosophy.[89]

I do not believe this view to be correct. The life and work of the philosopher Wittgenstein has received considerable scrutiny in this book. Perhaps more than anyone else discussed here, he has manifested compelling features of HFA/ASP while his influence on philosophy in the twentieth century has been nothing short of ground breaking. But more significantly his philosophy has been influenced by his genetic developmental disorder. In this respect, his 'instincts' rather than pure reason have swayed his thought. Certainly, within the discipline of philosophy, the nature of 'instinct' as a determinant of philosophical ideas has been relegated in favour of 'pure reason'. On this point, Albert W. Levi has reacted to the view that philosophers are pure reasoning machines:

> Schwarzschild in his book *Wittgenstein as an Alienated Jew* presents a completely abstract, a completely utopian picture of how philosophers proceed – as if they were pure reasoning machines and not men of flesh and blood. In fact, many philosophers do not reason, do not present arguments at all – they simply assert. Moreover, when they do present arguments, it is often to veil the existence of completely non-rational motivations at the heart of their philosophy. Not only Freud, but philosophers themselves have been well aware of this fact. David Hume, the master of common sense, asserted that 'reason is the slave of

the passions'. That profound critic F.H. Bradley, a noted meta-physician himself, admitted that 'metaphysics is the finding of bad reasons for what we believe upon instinct'. One interested in the history of ideas might well be interested in those 'passions' which lay at the foundation of Wittgenstein's 'reasons', that 'instinct' which governed his metaphysical pronouncements. At the back of Schwarzschild's strictures lies an unfortunate overestimation of the exclusively rational element in philosophic discourse.[90]

A major criticism of suggesting that an individual's work is dependent on personality is that it gives rise to a 'cult of personality'. If one is to agree with Stephen Logan that certain academic philosophers believe the 'cult of personality' an 'unfortunate distraction',[91] then one certainly will be critical of this book. But clearly Wittgenstein recognised the importance of both. When asked by Russell whether his work or his life was troubling him, Wittgenstein reportedly replied 'Both, of course'.

Levi, more than any other philosopher, has come close to pinpointing what is essential when devising a method of doing philosophy, thereby due recognition is given to influences beyond the sphere of philosophy *per se*:

> Method in the history of ideas requires that we pay equal heed not to one thing, but to three: (1) the logical content of a philosopher's ideas, (2) to those unique elements contributed by the individual personality, the character and conduct of life of the philosopher, and (3) unique moment in time, the social and historical elements which formed the matrix of the philosophy's appearance. Only so shall we understand for philosophy the human and societal conditions which gave it actuality.[92]

Interestingly, Wittgenstein did allude to the issue of philosophical instincts. Indeed, his words 'it is sometimes said that a man's philosophy is a matter of temperament, and there is something in this'[93] certainly validate the purpose of this book. However, it is not true to say that it is always a deliberate process on the part of the philosopher. Bouveresse claimed that Wittgenstein himself went to great lengths to avoid his philosophy appearing to be a 'direct expression of his personality'.[94] This was also the case with Kant. According to Kuehn, Kant in his philosophical works followed the motto, 'About ourselves we are silent'.[95] Kant was concerned with philosophical truths and wished to be recognised for advancing them, yet without reference to Kant the individual. Klagge, in assessing the relevance of biographical research in respect of Bouveresse's comments on Wittgenstein, is correct when he states:

> This constitutes an interesting challenge to the philosophical relevance of biographical research. While all thinkers hope that their best

thoughts are not merely subjective and idiosyncratic, it would be perverse to write in a way that was not an expression of one's self. This sort of self-cancelling approach to philosophical thought is not impossible, but it seems thoroughly disproven in Wittgenstein's case by the work of his two biographers.[96]

The 'self-cancelling approach' of philosophers towards their work is worthy of debate. Wittgenstein's biographer, W.W. Bartley, supports Ben Ami Scharfstein's thesis that a man's philosophical product is a 'disguised expression of his inner state – it is a sophisticated variant of "epistemological expressionism"' (i.e. the epistemological expressionism of Karl Popper).[97] In contrast to the world of academia, Bartley notes how there exists 'the popular idea that a man's work, whether art or philosophy, is an expression of his inner states, of his emotions, of his personality'.[98] I would agree with this view partially but not entirely, as it is too narrow in its explanation.

This inevitably raises the question of whether philosophers conceal more than they reveal. Scharfstein has stated, quite rightly, that most philosophers 'hide behind the facades: their ideas are indeed constructions intended to make these facades more difficult to penetrate'.[99] Indeed, Bartley points out that sometimes their ideas are the 'facades themselves'.[100] I agree with this view. George Steiner writes that 'languages conceal and internalise more, perhaps, than they convey outwardly. Social classes, racial ghettoes speak at rather than to each other.'[101] The same could be said of both philosophers and psychiatrists. It is worth noting that Steiner has claimed that Wittgenstein's personal temperament may indeed be 'relevant to his philosophy and especially to his treatment of human speech'.[102] It is interesting that some people with HFA/ASP have a problem with 'inner speech'.

The study of patterns in the dynamic between the creator and the material created is central to this book. Moreover, this book is concerned about individuals where the psychopathology of individuals matters enormously. There is a particular emphasis on the twentieth century, since technological and communication advances have increased our awareness of genius. Certainly, with the advent of mass media more biographies and information are at our disposal than ever before. Unquestionably, it is not possible to separate completely the creator from what is created. And finally it remains to be seen how far HFA/ASP impacts on the creative act. In this respect the words of Yeats are apt '*How can we know the dancer from the dance?*'

Conclusion

The book clearly will be relevant to all those people with HFA/ASP who show exceptional degrees of creativity and to parents and professionals who work with them. Gillberg[103] points out that:

the possibility that prominent individuals who have forever put their mark on history in the respective field might have had the condition described by Hans Asperger, is hopeful for all of those whose lives are touched by Asperger's syndrome. Maybe one could even speculate that historic progress has quite often been made by people with Autism Spectrum conditions. The perseverance, drive for perfection, good concrete intelligence, ability to disregard social conventions, and not worry too much about other people's opinions or critiques, could be seen as advantageous, maybe even a prerequisite for certain forms of new thinking and creativity.

Gillberg describes here precisely what I have attempted to set out to do in this book. He also states that people with high creativity give hope to all of those whose lives are touched by Asperger's syndrome. The book will also be relevant to a subgroup of highly creative individuals and to individuals interested in creativity, and will expand their knowledge of this. Clearly, only a minority of those with high creativity/genius will meet the criteria for HFA/ASP.

Chapter 2

Diagnostic issues

Introduction

Autism was first described by Leo Kanner in 1943.[1] Kanner[2] described 'the profound withdrawal from contact with people, an obsessive desire for the preservation of sameness, a skilful relation to objects, the retention of an intelligent and pensive physiognomy, and either mutism or the kind of language that does not seem intended to serve the purpose of interpersonal communication'.

In 1958 Kanner and Leonard Lesser[3] stated that 'there is no single pathogenic sign in early infantile autism', going on to state that:

> in considering the personalities of these parents, one may think of them as 'successfully autistic' persons. This suggests the possibility that they may represent mild or latent manifestations, while their children show the manifest forms of the disorder. One of the fathers in this group, a physician engaged in research, described mildly schizoid trends in his grandparents, more severe ones in his parents and himself and a full-blown picture of autism in his child.

Eisenberg[4] describes the fathers (some of whom would now be described as having HFA/ASP or the broader phenotype of autism) as having serious 'personality difficulties'. It is now known that autism is probably one of the most heritable or genetic conditions in child psychiatry.

Wing was of the opinion that only 10 per cent of children with autism met Kanner's definition, and recommended a broader definition.[5]

Hans Asperger's analysis

Hans Asperger trained in medicine in Vienna, and in 1931 worked at the Children's Clinic at the University of Vienna. In 1932 he worked in the Orthopaedic Department. He was influenced by Ludwig Klage's publication, *Foundation of the Science of Perception*.[6] He has become very influential since his death. Arn van Krevelen[7] introduced his work to the Anglo-Saxon world, but Lorna Wing has had the greatest influence in this respect with her 1981 paper on Asperger's syndrome.[8]

Autistic psychopathy

In 1943 Asperger described a condition similar to that which Kanner described the same year. Kanner wrote of 'autistic disturbances of affective contact'; Asperger wrote of 'autistic psychopathy'.[9]

Asperger noted a disturbance in social relationships: 'the fundamental disorder of autistic individuals is the limitation of their social relationships'.[10] In addition he identified communication difficulties, with 'abnormalities in the language of autistic individuals'. He also identified narrow interests and repetitive activities – 'special interests', 'abnormal fixations' and 'stereotypic movements'. He noted associated food fads and unusual reactions to sensory sensations, for example tactile and sound, as well as problems with attention. He was particularly taken with autistic intelligence, but nevertheless stated that the people in question had 'all levels of ability from the highly original genius . . . to the . . . mentally retarded individual'.[11]

High-functioning autism or autistic psychopathy?

Personality is the characteristic manner or style of a person's behaviour.[12] As with HFA/ASP, personality disorders are considered in dimensional rather than categorical terms, and multiple genes are involved in both HFA/ASP and personality disorders. Also, as in HFA/ASP, the behavioural and genetic components of personality can be recognised quite early in development; (genetic) polymorphisms contributing to personality traits are demonstrable in the first year of human development.[13] Ebstein and colleagues point out that the dimensions of autism overlap with 'areas of personality and social anxiety' and obsessive compulsive disorder.[14]

Lorna Wing did not agree that Asperger's syndrome should be classified as a personality disorder, instead she viewed it as a developmental problem on the autistic spectrum.[15] Her paper reflected Wing's desire for a broader conception of autism. She described Asperger's cases as well as her own, and changed the disorder's name from autistic psychopathy to Asperger's syndrome. Wing reasoned that the term 'psychopathy' was too often associated with antisocial behaviour and could cause confusion. Wing also included females among her cases, arguing that although Asperger's syndrome was more common in males, it clearly could occur in females as well.

The present author has expressed the view that we should retain the term 'autistic psychopathy', particularly when serious antisocial behaviour is involved (see Table 2.1).

Table 2.1   Similarities and differences between high-functioning autism/
Asperger's syndrome (HFA/ASP) and antisocial personality

Antisocial personality/psychopathy	Autistic psychopathy (HFA/ASP)
Superego deficits	Harsh superego
Morality reduced	Morality generally increased, but with very serious exceptions due to lack of capacity for empathy
Serotonin (low tendency)	Serotonin (high tendency)
Primary psychopaths have 'semantic aphasia'. This was first described by Checkley in 1950.[16] Semantic aphasia refers 'to meaning, and aphasia is broadly considered a class of disorders related to the understanding or production of language . . . Psychopaths suffer an inborn inability to understand and express meaning of emotional experience, even though their understanding of meaning is normal.'[17]	Difficulties in semantic pragmatic problems are very important in HFA/ASP, as are problems in understanding the meaning of experience
'The significance of embarrassment [and] shame [is] lost on them'[18]	Same features as in autistic psychopathy
Problems in understanding 'what makes people tick'[19]	Same
Problems in adapting to 'the alien world of the empathic and socialised'[20]	Same
'Unable to appraise a potentially dangerous situation by gauging their own fear, they plow ahead violently, regardless of risk'[21]	This can occur in autistic psychopathy
'Low in the desire to avoid harm, and low in dependence on external awards'[22]	This can occur in autistic psychopathy with violent propensities
Heredity element[23]	Higher heredity element
DSM-IV antisocial personality disorder:[24]	
1. Pervasive patterns of disregard for and violation of the right of others occurring since age 15 years	1. Autistic psychopathy occurs before and after 15 years
2. Failure to conform to social norms	2. Occurs in autistic psychopathy
3. Deceitfulness	3. Does not occur in autistic psychopathy
4. Impulsivity	4. Common in autistic psychopathy
5. Irritability and aggressivity	5. Not uncommon in autistic psychopathy
6. Disregard for safety of self and others	6. Can occur in autistic psychopathy
7. Repeated failure to maintain consistent work behaviour	7. Common in autistic psychopathy
8. Lack of remorse	8. Common in autistic psychopathy
Illness model is inappropriate for the concept of psychopathy[25]	Same
Persons who are given the diagnosis are not a homogeneous group[26]	Same
Could be a final common pathway for a series of different conditions[27]	Same

An example of autistic psychopathy: Adolf Hitler

A phrase that Winston Churchill coined with reference to Russia – 'a riddle wrapped in a mystery inside an enigma' – could usefully be applied to Hitler. Many of Hitler's traits seem very autistic.

Hitler was interested in art, but failed in his efforts to get into the Vienna Academy. He lived in poverty, unemployed or doing various menial jobs, until he went to Munich and volunteered for service in the First World War, during which he was decorated. It was said that he was quite courageous and never tried to evade dangerous assignments in the war. It is clear that the army gave him a structure that he could adapt to in his own way, and it took him off the streets. After the war he returned to Munich, became a member of the German Workers' Party and began his rise, basically as a mob orator. There then followed his relatively rapid rise to become leader of the German nation, the Second World War and his death by suicide.

He was a poor sleeper and had food fads. He recoiled from physical contact, was unable to forge genuine friendships, and showed an emptiness in his human relations.[28] His conversations in the Men's Home in Vienna were really harangues and invited no reciprocity, for which he lacked the capacity. In Munich he was distant, self-contained, withdrawn and without friends.[29] His comrades noted that he had no humanitarian feelings.[30]

He was extremely socially awkward and uncertain in small groups. He showed little human interest in his followers, and even one of his leading supporters accused him of 'contempt for mankind'.[31] In addition, a colleague, Gregor Strasser, thought that there was 'something other-worldly about Hitler . . . a lack of knowledge of human beings and with it a lack of sound judgement of them . . . he lived without any bonds to another human being'.[32]

His poor adaptation to people was perhaps most obvious in his relations with women.[33] During his life he took only a slight interest in a couple of women. One was his niece, Geli Raubal, who effectively became his prisoner and said 'my uncle is a monster';[34] she apparently committed suicide in his apartment. His second relationship was with Eva Braun, who apparently attempted suicide by shooting in 1932 and died with him in the bunker in 1945.

His colleagues regarded him as a remote figure: he was an obsessive, and obsessives rarely make good or interesting company, except in the eyes of those who share the obsession or those in awe of, or dependent on, such an unbalanced personality.[35] He was single minded and inflexible.

He spent a great deal of time with Albert Speer, examining architectural plans, and this remained a major focus throughout his life. His other major interest was in the music of Wagner. His greatest interest, clearly, was in control over people and power over people. His ability to achieve this control and power was extraordinary:

> he was able to extend that power until it became absolute, until field marshals were prepared to obey without question the orders of a former corporal, until highly skilled 'professionals' and clever minds in all walks of life were ready to pay uncritical obeisance to an autodidact whose only indisputable talent was one for stirring up the base emotions of the masses.[36]

He was an 'ideologue of unshakeable convictions'.[37]

Hitler had 'a bed compulsion, which demands that the bed be made in a particular way with the quilt folded according to a prescribed pattern and that a man must make the bed before he could go to sleep'.[38]

Hitler did not use language for the purpose of interaction with others, but only for the purpose of dominating others. He endlessly engaged in long-winded, pedantic speeches, with 'illogical arguments full of crude comparisons and cheap allusions'.[39] When Anton Drexler, the leader of the DAP,[40] first heard him speak in September 1919, he remarked: 'goodness, he's got a gob. We could use him.'[41]

Hitler was regarded as a great orator even though his voice could be 'distinctly unpleasant. It has a rasping quality and often breaks into a shrill falsetto when he becomes aroused.'[42] He was unable to carry on a normal conversation or discussion with people. Even if only one other person was present, he had to do all the talking. 'His manner of speech soon loses any conversational qualities it might have had and takes on all the characteristics of a lecture that may easily develop into a tirade. He simply forgets his companions and behaves as though he were addressing a multitude', repeating the same stories over and over again in exactly the same form, almost as though he had memorised them.[43]

After the First World War 'his awkward mannerisms' were noted.[44] At that time:

> in his gangster hat and trenchcoat over his dinner jacket, touting a pistol and carrying as usual his dog-whip, he cut a bizarre figure in the salons of Munich's upper-crust. But his very eccentricity of dress and exaggerated mannerisms . . . saw him lionized by condescending hosts and fellow-guests.[45]

In his early days he wore the Bavarian costume. His clothes were not clean with 'his mouth full of brown, rotten teeth and his long fingernails he presented a rather grotesque picture'. His gait was 'a very lady-like walk. Dainty little steps. Every few steps he cocked his right shoulder nervously, his left leg snapping up as he did so.' He also had a 'tic in his face that caused the corner of his lips to curl upwards'. People found his look 'staring and dead'.[46]

Herman Rauschning stated that 'anyone who has seen this man face to face, has met his uncertain glance, without depth or warmth, from eyes that seem hard and remote, and has then seen that gaze grow rigid, certainly has experienced the uncanny feeling: that man is not normal'.[47]

At the home of Ernst Hanfstaengl, an upper-middle-class American, the host noted 'his awkward use of a knife and fork'.[48]

He ate 'large quantities of eggs prepared in 101 different ways by the best chef in Germany, and a large variety of fresh vegetables prepared in unusual ways. In addition, Hitler consumes incredible quantities of pastries.'[49]

Adolf Hitler meets the criteria for autistic psychopathy described by Hans Asperger.[50] He was not schizophrenic. The combination of a person with autistic psychopathy and a nation in turmoil after the First World War (even though this nation was modern, cultured, and technologically advanced) caused Germany to sink into what Kershaw[51] describes as 'scarcely imaginable brutality and rapaciousness . . . a form of nuclear blow-out within modern society'.

Asperger's syndrome

Lorna Wing[52] renamed autistic psychopathy 'Asperger's syndrome', and emphasised the following issues in people displaying this syndrome:

1 a lack of normal interest and pleasure in people around them
2 a reduction in the quality and quantity of babbling
3 a significant reduction in shared interests
4 a significant reduction in the wish to communicate verbally or non-verbally
5 a delay in speech acquisition, and impoverishment of content
6 no imaginative play, or imaginative play confined to one or two rigid patterns.

Asperger noted that, unlike other children who struggled to progress from mechanical learning to original thought, children with Asperger's syndrome (AS) were capable only of forming their own strategies. They could not, or did not, follow those used by their teachers.[53] The people discussed in this book demonstrate what Asperger had in mind, and indeed most had major school difficulties of the type that he described. Asperger was also aware of the social value of these characteristics (he noted that many parents of such children were quite successful).[54] The originality of the people concerned is what this book is about.

In 1962 van Krevelen and Kuipers discussed Asperger's autistic psycho-pathology and emphasised the 'personal unapproachability' and the inability 'to distinguish between dream and reality'.[55] They also pointed out that 'the eye roams, evades and is turned inwards. The speech is stilted, it is not addressed to the person but into the empty space . . . it sounds false owing to exaggerated inflection.'[56] They identified a lack of 'childlikeness, his being old-fashioned in word and gesture':[57]

> They show signs of an original intelligence. They also develop their own methods. When they are gifted – and this is not infrequently the case – they are often characterized by specific interests. Some children are naturalists, others experimenters or would-be inventors. But they are not children. Their schoolmates' play does not appeal to them. When one observes them at play, one gets the impression that they handle their toys mechanically. They are tied to solitary pursuits. Accordingly, they read much, anything they can lay hands on; they often develop a veritable mania for reading.[58]

While empathy is reduced, it is rarely absent. This is well illustrated in some of the people described in this book. It is likely that people with Asperger's disorder are even more vulnerable to the stresses of life and family than other people. Likewise, notwithstanding the triad of impairments in autism mentioned below, the people in this book often show massive imagination, albeit an 'autistic imagination' of the Einsteinian type. Social imagination is impaired.

Tantam talks about 'people with Asperger's syndrome who make up stories, imaginary words or imaginary play comparisons', and states that when people with Asperger's syndrome 'act a part on the stage, they have difficulty in infusing it with a character other than their own'.[59] A number of people in this book illustrate this point. Lorna Wing pointed out that 'recognising patterns within this bewildering complexity is akin to classifying clouds'.[60]

A number of authors have subsequently suggested diagnostic criteria, but the six proposed by Gillberg[61] are among the most useful descriptions of Asperger's syndrome that I have found:

1 social impairments
2 narrow interests
3 repetitive routines
4 speech and language peculiarities
5 non-verbal communication problems
6 motor clumsiness.

This book gives considerable emphasis to Gillberg's criteria.

Descriptions of autism 1980s to 1990s

American Psychiatric Association DSM-III[62] criteria for autism were too narrow and were excessively childhood oriented. They were revised and broadened, quite rightly, in 1987.

Mesibov and colleagues[63] have noted that Twachtman-Cullen identified the following difficulties with DSM-IV criteria for Asperger's syndrome:

1   the DSM-IV definition uses the term 'clinically significant general delay in language', which is open to different interpretations
2   the milestone of single words at age 2 years, used as an example of normal language development, actually represents a significant expressive language delay
3   use of communicative phrases at age 3 years involves not just saying a sequence of words but also communication, meaning the appropriate use of language for social purposes, which is very frequently not normal in youngsters with Asperger's syndrome, even if they speak in phrases or sentences.

Another difficulty with DSM-IV criteria of delayed language development (noted by Mesibov and colleagues) is that it is becoming clear that empirical support is lacking for this as a differentiating factor between autism and Asperger's syndrome.[64] This is why the term HFA/ASP is used in this book.

The present author[65] makes the following suggestion for a future revision of DSM-IV in relation to Asperger's disorder, i.e. the deletion of:

(a) Section D. Communication: One of the following:

(1) No clinically significant general delay in language
(2) Delay in the development of spoken language
(3) Impairment in the ability to initiate or sustain conversation with others.
(4) Stereotyped or repetitive use of language or idiosyncratic language.

(DSM-IV)

and its replacement by:

(a) No clinically significant general delay in language development, or
(b) Impairment in speech and language.

This would at least allow researchers who are interested in Asperger's disorder with or without clinically significant general delay in language to study these groups separately.

Some of the people in this book would meet the DSM-IV criteria for pervasive developmental disorder not otherwise specified, which is part of the autism spectrum of disorders. This is characterised by 'a severe and pervasive impairment in the development of reciprocal social interaction or verbal and non-verbal communication skills or when stereotyped behaviour, interests and activities are present'. This category in DSM-IV needed revision, as the double inclusion of the word 'or' greatly diluted its meaning and grossly widened it as a category. *Diagnostic Criteria from DSM-IV-TR*[66] has corrected this error, requiring an impairment in reciprocal social interaction associated with an impairment in communication skills or with stereotyped behaviour, interests or activities. In the past, particularly in the USA, pervasive developmental disorder not otherwise specified was used as a synonym for Asperger's syndrome.

In a prevalence study of autism, Wing and Gould[67] identified a large number of children who failed to meet the diagnostic criteria for classic autism, but had a triad of impairments involving social interaction, communication and imagination, with additional repetitive stereotyped activities. This triad of symptoms, termed the 'autistic spectrum', was recognised at all levels of intelligence and is included in DSM-IV as a 'pervasive developmental disorder not otherwise specified', and in ICD-10[68] as 'atypical autism', 'other pervasive developmental disorders' or 'pervasive developmental disorders, unspecified'.

Autism versus Asperger's syndrome: similarities and differences

This debate has a long and continuing history. In 1971 van Krevelen[69] attempted to distinguish autism and autistic psychopathy (Asperger's syndrome) by listing the following criteria:

1   Early infantile autism
    • Manifestation age: first month of life.
    • Child walks earlier than he speaks; speech is retarded or absent.
    • Language does not attain the function of communication.
    • Eye contact: other people do not exist.
    • The child lives in a world of his own.
    • Social prognosis is poor.
    • A psychotic process.
2   Autistic psychopathy
    • Manifestation age: third year of life or later.
    • Child walks late, speaks earlier.
    • Language aims at communication but remains one-way traffic.
    • Eye contact: other people are evaded.
    • The child lives in our world in his own way.

- Social prognosis is rather good.
- A personality trait.

Van Krevelen stated that it is 'unmistakably clear that early infantile autism and autistic psychopathy are two entirely different nosological syndromes'. This has not been sustained, and is the opposite view to that of the present author. Nevertheless, while van Krevelen's distinctions are largely not supported in this book, there is the clinical view that people with autism don't want social contact and people with Asperger's syndrome don't know how to initiate it.

Van Krevelen also emphasises child originality, lack of common-sense and interest in abstract topics – the 'hypertrophy of the intellect at the expense of feeling'.[70] These traits are certainly shown by the people described in this book.

While a clear differentiation of autism and Asperger's syndrome appears impossible, I believe they may be at different points on the autistic spectrum, and it may be unwise to dismiss any differences completely. I have some sympathy for the research of Professor Luke Tsai,[71] who noted that the following features were more marked in Asperger's syndrome than in high-functioning autism:

1 Preoccupation with one or more stereotyped and restricted patterns of interest.
2 Talking, reading and drawing about violence and death.
3 Moody and easily frustrated, with tantrums.
4 Poor hygiene.
5 Failure to develop peer relationships.
6 Interested in heterosexual relationships.
7 Argumentative rules for others.
8 No insight into own disability.
9 Condescension.
10 Pedantic speech.
11 Likes to tell people his/her special knowledge.

The reader will see that there is support for Luke Tsai's position in relation to some individuals in this book. It might be premature to close the discussion of the differentiation between high-functioning autism and Asperger's syndrome.

Hans Asperger[72] states that 'it has become obvious that the conditions described by myself and Leo Kanner concern basically different types, yet in some respects there is complete agreement', and that his 'typical cases are very intelligent children with extraordinary originality of thought and spontaneity of activity though their actions are not always the right response to the prevailing situation'. These are the kind of people described in this book.

Asperger also states 'they are able for exceptional achievements' (people with autism are the 'salt of the earth').[73] He goes on to state something that this book attempts to illustrate, i.e. that:

> their thinking, too, seems unusual in that it is endowed with special abilities in the areas of logic and abstraction and these often follow their own course with no regard for outside influences. Often they are not directed towards the wider world but are canalised into rather abstruse subjects of little practical use. A further important difference from early infantile autism is that Asperger children, very early, even before they walk, develop highly grammatical speech and they may be uncommonly apt at using expressions coined spontaneously. There is a likeness here to the children described by Kanner. However, the children with Kanner's syndrome generally avoid communication, consequently they do not develop speech or develop it very late. But even autistic children with the Asperger's syndrome who have complete speech, do not usually use it for communication. It seems that they do not wish to convey information to others or do not want to get into contact with them; rather they hold forth on their own subject of interest and do not appear to care whether others wish to listen or whether they are speaking out of turn.[74]

As far as this book is concerned, their interests can be of enormous value.

Asperger notes that these children's school problems are due to their social integration difficulties. He mentions their originality, energy, and persistence, noting their interest in science. Even as small children they may have been able to formulate scientific formulae:

> Indeed, it seems that for success in science or art a dash of autism is essential. For success the necessary ingredient may be an ability to turn away from the everyday world, from the simply practical, an ability to rethink subject with originality so as to create in new, untrodden ways, with all abilities canalised into the one speciality.[75]

This is what this book attempts to illustrate.

Asperger states that:

> It was the astonishing similarities within these two groups which obviously accounted for the same choice of name. The two types are at once so alike and yet so different. When Kanner writes of an innate phenomenon of a peculiar disability to form affective contacts, then this is just as valid for the Asperger type. And all those who have tried to interpret the nature of the disturbance have made similar statements. We, in this country, speak of a defect in the 'thymic', the mind of the

personality. This defect would explain the disturbance in relationship to other people and of all that builds up human contact.[76]

Mesibov and colleagues note points made by Bosch[77] that 'remain relevant today':

> In describing autistic psychopathy, Bosch asserts that the difference between Asperger's syndrome and autism is a matter of degree, and that the same person can be diagnosed with each disorder at different points in life. Bosch asserts that many people with Asperger's syndrome would have been diagnosed with autism if they had been seen at younger ages. Likewise some of his patients with autism improved enough with age to be indistinguishable from his adult clients with Asperger's syndrome. The possibility of different diagnosis at different ages is still discussed today, though not adequately reflected in any of the diagnostic systems.[78]

These distinctions have been well described by Barbara Kugler,[79] who states that 'few definitive conclusions can be drawn'. Formal scientific research has not convincingly demonstrated a difference between autism and Asperger's syndrome. The author agrees with this, and has used HFA/ASP as the designation throughout this book (see Table 2.2).

In the past, clumsiness was stated to be a feature of Asperger's syndrome. Ghaziuddin and co-authors[80] found that individuals with either

Table 2.2   Differences between high-functioning autism and Asperger's syndrome

High-functioning autism	Asperger's syndrome
	Better verbal skills
	More originality of thought
Good fine motor skills	Clumsiness
Walks before talks	Talks before walks
Not following through in verbal interchanges	Long-winded
Lower verbal IQ than performance IQ	Higher verbal IQ than performance IQ
Better block design and object assembly than Asperger's syndrome	Better verbal memory and auditory perception than autism. Weaker spatial skills and visual memory than autism. Weaker visual-motor integration and visual-spatial perception than autism
Less interested in other people than individuals with Asperger's syndrome	More interest in making social contact but lacking 'know-how'
	More eccentric interests

high-functioning autism or Asperger's syndrome had 'problems with co-ordination'.

Mayes and colleagues[81] state that:

> DSM-IV criteria for autistic and Asperger's disorders were applied to 157 children with clinical diagnoses of autism or Asperger's disorder. All children met the DSM-IV criteria for autistic disorder and none met criteria for Asperger's disorder, including those with normal intelligence and absence of early speech delay. They conclude that a DSM-IV diagnosis of Asperger's disorder is unlikely or impossible.

Lorna Wing[82] notes that Kanner stated that 'it is well known in medicine that any illness may appear in different degrees of severity, all the way from the so-called *formes frustes* to the most fulminant manifestations. Does this possibly apply also to early infantile autism?' The answer is 'yes', and this is precisely what this book is attempting to demonstrate.

Wing also notes that 'the findings from research and clinical work are best explained on the hypothesis of a continuum of impairments of the development of social interaction, communication and imagination and consequent rigid, repetitive behaviour'.[83] This remains accurate except that the term 'spectrum' has replaced 'continuum'.

Originally Lorna Wing described autism as being on a continuum. According to Tsai, 'The central problem of the continuum is an intrinsic impairment in development of the ability to engage in reciprocal social interaction . . . the term continuum represents a concept of considerable complexity, rather than simply a straight line from severe to mild.'[84]

Then Lorna Wing felt that 'the autism spectrum' was a better description, because:

> the essential features of [autism] were a triad of impairments of social interaction, communication and imagination, the last being replaced by a narrow range of interests or activities. These are familiar features appearing in virtually all sets of criteria. The essential point of the spectrum concept is that each of the elements of the triad could occur in widely varying degrees of severity and in many different manifestations. For example, social impairment could be shown as passivity in social interaction or as active but inappropriate and repetitive approaches to others, not just aloofness as in Kanner's syndrome.[85]

Having observed this variability, she felt that 'spectrum' would be a better word, and now the accepted international term is autism spectrum disorders.

This book examines individuals at various points of the spectrum, and indeed all the people in this book could be described as meeting criteria for an autism spectrum disorder.

Wing states that:

> the continuum ranges from the most profoundly physically and men-
> tally retarded person, who has social impairment as one item among a
> multitude of problems, to the most able, highly intelligent person with
> social impairment in its subtlest form as his only disability. It overlaps
> with learning disabilities and shades into eccentric normality.[86]

Of course, the closer the individual is to simple eccentricity without
Asperger's disorder, the more difficult the diagnosis is; we don't have a
precise cut-off or blood test to make the diagnosis. According to Wing 'the
various clinical pictures of autism and related disorders depend upon the
combination of different impairments, which vary in severity independently
of each other, though they interact to produce the overt behaviour
pattern'.[87]

There is great heterogeneity within the spectrum. Wing states that:

> Kanner's and Asperger's syndrome are best regarded as falling within
> the continuum of social impairment (of which they form only a part)
> but characterised, at least in the earlier years of childhood, by some-
> what differing profiles of cognitive, language and motor functions.
> Thus, to emphasise the differences, the young classic Kanner's child has
> good visuo-spatial skills, good manual dexterity when engaged in his or
> her preferred activities but has delayed and deviant language develop-
> ment as well as social impairment of the aloof kind. Those with typical
> Asperger's syndrome have good grammatical speech from early in life,
> passive, odd or subtly inappropriate social interaction and poor gross
> motor co-ordination shown in gait and posture.[88]

Most people regard high-functioning autism and Asperger's syndrome as
synonymous. It is very likely in the long term that this autistic spectrum will
be subdivided into different subgroups, possibly using new genetic findings,
but this point has not yet been reached. The idea of dividing the people on
the spectrum into high, medium and low severity originated in clinical
practice and is helpful from a prognostic point of view. Indeed, many
people with HFA/ASP are described as being eccentric. At the same time
the majority of the people, in my experience, who have the word 'eccentric'
attached to them do not meet diagnostic criteria for HFA/ASP.

Eric Schopler[89] stated that:

> the boundary of a well-established diagnostic category like autism con-
> verges with other diagnostic labels – one such convergence occurring
> for learning disability, higher-level autism, and Asperger's syndrome.
> Moreover, since no behavioural distinction between higher-level autism

and Asperger's syndrome has yet been demonstrated, diagnostic confusion can be reduced if the Asperger's syndrome is not used, at least until an empirically based distinction from higher-level autism can be demonstrated for it.

Clearly Schopler was correct. He also points out that 'Gillberg concluded that he saw no basis for differentiating autism at higher levels of intellectual functioning from Asperger's syndrome'.[90]

Miller and Ozonoff[91] point out that all four original Asperger cases met criteria for autistic disorder rather than Asperger's syndrome or DSM-IV.

Prevalence of Asperger's disorder

The National Autistic Society[92] in the United Kingdom estimates the possible total prevalence rate of all autistic spectrum disorders at 91 per 10,000, broken down as follows. (1) People with learning disabilities with an IQ under 70: (a) classic autism, 5 per 10,000; (b) other spectrum disorders, 15 per 10,000. (2) People with average or high ability: (a) Asperger's syndrome/high-functioning autism, 36 per 10,000; (b) other spectrum disorders, 35 per 10,000. I agree with this 'estimate of prevalence', which would mean almost half a million people in the UK. The individuals discussed in this book are the kind of people who have been missed in the past.

Differential diagnosis of high-functioning autism/ Asperger's syndrome[93]

Attention deficit hyperactivity disorder (DSM-IV)[94] (see Table 2.3)

People with attention deficit hyperactivity disorder lack the classic impairment in reciprocal social interaction, narrow interests, repetitive routines and non-verbal problems that are found in individuals with HFA/ASP.

Obsessive-compulsive disorders (DSM-IV)[95] (see Table 2.3)

Where these differ is that people with HFA/ASP have obsessive interests that are not experienced as ego-dystonic and, indeed, are often enjoyed. Baron-Cohen was critical of the use of the term 'obsession' in people with autism, because the subjective phenomenon of resistance to repetitive activities could not be discerned in autism. He suggested instead the phrase 'repetitive activities'.[96]

Schizoid personality in childhood (DSM-IV)[97] (see Table 2.3)

Sula Wolff notes that 'schizoid personality disorder in childhood lies at one extreme of the autistic spectrum, where it shades into normal personality variation, while at the same time there is evidence for its relationship to the schizophrenia spectrum'.[98]

Tantam[99] has argued that the autistic-like abnormalities of social interaction characteristic of Asperger's syndrome are of a different kind to schizoid abnormalities of social relationship, evinced by emotional detachment, introversion and oversensitivity.

Tantam made an interesting point in differentiating schizoid, schizotypal and borderline personalities from Asperger's syndrome, saying that 'their social isolation arose from a failure to make relationships rather than from an abnormality of social interaction'.[100]

Borderline personality disorder[101] (DSM-IV)

Borderline personality, with its instability in sense of identity, problems in interpersonal relationships, impulse control, transient stress-related paranoid ideations, chronic feelings of emptiness, inappropriate intense anger, and moods could also be confused with Asperger's syndrome.

Schizophrenia spectrum disorders

Schizophrenia[102] (DSM-IV)

Because individuals with Asperger's syndrome have normal cognitive ability, restrictive behaviours and impairments in social interaction and communication can be misinterpreted as evidence of schizophrenia. People with Asperger's syndrome have difficulty understanding the subtleties of social behaviour, but this should not be confused with evidence of psychotic disorder.

Fitzgerald[103] pointed out that the terms simple schizophrenia and latent schizophrenia were formerly used for conditions that would now be called Asperger's syndrome.

Schizophrenia occurs in patients with Asperger's syndrome no more commonly than in the general population, but bipolar affective disorder is more common.

Schizotypal personality disorder[104]

The DSM-IV diagnosis of schizotypal personality disorder depends on odd beliefs or magical thinking; bizarre fantasies or preoccupations; odd thinking and speech; odd, eccentric or peculiar behaviour and appearance; lack

Table 2.3 Differential diagnosis of Asperger's syndrome[114]

Asperger's syndrome (DSM-IV)	Impairment in use of eye-to-eye gaze, facial expression, body postures	Failure to develop peer relationships to developmental level	Lack of spontaneous seeking to share enjoyment	Lack of social and emotional reciprocity	Preoccupation with one or more stereotyped patterns of interest
Autism (DSM-IV)	Yes	Yes	Yes	Yes	Yes
Schizoid personality in childhood[115]		Yes	Yes	Yes	Yes
Deficits in attention motor control perception[116]	Yes, sometimes	Yes, sometimes		Yes, sometimes	
Semantic pragmatic disorder[117]		Yes	Yes, sometimes	Yes	
Dyslogia[118]		Yes	Yes	Yes	Yes
Developmental learning disability of right cerebral hemisphere[119]	Yes	Yes		Yes	
Non-verbal learning disability[120]		Yes		Yes	
Multiple complex developmental disorder[121]		Yes		Yes	
Multidimensionally impaired disorder[122]		Yes		Yes	
Obsessive-compulsive disorder[123]			Yes, often	Yes, sometimes	Yes
Obsessive-compulsive personality disorder[124]			Yes, often	Yes, often	Yes
Attention deficit hyperactivity disorder[125]		Yes, sometimes		Yes, often	
Schizotypal disorder[126]		Yes	Yes	Yes	Yes, sometimes
Reactive attachment disorder[127]	Yes	Yes	Yes	Yes	
Schizophrenia[128]			Yes	Yes	
Avoidant personality disorder[129]	Yes	Yes	Yes	Yes	
Social phobia (to people outside family)[130]	Yes	Yes	Yes	Yes	
Cerebellar cognitive affective syndrome[131]	Yes, sometimes		Yes, sometimes	Yes, sometimes	
Autistic-like disorders	Yes	Yes	Yes	Yes	Yes
Over-focused child[132]	Yes	Yes	Yes	Yes	Yes

Inflexible adherence to specific non-functional routines or rituals	Stereotyped and repetitive motor mannerism	Persistent preoccupation with parts of objects	Clinically significant impairment in social or occupational functioning	No clinically significant delay in language development	No clinically significant delay in cognitive development or self-help skills
Yes	Yes	Yes	Yes		
Yes			Yes	Yes	Yes
	Yes (50%)	Yes, sometimes	Yes		
			Yes		Yes
			Yes	Yes	Yes
Yes					Yes
Yes			Yes		
			Yes	Odd language	
			Yes	Yes	
Yes	Yes, sometimes		Yes	Yes	Yes
Yes			Yes	Yes	Yes
			Yes	Yes	Yes
			Yes	Yes	Yes
Yes			Yes	Yes	Yes
	Yes, sometimes catatonic		Yes	Disorganised speech can be evident	
Yes			Yes	Yes	Yes
			Yes	Yes	Yes
Yes	Yes, sometimes		Yes	Yes, in childhood	Yes, in childhood
Yes	Yes	Yes	Yes		
	Yes	Yes	Yes	Yes	

of close friends and social anxiety. All these criteria can also occur in Asperger's syndrome, and Peter Szatmari states that Wolff regards 'Asperger's syndrome and schizoid/schizotypal disorders as interchangeable terms that identify roughly the same group of children'.[105]

Multidimensionally impaired disorder (see Table 2.3)

Criteria for multidimensionally impaired disorder include a poor ability to distinguish fantasy from reality, impairment in interpersonal skills, and multiple deficits in processing information.[106] Fitzgerald[107] has argued that multidimensionally impaired disorder should be categorised with autism or Asperger's syndrome because of the overlapping symptomatology.

Multiple complex developmental disorder (see Table 2.3)

Thought disorder and affective dysregulation are more characteristic of multiple complex developmental disorder subjects, whereas problems in social interaction, communication and behavioural adjustment are more typical of subjects with autistic disorder.[108] As the core features can also occur in Asperger's syndrome, the nosological status of multiple complex developmental disorder is uncertain according to Fitzgerald.[109]

Dyslogia (see Table 2.3)

The syndrome of dyslogia was described by Jordan[110] as the inability to apply logic and common-sense in decision making. Individuals with this difficulty make decisions based on partial facts and have difficulty in integrating data into a working whole. They have social difficulties similar to those of individuals with Asperger's syndrome, and dyslogia may simply describe the same population, as pointed out by the present author.[111]

The over-focused child (see Table 2.3)

Kinsbourne and Caplan[112] describe the over-focused child as having 'total concentration', 'encyclopaedic knowledge' of a single topic, and being more 'preoccupied with inanimate objects than with people'. These features are common in people with HFA/ASP.

Autistic-like disorders (see Table 2.3)

These disorders, which are really attachment disorders, can descriptively meet criteria for autism, but are due to gross early neglect. I have seen about eight children with this picture who had been in orphanages in

Eastern Europe. It was quite impossible for me and the adoptive families to reverse the more severe damage.

Rachel Yeung-Courchesne and Eric Courchesne[113] point out that the idea of finding a core behavioural deficit is 'meaningless' because of the 'known principles of neurodevelopment: that many paths can lead to the same signs and symptoms (convergence or equi-finality), and the same beginning can diverge into many different manifestations and outcomes (divergence or multi-finality)'. They go on to point out that 'autism and many other developmental psychopathologies are characterised by convergence heterogeneity and divergence heterogeneity, making the goal of finding a single, causative core behavioural deficit a meaningless effort in such disorders'.

Chapter 3

Psychology of high-functioning autism/Asperger's syndrome

Theory of mind and autism

It is necessary to understand the people in this book to understand something about the psychology of HFA/ASP. A key element in this understanding is the work of Simon Baron-Cohen in relation to theory of mind, which has been enormously influential in research on autism.

The expression 'Theory of mind' refers to 'being able to infer the full range of mental states (beliefs, desires, intentions, imagination, emotions) that cause action. In brief, to be able to reflect on the content of one's own and others' minds.'[1] This is an intellectual approach to the psychology of autism.

Digby Tantam[2] points out that people with autism have theories of mind that are 'stripped down', as if developed by a psychologist or an anthropologist naïve to the culture. They have to develop their own understanding of human beings.

Val Cummine, Julia Leach and Gill Stephenson[3] point out that people with Asperger's syndrome showed the following theory of mind features of impairment:

1 'Difficulty in predicting others' behaviour, leading to fear and avoidance of other people.'
2 'Difficulty in reading the intentions of others and understanding the motives behind their behaviour.'
3 'Difficulty in explaining own behaviour.'
4 'Difficulty in understanding emotions – their own and those of others, leading to a lack of empathy.'
5 'Difficulty in understanding that behaviour affects how others think or feel, leading to a lack of conscience, of motivation to please.'
6 'Difficulty taking into account what other people know or can be expected to know, leading to pedantic or incomprehensible language.'
7 'Inability to read and react to the listener's level of interest in what is being said.'

8 'Inability to anticipate what others might think of one's actions.'
9 'Inability to deceive or to understand deception.'
10 'No sharing of attention, leading to idiosyncratic reference.'
11 'Lack of understanding of social interaction, leading to difficulties with turn-taking, poor topic maintenance in conversation, and inappropriate use of eye contact.'
12 'Difficulty in understanding "pretend", and differentiating fact from fiction.'

Carlos Gomez[4] points out that theory of mind means that 'our knowledge of other minds is due to the operation of specialised mechanisms that build up a corpus of knowledge and presuppositions about subjectivity similar in many respects to scientific theories'. This means that 'knowledge of other minds must be based upon some kind of abstract representations, usually referred to as metarepresentations'. Metarepresentation, according to Gomez,

> can be roughly defined as the representation of a representation attributed to a subject – a representation being something unobservable, a 'theoretical' or 'imaginary' entity. A person's subjectivity is equated to the internal representations this person entertains about the world. Intersubjectivity, therefore can be achieved only if one is capable of representing the internal representations of the other person.[5]

Gomez points out that this focus is on the 'thinking' side of people. Metarepresentation deficits are a very common feature of autism.

'Much of the time,' Temple Grandin said, 'I feel like an anthropologist on Mars.' Sacks[6] referred to Grandin as being at pains

> to keep her own life simple . . . and to make everything very clear and explicit. She had built up a vast library of experiences over the years . . . They were like a library of videotapes, which she could play in her mind and inspect at any time – 'videos' of how people behaved in different circumstances.

Baron-Cohen regards Grandin's description as giving us 'a clue to how successfully adapted individuals with autism may have managed to circumvent their mind blindness'.[7] 'True, but it may also give us a clue as to why other individuals do not behave like scientists, having to construct or evoke a theory of mind.'[8]

People with HFA/ASP often use alternative strategies to understand situations. They may use intellectual strategies to process emotional situations. In an attempt to compensate, they can be excessively formal in their verbal and non-verbal behaviour. They have to be allowed extra time, therefore, to process social situations. Their social interaction can have a 'robotic' and mechanical feel, just like the robots in Stephen Spielberg's movie *A.I.* They often have difficulties with hypothetical thinking and theoretical processing, especially in the social arena. Ludwig Wittgenstein, possibly because of his HFA/ASP, was against theories of philosophy.[9] People with HFA/ASP find *things* easier to process than *people*. They have problems reading peoples' 'faces'.

In terms of emotional intersubjectivity, Sigman and Capps[10] summarise Hobson's perspective as follows:

> innate impairment in the ability to perceive and respond to affect in others, and . . . problems with joint attention and empathy. With this conceptual framework, autistic persons' repetitive, stereotypic behaviours and restricted interests are thought to be substitutes for the broader interests and directed behaviours that fail to develop as a consequence of limited social involvement.

This is the emotional approach to the psychology of autism or 'emotional intersubjectivity'.

Carlos Gomez[11] points out that 'an emotional intersubjectivity precedes and is inseparable from the intellectual intersubjectivity studied by authors working under the label of theory of mind', and that 'it is around 9 to 12 months that the two research traditions in intersubjectivity seem to meet', with the emotional intersubjectivity coming first.

People with HFA/ASP live in an autistic culture, i.e. one constructed by themselves as opposed to neurotypicals ('normal' people), who construct cultures interpersonally and in agreement with other people in that geographical area. They may therefore have a deficient sense of their own nationality and all that that means. They are then 'citizens of no country' or 'citizens of an autistic country'.

These are all the kind of deficits shown by the people in this book. What is interesting is the enormous variability in the way that their deficits are expressed.

Folk physics and folk psychology

Baron-Cohen[12] points out that 'folk psychology' refers to our 'understanding of other minds' and that 'folk physics' refers to 'searching for the physical causes of any other kind of event'. The people of genius discussed in this book showed their strengths mostly in the area of folk physics, with most showing a weakness in folk psychology.

People with HFA/ASP are very attracted to computer-style thinking. Indeed, efforts have been made 'to construct a scientific, a physicalist theory of the mind, and thereby resolve the ancient philosophical problem of mind and matter. They thought themselves capable of reconciling the world of meaning with the world of physical laws.'[13] According to Jean-Pierre Dupuy, there was an effort to construct 'a general science of how the mind works'. It was as if they were trying to create the autistic mind.

At times people with HFA/ASP treat other people as if they were thinking machines, almost like computer robots.

Language and autism

Persons with HFA/ASP show major pragmatic deficits and Simon Baron-Cohen[14] has pointed out that the pragmatic difficulties include:

1   'tailoring one's speech to a particular listener'
2   'adapting the content of one's speech to what one's listener already knows or needs to know'
3   'respecting conversational maxims such as being truthful, relevant, concise and polite'
4   'turn-taking so that there is space for both participants in the dialogue'
5   'being sensitive to the other person's contribution to the conversation'
6   'recognising what is the wrong or right thing to say in a particular context'
7   'staying on topic'
8   'helping your listener to follow when a topic change is occurring'.

Most of these features are common in the people in this book. It would be uncommon for one person to show all these difficulties. There is much variation in deficits.

People with HFA/ASP have great difficulty understanding works of fiction, which require a sophisticated capacity to understand the emotional interplay of the characters. They will often interpret the storylines in a very concrete way. Movies are also a very significant problem; a great deal is conveyed in a non-verbal way which they have difficulty interpreting.

Not surprisingly, they are interested in movies and television series like *Star Trek* and characters like Data in *Star Trek* – an android who functions in a way not unlike a person with HFA/ASP. Other movies that might be of interest to people with HFA/ASP would be 'autistic movies' such as *A.I.* (Artificial Intelligence) and *Robocop*. The increasing robotisation of movies might mean that they would be more attractive to people with HFA/ASP.

Tantam[15] points out that 'cognitive difficulties that parallel pragmatic speech problems include a fussiness and search for precision about concepts, which is doomed to failure because no definition exists for them, only competence in their use'. This is what Wittgenstein did in the *Tractatus*, and then in the *Philosophical Investigations* he understood the importance of use of language in the social context. This was an enormous achievement for him, and will be discussed in the next chapter.

Jill de Villiers[16] states that 'for individuals with autism, verbal mediation may be their only way of "hacking" out a correct solution to these tasks, which other children solve them using non-linguistic cognitive mechanisms'. This is possibly why Wittgenstein focused on linguistic philosophy.

Identity and autism/identity diffusion

Jean Quigley states that:

> Our extreme sensitivity to narrative and the tendency to narrative experience links one's sense of self and one's sense of others in the social world. In the view of some authors, not only does narrative provide privileged focus for examining the culture of language but there may also be a special affinity between narrative and self, such that narratives can be said to play a special role in the process of self-construction.[17]

She is referring here to the work of Bruner[18] as well as Miller and coworkers.[19] Similarly, Ochs and Capps point out that:

> personal narrative simultaneously is born out of experience and gives shape to experience. In this sense, narrative and self are inseparable. Self is here broadly understood to be an unfolding reflective awareness of being in the world, including a sense of one's past and future. We come to know ourselves as we use narrative to apprehend experiences and navigate relationships with others.[20]

This appears to be very true, and is precisely what people with autism have difficulties in doing and fail to do; this leads to their very deficient sense of self and sense of identity.

Identity is also partly built up by imitation and identification with parents and others. This partially fails in people with autism. The problems with eye contact, reading non-verbal behaviour, and understanding emotional aspects of verbal conversations also aggravate the normal development of a sense of self.

People with autism have a very distorted sense of self and a very unusual identity. Indeed, they may have very little sense of identity in the classic form. Persons with autism have difficulty in personalising memory, and this leads to a deficient sense of self.

Jean Quigley believes that 'the self-constructive implications of being skilled at linguistic, and especially narrative, practices' have a bearing on autism and identity.[21] She also points out that 'language and especially narrative, which remain problematic even for the most able of autistic individuals, are accorded a special role in the process of self-construction'.[22]

Quigley has investigated the idea, based on Wittgenstein's, of a sense of self constituted in, and by, language, rather than one arrived at through a special form of inner perception.

Ordinarily, people also build up identity by observing how they themselves affect their environment, how they affect people around them, and this power of action of themselves helps to give them a sense of self. People with autism have difficulty reading other people and other people's reactions to them, and are bewildered by these reactions: this is partially the effect of their non-development of a normal sense of identity. Identity probably begins with the baby's recognition of the mother's face, and different emotional reactions on that face. The person with autism has difficulty in reading the mother's face and therefore will have difficulty building up good psychological internalisations.

Jordan and Powell propose that the difficulties in autism might derive from the failure to develop 'an experiencing self'.[23] They appear to be correct in this assertion.

Margaret Prior and Sally Ozonoff[24] agree with Shapiro and Hertzig[25] that:

> integrative deficits . . . are central to any sensory and perceptual dysfunction, i.e. the autistic child is unable to coordinate and integrate varying kinds of sensory input and to form a coherent functional picture of the world. This applies across all modalities and may be fundamental to all the other deficits.

People with HFA/ASP are also unable to form a coherent picture of themselves, partly because of these integrative deficits.

Autobiographical memory and autism

Siegel points out something that is very important for autism, i.e. that 'recent neuroimaging studies suggest that memory for facts (semantic memory) – including events – is functionally quite distinct from memory of the self across time (episodic)'.[26] It is clear that people with autism are quite good with memory for facts.

According to Siegel, in contrast,

> autobiographical or episodic memory requires a capacity termed autonoesis (self-knowing) and appears to be dependent on the development of frontal cortical regions of the brain. The ability of the human mind to carry out 'mental time travel', to have a sense of recollection of the self at a particular time in the past, awareness of the self in the present,

and projections of the self into the imagined future, are the unique contributions of autonoetic consciousness.[27]

It would appear that this might be the area in which people with autism are poor, and therefore they have poor identity and poor sense of self.

Executive function deficits

According to Happe, executive functions include 'planning and monitoring of behaviour, set shifting inhibiting automatic actions and holding information on-line in working memory'.[28] Persons with HFA/ASP have significant executive function deficits.

Baron-Cohen points out that the repetitive behaviour of people with autism has been interpreted as an executive function deficit,[29] and that:

> much repetitive behaviour involves the child's obsessional or strong interest with mechanical systems (such as light switches or water faucets) or other systems that can be understood in physical-causal terms. Rather than these 'behaviours' being a sign of executive dysfunction these may reflect the child's intact or even superior development of their folk physics. The child's obsession with machines and systems, and what is often described as their need for sameness in attempting to hold the environment constant, might be signs of the child as a superior folk physicist: conducting mini-experiments in his or her surroundings, in an attempt to identify physical-causal principles underlying events. Certainly, our recent study of obsessions[30] suggests that these are not random with respect to content (which would be predicted by the content-free executive dysfunction theory), but that these tend to cluster in the domain of folk physics.

This is what many of the people in this book show.

Central coherence

Happe also discusses central coherence, which means 'the everyday tendency to process incoming information in its context – that is, pulling information together for higher-level meaning – often at the expense of memory for detail'.[31] Happe notes that this 'global processing predominates over local processing in at least some aspects of perception', and, in addition, central coherence relates to the tendency to recall the gist of a story 'while the detail is effortful to retain and quickly lost'.[32]

As mentioned above, Wittgenstein was aware of his problem with central coherence even though he did not call it by that name.[33] Sigman and Capps point out that:

a deficient drive for central coherence not only accounts for behaviours and abilities that are lacking such as joint attention and theory of mind. It also accounts for the visible symptoms, including the obsessive desire for sameness, repetitive and stereotypical movements, restricted range of interest, and fragmented sensations.[34]

Wittgenstein had many of these problems.

Cummine and colleagues[35] note that the following are the implications of the central coherence deficit:

1   'idiosyncratic focus of attention'
2   'imposition of own perspective'
3   'preference for the known'
4   'inattentiveness to new tasks'
5   'difficulty in choosing and prioritising'
6   'difficulty in organising self, materials, experiences'
7   'difficulty seeing connections and generalising skills and knowledge'
8   'lack of compliance'.

Baron-Cohen[36] points out that Francesca Happe[37] makes the case for:

> the weak central coherence theory having greater explanatory power. Note that folk physics relics on analysis of contingencies in the physical world, noticing spatial and temporal relations which may be causal. This is not confined to the visual world. More important, these two accounts are not necessarily mutually exclusive, as it may well be the case that weak central coherence is a prerequisite for having good folk physics.

Happe points out that weak central coherence could explain 'the high frequency of absolute pitch and the superior ability to learn note–name mappings at later ages'. She also notes that 'weak central coherence may underlie many of the "modular talents" found in autism'.[38] This possibly explains at a psychological level many of the individuals in this book.

Autistic savants

According to Radford:

> Savant memory seems to be more automatic and literal than that of a prodigy of any sort. However, the findings that calendrical and light-ning calculators use rules and rely on calculation rather than sheer memory, that musical savants use musicaltures, and that artistic savants use object classifications, all force us to reject any generalisation that

savants rely totally on 'dumb' rote memories. The very fact that savantism occurs only in domains that have clear, well-defined rules (visual realism, tonal piano playing, calculation, calendrical calculation) must be important.[39]

As defined in the literature, autistic savants have learning disability (mental retardation). In contrast, this book focuses on high-functioning creative autistic savants with probably above-average intelligence levels.

The brain and autism

Sacks[40] reports that, according to Temple Grandin, people with autism have:

> an impaired 'emotion circuit' in the brain (sometimes she speaks of 'empathy circuits'), and she imagines these serve to link the phylogenetically ancient, emotional parts of the brain – the amygdala and the limbic system – with the most recently evolved, specifically human, parts of the prefrontal cortex. Such circuits, she accepts, may be necessary to allow a new 'higher' form of consciousness, an explicit concept of one's self, one's own mind, and other people's – precisely what is deficient in autism.

The present author agrees with this.

Valerie Stone notes that Simon Baron-Cohen and colleagues[41] have 'suggested that it would be more accurate to think of theory of mind inferences as being computed by a distributed neural circuit, with different regions contributing different kinds of computations'.[42] The idea of problems in distributed neural circuits makes a lot of sense. The problems in autism are quite diffuse.

Schultz and colleagues[43] point out that:

> without normally functioning limbic structures, persons with autism spectrum disorders would fail to take special notice of faces and emotions expressed in faces and across early development they would be deprived of critical social learning opportunities. These earliest experiences may be necessarily precursors for achieving later developmental milestones, including the emergence of theory of mind, empathy, and emotional reactions to others that fuel the use of a theory of mind. In addition, failure of the amygdala [a part of the brain that processes social and emotional information] to transmit social–emotional information to cognitive and motor output centres of the frontal lobe would result in abnormal responses to social stimuli, such as faces, and difficulties conveying social–emotional information, e.g.

prosody [stress, pitch and intonation]. This early emotional learning failure could cause a cascade of neurodevelopmental events including the emergence of profoundly disturbed social relatedness.

Frith states that there is a suggestion from post-mortem studies of 'curtailment of neuronal development at, or before, 30 weeks' gestation in foetuses who develop autism as young children'.[44] According to Ratey, autism may be caused in part by migration problems.[45] 'Proper migration of neurons, therefore, is important for the development of normal brain function.'[46]

Cerebral cortex and high-functioning autism/ Asperger's syndrome

Right cerebral hemisphere

Schultz and colleagues point out that there has been a tendency to hypothesise about left-hemisphere dysfunction in autism and right-hemisphere dysfunction in Asperger's syndrome.[47] Clearly, the right hemisphere is involved in visuo-spatial and socio-emotional processing.

Frith notes that 'recent studies have highlighted the resemblances of the profiles [of persons with autism] to those of patients with frontal lobe and right-hemisphere lesions'.[48]

West states that the 'processing of visual images, spatial relationships, face and pattern recognition, gesture, and proportion are seen to be specialised in the right hemisphere' and that the 'right thinks visually, in pictures and images in three-dimensional space'.[49] Persons with autism have strengths in visuo-spatial areas.

The right hemisphere of the brain controls visuo-spatial functions. Some studies have shown 'reversed or absent lateralisation of brain activity in autism',[50] and that the right hemisphere was over-active in people with autism, but not all people with autism showed these patterns. Ludwig Wittgenstein had enormous strength in right-brain tasks such as architecture and engineering, and succeeded brilliantly in them from a very young age (ten years), when he developed a sewing machine, but later in life he focused on the language of philosophy (as discussed in the next chapter).

Left cerebral hemisphere

West states that 'abilities such as logic, language, orderliness, sequential time, and arithmetic are seen to be largely specialised in the left hemisphere' and that 'in general, one might say that the left thinks in words and numbers'.[51]

Gregory points out that the left hemisphere of the brain controls language and symbolic functions.[52] The ability to think spatially depends on a region of the right hemisphere between the occipital, parietal and temporal lobes, and a main region for mathematical thinking is in a similar part of the left hemisphere.

These sharp differentiations between the two hemispheres and between HFA and ASP have not been sustained in autism spectrum disorders. This is why the term 'HFA/ASP' has been used in this book.

West also states that 'it is becoming increasingly clear that most activities involve both hemispheres to one degree or another, as well as various combinations of structures within each hemisphere'.[53]

Brain size, gender and autism

There is no doubt that autism/Asperger's syndrome is more common in males than females, and of course the same goes for many other childhood conditions. My clinical experience with HFA/ASP is that it has the same features in women as it does in men. It is more easily missed in women. In my view there is no male autism or female autism – only autism. To date the enormous creativity of certain individuals with autism/Asperger's syndrome and genius has been largely shown in men. Some will say this is entirely cultural, but I don't believe that cultural factors can fully explain this. There does seem to be something unique about male creativity and autism. I believe that Temple Grandin showed autism, and not a 'female form of autism'. Nevertheless, males are more susceptible.

In this area I am very persuaded by the writings of Simon Baron-Cohen and his colleagues, who state that:

> deficits in folk psychology exist alongside superiority in folk physics. If it was partly the result of a genetic liability, there is every reason to expect that individuals with this sort of cognitive profile would have been selected for hominid evolution, since good folk physics confers the important advantages (e.g. tool use, hunting skills, construction skills). Indeed, it is a tautology that without highly developed folk physics (e.g. engineering), *Homo sapiens* would still be pre-industrial. It may be that the 'male brain' is an instance of this cognitive profile, given the evidence from the experimental studies of sex differences (female superiority in folk psychology, and male superiority in folk physics).[54]

As shown by the work of Baron-Cohen and Hammer[55] on this view, the autistic brain may be an extreme form of the male brain.

In terms of sex ratios, Rita Jordan[56] points out that 'the sex ratios seems to vary with ability; most girls with autism are at the lower end of the ability range, while at the most able end (including those with Asperger's syndrome) boys may outnumber 5:1'. Jordan also points out that Skuse is quoted in Schmidt as saying 'I suggest that girls are generally pre-programmed to learn almost by instinct, to interpret social cues; boys on the other hand do not have this advantage and have to work harder to get to the same point'.[57] 'Such a sex-linked view of the genetics of autism harks back to the view of Asperger in 1944 that autism represented the extreme form of maleness.'[58] Tony Attwood[59] asked the question 'do girls have a different expression of the syndrome?' He also points out, quoting Gillberg, that 'the boy to girl ratio for referrals for a diagnostic assessment is about 10 boys to each girl'. Attwood believes that:

> in general boys tend to have a greater expression of social deficits with a very uneven profile of social skills and a propensity for disruptive or aggressive behaviour, especially when frustrated or stressed. In contrast, girls tend to be relatively more able in social play and have a more even profile of social skills.

Attwood also 'noticed how girls with Asperger's syndrome seem more able to follow actions by delayed imitation. They observe the other children and copy them, but their actions are not well timed and spontaneous'. He points out that:

> girls with this syndrome are more likely to be considered immature rather than odd. Their special interest may not be as conspicuous and intense as occurs with boys. Thus, they can be described as the 'invisible' child – socially isolated, preoccupied by their own imaginary world while not a disruptive influence in the classroom.

Although girls are less likely to be diagnosed, they are more likely to suffer in silence.

An important issue for girls is that during adolescence the usual basis for friendship changes. Instead of joint play with toys and games using imagination, adolescent friendship is based on conversation that is predominantly about experiences, relationships and feelings. The young teenage girl with Asperger's syndrome may want to continue the playground games of the primary school and starts to reduce her contact with previous friends. They no longer share the same interests. There is also the new problem of coping with the amorous advances of teenagers. Here conversation is acceptable but concepts of romance and love as well as physical intimacy are confusing or abhorrent. In an attempt to be included in social activities, some teenage girls have described how they have deliberately adopted a 'mask'-like quality to their face. Attwood states that he has 'observed girls with the classic signs of Asperger's syndrome in their primary school years progress through the autism/Asperger's syndrome continuum to a point where the current diagnostic criteria are no longer sensitive to the more subtle problems they face'.

Christopher Gillberg[60] points out that:

> males are strongly over-represented in the clinical variant of Asperger's syndrome. Some of the salient features of Asperger's syndrome could be construed as extreme exaggerations of what some people would refer to as 'the male psyche' (tendency to social isolation, formalism, subdued expression of non-verbal communication, interest in only a few or narrow areas rather than a varied interest pattern). There is actually some, albeit limited, empirical evidence that this stereotype may not be a complete misrepresentation of realities. If, indeed, boys and men tend just a little bit towards the 'Asperger type personality', then a smaller gene dose or less severe brain damage would be needed to 'push' them 'over the edge' as compared with what would be required in the case of a female. This could account for some of the skewed gender ratio in Asperger's syndrome. Related to this reasoning is the notion that girls/women with the core problems of Asperger's syndrome may be missed in clinics where autism spectrum disorder is diagnosed. If females with the crucial characteristics show a slightly different phenotype (roughly equivalent to symptomatic presentation) as compared with males, then the male prototype – which was certainly what Asperger described – connected with our conceptualisation of the syndrome would lead to under-diagnosis in girls and women. Several recent studies have argued that this may indeed be the case, and females may receive a host of other diagnoses, including obsessive compulsive disorder/personality disorder, eating disorder, or atypical depression, when, in fact, Asperger's syndrome would have been a more appropriate (and more helpful) diagnosis.[61]

Gillberg points out that boys' interests are more factual and that 'girls' interests may sometimes, at least superficially, appear to be more "social", but, on further analysis, one often finds that they are also dependent on rote memory rather than meaning. Some girls (and a few boys) appear to have few or even no interests.'

Gillberg also makes the following statements:

> Girls and women with Asperger's syndrome sometimes show a slightly different constellation of symptoms than the one regarded as typical of the males with the disorder. It is quite considerable that such cases would be missed in epidemiological studies. This, in turn, infers the current prevalence estimates are underestimates, and that the proportion of females with the condition is larger than usually reported.[62]

> Those few girls who have been diagnosed with autism in the past have usually been severely affected, often with major signs of brain damage.

This could be because a large proportion of all girls with Autism Spectrum Disorders – specifically those that are higher functioning – may have been undetected in these studies, conveying the false message that when girls have autism they are more severely handicapped.[63]

The language of some girls with Asperger's syndrome whom I have met over the years has been less formal, less pedantic than the language of similarly aged boys. At present, however, there is no good empirical data to suggest that girls with Autism Spectrum Disorders generally differ from boys with similar conditions specifically in respect of language.[64]

It has been proposed that the same kind of underlying empathy disorder might be present in more girls than hitherto acknowledged. Girls could have the same type of core deficit as boys with autism, but they would not receive a diagnosis of autism because they do not show all the symptoms of autism which are typically associated with the male prototype. Girls in the general population appear to be more interested and participate more readily in two-way social interactions already at an early age. Their language development is earlier than that of boys. Their pattern of interest is definitely different in that they are not so exclusively devoted in mechanical aspects of objects and may not be equally insistent on routine.[65]

Uta Frith[66] states that 'there is no empirical evidence to suggest that autistic boys differ from autistic girls in terms of abstract thinking', and points out that Hans Asperger states that 'the autistic personality is an extreme variant of male intelligence'.

Obler and Fine speculate[67] that 'average non-exceptional abilities are the price that most of us pay for overall normal cognitive and emotional functioning'.

Studies have shown greater head circumference in males with autism. Schultz and colleagues note that 'males tend to be more strongly lateralised for functions than females', and, adjusting for body size, to have larger brains.[68] Schultz and colleagues also note that 'greater lateralisation in males is taken to be a reflection of increased modularity and decreased interconnectedness that is dictated by the physical constraints imposed by their larger brains'.[69] In autism and Asperger's syndrome we may be dealing with a male form of genius and creativity. Baron-Cohen and Hammer point out that 'the autistic brain may be an extreme form of the male brain'.[70]

Schultz and colleagues state that:

the larger brain in persons with autism spectrum disorders would be increased modularity of function, with less overlap and integration of functions (perhaps resulting in a lack of 'central coherence') that is posited in Frith's theory. There is a female advantage in such things as face recognition and emotion recognition and with the much lower rates of autistic disorder.[71]

Of course it is possible to have a big brain and not be autistic.

Pamela Wells points out that 'girls tend to be better at verbal tasks, and boys at mathematical tasks; boys are on average more aggressive than girls; boys are better at some visuospatial tasks and girls at others (so, for instance, men tend to be better at reading maps and women are, famously, better at finding things around the house)'.[72]

Happe notes that:

> some people with autism have larger or heavier brains than do comparison groups, with increased cell packing in several areas. It is possible that this reflects an abnormal number of neurons [nerve cells], perhaps because of a failure of pruning in brain development. In turn, processing with excess neurons could result in a failure to process information for gist – in other words, a lack of drive for cognitive economy, as a result of increased capacity for exemplar-based processing.[73]

Cohen has presented a computational model of autism, in which lack of generalisation results in an increase in the number of units – 'an intriguing example of how computational analyses can interact with neural anatomical data and psychological theory to help solve the puzzle of autism'.[74] Happe notes that 'it is intriguing to think that the cognitive style of weak coherence in autism, with its attendant assets and deficits, might result from "an embarrassment of riches" at the neural level'.[75] This may have implications for the people described in this book.

Chapter 4

Ludwig Wittgenstein

PSYCHOBIOGRAPHY

Introduction

Ludwig Wittgenstein was arguably the greatest philosopher of the twentieth century. His family background, personal development and psychopathology are of considerable importance in understanding his contribution to twentieth-century philosophy. Born in 1889 of mixed Jewish–Catholic heritage, he grew up in aristocratic splendour in Vienna, a city that could then claim luminaries such as Sigmund Freud, Karl Kraus and Alfred Loos among its inhabitants. Many of Wittgenstein's peers have attested to his remarkable genius.

While the study of a remarkable man can give clues to the origins of his greatness, genius itself is unique and a citizen of no nation. It does represent, however, a unique coming together of genes and environment. It would appear that some forms of great creativity can benefit from autistic psychopathology, while 'normality' – at least in the statistical sense – produces only replicate ideas. Though Wittgenstein's genius and the autism he manifested are largely genetically determined, the influence of culture was felt. The sharp sense of duty and moral rectitude that preoccupied him throughout his life was partially induced by his family, but is also a not uncommon characteristic of HFA/ASP. So virulent was his criticism of his culture that in 1946 he recommended dropping a few more atomic bombs on the region to make an end of 'our disgusting soapy water science'.[1]

Following his education at the Realschule in Linz, and a technical college in Berlin, he became a research student in aeronautical engineering in Manchester and made a significant contribution to the aircraft industry with his development of a propeller.[2] His interest in philosophy began after reading Bertrand Russell's *Principia Mathematica* and meeting the greatest logician since Aristotle, Gottlob Frege, at the University of Jena. Wittgenstein then studied philosophy at Cambridge under Russell and G.E. Moore, the leading philosophers of the day, spending five terms at

Trinity College from 1912 to 1913. The outbreak of the First World War saw him enlist as a soldier, a duty he embraced with fearless dedication and for which he was later decorated for bravery. Privately he continued to work on philosophy, which culminated in the post-war publication of *Tractatus Logico-Philosophicus*, one of the most important philosophy tracts of the twentieth century, which was to change the direction of philosophy. Following the war he trained as a primary school teacher and spent a number of years teaching in Austrian villages. After finally resigning from teaching he became a monastery gardener, but later returned to philosophical work at Cambridge via the Vienna Circle.

At the outbreak of the Second World War Wittgenstein became professor of philosophy at Cambridge but contributed to the British war effort as a medical orderly at Guy's Hospital, London, and later became a trauma researcher at Newcastle-upon-Tyne. He returned to Cambridge following the war but resigned from what he saw as a senseless job as professor of philosophy in 1947. He was then to spend long periods alone in Ireland writing his second major work, *Philosophical Investigations*. Throughout his life he sought the most isolated regions of Europe (Norway, the west of Ireland) in which to write. He died from cancer in 1951 at the home of his physician, Dr E. Bevan. His last words to his friends were 'I have had a wonderful life'.[3]

The focus of much of Wittgenstein's research was in areas that he had difficulties with himself: language and logic. His achievements can be described as colossal in many areas; e.g. he produced great philosophy, was a brilliant engineer, an architect, and a multi-decorated soldier, as well as a man who survived and coped with severe depression for most of his life yet died of natural causes.[4] His final monumental achievement was to overcome (partially) a severe deficit in communication and social interaction, i.e. HFA/ASP. Of course, this was only partially achieved as it is impossible to overcome it completely. This last achievement was as great as the others described above, but long unrecognised.

This chapter attempts to show how Asperger's description of autistic psychopathy (now called Asperger's syndrome) works out in practice with a person with HFA/ASP. It illustrates the strengths and deficits of such a person. There is particular focus on family history, social relationship difficulties, control issues, preservation of sameness, all-absorbing interests, problems with non-verbal behaviour often associated with identity problem issues, problems with aggression, depressive problems, special talent in engineering and philosophy. Considerable attention is given to Wittgenstein's philosophy in an attempt to show how his HFA/ASP impacted on his philosophical work. He continues to be a controversial figure and therefore more attention is given to him than to others in the book. This chapter sets out the issues in more detail than is possible in other chapters because of space constraints.

Family and social background

Wittgenstein was fortunate in having two superb biographers that give valuable insights into his life, first Brian McGuinness for his early life and second Ray Monk, who is particularly helpful on his later life.[5] Between them they were able to provide a telling account of his personality and character with its many eccentricities and peculiarities. Thus, the evidence for Wittgenstein's HFA/ASP is plain to see.[6]

Many of Wittgenstein's traits appear to be inherited from his grandfather and father. His grandfather, Herman Christian Wittgenstein, was born in 1802 in Korbach, Austria. He was a man, according to McGuinness, who showed 'a religious earnestness, a sense of life as a task, which was to reappear in many of his descendants'. In addition, Herman Christian was regarded as being stern, cold and very serious in conversation.[7] He also had the ability and determination to get things done properly and was obstinate, but had unquestioning confidence in his own authority. Indeed, Herman Christian appears also to demonstrate traits at the very least of an autism spectrum disorder while being 'not a little irascible'. The sharp sense of duty that Wittgenstein demonstrated throughout his life was possibly inherited from Herman Christian, who had 'a consciousness of their [family's] capacities and a strong feeling of a duty to realise them'. This sense of duty obligated the family to improve and educate others.[8] Certainly, the wish to control is very much a feature of autism.

Furthermore, despite his contribution to the great wealth of the Austro-Hungarian Empire with his varied mercantile and manufacturing interests, Herman Christian refused ennoblement or titles. McGuinness notes how the family had exceptional loyalty to chosen friends, but this was accompanied by a 'nervousness and a degree of sensibility' which made them difficult to live with unless offset by a placid and understanding companion.[9]

Wittgenstein's grandmother, Fanny Figdor, brought the more urbane world of Vienna to the family but was highly critical herself – being quicker to 'censure than to repine'.[10] She also showed a certain 'impatience and quickness of decision' according to McGuinness. In an energetic spirit she reared her family in a strict household and was unnecessarily frugal given the family's affluence.

Wittgenstein's father, Karl, was the sixth of ten children. Karl had a love for the 'bold and unconventional'.[11] A dislike of schooling led him to run away both from school and from home on numerous occasions. According to McGuinness, he too was impatient, quick to detect humbug but showed ingenuity and a practical bent, particularly in his childhood escapades.[12] These misdemeanours were usually punished by locking him in a room. He was 'a self-made man', who ran off to New York where he worked in a variety of low-paid jobs before eventually returning to Austria in 1867. From an early age he had a phenomenal ability for mathematical calculation. Not surprisingly, he later studied engineering and became a steel magnate. So extraordinary was his ability that he was able to give lectures with statistics from memory.

Karl was uncertain of spelling and punctuation (as was Wittgenstein). It is quite possible that he had HFA/ASP, or at the very least traits of the disorder.

In keeping with the life of a *grand seigneur*, Karl was a keen patron of the arts. He played the violin and horn, and associated with the leading composers and musicians of the day, such as Mendelssohn, Clara Schumann, Brahms, Joseph Labor, Bruno Walter and Pablo Casals. Musical recitals and concerts were often arranged at the Wittgenstein home. Karl was an avid art collector of modern pieces. However, his taste had a certain seriousness and calm to it, which his daughter Hermine identified as a 'stress on verticals and horizontals' that she considered 'ethical'.[13]

According to McGuinness, Karl showed 'insensitivity and at times brutality' and was certainly an autodidact.[14] Hermine, in her unpublished account of the Wittgenstein family life, *Familienerinnerungen*, remarked that 'a personality so out of the ordinary required . . . a development out of the ordinary'.[15] McGuinness notes that the world of 'moral absolutes' that Karl created could be perceived immediately. It was 'not assented to on balance and from which deviation was a complete failure'.[16] He lacked empathy and certainly was a perfectionist. He was insensitive and dictatorial to many of his children and, indeed, a number later committed suicide. The critical attitude so characteristic of his mother was also evident, and he showed an iron will in his dealings with others. Yet for all his shortcomings, Karl was idealised by Wittgenstein. This cannot be said for Wittgenstein's mother, Leopoldine (Poldi). Poldi had a rather anxious personality and was uncertain of herself. Unfortunately for her children, she was unable to protect them from her husband's lack of empathy and insensitivity. In fact, she took a position of abject submission to her husband. According to McGuinness, music was her chief means of contact with her husband and children.[17]

Wittgenstein was the youngest of eight children. As well as being rather delicate and sensitive, as a young adolescent he had a double rupture. He had many of the traits described in other family members, such as a religious earnestness, a sense of life as a task, a sense of duty, the need to improve and educate others, a willingness to suffer privation, a sense of melancholy and a lack of empathy. Not surprisingly, Wittgenstein described his childhood as unhappy and lonely.[18] There was a lack of parental warmth and empathy. His mother hardly figured in his life. Instead he had many nannies and tutors who were poorly supervised and often of dubious ability. Undoubtedly, he suffered in a major way from the severe morals of his family. He was very concerned about telling lies; more seriously, thoughts of suicide preoccupied him from the ages of 18 to 22 years. Nevertheless, the key to Wittgenstein was his HFA/ASP, not his environment. Indeed, suicidal thoughts are not rare in people with HFA/ASP.

It is possible that his sister Margarete (Gretl) may also have had traits of HFA/ASP. She was seven years senior to Wittgenstein and was 'at least as independent, and eccentric as Ludwig . . . [and] self-willed',[19] according to Paul Wijdeveld, architect and family friend. She was rebellious and studied mathematics and physics despite the conventions of the day discouraging the study of such subjects by women. However, her upper-class fancies were evident too. Wijdeveld noted that she liked to collect 'porcelain and china and chinoiserie'.[20] It is widely believed that she was psychoanalysed by Freud. Indeed, following the annexing of Austria by the Nazis in 1938, she arranged for his emigration to England in close co-operation with her friend Princess Marie Bonaparte.[21]

Speech and language

Christopher Gillberg emphasised a number of features in Asperger's syndrome (part of autism spectrum disorder), such as delayed development, superficially perfect expressive language, formal pedantic language, odd prosody and peculiar voice characteristics, and impairment of social comprehension including misinterpretations of the meaning of social interaction. Undoubtedly, Wittgenstein manifested all these features to varying degrees.

Wittgenstein did not begin to speak until he was four years old. He suffered from dyslexia and stammering, which can be associated with autism spectrum disorder. There was a family history of dyslexia. Anna Maija Hintikka notes that his sister Hermine in *Familienerinnerungen* claimed that both their mother and father had language problems.[22] Certainly, Wittgenstein stated that:

> my bad spelling in youth up to the age of about 18 or 19, is connected with the whole of the rest of my character (whole of my weakness in study) . . . I never more than half succeed in expressing what I want to express. Actually not as much as that, but no more than a tenth. That is still worth something. Often my writing is nothing but 'stuttering'.[23]

Throughout his life his spelling difficulties and stammer were widely observed. McGuinness elaborates on his language difficulties:

> [His] special difficulty with spelling presumably explains why, in German, he was actually given the failing mark of *nicht-genugend* in the written examination, redeeming himself only by obtaining *lobenswert* in the *viva voce*. It always cost him some effort to spell correctly and there are a fair number of misspellings, sometimes quite expressive ones, in

his rougher drafts. His written English naturally varied with the length of time he had been in or away from England; but at all times the spelling was shakier than the idiom. This shadow of a defect, possibly hereditary, can be associated with the slight stammer that Engelmann observed. The stammer had disappeared by the 1920s, when he spoke with the clear high voice not uncommon among those who have overcome an impediment.[24]

In Wittgenstein's case, the clear high voice is a feature of HFA/ASP. The odd prosody and peculiar voice characteristics, as listed by Gillberg, were marked in Wittgenstein's speech. His voice was quite distinctive in addition to the high pitch. His one-time student and later close friend, Norman Malcolm, remarked on the nature of his voice and intonation:

> Wittgenstein always spoke emphatically and with a distinctive intonation. He spoke excellent English, with the accent of an educated Englishman, although occasionally Germanisms would appear in his constructions. His voice was resonant, the pitch being somewhat higher than that of the normal male voice. His words came out, not fluently, but with great force. Anyone who heard him say anything knew that here was a singular person.[25]

The above intonation can occur in HFA/ASP. Certainly, Wittgenstein spoke English fluently with an eye for precision and exactitude.

Wittgenstein was educated at home with a string of tutors until 14 years old. He fared badly, and preferred subjects that he could teach himself. Failure to show the interest in schooling his father expected meant he was denied a grammar school (gymnasium) education. Instead he went to the Realschule in Linz for a scientific and technical education. In school he performed well below his ability, suffered from bullying and was regarded as somewhat odd. His poor performance was due to his learning difficulties, depression and HFA/ASP. Poor school performance is very common in people with HFA/ASP. McGuinness provides details of his school record:

> His performance in school subjects was far from distinguished. On the 5-point scale then used, he obtained in his Matura Certificate a 1 only for religious knowledge, a 2 for conduct and English; a 3 for French, for geography and history, for mathematics, for natural history, and for physics, and a 4 for German, chemistry, descriptive geometry, and freehand drawing.[26]

Interestingly, Adolf Hitler attended the same school but was a couple of years behind Wittgenstein. There is some controversy as to the extent of their interaction and mutual influence. Monk states that:

Hitler, though almost exactly the same age as Wittgenstein, was two years behind at school. They overlap only for the year 1904–1905, because Hitler was forced to leave because of his poor record. There is no evidence they had anything to do with one another.[27]

Clearly, this is the true state of the relationship or non-relationship.[28]

Wittgenstein's dyslexia was to have an influence on his early work in philosophy. Hintikka claims that Wittgenstein had 'earlier thought the preference of pictorial thinking culminates in the "picture theory of language" of the *Tractatus*. As a dyslexic, he was more comfortable in the visual, not to say geometrical medium than in the verbal one, even when it comes to language understanding.'[29]

[It is possible to consider almost all of Wittgenstein's] central writings as attempts to deal with problems of linguistic structure, of the meanings of words, and problems of language learning. Perhaps one could say that Wittgenstein was puzzled by the phenomena of language in the same way in which Einstein, another dyslexic, never ceased to wonder at the phenomena of the physical world. Einstein himself attributed the peculiarity of his slow development which enabled him never to lose completely a child's wonder at the world. Could it be likewise that Wittgenstein's slow linguistic maturing enabled him to wonder like a child at the formation of his own linguistic processes – and to recover an awareness of them for the rest of us who have lost the awareness in the course of their becoming routine? In *Philosophical Investigations*, Part 1, Section 129 'the aspects of things that are most important for us are hidden because they are simplicity and familiarity . . . the real foundations of his enquiry do not strike a man at all. Unless that fact has sometimes struck him. And this means: we fail to be struck by what once seen, is most striking and most powerful.'[30]

Undoubtedly Wittgenstein was more comfortable in the visual. Hintikka also points out that he used to communicate through drawing, and indeed 'had a friend whom he communicated with by drawing pictures'.

In conversation Wittgenstein often showed literalness and took people at their word. Though he had problems initiating and sustaining conversations, he was often insensitive to the listener's response. He was also very good with metaphor. According to Malcolm, on one occasion when feeling in a good mood because the day's work had gone well, Wittgenstein described it as 'making hay during the very short period when the sun shines in my brain'.[31] Wittgenstein's formality of speech was noted at the Realschule in Linz, where he addressed his teenage peers in the polite form of address, *Sie,* much to their amazement, leading them to think he had come from another world.

In his use of language he showed a concreteness, particularly evident in the *Tractatus*. It is possible that dyslexia and HFA/ASP can account for the shortness of the sentences and the aphoristic chains of ideas in his work. This possibly can be attributed to the relatively small amounts of working memory he may have had. The paradox here was that his problem led him to see things more clearly. Wittgenstein also talked to himself, a feature not uncommon in people with HFA/ASP. Tommy Mulkerns (caretaker of the cottage in the west of Ireland where Wittgenstein stayed) arrived one morning to hear voices inside the house. He remarked to Wittgenstein that he thought he had company, to which Wittgenstein replied 'yes, he had been talking to a very dear friend – himself'.[32] People with HFA/ASP can also have problems with inner speech. There is a question as to whether Wittgenstein had inner speech problems, which possibly later influenced his views on private language.

However, he had great difficulty in expressing himself and struggled for words; this was reflected in his mode of thought. Scharfstein used the word 'stammering' to characterise 'Ludwig's writing, speaking, and thinking'.[33] For him language was so full of both promise and danger that it could not be used simply as a neutral medium.[34] Though his stammering disappeared to a greater extent later on, according to Engelmann, his struggle for words was especially keen when trying hard to formulate a proposition.[35] Wittgenstein's ambivalent attitude to words as modes of expressing ideas is reflected in his stammering, according to Scharfstein:

> Wittgenstein's stammer, traces of which I think he always retained, was paralleled by his idea-stammer, by which I mean a fierce but blocked searching, a series of hesitancies, and then, sometimes, a sudden resolution. Stammering in the meaning of which I would like to include the stammering, not only of speech-sounds, but of ideas, may be the response to something the stammerer both wants and does not want to say, or the equally ambivalent response to the activity itself of speaking. Wittgenstein's stammering is likely to have been related to his peculiar interest in speech and deprecation of its powers and, often, of its use to his ambition and self-doubt; and to his at least mild exhibitionism, which was his need for an audience and his revulsion from an audience.[36]

Once again this may have been due to HFA/ASP, and one wonders whether his speech and language problems precipitated his interest in linguistic philosophy. However, his disjointedness had serious problems for his students, who were left thoroughly confused by his lectures. Ambrose and Lazerowitz point out that 'during the first term I felt that I was hearing a lecture in which there were gaps such as intermittent deafness might produce'.[37] Similarly, Gasking and Jackson note that the difficulty in following his lectures arose because 'it was hard to see where all this often repetitive concrete detailed talk was leading to'.[38] This is highly characteristic of HFA/ASP.

In a letter to his mother in 1923, Frank Ramsey, the mathematician/philosopher, wrote that '[Wittgenstein] often forgot the meaning of what [he said] within five minutes, and then remembered it later. Some of his sentences are intentionally ambiguous having an ordinary and a more difficult meaning which he also believes'.[39] During his lectures, without resorting to manuscripts or notes, Wittgenstein would entangle himself in questions, continually arranging and rearranging his thoughts and ideas, which to his audience would appear as silences and stammerings and passionate questioning. Asking ambiguous, seemingly irrelevant questions was no more than Wittgenstein's way of eliminating areas of study. In *Vermischte Bemerkungen* he declares that he would inspect a wide area only in order to exclude it from consideration.[40]

H.J. Glock claimed that Wittgenstein's handwriting was bad and his text littered with additions of individual words and phrases, often making the sequence of his remarks unclear.[41] This was possibly due to reading and writing difficulties. Interestingly, dictionaries were vital to Wittgenstein – so much so that he contributed to educational reform in his native country by producing a spelling dictionary for elementary schools when he was a schoolteacher in the village of Otterthal. While he worked in Ireland, according to J. Mahon, he was constantly using dictionaries.[42] None the less, Scharfstein suggests that there was something wilfully obscure in Wittgenstein:

> For his writing, his justification was that he had to write in his disjoined aphoristic style. As has been emphasised in the earlier discussion of his style, the Preface to *Philosophical Investigations* explains that he found his thoughts were soon crippled if forced against their natural inclination. Therefore, he said, he made remarks sometimes in a fairly long chain devoted to the same subject, but sometimes the remarks jumped suddenly from subject to subject. This insistence on at least surface disconnectedness applies as well to the *Tractatus*, which would have been unintelligible if not for its numbering.[43]

Because of his HFA/ASP, this was possibly the only way he could write. It was an autistic style – a kind of one-person psychology. It is not true to say that he was deliberately obscure; rather his condition made it more difficult for him to communicate and to connect to the outside world.

For much of his life Wittgenstein was subjected to teasing by nicknames and rhymes. Those with autism are commonly mocked and given nicknames. Indeed, Monk notes that his peers 'ridiculed him by chanting an alliterative jingle that made play of his unhappiness and the distance between him and the rest of the school . . . *Wittgenstein Wandelt Vehmuetig Widriger Winde Wegen Wienwaerts* (Wittgenstein wends his woeful windy way towards Vienna)'.[44] The nicknames continued into adulthood, though in private. During his time at Cambridge Wittgenstein was referred to as 'Herr Sinckel Winckel' by Lytton Strachey.[45]

Humour

Humour is an area that poses particular difficulty for people with HFA/ASP. David Pinsent considered his friend's sense of humour as 'heavy',[46] whereas Russell said that Wittgenstein was witty.[47] Edmonds and Eidinow agree there is little doubt that Wittgenstein did have a sense of humour; however, it was clearly childlike. This is often a feature of those with HFA/ASP. A favourite joke of his went as follows:

> A fledgling leaves the nest to try out its wings. On returning, it discovers that an orange has taken its place. 'What are you doing there?' asked the fledgling. 'Ma-me-aid,' replies the orange.[48]

The type of humour that Wittgenstein enjoyed most was found in the detective stories of the time, particularly American comic-style ones, to which he was 'addicted'. These stories have simple emotional lines and uncomplicated plots, which was as much as Wittgenstein could understand because of HFA/ASP. As he later came to realise, humour was seeing things from another person's point of view. He was particularly taken with the detective stories of Norbert Davis and their simple humour. Monk gives a typical scenario from one of Davis' novels, *Rendezvous with Fear*:

> after setting the scene by describing the tourists at the Azteca, a Hotel in South America, Davis introduced Garcia: all this was very boring to a man who, for the time being, was named Garcia. He sat and drank beer the general colour and consistency of warm vinegar, and glowered. He had a thin, yellowish face and a straggling black moustache, and he was cross-eyed. He should really have been more interested in the tourists coming from the Hotel Azteca, because in a short time one of them was going to shoot him dead. However, he didn't know that, and had you told him he would have laughed. He was a 'bad man'. When Doan shoots Bautiste Bonofile, another 'bad man', the romantic but naïve heroine, Jane, asks with concern: 'Is he hurt'? 'Not a bit', says Doan, 'he is just dead'.[49]

Because he read a vast number of detective stories, after a time, American phrases became part of his everyday vocabulary. Once, when talking about examining a property with Malcolm, he said 'let's go and case the joint!'.[50]

He also picked up the phrase 'hot ziggety!' from Norman Malcolm. This was a phrase commonly used in Kansas when somebody was particularly happy with something. Wittgenstein used it exhaustively when pleased with anything at all.[51] He loved the same repetitive phrases and this is common in people with HFA/ASP.

There was also an element of crudeness to some of his humour. One of his most humorous aphorisms, as recalled by George Kreisel, was 'don't try and shit higher than your arse'.[52] Equally, letters to his friend Pattison are 'astonishingly feeble', according to Monk. Closing an address that ended with WC1, he drew an arrow to WC and wrote that it didn't mean 'lavatory'. On the back of a postcard of Christ Church Cathedral, Dublin, he wrote 'If I remember rightly this cathedral was built, partly at least, by the Normans. Of course, it is a long time ago and my memory isn't what it was then.'[53] In this respect, Wittgenstein engaged in much nonsense humour, of which his friends Roy Fouracre and Gilbert Pattison appear to have been the main beneficiaries. Monk notes that Wittgenstein's correspondence with Pattison consists almost entirely of 'nonsense', which gave him enormous pleasure:

> In nearly every letter he makes some use of the English adjective 'bloody', which, for some reason, he found inexhaustibly funny. He would begin his letters 'Dear Old Blood' and end them 'yours bloodily' or 'yours in bloodiness'. Pattison would send him photographs cut out from magazines, which he called his 'paintings', and which Wittgenstein would respond with exaggeratedly solemn appreciation: 'I would have known it to be a Pattison immediately without the signature. There is that bloodiness in it which has never before been expressed by the brush.' In reply, Wittgenstein would send 'portraits', photographs of distinguished looking middle-aged men, ripped out of newspaper advertisements for self-improvement courses. 'My latest photo', he announced, enclosing one such picture. 'The previous one expressed fatherly kindness only; and this one expresses triumph.'[54]

Interestingly, Lewis Carroll too excelled at nonsense humour. When Tom Mulkerns realised how much processed food Wittgenstein ate while at Rosro, Co. Galway he declared 'tinned food will be the death of you'. Wittgenstein, probably not realising the humour in his response, answered 'people live too long anyway'.[55] It also indicates his misinterpretation of the literal and implied meaning common in those with HFA/ASP.

Wittgenstein had a considerable talent for mimicry, as observed by Peter Gray-Lucas:

> he was an absolutely marvellous mimic. He missed his vocation . . . he would have been a stand-up comedian. In his funny Austrian accent he could do all sorts of mimicry of accents, styles, ways of talking. He was

always talking about the different tones of voice in which you could say things, and it was absolutely gripping . . . that must have been part of his spell . . . that he could conjure up almost anything.[56]

Here we see Wittgenstein focusing on humour, which is supposed to be a deficit in people with HFA/ASP. The skill in mimicry is quite distinct from that of acting, where role-playing is required. Mimicry involves a one-dimensional interpretation of a character, and it is not surprising that Wittgenstein excelled at it. In contrast, taking on the persona of a character would have posed difficulties for him since he lacked empathy, consistent with HFA/ASP. Clearly, people with HFA/ASP are often good at mimicry but have problems identifying with a character.

Not surprisingly, Wittgenstein studied humour in his philosophy. Indeed, he believed that humour was not a mood but a way of looking at the world.[57] Humour was not something superficial that could easily be erased in a person, but something deeper. According to Monk, Wittgenstein wrote while in Rosro:

So if it is correct to say that humour was stamped out in Nazi Germany, that does not mean that people were not in good spirits, or anything of that sort, but something much deeper and more important . . . To understand what that 'something' is, it would perhaps be instructive to look at humour as something strange and incomprehensible: 'two people are laughing together, say at a joke. One of them has used certain somewhat unusual words and now they both break out into a sort of bleating. That might appear very extraordinary to a visitor coming from quite a different environment. Whereas we find it completely reasonable (I recently witnessed this scene on a bus and was able to think myself into the position of someone to whom this would be unfamiliar. From that point of view it struck me as quite irrational, like the response of an outlandish animal).[58]

Monk claims that understanding humour, like understanding music, provides an analogy for Wittgenstein's conception of philosophical understanding. It was not in the discovery of facts or construction of theories but in having the 'right point of view', i.e. from which to 'see' the joke, to appreciate music, clarify philosophy, etc. But the real problem was how to find a way to explain or teach the 'right point of view'.[59]

Social impairment

Wittgenstein demonstrated severe impairment in reciprocal social interaction, with an inability to interact with peers, a lack of desire to interact with peers, a lack of appreciation of social cues, and socially and emotionally inappropriate behaviour. There are many examples of his difficulties with interpersonal relationships.

Early life

While Wittgenstein idealised his father, this was contradicted to some extent by his comment that his childhood was unhappy. During his private education at home he was able to manage only one friend at a time, always finding friendships very problematic. His self-esteem may also have been undermined by his learning difficulties and speech and language problems. At the Realschule in Linz he concentrated all his affection on one friend, and became very upset when this friendship broke down. Much of the difficulty stemmed from Wittgenstein's wish to have control over his relationships, like a 'puppeteer'. He was extremely slow to build up trust and required his friends to be caring and warm in personality. Like most children with HFA/ASP, he was bullied and teased at school.

Clearly, both parents were not attuned to him emotionally, but this was not the fundamental problem. Indeed, Wittgenstein spent his life seeking emotional nurturance. Given that his childhood was unhappy and lonely, according to McGuinness, it is not surprising that he identified with Schopenhauer's 'proud and lonely spirit' as well as with 'Lenau's Faust who showed what despair was like and showed the powerlessness of man'.[60] Wittgenstein himself had admitted to the 'coldness' of his personality. In school he maintained a certain distance, as McGuinness points out:

> one of his contemporaries later told his sister that he seemed to come from quite another world. His way of life was entirely different. He addressed them as *Sie* (surely a deliberate distancing of himself from them) and all his reading and interests were quite different from theirs. It was painful for him (then as later in life) to sit in a class.[61]

In Schopenhauer's porcupine story, Wittgenstein found the picture of his ideal relationship with people. He often quoted this story, where the porcupines 'crowded together for warmth on a winter's day and then drew apart to avoid one another's spines and so moved to and fro until they found a moderate distance that they could support'.[62] The distancing continued throughout his life, most noticeably in that he addressed people by their surnames when he spoke. The exception, according to Wall, was Francis Skinner, with whom he had an intimate physical relationship and the only person he ever called by his first name, Francis.[63]

Teaching methods

Lorna Wing points out that social isolation, egocentricity and lack of interest in the feelings of others are characteristic of both Asperger's syndrome and autism.[64] Wittgenstein manifested these features very strongly. She also mentions the absence of language for interchange with others. This, too, occurred frequently in Wittgenstein's case. Much of his seminar and written work shows a lack of dialogue, where he appears to ignore the needs of the reader or the audience. His method of small group teaching was distinctly strange. He basically spoke his thoughts aloud in the presence of group members. In this fashion he was attempting to clarify his thoughts and directed occasional questions to the audience, who sat in deck-chairs. Thus, his conversations were more monologues than exchanges, except when they concerned a topic of intense interest, e.g. discussing philosophy with Russell and others. The philosopher A.J. Ayer notes Malcolm's description of Wittgenstein's classes: 'Here was Wittgenstein "wrestling with his thoughts, often falling into silences which no one dared to interrupt" . . . he could be impatient with any show of misunderstanding and brutal to anyone who made a remark he considered stupid.'[65] People with HFA/ASP are generally very poor teachers. Students found it difficult to know what point Wittgenstein was trying to make.

Lack of social cues

Wittgenstein's lack of tact and lack of appreciation of social cues is evident from his first contact with Russell, where he arrived without appointment or prior warning. Caroline Moorehead related the meeting as follows:

> When Wittgenstein appeared in his rooms, unannounced and insisting on speaking rather bad English, Russell was having tea with C.K. Ogden, later to become the translator of Wittgenstein's *Tractatus Logico-Philosophus*. He was intrigued by his curious visitor . . . [and said] 'I am much interested in my German and shall hope to see a lot of him'. A lot soon became too much. Wittgenstein haunted his rooms, arguing, debating, contradicting, appearing at midnight and then walking up and down Russell's small attic room like a tiger in a cage . . . At the time he grumbled about Wittgenstein's relentless arguing: 'he is armour-plated against all assaults of reasoning' and joked that he was unable to convince his new disciple of anything. 'I wanted him to consider the proposition 'there is no hippopotamus in this room at present'. When he refused to believe this, I looked under all the desks without finding one; but he remained unconvinced.'[66]

This kind of behaviour is typically seen in a person with HFA/ASP. Wittgenstein had no sense of propriety, no sense of what was considered an appropriate time to visit or converse. Shortly after the First World War he went to see Russell, then staying at a hotel in The Hague. Russell recounted how Wittgenstein 'came before I was up, and hammered on my door till I woke, since then he has talked logic without ceasing for four hours'. This is all very autistic inappropriate behaviour. It resembles the way the mathematician Paul Erdös[67] – who also had HFA/ASP – would arrive at people's doors to discuss mathematics at any time of the day or night.

While in Norway Wittgenstein received a visit from G.E. Moore, then professor of philosophy at Cambridge, and used him as a secretary to take dictation. He then became extremely agitated when Moore failed to understand his work fully. To use Moore, a celebrated philosopher, in this way was indicative of someone with no social cues, i.e. with autism. On another occasion, he wrote to Moore requesting his thesis be considered for his Bachelor of Arts degree. When told it was not in the right format for a degree, Wittgenstein wrote a furious letter in reply that unnerved and upset Moore for days. People with HFA/ASP can do things unknowingly that can be very upsetting. At his oral PhD examination in 1926 with two of the most respected philosophers, Russell and Moore, in attendance, Wittgenstein brought the proceedings to an end 'by clapping each of the examiners on the shoulder and remarking consolingly . . . don't worry, I know you'll never understand it'.[68] Monk adds that it was the most extraordinary PhD examination that possibly had ever taken place in the university. Nevertheless, the examiners recognised his PhD as brilliant and passed him.

By the same token, while writing the *Philosophical Investigations* in the west of Ireland, his isolation became unbearable, he asked Tommy Mulkerns if he could find a place for him in Mulkerns' own cottage as a guest. At that time the Mulkerns' cottage was grossly overcrowded and the request was clearly inappropriate.

Wittgenstein could be extraordinarily abrupt and impatient. M. Drury's widow, Eileen, spoke about an incident at the Savoy cinema in Dublin.[69] One day, Drury (a psychiatrist and friend of Wittgenstein), Eileen and Wittgenstein queued outside for a film, finding the queue too long Wittgenstein left abruptly without saying goodbye.

Wittgenstein made no distinction of class or creed when expressing any form of contempt. Monk notes that at Cambridge he took a dislike to an undergraduate monk whom he considered 'dishonest minded'. One evening at a gathering in Wittgenstein's room when the monk appeared, Wittgenstein criticised his reading material in an extremely insensitive way. Russell commented that Wittgenstein was very overbearing and indeed told the monk his opinion of him in an imperious manner more suited to his director of studies. The monk, however, took it quite well, convinced that Wittgenstein was a lunatic.[70]

These episodes relate the extent of Wittgenstein's social naïvety. The lack of tact and appreciation of social cues has led many to conclude, unwittingly, that those with HFA/ASP are 'simple'. Indeed, Russell described Wittgenstein as being 'a little too simple'.[71] It is hardly surprising that his friend David Pinsent admitted that 'he is if anything a little mad'.[72]

Unfortunately, that is not an uncommon description of a person with HFA/ASP.

Morbid sensitivity

Wittgenstein often misinterpreted people, partly because of a morbid sensitivity, according to Monk. Indeed, a misconception was noted by the economist John Maynard Keynes, who claimed that Wittgenstein misinterpreted a 'slight tension between them' when this was not so from Keynes's viewpoint.[73] The burden of such false impressions weighed heavily on his peers. On another occasion when Keynes informed his wife, Lydia Lopokova, that Wittgenstein planned to visit them in a fortnight's time, he asked rhetorically 'Am I strong enough? Perhaps if I do not work between now and then, I shall be.'[74] Scharfstein analyses the extent and nature of Wittgenstein's misunderstandings:

> he himself said that he had given hidden senses to his words and had omitted or barely hinted at what mattered most. And yet he complained that he was always misunderstood; and he anticipated further misunderstanding. It will be recalled that he felt he could really communicate the truth yet found only to some possible future individuals. Rejecting almost everyone, he anticipated rejection and usually spoke in rejecting, depressed or guarded words.[75]

People with HFA/ASP very often feel themselves to be misunderstood. As a result Wittgenstein could only share enjoyment with those who shared his own interests, i.e. discussing philosophy and music in particular. There is accumulating evidence of his problems in social and emotional reciprocity. Hence his controlling behaviour and obsessive interests made him extraordinarily demanding company. This is typical of people with HFA/ASP. According to Monk, Wittgenstein was given to emotional outbursts over some minor inconvenience or misunderstanding, and clearly needed robustness and understanding from people. For example, if he failed to receive a letter from a correspondent, it would fill him with anxiety. He was hypersensitive. A large measure of fear and paranoia about people stealing his ideas was also evident, not unlike Newton. Wittgenstein generally found it hard to be hopeful about a relationship or trusting of a person. Thus, it is all the more surprising that he was completely open, honest, and trusting with his psychiatrist, Professor J.N.P. Moore. This was my view of the interview with Professor Moore.[76]

Impairment in reciprocal social interaction

Wittgenstein's social relations were enormously difficult. He tended to talk at people, not to them. Accordingly, he tended to compartmentalise his friendships.[77] During the First World War, as a soldier at the front, he reflected that 'I miss greatly having people with whom I can communicate a little, it would invigorate me a great deal'.[78] The day after writing that note, Wittgenstein learnt that the poet George Trakl, whom he had hoped to meet, had just committed suicide. He was very upset by this loss, and wrote 'what unhappiness, what unhappiness!!!'. Without a doubt he was capable of grief.

Wittgenstein certainly showed narcissistic contempt for others and, according to Monk, 'most human relationships were irksome for him'.[79] His ambivalence about social relationships is also seen in his admission that 'normal human beings are a balm to me . . . and a torment at the same time'.[80] He also wrote 'although I cannot give affection, I have a great need for it'.[81] Here he was expressing the great problem people with HFA/ASP have in social relationships. Clearly such people can be affected by loss, as evidenced by Trakl's death, and indeed Wittgenstein was greatly distressed at the funeral of Francis Skinner, with whom he shared a close intimate physical relationship – at least one that he was able to acknowledge.[82]

Unquestionably, Wittgenstein had great difficulty in finding a comfortable distance in relationships, and vacillated between extremes. McGuinness noted that 'either he was shunning all contact, as when he wanted to live in the high tower of the Rathaus, or he was so involved in his friend's lives that their failings rankled'.[83] Conflict over distance and closeness is central to people with HFA/ASP. Ayer remarked that Wittgenstein suffered from 'not being really interested in the actual world',[84] which is an autistic position. In fact, it is interesting to note that people never remember him opening a newspaper. This is unusual behaviour and probably another manifestation of his autism, living in a world of his own observations and interests.

People with HFA/ASP have considerable difficulty with intimacy. Certainly Wittgenstein experienced feelings of claustrophobia in his relationship with Franz Parak, a writer he met while interned in a prisoner-of-war camp after the First World War. It possibly reminded him of his mother's anxious behaviour towards him, as noted by McGuinness:

> Parak, who was seven years younger than Wittgenstein, formed a respect for Wittgenstein that bordered on worship. He hung onto Wittgenstein's every word hoping, as he says in his Memoir, to drink in as much as possible of Wittgenstein's superior knowledge and wisdom. After a while, Wittgenstein tired of this and began to withdraw, like a 'mimosa', from Parak's attachment. Parak, he said, reminded him of his mother.[85]

Essentially Wittgenstein had an immature personality and liked his disciples to be immature emotionally, child-like, submissive, intelligent, and to have nice faces. Clearly, there was a homosexual element in these tendencies. He dominated them in the same way that Socrates – who most likely had HFA/ASP too – dominated his students. In later life Wittgenstein grew to acknowledge the other person, e.g. their faces and the importance of facial expression. Clearly, he had discovered the significance of what can be learned from other people's faces. This is an example of people with autism growing and developing interpersonally. Arguably, in his later writings he showed some insight and empathy for those with severe problems of communication. On the issue of people entering monasteries, he wrote 'were they stupid or insensitive people? – well, if people like that found they need to take such measures in order to be able to go on living, the problem cannot have been an easy one'.[86] Naturally such issues occur in those with autism.

Peers

Wittgenstein's treatment of academics at Cambridge was marked by intense and frequent criticism. However, the real problem was his autistic inability to relate to them. He wrote 'everything about the place repels me. The stiffness, the artificiality, the self-satisfaction of the people. The university atmosphere nauseates me.'[87] Unquestionably, Wittgenstein made many people uneasy. The novelist Iris Murdoch was acutely aware of the strain that he imposed on relationships, and remarked: 'with most people you meet them in a framework, and there are certain conventions about how you talk to them and so on. There isn't a confrontation of personalities. But Wittgenstein always imposed a confrontation on all his relationships.'[88]

G.H. von Wright succeeded Wittgenstein at Cambridge, but each conversation they had together was like living through the day of judgement, according to Edmonds and Eidinow: 'It was terrible. Everything had constantly to be dug up anew, questioned and subjected to the tests of truthfulness. This concerned not only philosophy but the whole of life.'[89] This fundamental searching is not uncommon in people with HFA/ASP.

A most demanding and exacting conversationalist, Wittgenstein criticised people for loose generalisations. Scharfstein adds that 'he could rebuke a friend with extreme harshness, and he tended to be suspicious of motives and character and fear of him helped to keep his students' attention at high pitch'.[90] There is general consensus that most of his relationships were tempestuous and unpredictable.[91] In addition, Wittgenstein intimidated students and visiting lecturers by frequently interrupting them while speaking.[92] There is endless evidence of his lack of empathy and his discourtesy.

Russell gave Wittgenstein considerable support both emotionally and intellectually. He showed enormous tolerance and forbearance as well as great sensitivity towards him, especially when, mindful of his deficiencies in philosophy, he tried to give him a thorough grounding in the subject.

Russell had arranged formal tuition in logic for Wittgenstein with Johnson, the esteemed Cambridge logician. However, Wittgenstein exasperated Johnson to the extent that the latter terminated the tuition. Wittgenstein came to his mentor afterwards in an agitated state, as described by Russell:

> Wittgenstein appeared in a great state of excitement because Johnson wrote and said he wouldn't take him any more, practically saying he argued too much instead of learning his lesson like a good boy. He came to me to know what truth there was in Johnson's feeling. Now he is terribly persistent, hardly lets one get a word in, and is generally considered a bore. As I really like him very much, I was able to hint these things to him without offending him.[93]

Nevertheless, by 1946 Wittgenstein felt only 'barely concealed contempt' for Russell.[94] He became highly critical of his mentor because he regarded his published work as lacking intellectual rigour. Russell was devastated by the criticism:

> his criticism, tho' I don't think he realised it at the time, was an event of first-rate importance in my life, and affected everything I have done since. I saw he was right and I saw that I could no longer hope ever again to do fundamental work in philosophy . . . Wittgenstein persuaded me that what wanted doing in logic was too difficult for me.[95]

One could surmise here that Russell over-reacted and was overpowered by Wittgenstein. Indeed, one wonders initially if Wittgenstein was not attracted to Russell because of some similarities in their personalities. In certain areas of his life, Russell showed a gross lack of sensitivity too. Edmonds and Eidinow discuss his lack of emotional insight from the standpoint of his estranged family, who accused him of 'coldness, salaciousness and cruelty towards them'.[96] Certainly, Wittgenstein and Russell had major problems in relationships. Monk suggests that Russell possibly saw in Wittgenstein a mirror image of himself 'or, perhaps more apposite . . . he saw him as his own offspring'.[97] Again and again, one comes across the word 'passion' in Russell's descriptions of Wittgenstein's genius: 'a pure intellectual passion' that Wittgenstein (like Russell himself) had 'in the highest degree'. Of course, this is an intellectual passion and not an emotional one. Despite Russell's high regard for Wittgenstein, their friendship was uneasy. Russell describes the 'heaviness' that comes from dealing with a person with HFA/ASP, especially involving his obsessive and exacting style of questioning:

> I had an awful time with Wittgenstein yesterday between tea and dinner. He came analysing all that goes wrong between him and me and I told him I thought it was only nerves on both sides and

everything was all right at bottom. Then he said he never knew whether I was speaking the truth or being polite, so I got vexed and refused to say another word. He went on and on and on. I sat down at my table and took up my pen and began to look through a book, but he still went on. At last I said sharply 'all you want is a little self-control'. Then at last he went away with an air of high tragedy. He had asked me to a concert in the evening but he didn't come, so I began to fear suicide. However, I found him in his room late (I left the concert, but couldn't find him at first), and told him I was sorry I had been cross and then talked quietly about how he could improve.[98]

Intimate relationships

Feelings of love and affection were extremely complicated for Wittgenstein, as indeed were all emotional events because of his HFA/ASP. He could relate in a positive emotional way to people who were gentle, submissive, timid and very sensitive to his needs. Monk puts it as follows:

in love, too, though he felt a deep need for it, he often felt himself incapable, frightened. And, of course, frightened of its being taken away from him, all too conscious of its possible impermanence and of its uncertainty. In 1946 – and it probably came as some relief to find that he was, after all, still capable of loving someone – he fell in love with Ben Richards, an undergraduate student of medicine at Cambridge. Richards had what one by now perceives as the qualities that warmed Wittgenstein's heart: he was extraordinarily gentle, a little timid, perhaps even docile, but extremely kind, considerate and sensitive.[99]

Wittgenstein was at pains to disguise the fact of his homosexuality, and that he could fall in love with people unbeknownst to them. This occurred in his relationship with Keith Kirk, his student in mathematics and mechanics in Manchester. The relationship was extremely intense from Wittgenstein's point of view, but Kirk was scarcely aware of this fact. Certainly, Kirk was not in love with him, according to Monk.[100] The lessons ended when Kirk moved away, and he later got married. He never corresponded with Wittgenstein again, which hurt Wittgenstein deeply. This scenario shows the enormous lack of understanding of other minds that people with HFA/ASP can demonstrate. In effect, it shows a theory-of-mind deficit.

The medical student, Ben Richards, was one of the last people that Wittgenstein fixated on; he believed that Richards had 'a thing' for him. Once again, as with Kirk, the assumption was groundless. Wittgenstein attributed more to the relationship than existed, notwithstanding Richards' great friendship and admiration for him. Richards later married.

In his coded remarks, Wittgenstein did allude to a homosexual contact with Francis Skinner. Wittgenstein recalls that he was 'sensual, susceptible, indecent' with him but afterwards was filled with shame. Whether this was the only occasion on which Wittgenstein and Francis were intimate we do not know.[101] However, there is much anecdotal evidence of Wittgenstein's widespread promiscuity in Vienna. In terms of reconciling the intimacy of such situations, Wittgenstein held the belief that love and sex were mutually exclusive.

In later life Wittgenstein showed some evidence of overcoming an element of his autism by recognising the value of empathy, especially when inspired by love. 'It is the mark of a true love that one thinks of what the other person suffers. For he suffers too, it is also a poor devil.'[102]

Female friendships

Wittgenstein had enormous difficulty in communicating at an emotional level and was unable to manage social relationships with women; this often led to bizarre behaviour. Eileen Drury remarked that Wittgenstein would barely acknowledge her presence when she was with Drury.[103]

When studying mechanical engineering in Berlin, Wittgenstein lodged with a family called the Jolles. Frau Jolles became very affectionate towards him, but some time later Wittgenstein found this oppressive and rejected her in a harsh, unempathetic way. In reply to one of her letters, he wrote that her journalistic ways of expressing herself filled him with 'repugnance'.[104] He failed to see that his brutal openness and frankness could be seen as harsh and rejecting. Relationships could only be conducted on his own terms, where he had total control. He considered Frau Jolles' friendship as nothing more than an imposition, which indicates the extent of his impairment in reciprocal social interaction.

Despite being homosexual, there is one known example where he fell in love with a woman, the much younger Viennese-born Marguerite Respinger. She did not realise the depth of his attachment until he discussed it with her 1 hour before her wedding to someone else. He had in mind an 'autistic marriage' which would be 'platonic, childless' for them.[105] They cut an odd pair in fashionable Vienna. The much older Wittgenstein went about with the very elegant lady in a 'jacket worn at the elbows, an open neck shirt, baggy trousers and heavy boots'.[106] The inappropriateness of his attire never disturbed him. Indeed, he liked to wear the same clothes for very long periods.

In relation to female emancipation, he was unquestionably misogynistic and opposed to any progress on 'women's suffrage'.[107] By and large he also disapproved of women studying philosophy. Elizabeth Anscombe was the exception. She became a major disciple and later one of his literary executors, and 'a notoriously intractable literary executor' at that.[108] During

Wittgenstein's life she took up a position of abject submission to him that lasted for a number of years after his death, as noted by Monk:

> [Anscombe became] one of Wittgenstein's closest friends and one of his most trusted students, an exception to his great dislike of academic women and especially of female philosophers. She became, in fact, an honorary male, addressed by him affectionally as 'old man'. 'Thank God we have got rid of the women!' he once said to her at a lecture on finding to his delight that no (other) female students were in attendance.[109]

Evidently she had gender identity issues as he had, where the 'male' aspect of her personality was more highly developed. The fact that she was more man-like than female obviously made Wittgenstein comfortable in her company. It stood in stark contrast to his encounter with Virginia Wolff and the Bloomsbury Circle, where their frank discussion on sex horrified him speechless, and forced him to leave their company abruptly. Indeed, Anscombe was Freud's 'phallic woman'. She was described by Mary Warnock as a woman who 'dressed in shapeless black trousers and a nondescript baggy sweater, though her hair was longish, greasy . . . [with] a cast in one eye'.[110] Anscombe could be as controlling as Wittgenstein, and was extremely critical of Warnock when she went to study philosophy at Oxford.[111] According to her obituary in *The Irish Times* she became Wittgenstein's 'close friend and proselytiser, even adopting his mannerisms – the anguish in the hands, furrowed brow, long silences, and the tinge of an Austrian accent'.[112]

Austrian villagers

Wittgenstein's poor social interaction was not confined to his peers at Cambridge. He had great difficulty relating to the villagers of the three Austrian villages he taught in, and treated them with gross contempt. In the winter of 1922 after arriving at the first school in Hassbach, he described the people as 'not human at all but loathsome worms'.[113] After a month he switched to a primary school at Puchberg and wrote to Russell that the people there were 'really not people at all but one quarter animal and three-quarters human'.[114] Later, when teaching at Trattenbach, according to Ayer, he wrote to Russell saying that he was surrounded as ever by 'odiousness and baseness'.[115]

In Trattenbach and Otterhal, Wittgenstein came to avoid adults as much as possible. But when he did encounter them, he never lied, which can only mean that his bluntness made him unpopular. In fact, Wittgenstein was scrupulously honest throughout his life, a feature common in those with autism. It is interesting that Wittgenstein lacked this ability to lie and was rather naïve in that respect. Certain kinds of lying are part of normal social interaction, arising out of a need not to hurt people unnecessarily. Indeed, Wittgenstein was socially naïve, leading his sister Gretl to remark 'all Luki's swans are geese'.[116] According to Bartley, the adult Trattenbachers encountered only an 'aloof awkwardness from him that came across as gruffness';[117] in short, HFA/ASP. His dislike for such people distanced him from them.

Fellow soldiers

The complexity of Wittgenstein's social relationships was also evident during the First World War, when he deplored the company of his fellow soldiers:

> [A] company of drunkards, a company of vile and stupid people . . . the men, with few exceptions, hate me because I am a volunteer. So I am nearly always surrounded by people that hate me. And this is one thing that I cannot bear. The people here are malicious and heartless. It is almost impossible to find a trace of humanity in them.[118]

This, of course, is a view of human beings from an autistic perspective. However, Wittgenstein did struggle in his autistic way to understand them and considered how misunderstood and limited they were. He wrote:

> the people around me are not so much mean as appallingly limited. This makes it almost impossible to work with them, because they forever misunderstand. These people are not stupid, but limited. Within their circle they are clever enough. But they lack character and thereby breadth.[119]

When put in charge of a workshop forge he fared badly because of an inability to relate to his fellow soldiers. He was at a loss as to how to behave like an empathic supervisor, complicated by his authoritarianism. He became suicidal and depressed. People with HFA/ASP have major difficulties in supervisory roles. It is hardly surprising that during the war he volunteered to do the most dangerous and solitary duties. One was on the look-out on a ship, manning a searchlight at night. The reason was twofold. First, it allowed him to get away from his comrades, and second, it helped, as he saw it, to purify himself of his sins and guilt and so become a better person. When at the front, he also asked to be assigned to the observation post, the most dangerous of places, thus ensuring that he would be the target of enemy fire. The assignment resulted in him being cited for bravery. 'His exceptionally courageous behaviour, calmness, sang-froid, and heroism', according to the military report, 'won the total admiration of the troops' and he was awarded the Band of the Military Service Medal with Swords.[120]

Children and animals

In sharp contrast to adults, Wittgenstein could generally relate exceptionally well to children and indeed did genuinely care for them. While teaching in Austria, he would bring food to school if he thought the children needed it. Many of the children adored him, and they even helped in teaching one another.[121] It is clear that people with HFA/ASP frequently relate much better to children than to adults. His relationship with children was marred, however, by incidents of brutality towards them. As a consequence he was later charged in court and resigned from his teaching job. Any violence towards them arose when they failed to learn in the fashion he deemed appropriate. Indeed, it could be argued that it was excess concern for their education that prompted such behaviour.

Similarly, Wittgenstein could relate extremely well to birds, and this became apparent in Ireland towards the end of his life. People with HFA/ASP sometimes can communicate well with animals, and Wittgenstein was no exception. At Rosro, he used to talk to and feed the birds daily, and indeed tamed many of them to the point that some died shortly after he left the area. He also became knowledgeable of their names and ways. Indeed, Wittgenstein's similarity to both St Francis of Assisi and the Irish St Kevin in their remarkable way with birds and regard for animals is noted by Wall.[122] Also, it would appear that, like Wittgenstein, St Kevin also sought solitude.

Social isolation

The willingness to distance himself from people led to the frequent need for isolation. In a letter to Russell, Wittgenstein confessed that 'being alone does me no end of good, and I do not think I could now bear life among people. Like me, everything is in a state of ferment.'[123] His desire to exile himself was very pronounced, and he spent long periods in remote parts of Norway and Ireland.

Another factor influencing his decision to go to Norway was that he effectively fled when he learned that his sister Gretl and her American husband were coming to live in England. The idea of frequent visits from them could not be tolerated. In addition, people with HFA/ASP can have problems with concentration and certainly Wittgenstein found Cambridge a great distraction. An excellent example of his difficulties is described by his close friend, Pinsent:

that he should exile himself and live for some years right away from everyone he knows – say in Norway. That he should live entirely alone and by himself – a hermit's life – and do nothing but work in Logic. His reasons for this are very queer to me – but no doubt they are very real for him: firstly he thinks he will do infinitely more and better work in such circumstances, than at Cambridge, where, he says, his constant liability to interruption and distractions (such as concerts) is an awful hindrance. Secondly he feels he has no right to live in an antipathetic world (and of course to him very few people are sympathetic) – a world where he perpetually finds himself feeling contempt for others, and irritating others by his nervous temperament – without some justification for that contempt, etc. such as being a really great man and having done really great work.[124]

Maud Kingston, in whose house in Co. Wicklow Wittgenstein stayed for some months, remembered 'the lonely, taciturn visitor who always took his meals – up to three a day – in his room, who liked to sit in the sun in front of the big window and who for days did nothing but write, without any contact with the family'.[125] Wittgenstein could work alone in the most extraordinary of places, for example the Palm House of the Botanical Gardens in Dublin. Naturally, the building was heated and he would sit there during the winter months, writing philosophy into notebooks for hours.

At other times it appeared as if Wittgenstein was searching for the most isolated place on the planet to work. As we have seen, he liked remote spots where an autistic person could work. Indeed, at one point he considered going to the Faroe Islands, Orkney, Shetland or the Hebrides, according to Wall.[126] Kirkpatrick in Wicklow, where he resided with the Kingstons in 1947, was not isolated enough, forcing him to move to a much more secluded place in the west of Ireland.[127] After staying at Rosro for some months, again he found it not isolated enough and considered building a small house on an island off the coast of Connemara. However, this plan was not feasible. A philosopher, Fr Fechim O'Doherty recalls Wittgenstein as saying that he could think best in the dark and that in the west of Ireland he had found one of the last 'pools of darkness' in Europe.[128]

The solitary figure of Wittgenstein walking the fields was a common sight in Rosro. In a radio interview with Festie, a local boat maker – Wittgenstein fell out with him because of walking along his ridges of potatoes – the broadcaster Joe Duffy tried to get the measure of the philosopher:

JOE DUFFY [what about] the philosopher's propensity for hill walking?
FESTIE We thought he was a man that was expecting a submarine or something. Now that's the truth.
JOE DUFFY He was very interested in language and communication.

FESTIE   Well, damn it, he wasn't. No thanks, [that's what was] wrong about
him anyhow. He didn't want to talk to anyone.[129]

Commenting on the radio show, journalist Harry Browne pointed out that
Wittgenstein's stay in Ireland came across as 'a continuous and continually
frustrated quest for silence'. And the reason he wanted to live on an island
was because the noises of a fishing pier and a nocturnal sheepdog 'drove
him around the twist at the back end of County Galway'.[130]

Some commentators have remarked on how landscapes can affect an
individual. Referring to where Darwin meets Malthus, Edward Skidelsky
supported E.O. Wilson's explanation 'of our preference for certain types of
landscape in terms of the survival requirements of the African savannah'.[131]
It is valid here to have a hypothesis about why Wittgenstein liked the west of
Ireland or indeed Norway. He depended on isolated regions for his work at
times. Wall has suggested that the landscape of Ireland had a great effect on
his thinking in philosophy. I'm not entirely sure. It is true that he was very
taken with the light and colour of the landscape, particularly in County
Galway. Colour had great significance for him, and his thoughts on the
subject form part of his work in philosophy. That said, I do believe that it
was not the barren landscape that was primarily important to him but his
autistic condition of having no desire to interact with his peers. Alterna-
tively, does the barren landscape reflect an inner state of mind? In
Wittgenstein's case, his desire to withdraw arose from his lack of empathy
with people, which in turn gave rise to some guilt. Pinsent has already
remarked how Wittgenstein felt he was in a world where he perpetually
found himself feeling contempt for others, and irritating others by his
nervous temperament, and so had to produce some memorable piece of
work to counteract it.[132] Thus the desire to distance himself from his peers
compelled him to seek out isolated locations where he was free to concentrate on his work.

Privation and austerity

Wittgenstein reduced his life to the minimum in terms of food, money and
comforts. Despite his privileged upbringing he lived extremely frugally,
especially in rural Austria and the west of Ireland. According to Bartley, as
a schoolteacher he lived in 'ostentatious poverty'.[133] He was a minimalist in
every sense, and this extended to his ideas in architecture and philosophy. It
appeared that all those things that would interfere with his objective in life
to produce works of genius were discarded. Clearly, the absence of ornamentation or excess did not put people at ease. Iris Murdoch remarked that
Wittgenstein's extraordinary directness of approach and lack of any sort of
paraphernalia 'were the things that unnerved people'. She added there was
'an unearthly, even alien, quality to Wittgenstein's dealings with others'.[134]

After the First World War Wittgenstein gave away his vast fortune. Disposing of his money was an effort to pare his life down to the minimum, which in itself is an autistic act. Moreover, he did not want people to relate to him because of his money. When he was giving it away, a notary commented 'you want to commit financial suicide?'[135] He did. Only a person with HFA/ASP would successfully carry out such an action. For him money was absolutely corrupting and damaging. However, this was only one of many bizarre acts for which he is famed. Throughout his life, Wittgenstein made efforts to atone for acts that filled him with guilt. One might ask also whether the giving away of his money was a way of atonement for his homosexual behaviour. Equally corrupting for him was the influence of those in positions of power. When interned in a prisoner-of-war camp in Italy, he refused all help, political and otherwise, offered on his behalf by friends and relations.

Equally, his rooms in Cambridge were sparsely furnished. He was against ornamentation and any unnecessary additions, which even extended to beds having wheels. When students came to his rooms, they sat on deck-chairs and had refreshments from beakers. Ayer describes the Spartan state of Wittgenstein's rooms:

> His rooms . . . situated at the very top of a high staircase, the sitting-room like a monk's cell, with no ornament, a table and chair for Wittgenstein's own use, no armchairs but two deckchairs brought out for visitors.[136]

Scharfstein notes that when Wittgenstein attended a lecture in Vienna by Moritz Schlick, the eminent head of the Vienna Circle of philosophers, and others, the students thought he 'was a tramp because of his tattered and patched clothes'. Oscar Fuchs, the shoemaker in the Austrian village, Trattenbach, observed that Wittgenstein was 'ascetic'. However, he did add that such men are taken to be crazy, but 'one just oughtn't to measure them by ordinary standards'.[137] This is certainly true of people with HFA/ASP.

Imposition of control

There is no doubt that Wittgenstein's autistic dominance frightened people. Many of his contemporaries tended to avoid his company, and indeed as far as the fellows of Trinity College, Cambridge were concerned, he had little contact with them except for the mathematician G.H. Hardy, who also had HFA/ASP. Klagg quotes from *Wittgenstein and Norway*[138] that Wittgenstein was a 'highly demanding and unusual figure'.[139] His wish to dictate the terms of social contact did occasionally lead to friction. The villagers in Skjoden described him as 'austere and dominating, perspicuous and determined'. On one occasion a local worker was asked to tar Wittgenstein's cottage. The man arrived 5 minutes late for an appointment to discuss the work. This greatly angered Wittgenstein, who felt that anyone who would make this kind of mistake should have his head 'chopped off'.[140]

Wittgenstein exerted considerable control over people, whether discussing philosophy or dictating a food regime. When visiting Drury in the west of Ireland, Wittgenstein imposed dietary restrictions on the group. After finishing a lavish meal on their first day, Wittgenstein declared 'now let it be clear that while we are here, we are not going to live in this style. We will have a plate of porridge for breakfast, vegetables from the garden for lunch, and a boiled egg in the evening'.[141] According to Wall, nobody dared contradict the 'Master' once he had spoken. This was not unlike the psychoanalyst Lacan.

Treatment of Bertrand Russell

In many ways, Wittgenstein was an autodidact, typical of people with HFA/ASP. As a consequence, he was not attuned to learning from others, even mentors. As previously mentioned, Russell and Wittgenstein were constantly at loggerheads, prompting Wittgenstein on one occasion in Norway to break off all communication:

> Our latest quarrel, too, was certainly not simply a result of your sensitiveness or my inconsiderateness. It came from deeper – from the fact that my letter must have shown you how totally different our ideas are, e.g. of the value of scientific work. It was of course stupid of me to have written to you at such length about this matter: I ought to have told myself that such fundamental differences cannot be resolved by a letter. And this is just ONE incident out of many . . . I shall not write to you again.[142]

Nevertheless, he did write to Russell again:

> You may be right in saying that we ourselves are not very different, but our ideals could not be more so. And that's why we haven't been able and we shan't ever be able to talk about anything involving our value judgements without either becoming hypocritical or falling out. I think this is incontestable; I had noticed it a long time ago; and it was frightful for me, because it tainted our relations with one another; we seemed to be side by side in a marsh.[143]

The idea of being 'side by side in a marsh' is a perfect description of a person with HFA/ASP in terms of social interaction and problems associated with emotional relations. Wittgenstein suggested that a relationship with Russell could only be conducted by restricting their relationship to the communication of facts that could be established objectively.[144] Of course, facts are what people with HFA/ASP are most able to deal with. Wittgenstein saw major problems in value judgements between himself and Russell. Clearly, values are more subjective and consequently more difficult for a person with HFA/ASP to understand.

There is little doubt that Wittgenstein's treatment of his mentor Russell was grossly insensitive but arose from an inability to appreciate social relationships fully. Wittgenstein accused Russell of not having proper standards in his published work while his own standards were extremely perfectionistic and exceptionally high. Russell put it in perspective in the following way: he 'must understand or die . . . he has more passion about philosophy than I have; his avalanches make mine seem mere snowballs'.[145]

Treatment of students

Wittgenstein made considerable demands on his students and was extremely controlling. According to former students, he demanded 'complete honesty',[146] emphasised punctuality and required students to attend for the whole term.[147] His displeasure at being misunderstood prompted him to take extreme measures to censure his peers. Warnock pointed out that 'Wittgenstein's pupils, or disciples rather, were excommunicated from time to time for publishing extracts from his lectures, or simply for getting things wrong, or failing to understand the teachings of the Master'.[148] The excessive control exerted over students and general interaction with them caused von Wright to remark that 'his influence as a teacher was, on the whole, harmful to the development of independent minds in his disciples'. Von Wright also believed that those who loved Wittgenstein most and shared his friendship also feared him.[149] Wittgenstein persuaded many of his students to seek careers outside academia, namely Francis Skinner, Drury, Arvid Sjogren, and Hijab, among others. Hetherington claimed that Wittgenstein was vehemently opposed to any of his students taking academic posts. Moreover, he notes how Wittgenstein regarded the teaching of philosophy as 'demeaning, dishonest and a useless occupation'.[150] Instead of pursuing a normal university career, he made Skinner and Sjorgen become mechanics, which was very odd and controlling and probably damaging to their careers.

In the same way, he counselled Yorick Smythies to work with his hands, even though Smythies was so ill co-ordinated that he had difficulty in tying his shoelaces. Wittgenstein simply told him that manual work was good for the brain. The parents of both Smythies and Skinner might well have regarded Wittgenstein as a malign genius for persuading their intellectually gifted sons to forsake academia, according to Edmonds and Eidinow. Clearly Wittgenstein could be extraordinarily destructive but appeared to have little insight into this fact at the time.[151] From their first meeting in

1929, he controlled almost every decision in Drury's life. At first Wittgenstein wanted him to get a regular job among ordinary people and not to become a priest, which Drury was then considering. Drury then became a medical doctor at Wittgenstein's suggestion. The only major decision that Wittgenstein did not influence was Drury's decision to get married, which was arranged just before Wittgenstein died. Certainly, the actions of people with HFA/ASP are not always in the best interests of their adherents. That said, Wittgenstein later did become aware that his influence was harmful to his disciples. Von Wright has stated:

> Wittgenstein himself thought that his influence was on the whole, harmful to development of independent minds in his disciples. I am afraid he was right. To learn from Wittgenstein without coming to adopt his forms of expression and catch-words and even to imitate his tone of voice, his mien and gestures was almost impossible.[152]

This shows some of the dangers that people with HFA/ASP can demonstrate when in positions of authority because of a lack of empathy.

Control

Wittgenstein's exacting standards and demand for control extended beyond his relations with others and philosophical discourse. The extent of his absolute control was apparent in the building of a house on Kundmanngasse in Vienna for his sister, Gretl, in 1926. Their sister Hermine noted that though Paul Engelmann was the architect, it was essentially Wittgenstein who was responsible for the design of the house:

> Engelmann had to give way to the much stronger [character], and the house was then built, down to the smallest detail, according to Ludwig's plans and under his supervision. Ludwig designed every window, door, window-bar and radiator in the noblest proportions and with such exactitude that they might have been precision instruments.[153]

The architect, Wijdeveld, points out that Wittgenstein was a man of tremendous willpower, who made high demands on those around him because of his 'almost childlike straightforwardness and unwillingness to compromise'.[154] The precision that Wittgenstein demanded sometimes appeared unattainable and 'drove the engineer of the company making the doors into a state of hysteria', according to Scharfstein.[155] In this undertaking Wittgenstein was utterly controlling and a perfectionist. Engelmann recalls that while building the house a locksmith had commented 'tell me, Herr Ingenieur, does a millimetre here or there really matter to you?' Even before he had finished speaking Wittgenstein replied with such a deafening 'Ja!' that the man nearly jumped with fright.[156]

Despite the enormous control that Wittgenstein felt he needed to exert, he also had 'an organ of reverence' in him, according to McGuinness.[157] He behaved in this way with very few people – Frege and Russell initially, and then Professor Moore, his psychiatrist. He also revered manual workers; the composers, Beethoven and Brahms; and in literature the figure of Father Zossima from *The Brothers Karamazov*.

Preservation of sameness

Wittgenstein had restricted, repetitive and stereotyped patterns of behaviour, interests, and activities, as demonstrated by his overwhelming interest in philosophy and machines. The desire for ritual and preservation of sameness is acute in those with HFA/ASP. Wittgenstein was genuinely interested in ritual and, as a child, was acquainted with Catholic ceremonies and traditions. Interestingly, his friends thought that he would appreciate a Catholic burial, and provided one following his death, despite his repudiation of religion when alive.

Preservation of sameness was evident in many aspects of his life. It could certainly be said that he was the ultimate creature of habit. Like Russell, Wittgenstein wrote a great deal and had established writing rituals. Because of his poor memory he always took notebooks with him and made immediate notes of his thoughts. He spent a considerable time arranging and rearranging his philosophical remarks and transferring them from one copybook to another. By rearranging his ideas, he was able to refine and condense remarks. He first wrote his ideas into one small notebook and then transferred them into a larger one and eventually to typescript.

Other areas where preservation of sameness was evident include his dietary habits in Dublin. According to Monk, he would eat exactly the same food every day in Bewley's Café on Grafton Street. Towards the end of his life when he stayed with his physician, Dr Bevan, in Cambridge, he requested exactly the same food every day.[158] When he briefly visited Malcolm in America his eating habits never varied:

> My wife gave him some Swiss cheese and rye bread for lunch, which he greatly liked. Thereafter he more or less insisted on eating bread and cheese at all meals, largely ignoring the various dishes that my wife prepared. Wittgenstein declared that it did not matter to him what he ate, so long as it was always the same.[159]

Indeed, food fads are common in people with HFA/ASP. Wittgenstein was quick to establish routines which persisted to the very end. According to Monk, Wittgenstein and Mrs Bevan quickly established the pattern of walking to the local pub at 6 o'clock each evening. Mrs Bevan remembers, 'we always ordered two ports, one I drank and the other one he poured with great amusement into the Aspidistra plant – this was the only dishonest act I ever knew him to do'.[160]

Attire

Wittgenstein demonstrated an unchanging attitude to his attire. After he had disposed of his family fortune, he always wore the same type of clothes but with meticulous care. Malcolm recalls him wearing 'light grey flannel trousers, a flannel shirt open at the throat, a woollen lumber jacket, or a leather jacket. Out of doors, in wet weather, he wore a tweed cap and tan raincoat. He nearly always walked with a light cane.'[161] Having spent the duration of the First World War as a soldier, Wittgenstein continued to wear his military uniform for years after the war, another example of his wish to keep things the same. Bartley records that in his period as an elementary school teacher Wittgenstein carried a bamboo walking stick and was often seen on solitary walks with an old briefcase or a notebook tucked under his arm.[162]

Music

Music was enormously important to Wittgenstein. Given his family passion for music and their liaison with famous composers such as Mendelssohn, Brahms, Mahler, Walter, Labor, Clara Schumann and Casals when in Vienna, it was part of his daily diet. He even conducted a few musical experiments on rhythm with Pinsent.[163] Even so, he tended to listen to one piece of music over and over again in classic autistic fashion. Wittgenstein was very much an autodidact in the classic autistic-spectrum sense, and like his father was keen on subjects and instruments that could be self-taught, e.g. the clarinet or violin. He was also a superb whistler of tunes. His taste in classical music was strictly restricted to those composers before Brahms. He claimed that one could hear the 'machinery' in the work of composers after Brahms, and consequently such music held little appeal for him. Temple Grandin, diagnosed with autism, mentioned an autistic composer who 'would take bits and pieces of music he had heard and rearrange them'.[164] This is in keeping with HFA/ASP and, as we have seen, Wittgenstein would also rearrange his philosophical remarks over and over again.

All-absorbing interest

Many of Wittgenstein's peers have drawn attention to the way he drove himself fiercely. Malcolm observed that Wittgenstein's intense focus was as if 'his whole being was under attention'.[165] In the same light, Edmonds and

Eidinow describe how, when a topic under discussion caught Wittgenstein's interest, he would 'become utterly engrossed, oblivious to his surroundings'. Undeniably Wittgenstein was thoroughly focused and showed a repetitive adherence to his interests. Interestingly, Gillberg downplays meaning in relation to all-absorbing narrow interest in people with Asperger's syndrome. Wittgenstein was interested in solving linguistic puzzles.

Wittgenstein felt that nothing was worth doing except producing great philosophical works. Indeed, he dedicated his life to his work. Russell has described Wittgenstein's intense focus as a pure intellectual passion that both of them shared; however, Wittgenstein had it in the 'highest degree'.[166] He showed 'the characteristic of logicians . . . his faults are exactly mine – always analysing, pulling things up by the roots, trying to get the exact truth of what one feels towards him'.[167] On the other hand, Wittgenstein's zealousness stood in contrast to Russell's. The similarity that Russell believed they embodied was a view not shared by Wittgenstein. He grew increasingly dissatisfied with what he considered Russell's lack of intellectual rigour. Russell, he claimed 'was a traitor to the gospel of exactness'. Similarly, Monk has remarked that Wittgenstein's intense single-mindedness made Russell feel like a compromiser.[168] This is typical of people with HFA/ASP.

Wittgenstein's all-absorbing narrow interest involved the exclusion of other activities, with repetitive adherence. It often meant sacrificing meals or good manners. McGuinness records that Wittgenstein could ignore midday breaks and carry on working till evening despite the presence of company.[169] Drury recalls an incident of such absolute absorption: he arranged to meet Wittgenstein at lunchtime in his hotel in Dublin. After he arrived, Wittgenstein said 'just wait a minute till I finish this'.[170] The minute turned into 2 hours, leaving Drury hungry.

Similarly, in his early days at Cambridge Wittgenstein would visit Russell's room late in the evening and stay until the early morning. His pursuit of ideas was intense and unflagging, indeed often argumentative and tiresome. He constantly badgered Russell, discussing philosophy as he paced up and down, often with exasperating results. Russell wrote 'my small ferocious German came and argued at me after my lecture. He is armour-plated against all assaults of reasoning. It is really rather a waste of time talking with him.'[171] Clearly, it was all typically autistic behaviour. Not surprisingly, Russell described Wittgenstein as a 'tyrant'.[172]

Wittgenstein was also able to focus exclusively on one area of philosophy – namely philosophic language – to the exclusion of all others, regardless of how much they interrelated or overlapped, as noted by Will Self:

> [Wittgenstein] imposed a Wittgensteinian agenda on the meetings of interested students and faculty, asking that visiting speakers be required to discourse solely on problems of philosophic language,

rather than the whole range of metaphysical, ontological, teleological and epistemological questions to which, at that time, philosophers still felt themselves, to a greater or lesser extent, capable of providing answers.[173]

The repetitive adherence to interests was also seen in other areas. Throughout his life Wittgenstein would return again and again to a passage of music or a poem that said something to him in order to deepen his understanding of it. According to McGuinness, Wittgenstein was never one for learning a multiplicity of things just because it was expected of him.[174] Instead, he preferred to read intensively rather than extensively, and could bring intensity of concentration to any task. Indeed, McGuinness notes that a peculiar excellence of his mind was his capacity for concentration.

Non-verbal behaviour

Distinctive forms of non-verbal behaviour occur in people with HFA/ASP. Non-verbal communication problems, as defined by Gillberg, include limited use of gesture, clumsiness/gauche body language, limited facial expression, inappropriate expression and a peculiar stiff gaze. There are many accounts of peculiarities in relation to Wittgenstein's face, gait and gestures. Malcolm observed the fierce concentration Wittgenstein laboured under, often accompanied by unusual gestures: 'As he sat in the middle of the room on a plain wooden chair and struggled with his thoughts, sweat poured down his face. There were long tense silences during which he sat in painful concentration, his hands making arresting movements.'[175]

Malcolm also recalls that Wittgenstein would walk in spurts, 'sometimes coming to a stop while he made some remark and locking into my eyes with his piercing gaze . . . Then he would walk rapidly for a few yards, then slow down, then speed up or coming to a halt, and so on.'[176] Motor clumsiness is also associated with HFA/ASP, but the extent of that feature is not clear in Wittgenstein's case. After holidaying with him in Norway, Pinsent noted in his diary that Wittgenstein was clumsy at sailing and clambering on rocks.[177] Yet he showed a particular talent for cutting sections of frozen lung as a trauma researcher in Newcastle-upon-Tyne.[178] His supervisor, E.G. Bywaters, reported that she was 'pleased with his meticulous and conscientious approach to the frozen sections of lung and other organs that he prepared' for her.[179] Evidently, his fine motor skills must have been good.

A peculiar stiff gaze can certainly be seen in all photographs of Wittgenstein. Sir John Vinelott, an ex-pupil, describes his penetrating eyes and remarkable facial appearance:

[He was] very withdrawn, [had] a huge great forehead, very penetrating eyes, but above all, when he concentrated, standing up talking to someone . . . he had so many anxiety lines on his forehead that they made a chequer board. I have never seen a human face like it in my life before.[180]

Facial expressions

Facial expressions are highly problematic for people with HFA/ASP. They themselves often have limited facial expression and in turn find it difficult to interpret the facial expressions of others. Wittgenstein became acutely aware of this in later life, and it became the concurrent focus of his philosophy. On one occasion he and Drury were out walking in Galway and came upon a 5-year-old girl sitting outside a cottage. Wittgenstein remarked: 'Drury, just look at the expression on that child's face . . . you don't take enough notice of people's faces; it is a fault you ought to try to correct.' Monk comments that it was a piece of advice that is implicitly embodied in Wittgenstein's philosophy of psychology; that 'an inner process stands in need of outward criteria'.[181] However, outward criteria require close scrutiny. He sought to clarify by observing someone's external behaviour whether it was possible to observe his or her state of mind, or whether 'inner life' was always mysterious. Monk claims that Wittgenstein concluded that the 'commonality of experience' required to interpret the 'imponderable evidence' and the 'subtleties of glance, gesture and tone' would be missing.[182] In addition, Monk notes that, for Wittgenstein, one of the most difficult distinctions to make was that between a genuine and an affected expression of feeling. He reiterates Wittgenstein's query as to whether there is such a thing as 'expert judgement' about the genuineness of expressions of feeling.[183] Wittgenstein was aware that in this regard there are those whose judgement is 'better', and conversely those whose judgement is 'worse'.[184] However, he did believe it was possible to learn this knowledge only through experience:

> Correcter prognosis will generally issue from the judgements of those with better knowledge of mankind. Can one learn this knowledge? Yes; some can. Not, however, by taking a course in it, but through 'experience' – Can someone else be a man's teacher in this? Certainly. From time to time he gives him the right tip – This is what 'learning' and 'teaching' are like here – What one acquires here is not a technique; one learns correct judgements. There are also rules, but they do not form a system, and only experienced people can apply them right. Unlike calculating rules.[185]

It is interesting that Wittgenstein himself was able to learn from experience. Baron-Cohen is correct in saying that one can't learn these facts using 'folk physics' but only from 'folk psychology'.[186] Monk cites the figure of Father

Zossima in *The Brothers Karamazov* as someone who could possibly be such a teacher:

> it was said by many people that the elder Zossima, by permitting everyone for some many years to come to bare their hearts and beg his advice and healing words, he had absorbed so many secrets, sorrows, and avowals into his soul that in the end he had acquired so fine a perception that he could tell at first glance from the face of a stranger what he had come for, what he wanted and what kind of torment racked his conscience.[187]

At one level that kind of perception is what an experienced psychiatrist achieves. Monk recognises that in describing Father Zossima, Dostoyevsky has succeeded in describing the ideal psychological insight. When, after being persuaded by Wittgenstein to read *The Brothers Karamazov*, Drury reported that he found the figure of Father Zossima very impressive, Wittgenstein replied 'yes there are really people like that, who could see directly into the souls of other people and advise them'.[188] At a fundamental level Wittgenstein is referring to the development of empathy, and showed the considerable progress he made in achieving it, which is certainly the goal of therapy for people with HFA/ASP.

Effect on people

Wittgenstein had a profound effect on people, whether for the good or bad. His ways were plainly eccentric, as noted by Drury.[189] Wijdeveld too has documented how hard it was for Margarete Wittgenstein to cope with her brother's 'terrible fussiness and lack of practical sense' as well as his meticulousness and perfectionism. One day she invited Engelmann, Moritz Schlick and Wijdeveld to tea. Engelmann observed that 'the rich lady had a half-idiotic brother (Ludwig) whom she would like to do a favour; [he had a] stammering way of formulating his philosophical thoughts, vacillating between modesty and rudeness, [and] did not produce the effect the hostess had expected'.[190]

Because of the effect on those that came into contact with him, many described him as messianic, godlike, bewitching. Much of Wittgenstein's influence can be attributed to the sheer conviction he displayed, whether it related to philosophical problems or everyday issues. Moore remarked that he could not do justice 'to the intensity of conviction with which [Wittgenstein] said everything which he did say, nor to the extreme interest which he excited in his hearers'.[191] This was not unlike Hitler, who had autistic psychopathy.

Most of Wittgenstein's Cambridge peers point to his personality as commanding and even imperial. His sheer strength, according to one of his students, Hijab, was 'like an atomic bomb, a tornado – people just don't appreciate that'.[192] The architect, Sir Colin St John Wilson, claimed he was 'a magician and had qualities of magic in his relations with people'.[193] However, that magic was not always of a positive form. Edmonds notes that for Karl Popper, 'Wittgenstein was the sorcerer who had dogged his career'.[194] Similarly, Fania Pascal remarked that 'he cast a spell' (like Hitler). As a result, deciding whether he was a charlatan or genius occupied the minds of his contemporaries. Brian Morton states that:

> Wittgenstein is the sacred monster of modern thought. Undergraduate Julian Bell's satirical 1930 Epistle has him spot on: 'Ludwig's omniscient; well, I would be civil – but is he god almighty, or the Devil?'. Ascetic, sensuous, vain, mystical, power-obsessed.[195]

Many spoke of him in tones describing a deity. Indeed, Vinelott likened him to a 'charismatic prophet'.[196] On Wittgenstein's return to Cambridge after several years' absence, J.M. Keynes remarked to his colleagues 'God has arrived, I met him on the 5.15 train'. Despite the levity, the implication is unambiguous. Smythies points out that Wittgenstein's influence was due to his 'remarkable hypnotic, even demonic, personality'. In fact, the same things were said about Hitler. Ayer informed Smythies that the vast majority of philosophers at Cambridge were terrified of Wittgenstein and 'his ferocious and overbearing style' of philosophical debate.[197] Indeed, Wittgenstein's influence stretched across Europe from Vienna to Cambridge. Ayer related to Isaiah Berlin in 1933 how central Wittgenstein was to the Vienna Circle: 'Wittgenstein is a deity to them all . . . Russell is thought of as in many respects an old fashioned metaphysician but definitely a forerunner of the Christ (Wittgenstein)'.[198]

Significantly, Edmonds and Eidinow described him as a 'messiah' too.[199] Rudolf Carnap noted how Wittgenstein was more akin to a 'religious prophet or seer' than a scientist:

> his point of view and his attitude towards people and problems, even theoretical problems, were much more similar to those of a creative artist than to those of a scientist; one might almost say similar to those of a religious prophet or a seer. When he started to formulate his views on some specific philosophical problem, we often felt the internal struggle that occurred in him at that very moment, a struggle by which he tried to penetrate from darkness to light under an intense and painful strain, which was even visible on his most expressive face. When finally, sometimes after a prolonged arduous effort, his answer came forth, his statement stood before us like a newly created piece of art or a divine revelation. Not that he asserted his views dogmatically . . . But the impression he made on us was as if inside it came to him as

though a divine inspiration, so that we could not help feeling that any sober rational comment or analysis would be a profanation.[200]

Wittgenstein had enormous dominance and 'autistic control' over others. So influential was his effect on an entire generation of younger philosophers that it did not stop at the replication of his ideas. As Will Self has written, 'his personal quirks and mannerisms' had just as great an effect: 'Wittgenstein's acolytes dressed like the great man, spoke like the great man, and wrote like him . . . [Wittgenstein showed] effortless dominance'.[201]

On this point, Edmonds and Eidinow report how a former graduate student was able to recognise another, in Australia, many years later, simply by the way that he struck his forehead when concentrating on a philosophic problem. Wittgenstein's legacy continues to this day. In 1995, J.C. Marshall commented on the cult-like status it has reached:

> some 40 years after his death, the cult of Ludwig Wittgenstein burns more fiercely than ever. Scarce a week goes by but that some elderly gentleman remembers (and publishes!) a chance remark that Wittgenstein made when tying his shoelaces: for every (relatively lucid) sentence that Wittgenstein wrote there must now be thousands of pages of (exceedingly dense) exegesis in print. Here, then, is one of the profound mysteries of the 20th century . . . how did a minor Viennese aphorist come to be regarded (in some circles) as a great philosopher. It seems extraordinary that the reaction to Wittgenstein is very much the same reaction that is to Jacques Lacan.[202]

Even outside academic circles he exerted considerable influence. He had a profound effect on Drury's mother, as Wall points out. Before she met him, she was rather suspicious of Wittgenstein, who as she saw it had needlessly interfered with her son's career. But on meeting him she was completely won over.[203]

Comparison with Lacan

Much comparison has been made between Wittgenstein and Jacques Lacan, in relation not only to their approach to philosophy but also to their personality traits. In terms of a philosophical outlook, Lacan, too, focused on linguistic theories of psychoanalysis, but Wittgenstein posited that 'language is everything' well before Lacan ever did.[204] Raymond Tallis, in a review of 'the shrink from hell', discredited much of Lacan's work, believing him to hold 'crackpot theories, partly expropriated from Salvador Dali'.[205]

However, the area that draws the greatest comparison is the manner in which their students venerated them. Both were referred to as 'the Master'.

The most powerful support for Lacan's doctrines came from his students, caught up in the aura that surrounded him. Lacan was a 'handsome dandy' who was able to command unconditional love like many physically attractive psychopaths can, according to Tallis. He exploited this to the utmost in support of an insatiable appetite for wealth, fame and sex. Though Wittgenstein obviously differed in that respect, his disciples were similarly mesmerised. Tallis notes that Lacan's disciples:

> worshipped him like a god and treated his teachings like a holy rite . . . in constant fear of excommunication; the absence of Lacan was an ontological catastrophe equal to the absence of god. Anyone who fell under the spell of the Master laid aside the critical sense. He justified his intellectual terrorism on the grounds that he was surrounded by enemies whom he had to fight. His lunatic legacy lives on in places like departments of literature whose inmates are even now trying to, or pretending to, make sense of his utterly unfounded, gnomic teachings and inflicting them on baffled students.[206]

Interestingly, Lacan, like Wittgenstein, could also arouse the most virulent dislike.[207]

Sensory sensitivities

Sensory sensitivities can feature in HFA/ASP. Certainly, there are numerous accounts of Wittgenstein's sensitivities. He was particularly hypersensitive to auditory intrusions. When he first went to work as a teacher in Austria he lodged in a small upstairs room in the local guesthouse, Zum braunen Hirschen. Monk notes that Wittgenstein quickly found the noise of the dance music coming from below too much to bear. He abruptly left the building and made a bed for himself in the school kitchen.[208] While staying with the Kingstons in Wicklow he had similar problems. There was a great deal of noise in a room adjacent to his and he 'hammered violently on the wall several times' to put an end to it.[209] He also complained about people talking late at night, where the continual murmur of their voices drove him crazy.[210]

People with autism can be insensitive to cold; Wittgenstein is no exception in this regard. After the First World War he arranged to meet Russell in The Hague during December. When he arrived at the hotel, Russell was shocked to discover that despite the winter cold Wittgenstein had no coat.[211]

Identity diffusion

Wittgenstein's life was unquestionably full of diversity, not least in terms of frequent changes in occupation. Indeed, the literary theorist Terry Eagleton has described Wittgenstein as an 'arresting combination of monk, mystic and mechanic'.[212] Wittgenstein's 'restless spirit' was noted too by Maria Baghramian.[213] These features are often associated with HFA/ASP. Moreover, identity diffusion and lack of sense of self are central issues. Wittgenstein was largely engaged in a search for a sense of self throughout his life. The American critic, Marjorie Perloff, claims that Wittgenstein appears as the 'ultimate modernist outsider, the changeling who never stops reinventing himself'.[214] The desire to reinvent himself was often motivated by deep unhappiness associated with his character, where he 'judged himself to be vain, desirous of admiration, easily given to irritation, anger, contempt for others', according to Malcolm.[215]

At various times Wittgenstein wanted to become a monk. He did succeed in becoming an architect for a period. At another stage he wished to be an orchestral conductor, but became a schoolteacher instead. After he resigned his teaching post because of brutality towards pupils, he became a gardener in a monastery that adjoined a graveyard. When friends questioned his latest career choice they were met with a typical quasi-humorous response: 'the dead don't talk'.[216] None the less, he became an excellent and highly industrious gardener, according to Bartley.[217] His job as gardener can be viewed as a way for him to cope with his interpersonal difficulties through manual labour. Indeed, it was something he recommended to his academic disciples, however inappropriate and unsuitable for them. It is possible that gardening and the idea of physical work grounded him. The prospect of becoming a manual labourer in Stalinist Russia also appealed to him, and he undertook a short holiday there on a fact-finding mission. He lost interest, however, when the only form of work offered to him was as a philosophy lecturer in Moscow.

His volunteer work during the two world wars was also varied. He served as a soldier during the First World War and later, in the Second World War, as a medical orderly at Guy's Hospital, and later again as a trauma researcher at Newcastle-upon-Tyne. While there he even found the time to design a medical apparatus. Wijdeveld, among others, claimed that Wittgenstein showed enormous self-control and absolute dedication at whatever job he undertook:

> although he was not trained as a professional architect his own conception of ethical aesthetics implied that complete dedication and perseverance in an effort for clarification would necessarily lead to a satisfying result in at least those aspects of architecture to which his talents were relevant (the remaining architectural responsibility lay, of course, in the hands of Jacques Groag). As soon as Wittgenstein had agreed to take the commission, he regarded architecture not so much as a profession but as a vocation. He acquitted himself of the tasks with the same devotion as he had shown before in designing the jet propelled

engine, in devising the *Tractatus Logico-Philosophicus*, and in teaching children, and would demonstrate again in philosophy after the completion of the Kundmanngasse [the house he designed] and in designing a medical apparatus while working as a volunteer during the Second World War.[218]

Undeniably, the problems of identity preoccupied him. In Norway, in 1913, he wrote 'just now I am troubled with identity that I really cannot write any longer'.[219] Without a doubt, not being able to write made him despondent. Writing was inextricably linked to his identity and he wrote an enormous amount in his lifetime, albeit mainly unpublished work. 'I think, therefore I am' and 'I write, therefore I am or I exist' appeared to be his credo: so much so that he continued to work intensely up to two days before his death. Evidently, he believed that his writing could be seen as distinctly belonging to him. For him not to think or reflect on ideas was not to exist. In fact, his last words to Drury before he died were 'whatever becomes of you, don't stop thinking'.[220] Indeed, it is fair to say that 'thinking' is what people with HFA/ASP habitually do.

A study of Wittgenstein reveals that his own identity and sense of self were fragmented in the same way that his view of the world was fragmented. Ultimately his philosophy was fragmented too. He was unable to put his later work, the *Philosophical Investigations*, together under a coherent framework and, indeed, wanted to call it at one point 'philosophical remarks'. This is linked with his lack of both identity and sense of self. For the first half of his life he focused on one segment, language, and was unable to see the bigger picture in terms of human interactions.

It is possible to see Wittgenstein's remarks as an attempt to construct a cohesive sense of self. As mentioned above, his identity was equal to his writings. He could see small rhetorical differences and perhaps, like the classic obsessional personality, he was trying to create the absolutely perfect work. The *Philosophical Investigations* are a series of anxious questionings. Trying to find the answers to these slightly obsessional questions was probably his way of reducing anxiety. From the psychiatric and scientific points of view, Wittgenstein claimed that it was not human agreement that decided what was true or false, but what people did that was true or false.

Narcissism

Wittgenstein displayed elements of narcissism throughout his life, which often gave rise to feelings of guilt. On the occasion of his being made professor of philosophy at Cambridge in 1939, Wittgenstein wrote to a previous colleague, William Eccles:

having got the professorship is very flattering and all that, but it might have been much better for me if I got a job opening and closing crossing gates. I don't get any kick out of my position (except what my vanity and stupidity sometimes gets).[221]

Indeed, he admitted to Rhees that 'we all want to be admired'.[222] But when he attempted to purge himself of such guilt he found that it was replaced by more vanity. 'I thought that when I gave up my professorship that I had got rid of my vanity. Now I find I am vain about the style in which I am able to write.'[223] When his contemporaries at Cambridge tried to publish commentaries on his ideas that would form the basis of *Philosophical Investigations*, in circulation at the time, he was disturbed at the form in which they were presented. He later stated in its preface that it 'stung my vanity and I had difficulty quietening it'.[224] Giddens, in a review of Ernest Gellner's *Anthropology and Politics*, reported that Gellner considered Wittgenstein to have had 'a genius for publicity', while seeming to avoid it.[225] In this case the 'genius for publicity' cannot be looked at in terms of exhibitionism. There is no element of deliberately courting publicity in Wittgenstein's case. Rather, his non-verbal behaviour indirectly attracted as much publicity as his work in philosophy. It is interesting that the 'greatest genius for publicity' ever, Adolf Hitler, had autistic psychopathy.

Obsessive compulsive phenomena often form part of HFA/ASP. Wittgenstein was, by and large, a perfectionist. He was remarkably precise about his use of language, as noted by Peter Winch in *Wittgenstein: a Religious Point of View*: 'by most people's standards Wittgenstein was obsessively precise about the way he expressed himself'.[226] This search for precision and exactness was seen in his philosophical remarks over and over again, especially when he considered his work not right for publication, never quite good enough. Indeed, he did confess 'of course I want to be perfect'.[227] The striving for perfection was motivated by fear of loss of control and loss of identity. He did express his fears over his loss of identity in the words 'I am afraid of disintegration (of my disintegration)'.[228]

Violent behaviour

Wittgenstein displayed a certain 'autistic aggression' when interacting with people. Aggression is sometimes found in those with HFA/ASP. Certainly, Leonard Wolff claimed that Wittgenstein had an aggressive and cruel streak.[229] Similarly, Edmonds and Eidinow describe him as 'bullying, aggressive, intolerant, and self-absorbed'.[230] In fact, Wittgenstein's moods were so savage that once Russell feared he would break all the furniture in his room. However, Wittgenstein did admit to his aggressive tendencies and bouts of anger:

When I am furious about something, I sometimes hit the ground or a tree with a stick, and the like. But I certainly don't think that the ground is to blame or that this hitting can help at all. I give vent to my anger. And that is what all rights are like . . . the important thing is the similarity with the act of punishing, but nothing more than similarity is to be found.[231]

One of the most serious allegations made against Wittgenstein was of child brutality. From pupil reminiscences, the punishment meted out to them often took the form of *Ohrfeige* (ear boxing) and *Haareziehen* (hair pulling), according to Monk. Monk considers that for children with poor ability, the type of mathematics that Wittgenstein attempted to teach them was well beyond their ability. In those cases he likely came across as a tyrant, showing a clear lack of empathy and poor judgement. This was apparent in an episode described by one of his pupils, Anna Brenner. She reported that one day she, along with her friend Anna Volker, decided not to give any answers in class. When Brenner was asked how many metres there were in a kilometre, she said nothing and received a box on the ears. After the lesson Wittgenstein took her to the office to discover why she had said nothing. When asked if she was sick she lied and said yes. Wittgenstein, overcome with remorse, was deeply apologetic and asked her to forgive him as he held up his hands in prayer. Wittgenstein's absolute inability to detect the lie demonstrates a certain naïvety, found in people with HFA/ASP.[232]

When interviewed by Adolf Hubner, another pupil, August Riegler, gave an insight into a more alarming episode of brutality, as quoted by Monk:

Joseph Hidbaur was an 11-year-old pupil of Wittgenstein's whose father had died and whose mother worked as a live-in maid for a local farmer named Piribauer. Hidbaur was a pale, sickly child who was to die of leukaemia at the age of 14. He was not the rebellious type, but possibly rather slow and reticent in giving answers in class. One day, Wittgenstein's impatience got the better of him, and he struck Hidbaur two or three times on the head, causing the boy to collapse. On the question of whether Wittgenstein struck the boy with undue force – whether he ill-treated the child – a fellow pupil, August Riegler, has (with dubious logic) commented 'it cannot be said that Wittgenstein ill-treated the child. If Hidbaur's punishment was ill-treatment, then 80% of Wittgenstein's punishments were ill treatment'.[233]

Evidently Piribauer, who instigated the charge against Wittgenstein, believed that 'he wasn't a teacher, he was an animal trainer'.[234] The police were informed and Wittgenstein brought to trial. He was eventually acquitted after he underwent a compulsory psychiatric examination to determine his mental responsibility, and lied about the level of corporal punishment he had administered in the classroom.[235] The sense of moral failure that this brought 'haunted him for over a decade' and he eventually returned to apologise to the victims.

Wittgenstein's legacy continues today in the rural areas of Austria where he taught. A waitress in a café in Kirkberg-am-wechel in 1997 similarly remarked that 'Ludwig Wittgenstein hit children with his fist'.[236] She did add, however, that it was normal for children to be hit in Vienna. Furthermore, people did not like Wittgenstein as they could not follow his thoughts. Consequently, they 'couldn't see the reason why he hit them'.

Considerable debate still rages over whether Wittgenstein used a poker to make a philosophical point or simply to threaten Karl Popper; or indeed, whether Popper lied about being threatened with a poker, according to Edmonds and Eidinow.[237] Brian Morton points out that Popper's claim that he 'bested' Wittgenstein was no more than an act of rather 'lame and posthumous revenge'.[238] The poker incident occurred at a meeting of the Moral Sciences Club at Cambridge in 1946, when the much younger Popper considered himself 'to be the sole important critic of the Vienna Circle' rather than Wittgenstein, as suggested by Will Self. Moreover, Popper had 'resolved to lock antlers with a man he perceived as trivialising the quest for certain knowledge'. Self rejects Popper's version of events:

> Karl Popper 'glossed' over (which is what academics do when they are lying) the episode in his autobiography and had himself effortlessly facing down an irate, poker-wielding Wittgenstein – who was aggressively challenging him to give an example of a moral statement – with a cool riposte, 'not to threaten visiting lecturers with pokers'. He was still performing to an audience whom his opponent had regarded all along as a lot of swine, with their feet jammed in their mouths. It is this imbalance between the two men – Popper obsessed by Wittgenstein, Wittgenstein utterly unconcerned by Popper . . .[239]

Regardless of the true nature of the incident, the fact remains that Wittgenstein's aggressive display in wielding a poker in such a lecture setting was evidence of his 'autistic aggression'. So, too, is the manner of his contemptuous disregard for Popper.

Physical illness

On the physical side, Wittgenstein developed anaemia while in Dublin but it was probably the result of carcinoma of the prostate, which was finally diagnosed in the United Kingdom in November 1949 and led to his death in 1951.

Psychiatric co-morbidity

Undoubtedly, Wittgenstein came from a unique and great family with a history of mental illness. The major illness that dogged Wittgenstein was a depressive disorder of a recurrent and chronic type.[240] It would appear there was a genetic loading in the family for depression (as well as dyslexia and possibly autism spectrum disorder, especially HFA/ASP). Monk uses the phrase 'the laboratory of self-destruction' to describe the Wittgenstein home.[241] Indeed, major genetic factors were largely responsible for his condition.

His father more than likely had HFA/ASP traits, e.g. lack of empathy which interfered with his ability to parent his children and treat them with the sensitivity they craved. The harsh parenting style in all likelihood undermined the boys' self-esteem, sense of themselves and self-confidence, and made them more vulnerable to the stresses of life. According to McGuinness, Wittgenstein's aunt had a 'severe nervous disorder'.[242] This was probably schizophrenia but could have been HFA/ASP, as the two are often confused. McGuinness notes that Wittgenstein had thoughts of suicide from his tenth or eleventh year.[243] Therefore, it is highly likely that he suffered from childhood depression. From the age of 11 years he suffered from what he described as:

> terrific loneliness (mental – not physical): that he continually thought of suicide then, and felt ashamed of never daring to kill himself: he put it that he had 'a hint that he was *de trop* in this world' but that he had disregarded it.[244]

It is also possible that Wittgenstein's poor performance at school was partly due to an adolescent depression, but HFA/ASP was clearly the major factor. Wittgenstein seriously considered suicide at the age of 15 years and again from about the ages of 23 to 24 years, but resisted because his 'code of behaviour' did not permit it.

Klin and Volkmar suggest that there are increased affective disorders among relatives of people with autistic spectrum disorder and about 15 per cent of people with Asperger's syndrome have depression.[245] There is also a link between suicide and Asperger's syndrome. Certainly, Wittgenstein thought about suicide for much of his life. Three of his older brothers committed suicide. The eldest, Hans, appears to have done so because his father pressurised him into becoming a businessman when he wanted to be a musician. Kurt killed himself for reasons still unclear, but which appear to be related to his supervision of soldiers after the defeat of the Austro-Hungarian army in the First World War. Lastly, Rudolf (Rudy) committed suicide by taking cyanide, possibly because he could not come to terms with his homosexuality and other difficulties with the direction his life was taking. The eldest sister, Hermine, considered that all her brothers had 'a lack of the will to live' – of *Lebenskraft, Lebenswille* or *jugendliches, Lebensgefühl*, as she variously called it.[246]

Depression

Wittgenstein had low periods of depressed mood for most of the day and nearly every day for long periods. This was associated with a markedly diminished interest and pleasure in almost all activities as well as psychomotor agitation and feelings of worthlessness. There were, in addition, feelings of excessive and inappropriate guilt. Judging from the various accounts of him, he had diminished ability to think and concentrate as well as recurrent thoughts of death and suicidal ideation. These interfered with his social and occupational functioning as well as causing him major distress.

He was in better spirits in the afternoon, which is typical of those with biological depression.[247] Russell, in his autobiography, stated that Wittgenstein would visit him and pace up and down his room 'like a wild beast in agitated silence'.[248] He would talk constantly about his faults and his fear of a 'premature decay of his intellect'. In 1914 Wittgenstein wrote to Russell relating the depths of this depression:

> It is very sad, but I have once again no logical news for you. The reason is that things have gone terribly badly for me in the past weeks. Everyday I was tormented by a frightful *Angst* and by depression in turns and even in the intervals I was so exhausted that I was not able to think of doing a bit of work. It is terrifying beyond all description the kinds of mental torment that there can be! It wasn't until two days ago that I could hear the voice of reason over the howls of the damned and I began to work again. And perhaps I will get better now and be able to produce something decent. But I never knew what it meant to feel only one step away from madness – let's hope for the best![249]

Wittgenstein had considerable fear of mental illness, and wrote 'I am frightened of the onset of insanity. God alone knows whether I am in danger', and later 'I often believe that I am on the straight road to insanity'. His fear of insanity also stemmed from a failure to distinguish whether or not his fears were groundless. 'I am afraid of madness. Do I have any reason for assuming that this fear does not spring from, so to speak, an optical illusion: taking something to be an abyss right at my feet, when it is nothing of the sort?'[250]

When Wittgenstein was filled with despair, his friends made considerable efforts to help him. Monk quotes from Wittgenstein's writings in April 1942: 'I no longer feel any hope for the future of my life . . . I cannot imagine any future for me other than a ghastly one, friendless, joyless'.[251] While staying in Wicklow, Wittgenstein wrote that at first he suffered from terrible depressions and later insomnia. He came to Drury and said: 'what I have already dreaded: that I would no longer be able to work. I have done no work at all for the past two weeks. And I can't sleep at night.'[252] Drury prescribed sleeping pills for him, possibly sodium amytal, the barbiturate most commonly prescribed as a sedative at the time.

While at Cambridge, his mental state was a source of concern to Russell. Russell communicated his distress to Lady Ottoline Morrell at seeing him so depressed. 'Wittgenstein is on the verge of a nervous breakdown, not far removed from suicide, feeling himself a miserable creature full of sin. He makes me terribly anxious and I hate seeing his misery.'[253]

Wittgenstein's constant change of career was a source of anxiety to his family. On one occasion, when his sister Hermine took him to task for abandoning academia for elementary school, his reply left her in no doubt of the mental turmoil he was enduring:

> I told him . . . that imagining him with his philosophically trained mind as an elementary school teacher, it was to me as if someone were to use a precision instrument to open crates. Thereupon Ludwig answered with a comparison which silenced me, for he said 'you remind me of someone who is looking through a closed window and cannot explain to himself the strange movements of a passer-by. He doesn't know what kind of storm is raging outside and that this person perhaps is only with great effort keeping himself on his feet'. It was then that I understood his state of mind.[254]

Indeed, this state of mind would not be uncommon for a person with HFA/ ASP.

Ethics of suicide

The self-critical and negative thinking style typical of the depressive is evident in Wittgenstein. In his case there is a clear link between depression and suicide, much of it prompted by guilt and sin, as he understood them. The idea that there was something morally wrong with homosexuality was a matter of enormous conflict and guilt for people in Vienna at the turn of the twentieth century. Yet, despite his depression, he questioned the ethics of suicide:

> in fact I am in a state of mind that is terrible to me. It is a pitiable state, I know. But this is just like what happens when a man who can't swim has fallen into water and flays about with his hands and feet and feels that he cannot keep his head above water. That is the position I am in

now. I know that to kill oneself is always a dirty thing to do. Surely one cannot will one's own destruction, and anybody who has visualised what is in practice involved in the act of suicide knows that suicide is always a rushing of one's own defences.[255]

Essentially, Wittgenstein felt that committing suicide would be failure. He felt that if suicide was permitted, then everything else was accordingly permitted. 'If anything is not allowed then suicide is not allowed. This throws light on the nature of ethics, for suicide is, so to speak the elementary sin.'[256] These words echo those of Albert Camus who, at a later stage, believed suicide to be the only philosophical problem. Wittgenstein was convinced that his life would be short, which is in keeping with the pessimistic style of thinking of those with HFA/ASP. In 1913 he was afraid that he would die some time between the succeeding 2 months and 4 years.[257] Moreover, he was fearful that he would die before he had written his ideas in an intelligible form. Sigmund Freud was equally preoccupied with death. This leads one to believe that geniuses are often fearful of dying before they have produced their great works. Indeed, if he did not succeed in producing a work of genius, Wittgenstein feared that his life's work would have been in vain. Additionally, he feared that his nervous temperament had caused him a life of misery and other considerable inconveniences.

Schizophrenia

A debate has occurred in the literature about whether Wittgenstein had schizophrenia or depression. According to Smythies, Canon Raven told him that Wittgenstein 'suffered from paranoid delusions'.[258] Smythies elaborates on a speech disorder known as 'schizophreneze', which he links to Wittgenstein. He claims that he attended the weekly meetings of Wittgenstein's disciples and found the thoughts produced by this group 'very like the thoughts and mode of thinking that trouble my schizophrenic patients'. According to Matthews, Smythies' claims were welcomed by those who had failed to understand Wittgenstein but attacked by academics as being 'little more than hearsay'.[259] Indeed, Wittgenstein was aware of the dangers of such classification, as indicated by E. Eloma:

> in the Wittgensteinian sense, the concept of schizophrenia could even be seen as a furious attempt to grasp and classify human madness in scientific terms, and Smythies's letter is a warning of what may happen when people are privileged by virtue of their psychiatric training and identification to decide what is sound and scientific. The following note by Wittgenstein demonstrates that he was deeply aware of the hazards inherent in this way of thinking, doubting and perceiving the world: I

am sitting with a philosopher in the garden, he says again and again 'I know that that is a tree', pointing to a tree that is near us. Someone else arrives and hears this and I tell him 'this fellow isn't insane'. We are only doing philosophy'. Thus the claim that the writings of Wittgenstein should be read as nonsense poetry lacking a scientific dimension is not surprising. I have referred to Wittgenstein's studies on certainty in support of my theory that Shakespeare approached the mystery of madness in an experimental way by studying the genesis and consequences of a 'false experience of truth' (*Othello*, *Macbeth*), and what happens when our natural inclination to act according to the experience of truth is lost (*Hamlet*). I now propose that Wittgenstein, instead of being labelled a schizophrenic, should rather be regarded as a universal Hamlet figure of our time.[260]

However, Professor Norman Moore sheds some light on the true nature of Wittgenstein's depression. On 12 November 1993, Moore commented on Smythies' claims to the present author and David Berman, professor of philosophy at Trinity College Dublin. Moore had been professor of psychiatry at Trinity College Dublin and the leading Irish psychiatric clinician of his day. In the late 1940s Wittgenstein had been referred to Moore for another opinion by Drury, then working as a psychiatrist at St Patrick's Hospital, Dublin. Drury, according to Moore, was worried about Wittgenstein, who was on an extended visit to Ireland. Unlike Smythies, who had no personal contact with Wittgenstein, Moore saw Wittgenstein about five or six times. He describes Wittgenstein when he first saw him as a 'depressed and sad man' who was 'down with depressed affect' and 'gloomy'. He spoke slowly and was 'slowed down'. Moore found him a rather sensitive, withdrawn person. At this time Wittgenstein was a typical depressive with a pyknic build, who spoke in a very slow manner, again typical of depression. He did not discuss philosophical topics with Moore, and Moore diagnosed him as having a depressive disorder.[261]

John Hayman, philosopher at Queen's College, Oxford, was 'relieved' by this finding and told Matthews that the reason people have problems with Wittgenstein is partly because 'the ideas are very difficult and partly the way they are composed'.[262] In the same article Dr Raj Persaud of the London Institute of Psychiatry suggested that 'a lot of Wittgenstein does not make sense'. This viewpoint, however, seems close to Smythies' original position. Just because one has a difficulty with philosophy does not necessarily mean that it was written by a person with schizophrenia.

Neuropsychology

Psychologically Wittgenstein had weak central coherence, i.e. he had difficulty in seeing the big picture. However, he had a certain awareness of this fact. He felt, metaphorically speaking, that he took students down too many side-streets and did not show them direct routes. In *Vermischte Bemerkungen* there is an interesting quotation from Wittgenstein: 'I'll ask innumerable irrelevant questions . . . I hope I will be able to make my way through this forest'. But he then adds 'I keep entangling myself in details, without knowing whether I should talk about these things at all; and it seems to me that I perhaps inspect a wide area only in order to exclude it at once from consideration'.[263]

Causes of depression

There is a misconception that people with HFA/ASP are not vulnerable to losing people or fail to notice loss because they are in an autistic world. Nothing could be further from the truth. When Wittgenstein's ex-lover, Francis Skinner, died in 1941, he was tremendously upset and behaved, according to Rush Rhees, 'like a frightened wild animal during the funeral'.[264] Grief can give rise to depression, but equally Wittgenstein's guilt at the way he mistreated his friends distressed him. As with so many people with depression, a minor quarrel could cause great upset. Another typical factor of depressives is the idealisation of a parent, and in this case Wittgenstein idealised his father. Wittgenstein had an upbringing not unlike that of John Stuart Mill, who also suffered from depression and believed that he failed to live up to his father's standards. Clearly, people with depression suffer from low self-esteem and a gross lack of empathy, where criticism does play a role, which indeed figured highly in Wittgenstein's family. Furthermore, Wittgenstein was hypersensitive to minor reverses in his work or minor stresses in his relationships. As Storr points out:

> the depressive personalities are, as one might expect, particularly vulnerable to criticism. All creative people identify themselves to some extent with what they produce, for every piece of work, even if it consists of mathematics or observations requiring maximum scientific detachment, contains part of themselves.[265]

Wittgenstein's identity (even if diffused) was rooted in his work and resulted in severe perfectionism, as outlined above. His reluctance to publish work was likely because of a fear of hostile criticism, which is characteristic of patients with depression.

In their work on cognitive therapy of depression, Beck and colleagues point out that depressed patients anticipate that their current difficulties or suffering will continue forever.[266] All they can see ahead is a life of misery. The cognitive triad set of negative attitudes to the world as self and the future are typical of people with depression. This was certainly the case with Wittgenstein. Moreover, he was narcissistic in that his libido was largely invested in his ego or the self and in his ideas. As a consequence he came to see Dr Drury (his psychiatrist friend in Dublin) for 'narcissistic supplies' and support for his depression.

Meisner makes a point which I think is quite relevant to Wittgenstein, and may help explain some of his conflicting emotions and behaviour:

> depressive patients find it more comfortable in some sense to live in terms of their own sense of vulnerability, victimisation and narcissistic depletion. However, further clinical investigation often reveals the opposite configuration operating at a different level of conscious awareness and interpsychic availability. Thus depressive patients are often found to harbour repressed and well-concealed hostility, aggressive and destructive wishes, wishes for vengeance, and impulses to inflict sadistic, hostile and demeaning injury upon others.[267]

Nevertheless, it appears that these phenomena can be attributed to his HFA/ASP. By all accounts Wittgenstein certainly inflicted sadistic and hostile impulses on the 'rough youths' he engaged in homosexual relations in the Prater in Vienna. And as we have seen, when teaching he knocked a child with leukaemia unconscious.

Positive view of psychiatry

Wittgenstein took an interest in psychiatry and had encouraging views on *Physical Treatments in Psychiatry* by Sergeant and Slater because these concerned the more 'simple' treatments in biological psychology. Nevertheless, he felt that their work on biological psychiatry did not provide all the answers. That said, he was fearful of psychoanalysis in the sense that someone could really get to know him. He confided in Drury that 'he did not think it right to reveal all one's thoughts to a stranger'. More than likely he was fearful that his homosexuality would become known. Evidently, he was impressed with Freud's *Interpretation of Dreams* and, when he first read it, he exclaimed 'here at last is psychology that has something to say'.[268]

It is hardly surprising then that Wittgenstein took an interest in psychiatry, given his own lifelong chronic depression and family history of mental illness. At one time he wanted to study medicine at Trinity College Dublin, but did not pursue it. Indeed, his wish to become a psychiatrist was probably motivated by a wish to get treatment for his chronic depression. At another stage Wittgenstein had the choice of staying in Cambridge with Francis Skinner or going to Dublin to see Drury to get psychiatric attention. He opted for Dublin. His 'personal psychiatrist', Drury, even arranged for him to see patients in St Patrick's Hospital (founded in the eighteenth century with a bequest from Jonathan Swift). After a visit

Wittgenstein had said 'see the sane man in the maniac! (and the madman in yourself)'.[269] He also commented that one elderly patient was far more intelligent than his doctors.[270]

Coping mechanisms

Wittgenstein lacked what Bion called a psychological 'container' in terms of having secure thoughts.[271] Nevertheless, a more important factor was his autism. As an individual, he certainly could be described as a fragile man. Initially, Drury and Russell, among others, were empathetic to him and admired him and his philosophy, and this had a healing effect on his psyche. Indeed, Russell at first had unswerving faith in him and expressed the view that the next great advance in philosophy would come from Wittgenstein. Of course, the good support of his peers was not curative but it did prevent him from committing suicide. His friends helped him to restore partly and temporarily his sense of self and to make up for his sense of psychic deficiency.[272] Discovering Frege, Russell and philosophy for which he had a great aptitude was clearly important. Furthermore, he formed critical relationships throughout his life with men that were enormously vital to him, namely Hänsel, Drury, Russell, Malcolm, Eccles and Engelmann.

Undoubtedly he was a prickly character and relationships only worked well when his partner was placid, sensitive and tolerant. His intimate friendships with Francis Skinner and Ben Richards clearly brought him moments of happiness. The reason Wittgenstein got on so well with Drury was that they both had quite similar personalities and interests – both tried to understand people; Wittgenstein through philosophy and Drury through psychiatry. Drury was also a highly ethical and moral man, and indeed a workaholic like Wittgenstein.

Wittgenstein described his psychological problems in very concrete terms, e.g. 'nerve-racking' and 'mind-racking'. Storr points out that those who are temperamentally inclined towards depression, except when they are ill, 'cope successfully with their underlying tendency' by being overactive. He cites Balzac and Winston Churchill as examples.[273] Indeed, Wittgenstein did feel the beneficial effects of activity when he worked as a porter at Guy's Hospital. He found that the best way to counter depression was ceaseless activity. He wrote 'if you can't find happiness in stillness, find it in running! . . . like a cyclist I have to keep pedalling, to keep moving, in order not to fall down'.[274]

Wittgenstein also kept depression at bay by incessant research on philosophical matters, except when it overwhelmed this defence. Work was his antidepressant, and while writing *Philosophical Investigations* in Ireland he said that he was 'philosophising for all his worth' and doing the 'only work that really bucks me up'.[275]

During the First World War Wittgenstein kept a copy of Tolstoy's *Gospel in Brief* on his person, which had a positive impact on him. He wrote that it simply 'kept him alive'. In fact it allowed him to have a kind of religious conversion which he found beneficial. Some religious conversions can be very positive to mental well-being. Indeed, there is some evidence from the scientific literature of the positive impact of organised religion on mental health.[276] Wittgenstein was also happy during military action as it gave him an opportunity to be – as he saw it – a decent human being, capable of doing great good and of purging past guilts.

His musicality and the enormous satisfaction he got from music was another protective factor against suicide. He also relaxed by going to silent movies and preferred them to the later 'talking pictures', as the dialogue introduced an intellectual aspect 'with all its dangers and deceptions'.[277]

In terms of medical therapy, Drury prescribed sleeping tablets for Wittgenstein.[278] Moore also prescribed sleeping tablets – sodium amytal – which he took very carefully and in very small doses. Antidepressants as we know them today were not available at that period. The amphetamine, Benzedrine, was considered, but there is no evidence that Wittgenstein ever actually took it. Indeed, he was terrified of addiction.[279]

'Autistic superego'

Wittgenstein's father created a world of moral absolutes where failure was not tolerated.[280] The greatest fear of Wittgenstein's mother was to have incommoded someone or failed in her duty. Effectively, Wittgenstein and his siblings acquired from both their parents too strong a sense of duty, whereby their role in life was 'to change the world in some way'.[281] Enormous emphasis was placed on the correct use of language in the family, leading Wittgenstein to comment 'it would not matter what you had done, you might have killed somebody; what would matter would be how you talked about it'.[282] There is no doubt that people with HFA/ASP, like Wittgenstein and his father, live in a world of moral absolutes.

In personality, Wittgenstein was extremely perfectionistic, as noted above. He had a very harsh superego that led to feelings of guilt and an extremely demanding ego-ideal which was impossible to reach. Not surprisingly, he published only one book in his lifetime, as all other works fell short of his ideals. Laplanche and Pontalis described the ego-ideal as a distinct agency that constitutes a model to which the subject attempts to conform.[283] Freud, too, states that the ego-ideal 'constantly watches the actual ego and measures it by the ego-ideal'.[284] Lagache claims that the ego-ideal corresponds 'to the way in which the subject must behave in order to respond to the expectations of authority'. Interestingly, Nunberg points out that the ego-ideal is said to be formed principally on a model of love objects.[285] In Wittgenstein's case his ego-ideal was influenced by his grandfather, Herman Christian, who had the determination to do things properly, and similarly with his father. But it had none of what McGuinness describes as 'the competitiveness that goes with a feeling of inferiority and is often ascribed to families of Jewish origin but a much more aristocratic attitude, a consciousness of their capacities and a strong feeling of duty to realise them'.[286]

From all accounts Wittgenstein was plainly obsessed with his 'badness'. He blamed himself for anything that went wrong in his childhood, and was constantly examining his childhood for sins. The writings of St Augustine, Kierkegaard and Tolstoy appealed to him most, because 'over and over again in the works of each one of these is the expression of a sinful or a guilty sexuality', as Levi notes.[287] Wittgenstein did give an indication of the importance of sexuality in his life, referring to it in the following way: 'some trouble, or with some problem which is a big thing in your life – as sex is, for instance'.[288] This gives us a clue about his central conflict and what cannot be spoken about so easily.

Weininger

A book that was to have a potent effect on the young Wittgenstein was Otto Weininger's *Sex and Character*, which first appeared in 1903. It expressed similar problems to the ones Wittgenstein encountered: both were conflicted about their Jewish heritage and sexuality. It also appears that Wittgenstein had a similar outlook on guilt and atonement, and, not surprisingly, was preoccupied with sin and guilt throughout his life. Weininger claimed that 'every true and perennial problem is equally a true and perennial guilt; every answer is an atonement, every piece of knowledge won a conversation'.[289] Weininger's influence on the young Wittgenstein was crucial, as McGuinness points out:

> [the significance of Weininger for Wittgenstein] resided in his attitude towards suicide – it was the decent man's way out when he felt he was finally becoming evil: so Weininger said, that his practice differed from it only a little, since he committed suicide shortly after his book appeared because with his inheritance he could not meet the moral demands he made of himself.[290]

However, Wittgenstein differed from Weininger in that the former's philosophical work was an effort to purify him from any guilt, and produce philosophy of the highest order. That was the path he chose, while Weininger in fact chose suicide. Nevertheless, Wittgenstein did entertain the notion of death during the First World War as one way of meeting the moral demands he placed on himself. Malcolm claims that the single most important thing for Wittgenstein during the war was not to avoid death but 'to meet it without cowardice and without losing control of himself'.[291] Being in control is enormously important to people with HFA/ASP. Engelmann stated that the notion of a last judgement was of profound concern to Wittgenstein.[292] Dying a noble death was an all-pervasive thought, and he kept putting himself in danger in order 'to force himself to be a decent human being as he conceived it', according to McGuinness.[293]

On the question of ethics, Weininger stated that 'logic and ethics are fundamentally the same . . . they are no more than a duty to oneself'.[294] In Wittgenstein's case, his duty was to purify himself, especially from cottaging in the Prater in Vienna. Indeed, the greatest conflict in his life was between logic, ethics and sex with 'rough youths', whether in Vienna or elsewhere. It is interesting that one of Russell's favourite anecdotes about Wittgenstein encapsulates this:

> Once I said to him . . . 'Are you thinking about logic or about your sins?'. 'Both,' he replied, and continued his pacing. I did not like to suggest that it was time for bed, as it seemed probable both to him and me that on leaving me he would commit suicide.[295]

The issue of Jewishness was also treated in Weininger's book. At the turn of the century Jewishness was regarded in a highly negative way, as was homosexuality. None the less, there is little doubt that Wittgenstein felt far more alienated by his homosexuality and by HFA/ASP than his Jewishness. Clearly he did not know he had HFA/ASP. However, for most of his life he was careful not to reveal the extent of his Jewish lineage, feeling somehow tainted by his roots.

Clearly, Wittgenstein was an example of Freud's 'guilty man'. He was tormented with guilt throughout his life, particularly about homosexuality. He was also guilty about all imperfections, however minor, in his work. Pride, too, was central to his guilt. He was guilty that pride prevented him from living up to the extreme and unreasonable ideals of his family and himself in relation to duty and doing good works. By way of atonement he made a number of confessions in his life, and wrote letters to select friends describing times when he had been 'weak and dishonest' in order to 'dismantle his pride'.[296] Curiously, in his confessions he always omitted any reference to guilt associated with homosexuality, which he was very conscious of.

Badness

Oliver Sacks in *An Anthropologist on Mars* describes 'real badness' in respect of Temple Grandin, who had autism and believed it could have 'terrifying, instantly lethal consequences'.[297] Grandin felt that if she ever did anything really bad, God would punish her, for instance in a motor accident. There is a tremendous superego quality described here which bears some similarity to Wittgenstein. Indeed, one can surmise that people with HFA/ASP can frequently have a very severe superego.[298]

Evidently Wittgenstein would fly into a rage if he felt that time had been squandered or spent unwisely. Russell describes how he spent an afternoon with Wittgenstein watching North (son of his colleague, Whitehead) in a boat race. Wittgenstein was very critical of how they spent the afternoon, and declared that it was 'so vile that we ought not to live, or at least he ought not, that nothing is tolerable except producing great works or enjoying those of others, that he has accomplished nothing and never will'.[299] It was hardly surprising then that Wittgenstein suffered from depression, having such an inordinately demanding superego and ego-ideal, since it would inevitably lead to low self-esteem when its demands were not met.

As far as is known, the only time he spoke honestly about his homosexuality was to his psychiatrist, Professor Moore. I believe he was speaking about himself when in 1944 he wrote 'people are religious to the extent that they believe themselves to be not so much imperfect, as ill . . . Any half-way decent man will think himself extremely imperfect, but a religious man believes himself wretched.'[300]

In his coded remarks, Wittgenstein did allude to a homosexual contact with Francis Skinner. Monk notes the meeting with Francis and Wittgenstein in Norway. Wittgenstein was 'sensual, susceptible, indecent' with him: 'Lay with him two or three times. Always at first with the feeling that there was nothing wrong in it, then with shame.'[301] Levi points out that in the letters from Wittgenstein to Engelmann an important insight was given into Wittgenstein's character:

> From 1917 through 1925 was one long dirge of self-accusation and guilt. He speaks of himself as '*schlecht*', as a '*schweinehund*'. He is even more explicit about his '*Unanstandigkeit*'. To call oneself 'bad' or 'a swine' can have generalised reference but '*Unanstandigkeit*' (indecency) has the same sexual connotation in German which it has in English. He obviously did not see himself to be normal, '*die normalen Menscher sind*'.[302]

As a consequence of his feelings of disgust and indecency, Wittgenstein sought to atone for his guilt, as noted by Malcolm:

> Wittgenstein did once say that he thought he could understand the conception of God, in so far as it is involved in one's awareness of one's own sin and guilt. I think the ideas of Divine judgement, forgiveness, and redemption had some intelligibility for him, as being related in his mind to feelings of disgust with himself, an intense desire

for purity, and a sense of the helplessness of human beings to make themselves better . . . Wittgenstein himself possessed a stern sense of duty.[303]

Clearly, how to rid himself of, or atone for, this homosexual guilt constantly preoccupied him. Nevertheless, his superego or, in broad terms, his conscience failed to prevent him from 'sinning', i.e. from cottaging, which was sinning for him. Throughout his life he did attempt to realise his sense of duty, to do something responsible in his roles as soldier and elementary school teacher. But his duty to change the world in some way could only be done by producing first-rate philosophy. It became his ego-ideal.

Religious disposition

Many commentators have remarked on the religious dimension of Wittgenstein's work. A religious disposition is a recurring feature in people of genius with HFA/ASP – Newton, Ramanujan, Lewis Carroll, among others. According to Edmonds and Eidinow, the image of Wittgenstein as a religious figure, saint-like and suffering, runs through many accounts of him. Indeed, Wittgenstein told Drury, 'I am not a religious man but I cannot help seeing every problem from a religious point of view'.[304] If anything he was a 'religious atheist'. Though raised as a Roman Catholic and excelling at religious subjects in school, his faith as a teenager was undermined by his sister Gretl. Nevertheless, it reawakened at the front during the First World War, when he had a religious conversion after reading Tolstoy's *Gospel*.[305] It persisted during his teaching period in Austria, when he used to pray with his pupils every day. Searle elaborates on Wittgenstein's ambivalent attitude to God:

> I think most people who knew him would say that he was an atheist. Now in a way, when you read his remarks about God, you almost feel that he wants to have it both ways. He wants to talk about God and still be an atheist. He wants to insist that to understand religious discourse we need to see the role that it plays in people's lives. And that is surely right. But of course, you would not understand the role that it plays in their lives unless you see that religious discourse refers beyond itself. To put it bluntly, when ordinary people pray it is because they think there is a God there listening.[306]

Clearly, the time spent at the front during the First World War was a heightened religious period for him. He always asked to be assigned to the most dangerous places in search of redemption: 'perhaps the nearness of death will bring the light of life. May God enlighten me. I am a worm, but through God I become a man. God be with me amen.'[307] In an account provided by McGuinness, he shows evidence of religious feeling at that time too: 'Yes, not my will, but thine be done', which plainly was an identification with Christ on the cross.[308] His diary contains the words 'God is all that man needs'.

It has been documented that religious beliefs and organised religion can be very positive to mental health.[309] Wittgenstein was sympathetic towards Catholicism and interested in its ritual. Certainly, the issues of sin, confession and forgiveness are an integral part of Catholicism and obviously attracted him. Moreover, McGuinness points out that his thoughts 'ran on sin and guilt and good and evil spirits' and that 'much of the machinery of religion and eschatology seemed to be for him the natural expression of moral realities'.[310] In keeping with this outlook, his friends arranged for him to have a Roman Catholic requiem and burial at St Giles Church, Cambridge.

Visuo-spatial ability

Visuo-spatial relations can be highly developed in autistic people. As a result they are often talented at architecture and work with external materials which they handle well, such as concrete and steel. Wittgenstein showed an exceptional visuo-spatial ability, manifested both in engineering and architecture. He maintained an interest in the logic of machines throughout his life, and often made schematic drawings of them.[311] Indeed, McGuinness notes that by the age of 10 years, Wittgenstein's technical interests were so far advanced that he made a model of a house sewing machine with wood and wire. The model was a success and able to sew a few stitches.[312] Shortly after arriving in England for the first time in 1908 he developed a propeller, which was used successfully during the Second World War. Drury also records how Wittgenstein invented a device for measuring pulse pressure when he worked in a hospital research laboratory in Newcastle.[313]

The 'autistic house'

The building singularly associated with Wittgenstein the architect is the house he designed for his sister Gretl on Kundmanngasse in Vienna. Indeed, Kundmanngasse was designed so brilliantly that his sister Hermine described it as 'a house for the Gods', it 'embodied logic, monumentality and perfection'.[314] Indeed, Wittgenstein applied the same precision to its design and construction as he did to his philosophy or any other job he undertook.

When working as an architect, according to Whyte, Wittgenstein's intention appears to have focused principally on issues of 'proportion, axes of symmetry and detail':[315]

And just as linguistic expressions are significant in that they refer to something, so architectural devices are significant in that they refer to the activities of living. In place of the cartouche and the swag, Wittgenstein offered the immaculately detailed window frame and the exactly placed light-bulb. As befitted a trained engineer whose father had made a fortune out of the Austrian steel industry, Wittgenstein was especially drawn to the design of metal door and window fittings, locks, catches and the like, on which he lavished endless attention.

Wittgenstein's 'autistic perfectionism', however, became more apparent in the main salon of the house just as the building was nearing completion. He considered the ceiling too low, and forced the builders to tear it down and rebuild it 3 centimetres higher. However, Hermine noted that his 'educated instinct' was absolutely correct, as the new ceiling struck a more pleasing note than the old one. Always the emphasis was on achieving the appearance of balance and symmetry, even if that meant putting up sham or artificially thickened walls – reaching a compromise between Wittgenstein's ideal concepts and the practicalities of the builders.

Following its completion, however, the difference between building a house and a home were patently obvious. In *Vermischte Bemerkungen*, Wittgenstein noted with a certain irony that the house he built for Gretl was a product of a 'decidedly sensitive ear and good manners, an expression of great understanding (of a culture, etc.). But primordial life, wild life striving to erupt into the open – that is lacking.' According to Hermine, the house fitted their sister Gretl 'like a glove'.[316] But though she admired the house very much, Hermine herself had no wish to live in it:

> It seemed indeed to be much more a dwelling for the gods than for a small mortal like me, and at first I even had to overcome a faint inner opposition to this 'house embodied logic'.[317]

It was in reality an 'autistic house' with an emphasis on functionality rather than comfort. Monk suggests that it was easy to understand this 'slight abhorrence':

> The house was designed with little regard to the comforts of ordinary mortals. The qualities of clarity, rigour and precision which characterise it are indeed those one looks for in a system of logic rather than in a dwelling place. In designing the interior Wittgenstein made extraordinarily few concessions to domestic comfort. Carpets, chandeliers, and curtains were strictly rejected. The floors were of dark polished stone, the walls and ceilings painted a light ochre, the metal of the windows, the door handles and the radiators were left unpainted, and the rooms were lit with naked light-bulbs.[318]

According to Whyte, Wittgenstein rid the house of any classical decoration and reduced it to 'an austere composition of lines, planes and volumes'.[319] Furthermore, he had in mind an architectural language of 'great exactitude and resolution' with a palatial sequence of interlocking cubes. His idea was to resist the temptations of earlier architects. As he subsequently noted in *Vermischte Bemerkungen*, it was the essential difference between a good and bad architect: 'Today the difference between a good and a poor architect is that the poor architect succumbs to every temptation and the good one resists it'.[320] Certainly, the maxim that came to dominate twentieth-century architecture – less is more – was central to Wittgenstein's viewpoint.

Small wonder, then, that Wittgenstein told Drury that the problems of philosophy were nothing compared to those of architecture. In this respect Whyte concluded that 'Wittgenstein was no Fischer von Erlach'. Wijdeveld suggests that Wittgenstein's response to weak and inauthentic contemporary architecture was to make Kundmanngasse a statement of purification. In a search for authenticity it was Wittgenstein's own assessment of his architectural enterprise. Wijdeveld saw it as 'a uniquely unified, elegant and austere example of early architecturalism'. Furthermore, Kundmanngasse has often been regarded as the 'concrete embodiment of Wittgenstein's ideas' and is undeniably one of the few dwellings designed by a great philosopher.[321] In fact, it was a perfect example of an 'autistic house'.

Originality of thought

Asperger has commented on his patients' originality of thought and the frequency with which their interests were 'canalised into rather abstract subjects of little practical use'.[322] He also emphasises the high intelligence and special abilities in the area of logic that his patients demonstrated. This fits perfectly with Wittgenstein, given that he spent considerable time working in the area of logic.[323]

Wittgenstein was single-minded in his approach to logic and language, which concentrated his mind for the entirety of his philosophy career. He tended not to focus on the larger picture, i.e. presenting doctrines or theories of reality, thus making his philosophy lack a 'central coherence' for some commentators. It is true to say that Wittgenstein's engagement in philosophy, or indeed whatever else he undertook, was serious and unrelenting. People of genius with autism concentrate their minds on fundamental questions or abstract ideas, which they believe are central to their chosen discipline. People with HFA/ASP appear to 'merge' with their work.

In this sense Russell is correct when he states that Wittgenstein had 'too little wish for a broad survey of the world', he insisted on too great a degree of exactness from infant theories, and showed little patience with 'inconclusive considerations' and unsatisfactory points of view. Monk suggests that perhaps faced with Wittgenstein's single-mindedness, Russell came to think that a love of the big generalisation was not such a bad thing after all. Wittgenstein's absorption in logical problems was complete. 'They were not part of his life but the whole of it.'[324]

Furthermore, Wittgenstein's lack of 'central coherence' became a strength in the eyes of others. His dissatisfaction with systematic structured philosophy made him think beyond such frameworks. In fact, it was central to his genius. Ramsey, in an opinion piece written for the university, praised Wittgenstein highly: 'In my opinion, Mr Wittgenstein is a philosophic genius of a different order from anyone else I know'. Ramsey went on to state:

> this is partly owing to his great gift for seeing what is essential in a problem and partly to his overwhelming intellectual vigour, to the intensity of thought with which he pursues a question to the bottom and never rests content with mere possible hypotheses. From his work more than that of any other man I hope for a solution of the difficulties that perplex me both philosophically generally and in the foundations of Mathematics in particular. It seems to be, therefore, peculiarly fortunate that he should have returned to research.[325]

Wittgenstein's temperament impressed Russell as being like an 'artist, intuitive and moody' in beginning his work each morning with hope and ending each day in despair.[326] Russell quickly realised that Wittgenstein had a great philosophical talent, and saw him as his heir in philosophy: 'I think he has genius. In discussion with him I put all my force and only just equal his . . . I love him and feel he will solve the problems I am too old to solve.'[327] Moreover, Russell believed that Wittgenstein was 'perhaps the most perfect example I have ever known of genius as traditionally conceived, passionate, profound, intense, and dominating'.[328] Indeed, he could have added 'autistic' to the list. In the same way, Wijdeveld refers to 'the compelling power of Ludwig Wittgenstein's genius', which changed the course of Western philosophy and emerged unmistakably in everything he did.[329] Under these circumstances, it was not surprising that Wittgenstein would be known as a 'sonderling', 'an eccentric, someone out of the normal run' as McGuinness notes.[330]

Alper speculates on the nature of Wittgenstein's genius: 'it may be that the bizarre conjunction of profound originality, of first rate genius, and pronounced paranoid style creates much of the tension that goes into his unique, oracular style'.[331] Because of this, Alper suggests that part of our fascination with Wittgenstein is perhaps 'our fascination at seeing a genius literally trying to think his way out of despair'. Yet as Alper is only too well aware, psychoanalysts know better than anyone that it cannot be done, 'not even by Wittgenstein', as he rightly adds. Alper considers Wittgenstein's philosophical style to be the opposite of psychoanalysis. Where

Wittgenstein restrains, purifies and delineates language, psychoanalysis widens the range of language. It does this chiefly by spreading the network of personal meaning by means of 'listening for and discovering unsuspected, hierarchal levels of meaning'.[332]

Allowances and excuses

Despite Wittgenstein's controlling behaviour, many of his contemporaries and friends made special allowances for his ways, most noticeably for what they recognised as his quality of genius. The critic, F.R. Leavis, believed that Wittgenstein's behaviour was:

> a manifestation of the essential quality that one couldn't be very long with him without becoming aware – of the quality of genius: an intensity of concentration that impressed itself on one as disinterestedness. Nevertheless, there was some criticism, in that argument once started, he exercised the complete command that left other voices little opportunity – unless they were prepared to be peremptory, insistent and forceful.[33]

This is an autistic style of discourse. His extraordinary demands were made to fit his academic life. In terms of how his requests should be dealt with at Cambridge, according to McGuinness, Wittgenstein felt that his individuality should be recognised: 'Exceptions must be made for it, rules must be circumvented. The world must be made to fit his gifts. It was the only way he could make use of them.'[334] The Vienna Circle equally was very reverential and cautious in dealing with Wittgenstein. Rudolf Carnap, a member of the Circle, recalls how Moritz Schlick, then professor of philosophy at the University of Vienna, handled Wittgenstein:

> before the first meeting Schlick admonished us urgently not to start a discussion of the kind to which we were accustomed in the Circle, because Wittgenstein did not want such a thing under any circumstances. We should even be cautious in asking questions, because Wittgenstein was very sensitive and easily disturbed by a direct question. The best approach, Schlick said, would be to let Wittgenstein talk and then ask only very cautiously for the necessary elucidations.[335]

This is the kind of sensitive approach necessary for a person of genius with HFA/ASP. Needless to say, Schlick, too, held the view that Wittgenstein was one of the greatest geniuses on earth.[336] Carnap observed at first hand how controlling and one-sided Wittgenstein was in his interaction with the Vienna Circle. At their meetings, Wittgenstein 'tolerated no critical examination by others, once the insight had been gained by an act of inspiration'.[337]

He would then turn his back on them and read poetry instead – further evidence of his social impairment and controlling behaviour, which was courteously tolerated by the members of the Circle.[338]

From a discussion in February 1995 between David Berman, Drury's wife Eileen and the present author, it appears that there was one rule for Wittgenstein and another that applied to everyone else. Eileen remarked that 'one had to go by his rules and he had to be in control'. People with autistic disorders demand the world to fit with their requirements. They refuse to adapt to the world. Wittgenstein operated on what psychoanalysts call a 'part-object' relationship, which means not seeing other people as full human beings in their own right but as inanimate objects to be controlled. This is also an autistic form of relating.

In this respect, Wittgenstein considered himself not quite of the same order as his colleagues and friends. Academic circles were not suitable places for a man of his disposition. He described Oxford as 'a philosophical desert'[339] and was contemptuous of the majority of philosophers that preceded him. Indeed, he had a high degree of contempt for most academics and academic departments of philosophy. Monk notes that he told Drury that there was 'no oxygen for him in Cambridge' and insisted he get a working-class job instead, which in itself is extraordinary advice from a professor of philosophy. Just how autistic Wittgenstein's way of thinking was can be seen in his statement 'I manufacture my own oxygen', by which he indicated how much he was set apart from his philosophical co-workers. Clearly he was stating that he did his best work alone.

Conclusion

Wittgenstein would fit what Lorna Wing describes as an active but odd syndrome of autism.[340] He spoke late and had literal interpretation of words at least up to the First World War (at the outbreak of which he was in his mid-twenties), when he wrote the *Tractatus*. In his early life he had 'a lack of ease with colloquial turns of phrase' which he overcame when writing the *Philosophical Investigations* in his forties and fifties. In a study of those with autism, Wing states that vocal intonation was monotonous and interests were pursued relentlessly.[341] There was clumsy social interaction and over-sensitivity to criticism. She emphasises that contact with other people is made in a 'peculiar, naïve and one-sided fashion'.[342] Wittgenstein tended to talk at people and conversations lacked reciprocity. He had problems with social conventions, which persisted throughout his life. To his last days he did not succeed in overcoming this problem. Wing also cites inappropriate movements of face and limbs when speaking.[343] This was not unlike Wittgenstein's style of communication in seminars.

People with autism can have a special interest in birds, as Wing noted, and indeed Wittgenstein had this special awareness.[344] She also notes that children who are active, but odd in social interaction, tend to be clumsy. They are wary of balancing and climbing, and they have an odd immature gait and posture.[345] Wittgenstein, too, was described as clumsy in climbing. They are increasingly sensitive to criticism, which Wittgenstein certainly was.

Criminality can become an issue, though unwittingly. Wing notes that they can come into conflict with the law 'partly because they may lack understanding of social rules . . . and as a consequence of misinterpretation'.[346] As a teacher, Wittgenstein was guilty of child brutality and brought to trial, but resigned from his job. Similarly, Erdös[347] the mathematician, was arrested because he drifted into a secured area in the USA during the Second World War: obsessed with mathematical calculations at the time, he wasn't concentrating on the signs on the road. In Erdös's case, it was 'autistic naiveté'.

Wittgenstein showed many of the features of an obsessional person with scrupulosity, rigidity, honesty (with rare exceptions), tension, anxiety, obstinacy, parsimoniousness, relating in an authoritarian way with philosophers in Cambridge or else in a submissive way with his psychiatrist, Professor Moore, and only relating in terms of either superiority or inferiority. In reality his relations were mostly in terms of superiority. He was meticulous in his choice of clothes in later life. His perfectionism probably also meant that he could only publish one book in his life although he had written many.

All the above can be subsumed by his HFA/ASP. In the same way he showed the following features of schizoid personality: a sense of futility and meaningless of life, an air of superiority, a fear of intimacy, a fear of being dominated, a fear that he would harm people, intellectualism and sado-masochistic traits which he showed with the 'rough youths' in the Prater in Vienna and its associated high-risk behaviour. He was often described as being cruel.

In addition, he showed many of the features of a narcissistic personality: grandiosity, hypersensitivity to other people's assessment of him, criticism of himself, lack of empathy, difficulty in taking satisfaction from his work, extreme upset when he did not live up to his own ideals, a sense of entitlement of favourable treatment, automatic compliance with requests even if against university rules (as in the case of his first degree) and interpersonal exploitation with arrogant or haughty behaviour and attitudes.

It appears to me that patients with HFA/ASP are often narcissistic and grandiose. Bartley notes that Wittgenstein wanted to die in 'a moment of brilliance',[348] while Russell remarked that he had 'the pride of Lucifer'.[349] It was hard for Wittgenstein to admit that he got narcissistic gratification from being professor of philosophy at Cambridge; he was guilty about this and stated 'I don't get any kick out of my position except what my vanity and stupidity sometimes gets'.[350] After writing the *Tractatus* he felt he had solved all philosophical problems, which was clearly grandiose. In the same way, he once wrote jokingly to Pattison that he was 'the greatest philosopher that ever lived'.[351] There is also some similarity with Freud's patients with narcissistic neurosis and other psychosomatic patients who have alexithymia, i.e. problems in expressing affect. All things considered, he was largely acknowledged as the greatest philosopher of the twentieth century.

INFLUENCE OF WITTGENSTEIN'S PERSONALITY ON HIS PHILOSOPHY

Walter Kaufman, in his preface to Bartley's *Wittgenstein*, reiterated that every great philosopher has given philosophy a new direction, but only Wittgenstein did it twice: first with the *Tractatus*, published shortly after the First World War, and then with the ideas that culminated in the *Philosophical Investigations*.[352] Similarly, Glock points out that Wittgenstein occupies a unique position among the great philosophers of the modern era. He developed 'two fundamentally different and self-contained outlooks', which in turn were to influence two major philosophical movements. The *Tractatus*, he believed, 'heralded the linguistic turn of 20th century philosophy and inspired the logical positivists', while *Philosophical Investigations* was a major force between the 'conceptual analysis which dominated Anglophone philosophy until the 1970s and continues to stimulate analytical and continental philosophers alike'.[353]

Early work – the *Tractatus*

Wittgenstein's life was by and large minimalist – pared down to the essentials. So, too, his work in philosophy. He dealt with what he saw as fundamental questions in philosophy, not those of philosophical doctrines, systems or models. In doing so he placed the study of language at the core of philosophy. For Wittgenstein, language was the subject matter of philosophy.[354] And he, effectively, was 'reducing logic to language' according to Monk.[355] But the shift in focus was not what was being said or why but in showing *how*.

The placing of language at the centre of philosophy arose from Wittgenstein's own difficulties with language and communication. The limitations of his early work in philosophy were influenced by his autism. He produced a philosophy that only an autistic person in truth could produce. In this regard Ayer was correct when he asserted that Wittgenstein suffered from not being really interested in the actual world.[356] Attention has already been drawn to Wittgenstein's lack of empathy. This is certainly evident in his early work. Alper goes further and asserts that Wittgenstein's early work was an attempt to impose a personal control over his world; 'we see Wittgenstein's early yearning to construct consummately logical language, as a paranoid attempt to cleanse his private conceptual universe of every irritant and impurity he cannot personally control'.[357] This is typical of people with autism.

The difficulties that Wittgenstein himself faced with language and discourse – open to everyday misunderstandings, lack of clarity, etc. – paved the way for him to address the central issue that philosophy can only be evaluated through language. Hacker states that:

> the *Tractatus* propounded an unprecedented conception of philosophy as a non-cognitive, elucidatory, analytic discipline, discontinuous with the sciences. All philosophy, it declared in a remark which heralds the linguistic turn characteristic of 20th century analytical philosophy, is a critique of language. Its task is to eliminate misunderstandings, resolve conceptual unclarities and dissolve philosophical confusions by depth analysis of propositions into their primitive unanalysable.[358]

Calculating machine

Many commentators have remarked on the mechanical and calculating style of the *Tractatus*. Alper considered that there was no greater example of the 'mechanisation of thought and language in the history of philosophy than Wittgenstein's great masterpiece, the *Tractatus*'.[359] In this respect, Wittgenstein had the autistic mechanical mind. The *Tractatus*, in effect, calculates what can meaningfully be said in language in order to show what is beyond language. Not surprisingly, Wittgenstein has been called the 'architectural' or 'engineering' philosopher, the philosopher of machinery. Indeed, in Europe the mechanised spirit of the times was sweeping through many disciplines. On music composed after Brahms, Wittgenstein had said: 'I can begin to hear the machinery'.[360] In many respects, what Wittgenstein did to philosophy was no different to what contemporary composers did to music. The newly conceived world could only be experienced through mechanical functioning, according to Wijdeveld:

> the logic expounded in *Tractatus* goes further, therefore than a mere body of rules, the one to be rationally deduced from the other like the axiomatic system of Euclidean geometry, by incorporating the idea of *a priori* activity into it. It must be conceived of as the functioning of a mechanism. Wittgenstein borrows the idea of *a priori* activity as the basic state of experiencing the world and showing logic and ethics–aesthetics through it from his experience with mechanical functioning.[361]

Engelmann endorses this view of Wittgenstein: 'the machine was for him before all else the paradigm of a logically organised and consistently interlocking, and because of that *de facto* functioning, whole, and valid as a real, irrevocable proof for the rightness of such thought'. The *Tractatus* itself, according to Engelmann, 'shows its point by thinking it, it should therefore be compared to a calculating machine, not to a calculation'. This reflects a mechanistic position in the mechanical mind. The format of the *Tractatus* also displayed the self-evident logic of a mechanism, as noted by Wijdeveld:

> the *Tractatus* is a system of assertions, of proportions, founded on seven basic propositions meant as self-evident truths, very much like the Euclidian system of geometry, or the ethical system more geo-metrico of Spinoza. The propositions are given decimal numbers according to their relative role within the whole; thus the sixth basic proposition has number 6, which is elaborated by propositions number 6.1, 6.2, 6.3, etc. and the last number in its turn is further elaborated by 6.4.1, 6.4.2, and so on. As Wittgenstein was an engineer, we could regard the *Tractatus* as a complex mechanism receiving its energy from seven main gear wheels, which in their turn drive the wheels subordinated to them. Once set in motion, the logic of its mechanism as a whole will become self-evident. The *Tractatus* 'calculates' what can be meaningfully be said in language, in order to show what is beyond language.[362]

This approach to solving philosophical problems in turn came to be called the 'method' of logical clarification, which is a style of clarification very attractive to people with autism.

The description of the *Tractatus* as a 'calculating machine' is very accurate because it refers to a mechanical style of thinking, the thinking of the mind machine, the thinking of a person with autism. One could hypothesise that people with HFA/ASP think in the style of a calculating machine. Certainly, the autistic person wants the world to have 'a fixed structure'. Because Wittgenstein found the social arena particularly difficult, especially up to about 1932, he wished that people had 'mind machines' that would behave in an objective and predictable fashion. In a way, the 'autistic mind' is effectively a 'mechanical' mind.

Edmonds and Eidinow describe the *Tractatus* as 'remarkable for its combination of luminosity and oracular brevity, its impregnable confidence teetering on the end of dogmatism and its unwillingness to demean itself by supporting its numbered propositions in any conventional way'.[363] Indeed, the brevity of the *Tractatus* is extraordinary and I have seen this in a number of people with HFA/ASP, who likewise communicate with extreme brevity. It is also written in the autistic style of mathematics, with numbered paragraphs. C.D. Broad referred to it as the highly 'syncopated pipings of Herr Wittgenstein's flute', which I believe are really 'autistic pipings'. Broad, among others, observed that the *Tractatus* is composed of a system of assertions like Euclidian geometry.[364] In essence it is in the autistic–mathematical–cognitive style of people with autism.

Visuo-spatial ability

Both the *Tractatus* and the house on Kundmanngasse show Wittgenstein's exceptional visuo-spatial ability. Wijdeveld makes the point that similarities between Wittgenstein's architecture and philosophy refer to certain stylistic ones only, which ultimately explain very little. Nevertheless, he maintains that they do affirm a common mental attitude in their creator which is consistent with Wittgenstein's conception of aesthetics between 1916 and 1930:

> Apart from recognising the adage that the aesthetic principle underlying both Kundmanngasse and the *Tractatus*, it still remains difficult to compare the connections between architectural precision, consisting in visual–spatial–tactile relationships and in a certain use of building elements, with philosophical or linguistic precision, consisting in semantic relationships and in a certain use of words and concepts.[365]

In keeping with Wittgenstein's propensity for mechanical thinking, simplicity and truth were integral concepts of his work, as Wijdeveld notes:

> Wittgenstein's training as a mechanical engineer and unnerving feeling for the logic of mechanical construction enabled him to design the moving parts of the house with the same precision that served him in his philosophical pursuits. The design of the fastenings, latches, and locks clearly imply a mechanical interpretation of Occam's Razor, 'simplicity is the hallmark of truth' (*simplex sigillum veri*).[366]

Both the Kundmanngasse and *Tractatus* express *simplex sigillum veri*, although in different material forms, according to Wijdeveld; building materials in the case of the former and language elements in the latter. Clearly, the need for simplicity at the heart of his work is inextricably linked to Wittgenstein's disposition; first to express a 'subtle sense of proportion', second to create an 'austere atmosphere' and finally an 'effort for precision'. The sense of proportion in the *Tractatus* can be seen, for example, in the seven main propositions, the system of decimal numbering, the logical symbolism expounded, and so on. The austere atmosphere is created in its concise use of language, compellingly making its point with 'uncompromising restraint', according to Wijdeveld, and corresponds to a profound lack of ornament in the Kundmanngasse too. It is Wittgenstein's desire for simplicity, the *simplex sigillum veri*, that can be equated with his 'effort for precision'. Wijdeveld draws these comparisons only as an attempt to offer a semiotic explanation for the stylistic affinity between the Kundmanngasse and Neoclassicism on the one hand, and the Kundmann-gasse and the *Tractatus* on the other.

Pictorial thinking

Wittgenstein's highly developed visuo-spatial ability helps explain why the *Tractatus* puts forward a picture theory of reality, where words are concrete objects. As noted by Hintikka, Wittgenstein's preference for pictorial thinking culminates in the 'picture theory of language' of the *Tractatus*. Kenny points out that in ordinary language there is a perceptively pictorial element.[367] Undeniably, spatial relationships exist between things, such as the arrangement of cutlery on a table. But in Wittgenstein's philosophy the spatial representation is pictorial in a very straightforward way. The pictorial theory is an example of concrete thinking, which in turn is characteristic of those with HFA/ASP.

Early in the development of language, according to P. Giovacchine, 'words are symbols for concrete objects; the unconscious, a primitive psychic system, treats the world as if it were, in itself, a concrete object, a "thing" as Freud stated. This is also characteristic of primary process thinking.'[368] Clearly the *Tractatus* has a more primary-process thinking style, while, as we shall see, the *Philosophical Investigations* has a more secondary-process thinking style. By having concrete or primary-process thinking Wittgenstein was able to make statements such as 'whereof one cannot speak, thereon one must remain silent'.[369] I would hypothesise that for Wittgenstein one can say what a person with HFA/ASP can say. In the *Tractatus*, Wittgenstein declares there are indeed things that cannot be put into words. Here I believe he is talking about a person with autism not being able to put certain things into words. In addition in Wittgenstein's case he was referring to his homosexuality.

In sum, the picture theory is a concrete autistic-type theory. It is written without any gesture or effort to clarify matters for the reader, but in any case a person with autism has enormous difficulty in seeing another person's point of view, effectively having a theory-of-mind deficit. It is really a one-person philosophy – in this case, written from Wittgenstein's own perspective.

Wittgenstein's assertion that the *Tractatus* provided definitive solutions to all problems of philosophy is also very concrete and autistic. This raises the question about what a person with HFA/ASP can or cannot say. What limitations does HFA/ASP put on a person's ability to create new philosophy? In all likelihood it relates to the socio-emotional aspects of philosophy. If anything it heightens the significance of non-verbal methods of communication, not least from the perspective of the person with HFA/ASP. Wijdeveld notes:

> by showing what cannot be said the *Tractatus* is, in that sense, also a gesture; in fact, the problem of the unbridgeable gap between what can be expressed in language and what can only be expressed in non-verbal ways of communication lies at the foundation of the philosophy of the *Tractatus* and it was, among other problems, the problem of the meaningful gesture that led Wittgenstein to his later revised philosophy of the *Philosophical Investigations* built around the idea of language games.[370]

Interpreting the Tractatus

The extent to which Wittgenstein's own moral dilemma influenced the structure of his ideas and philosophy is the subject of much debate. Levi has attempted to explore its implication for Wittgenstein's own thought, where he assumes, like Hegel, 'the far-flung interconnectedness of all things, with its consequence that if there is some sexual problem which it might naturally be expected to have some influence upon the content and structure of your ideas.'[371] Undeniably, not being able to accept his homosexuality led to the greatest problem with his philosophy. Essentially it was a problem of language and ethics, which resulted in one of his most famous statements about what can and cannot be shown: 'What can be said at all can be said clearly, and whereof one cannot speak thereof one must be silent'.

In the *Tractatus* Wittgenstein states 'everything that can be put into words can be put clearly'.[372] He did not follow this guideline in the sense that he never spoke about his homosexuality, with one exception: 'philosophy will signify what cannot be said by presenting clearly what can be said. There are, indeed, things that cannot be put into words. They make themselves manifest. They are what is mystical.'[373] From a reading of Bartley's *Wittgenstein*, Levi has suggested that the last pages of the *Tractatus* must be understood in terms of a guilty homosexual:

> the anguish so clearly expressed in *Letters to Engelmann* was that of a guilty homosexual and thus it enabled a reconsideration of the last few pages of the *Tractatus* and of the 'Lecture on Ethics' as the expression not of moral rationality but of unconscious guilt. Thus, Wittgenstein's ethics (and philosophy of religion), philosophically unconvincing, could at least be reasonably accounted for. Wittgenstein's ethics and philosophy of religion – so paradoxical, so unsatisfying, so deeply unconvincing – could now at least be explained. Can the history of ideas pretend to do more?[374]

Levi adds that the logical structure of the biographical sources of Wittgenstein's ethics is thus at least clear. Indeed, Levi is correct when he states that confining homosexuality to a transcendental sense precludes all moral condemnation and judgement of it:

> Bartley's assertion of Wittgenstein's homosexuality provides an interpretation of the *Letters to Engelmann* for it resolves Wittgenstein's self-castigation and self-loathing into the consequences of guilty homosexuality and this perception of Wittgenstein's extreme guilt feelings in turn explains his 'transcendental' ethics as an unconscious attempt to outflank the moral condemnation of his fellow men and awe, guilt and deification of safety of the Lecture on Ethics as a consequence of his own dangerous moral dilemma.[375]

While it is simply too reductionistic to say that homosexuality is implied in the final pages of the *Tractatus*, evidently in Wittgenstein's case it was a subject that could not be put clearly into words. This does raise the possibility that Wittgenstein was motivated, not from a desire to withhold all knowledge of his moral dilemma, but from a failure to clearly express what it *meant* to him. He could not interpret his homosexuality in terms of language. He could not rationalise it because he could not control it. As Malcolm asserts, Wittgenstein's life was one of exceptional striving for moral and spiritual purity.[376] The ethical question he failed to come to terms with was his own behaviour. His helplessness translated into silence.

Later work – *Philosophical Investigations*

The catalyst for the change from the *Tractatus* to *Philosophical Investigations* is attributed to the brilliant Italian economist and friend of Wittgenstein, Piero Sraffa. One day Sraffa made a Neapolitan gesture of brushing his chin with his finger tips and asked Wittgenstein 'what is a logical form of that?'[377] This broke Wittgenstein's belief that a proposition must be a picture of the reality it describes. In *Philosophical Investigations* he asks 'is there such a thing as a picture that forces a particular application on us; so that my mistake lay in confusing one picture with another?'[378] Essentially, the outcome of talking to Sraffa was that Wittgenstein gained an 'anthropological' way of looking at philosophical problems, as he later remarked to Rush Rhees.[379]

Correcting his error resulted in a 'two person philosophy'. He discovered social context, which is central to the *Philosophical Investigations*. The importance of interpersonal relations, facial expression and of recognising the other person's point of view became his new focus. The philosophy of the second phase concentrated on the 'language-game' and the importance of how language was used in the social context. Except for the narrowness of his philosophy, he showed evidence of having moved beyond HFA/ASP. He was now in the real interpersonal world. It is fascinating that he uses the word 'anthropological' to describe his work, which reminds one of Sacks' *An Anthropologist on Mars*, which focused, among other matters, on Temple Grandin who also had HFA/ASP.[380]

Language game

Central to the *Philosophical Investigations* is the notion that no real problems with philosophy exist – only linguistic puzzles. All linguistic utterances are games, and to engage in a particular language game is to engage in a certain form of life. Wittgenstein considered the work of the philosopher in such circumstances as being 'to describe the many different sorts of language-games and the forms of life in which they were embedded',[381] according to Bartley. Monk contrasts it with Wittgenstein's earlier work:

> whereas the *Tractatus* deals with language in isolation from circumstances in which it is used, the *Investigations* repeatedly emphasises the importance of the 'dream of life' which gives linguistic utterances their meanings: a 'language-game' cannot be described without mentioning their activities and the way of life of the 'tribe' that plays it.[382]

According to W.A. Hijab, Wittgenstein was always looking for concrete examples. Hijab points out that 'the reason why a truth seeker is beguiled into the metaphysical mode is that he becomes entrapped by paradigms and precursor concepts that are deeply engrained in our language'.[383] This is different for people with and without HFA/ASP. The great task for a person with HFA/ASP is to discover the various 'forms of life' or language-games of people without autism. Klagg notes what social context came to mean for Wittgenstein:

> the social context for understanding such crucial notions as meaning and rule-following. In fact a social context of considerable agreement in judgements and actions seems to be a presupposition of communication. Communication presupposes community. Furthermore, when we try to discern what it is that gives normative force to our judgements, it seems to depend on conformity to that communal agreement. This line of thinking has led to so-called 'collectivist' construal of Wittgenstein's thought: normality does not derive from some mental intention or objective standard, but from the patterns of behaviour of the community in which the judgement is made. Marching 'in step' is marching that is in time with that of most others. To follow a rule is to form to a

custom. As Wittgenstein put it, 'to obey a rule, to make a report, to give an order, to play a game of chess, are customs (useless institutions)'[384] and their being done correctly depends on the roles in common life. To continue a series correctly is to continue it 'as we do it'.[385,386]

As outlined, rules are very important for Wittgenstein and present a way of making sense of the world. People with HFA/ASP are particularly attracted to rules as they anchor them in life. Wittgenstein's later philosophy can be viewed as someone with HFA/ASP trying to work out what the social context is and what the rules of society are; and, especially, what the rules of communication are in a society where most people do not have HFA/ASP. In this respect, Klagg, like Ayer, believed that Wittgenstein was in the community, but not of the community.[387] This is an excellent description of a person with HFA/ASP. Indeed, Klagg adds 'the community that plays such a central role in his philosophical thinking seems largely lacking in his own experience of life'.[388]

The language game remained entwined with the object of the game.[389] It was not until he was about 40 years of age that Wittgenstein was able to move from an exclusive focus on himself and language to recognise social context and the increasing complexity of social relations. Wittgenstein only achieved this through enormous effort over many years. This was particularly reflected in his shift from the 'picture-theory' of language to the 'language-game'. In the *Philosophical Investigations* he achieved what Hobson describes young children as achieving, i.e. 'objects can have multiple meanings for people, and people can have multiple attitudes to given objects',[390] which for Wittgenstein would depend on the language-game.

It was in Connemara in the west of Ireland when writing *Philosophical Investigations* that Wittgenstein moved into a relatively non-autistic style of philosophising. He discovered context and 'aspect seeing', which formed an integral part of his later work.[391] The issue arose from the fact that while the aspect changes, the object remains the same, and he used the duck–rabbit drawing in Jastrow's *Fact and Fable in Psychology* to illustrate the point.[392] Wittgenstein believed that leaving philosophy alone but changing the aspect or the way in which we look at things – even though the object doesn't change – is effectively a radical change. Some pessimism arose because he thought that 'aspect seeing' was largely determined by culture and somehow resistant to change. Of course, Wittgenstein's own life was largely based on moving from the 'aspect seeing' of a person with autism to the 'aspect seeing' of a person who had to some extent overcome certain autistic features.

The language game is also superficial and indeed rather grandiose, with the notion that all that is required is to sort out linguistic knots in philosophy. It is an excessively reductionistic view of philosophy.

Wittgenstein did become aware of the notion of expert judgement, where some people can skilfully distinguish between a genuine and an affected expression of feeling. Clearly, people with autism have the poorest judgement of all in this area and lack empathy skills for largely genetic reasons. Wittgenstein believed that empathy skills could not be taught, but nevertheless could be learned through experience. Clearly, this is autobiographical in that he did make significant progress in this area by learning from experience. In particular, he recognised that Father Zossima in Dostoevsky's *The Brothers Karamazov* had a special skill or capacity for empathy. Unquestionably, the figure of Father Zossima was to have an enduring effect on him.

I would argue that this approach is less autistic and an example of a person with HFA/ASP growing and developing as they can. It represents a more humanistic approach, where the notion of the other person being present is acknowledged. In this context we can clearly see how the *Tractatus* is based on one-person philosophy and the *Philosophical Investigations* on two- or more-persons philosophy.

As outlined in this book, people with HFA/ASP have to make enormous efforts to understand people – they have to try to build up an understanding as they have a deficit in theory of mind and a deficit in the capacity for affective relating. Wittgenstein turned what for him was a deficit into his greatest strength, which we witness in the *Philosophical Investigations*. He had to become extremely observant of people. Moreover, he had to observe people's faces far more often and with greater intensity than the average person in order to understand the meaning of facial gestures. Given the limitations imposed on him by HFA/ASP, what he achieved in this domain is truly amazing. Of course, it took many years to make this achievement. People with HFA/ASP experience our society as alien and have difficulty understanding the culture of those without HFA/ASP. It is to Wittgenstein's credit that he attempted to bridge the gap.

Philosophy as an activity

The notion of philosophy as an activity and not a theory was crucial to Wittgenstein. Understanding rested in the usage and not the meaning of language. On this point, Searle points out that Wittgenstein's favourite slogan was 'don't ask for the meaning, ask for its use'.[393] Similarly, Kenny notes:

> despite the difference between the *Tractatus* and the *Investigations* there is continuity in Wittgenstein's conception of the nature of philosophy. He continued to regard philosophy as an activity rather than a theory, as the activity of clarifying propositions and preventing us from being led astray by the misleading appearances of ordinary language. But

now the way to clarify propositions is not to analyse them to reveal their hidden structure, but to show how they are applied in language. Wittgenstein still denies the possibility of philosophical theses; the aim of philosophy is a therapeutic one, the cure is from talking nonsense and being tormented by problems for which there is no solution. When philosophy achieves clarity, this is not by the solution of philosophical problems but by their disappearance. 'Why is philosophy so complicated?' Wittgenstein once asked himself. His answer sums up his conception of its nature: 'Philosophy unties the knots in our thinking, which we have foolishly put there; but to do that it must make movements which are just as complicated as those knots. The complexity of philosophy is not in its subject matter, but in our knotted understanding.'[394]

Undeniably, people with HFA/ASP experience very 'knotted thinking', and this was Wittgenstein's effort to untie some of his own knotted thinking and that of others. As with theories, doctrines or models of philosophy, the notion of essences is similarly rejected by Wittgenstein, i.e. that the essence of language exists in some unified shape or form. Instead he puts forward the notion of 'family resemblance', as outlined by Searle:

[Wittgenstein] is always anxious to insist in the Investigations that language is indefinitely extendable, and there isn't any single essence that binds all uses of language together. There isn't any single feature that runs through all of language that constitutes the essence of language. And indeed, for particular words, there needn't even be any particular essence that constitutes the definition of that word. He thinks of many words as having only a 'family resemblance' among their various uses. He gives as an example the word 'game'. And he asks us, what, if anything, do all games have in common? And here, as always, he keeps insisting: don't just think that they must have some one thing in common, but rather, look and see what you can find. And then he says that, if you consider the enormous variety of different kinds of games – board games, Olympic games, gambling games, ball games, and so on – what you find that there isn't any single essence of gamehood, there isn't any single thing that all games have in common, but rather there are a series of criss-crossing and overlapping similarities. It is this phenomenon which he calls family resemblance.[395]

Monk states that Wittgenstein's remark that philosophy 'leaves everything as it is' is often quoted, but it is less often realised that, in seeking to change nothing but the way we look at things, Wittgenstein was actually attempting to change everything.[396] Not surprisingly, he was pessimistic and depressed that his work would be received negatively, as noted by Maria McGinn.

Wittgenstein was notoriously pessimistic about the chances of his work being understood. This was not because he saw his writings as placing great demands upon the intellect, but because he believed philosophers to be resistant to the style of investigation in which he was engaged. From his earliest writings, Wittgenstein combined a sense of depth of philosophical problems with a conviction that they arise from a failure to understand the workings of our language. Escape from these problems does not call for the formulation of explanations or theories, but for a form of clarification which he describes as an 'activity' and which he dissociates from the expression of doctrines.[397]

Pessimism about the effectiveness of his work also relates to Wittgenstein's conviction that the way we look at things is determined not by our philosophical beliefs, but by our culture and upbringing. And in the face of this, as he once said to Karl Britton, 'What can one man do alone?'[398] However, people of genius with HFA/ASP are largely interested in new knowledge; in Wittgenstein's case, in new methods of philosophising. Thus, whatever the negative reaction to his work, the urge for originality persists.

In making philosophical problems an activity rather than a theory, Wittgenstein saw the value of philosophy as therapeutic. People with HFA/ASP are often atheoretical. Scharfstein notes that Wittgenstein's interest in the peculiarities of language resembled that of a sculptor who organises his sculpture around the 'knots and projections of the wood' he is using. He hopes to escape by focusing his vision clearly on details. His intention is not to change but to become adapted to the reality through clear unaided vision. Like Freud, Wittgenstein believed that the capacity to see was in itself 'therapeutic'.[399]

The therapeutic value lay in bringing about a state of reflective awareness in his students. McGinn states that 'the difficulty of Wittgenstein's open and fragmentary text is not, therefore, a mere pedagogic ruse designed to force his readers to think for themselves, but an essential part of an approach which sets out to subvert our mistaken desire for philosophical doctrines. The method is not concerned with informing the reader of anything but with exploiting his practical grasp of language to bring about a state of reflective awareness in which the questions with which he began have ceased to plague him'.[400] Similarly, Hacker outlines Wittgenstein's therapeutic approach to philosophy:

[Wittgenstein] held philosophy to be therapeutic, not theoretical. It destroys idols, but does not replace them. It is the quest for a survey of grammar, not for an armchair preview of future science. Achievement in philosophy consists in dissolution of philosophical questions, not in acquisition of new information that provides answers to them. Understanding is indeed attained; but it consists in arriving at a clear vision of what is known and familiar, rather than in grasping the articulations of a new theory about the nature of things. Theory construction lies within the problems of science and philosophy – in its questions, methods, and results – it is wholly distinct from science.[401]

Undeniably, philosophising was therapeutic for Wittgenstein and kept him from suicide. It is interesting that one of the current key theories on autism and Asperger's syndrome concerns a lack of theory of mind. Edmonds and Eidinow, too, note the 'sort of linguistic therapy' aspect of Wittgenstein's work.[402] But the question remains: who is the therapy for? Was it self-therapy for Wittgenstein? Or was it to be useful for other philosophers? Both are probably true. Clearly Wittgenstein's aim in teaching was to persuade people to change their style of thinking.[403] However, he did not want the thinking style of the natural scientist to be mixed up with the thinking style of the philosopher.[404] What is surprising is that in his earlier work he wanted people to assume an autistic thinking style.

Private language

One of the most controversial aspects of Wittgenstein's philosophy has been the famous 'private language' argument. According to Magee, Wittgenstein argued that for language to mean anything, its use must follow certain rules. Given that many of the criteria of what constitutes a rule or the following of a rule are socially derived, Wittgenstein concluded that there could be no such thing as a private language.[405]

Wittgenstein's attack on private language appears to suggest that private language cannot be part of the language game, that language must always be interpersonal and have a social context. This again does not particularly make sense, because he often talks about his works being dialogues with himself. It is also possible that his attack on private language was due to a metarepresentational deficit, i.e. his difficulty in working out a theory about other minds. Indeed, Wittgenstein denied the very possibility of a private language in referring to inner experiences. In this respect Wittgenstein rejected Descartes' theory of mind.[406] Language, he contended, must be public.[407]

It is possible that arguments with Russell over values are evidence of Wittgenstein's metarepresentational deficit. At that time in Cambridge he had difficulty in understanding concepts such as values, especially in seeing things from another person's point of view.[408] Many philosophers, notably Ayer and Searle, maintain that Wittgenstein's private language argument can be seen as a *reductio ad absurdum*. According to Rogers, Ayer was never remotely convinced by it:

[Ayer] first criticised it in an article in the *Proceedings of the Aristotelian Society* in 1954, and returned to the attack time and again over the next 30 years. Wittgenstein's case against the logical possibility of a private language rested on what was in effect a *reductio ad absurdum*: the inventor of a private language used to refer to mental sensations would not be able to distinguish between actually using a word properly and just thinking it was being used properly; there would be no objective linguistic rule against which he could check his own usage; but if there was no distinction between really getting it right and just thinking we have got it right, then the concept of rightness has no content at all. The problem with this position, Ayer contended, was that even in the case of a public language, the same situation arises: I can check my understanding of a term against other people's usage or against dictionary definitions, but then in turn, I might misunderstand the meaning offered to me. Ultimately, Ayer argued, all language rests on what he called an act of 'primary recognition', which itself contains no guarantee that the recognition is valid.[409]

Opposition to Wittgenstein's argument was especially strong when viewed from the perspective of analysing sensory data or 'mental psychology'.[410] Kenny notes that the outcome of Wittgenstein's attack is that there cannot be a language whose words refer to what can only be known to the speaker of the language. He cites the language game with the English word 'pain' as not constituting a private language, because whatever philosophers may say, other people can very often know when a person is in pain: 'It is not by any solitary definition that "pain becomes a name of a sensation": it is rather by forming part of a communal language game'.[411] This is probably true of people in severe pain, but if somebody is in minor pain there is absolutely no way that anybody can know unless told about it. Greenfield, too, in a discussion on private language supports the impossibility of a private language. Moreover, it constitutes a powerful critique of the tendency 'to offer objectifying accounts of the subjectivity of psychological states'. This is perhaps best exemplified, he believes, by the 'uncritical willingness of many scientists to model the cognitive space of the subject, the subject's "inner life" on the literally inner goings-on of a computer'.[412]

P.F. Strawson, in a review of John McDowell's *Mind and Matter*, shows that the private language argument concentrated on the impressions of 'outer sense', i.e. sensible experience of objects in the world which exist independently of our awareness of them. However, the same conclusion applies in the case of 'inner sense', i.e. subjective experiences whose objects have no existence independent of our awareness of them. McDowell is compelled to reject from a human standpoint the notion of 'the blind intuition, the non-conceptual Given'. By doing so, he shows that we can then more fully appreciate the significance and coherence of Wittgenstein's private language argument.[413]

Loizzo sees the private language argument as the crux of Wittgenstein's mature views on the mind. The argument records his shift from the modern egocentric paradigm of mind to an intersubjective one.[414] According to Loizzo, Wittgenstein's 'communicative methodology' can help clinicians:

> the promise of Wittgenstein's language therapy extends from theory to practice. Wittgenstein's method can help us build the communicative skills it takes to treat any free speaking agent responsibly, clearing egocentric distortions from the doctor/patient field more fully than current methodologies. His 'clarity' redefines our 'objectivity' and 'neutrality' in communicative terms, as freedom to see the emptiness of our signifying habits; his 'sympathy' redefines 'participant observation' and 'empathetic concern' similarly, as the altruistic act of drawing others into the language-game. So his communicative methodology can help centre the clinician as a self-critical and responsible agent of intersubjective agreement.[415]

Loizzo also shows how Wittgenstein's intersubjective method avoids the excesses of behaviourism and phenomenology. Instead it offers a distinctively human way to adjust 'mechanistic and interpretative means to the communicative ends of psychiatry'.[416]

Patients with HFA/ASP have problems with inner speech and show metarepresentational deficits. Once again, perhaps Wittgenstein's statement that there is no such thing as a private language really reflects his personal view, which is an autistic view. Certainly, Wittgenstein's philosophy might be examined from the viewpoint of a metarepresentational deficit, i.e. his difficulty in working out a theory about other minds and autistic problems with inner speech.

Criticism of Wittgenstein's philosophy

Much of the criticism levelled at Wittgenstein concerns the lack of theory in his work. Marshall notes that modern philosophers – like Wittgenstein – have no theory of thought to speak of:

> In the specific case of Quine and Wittgenstein . . . the restrictions that they impose simply exclude from serious study the many fascinating questions they themselves raise. In the absence of 'any definite conception of body', the question of the irreducibility of the mental to the physical cannot even be formulated. LISP is no more (and no less) a 'private language' than is English. Certain aspects of 'consciousness' can be studied within the framework of natural science. But as Wittgenstein

himself wrote: 'nothing seems to me less likely than that a scientist or mathematician who reads me would be seriously influenced in the way he works'.[417]

Similarly, Fodor claims that Wittgenstein believed that philosophy should somehow be atheoretical: '[Wittgenstein] hated theories impartially, [and] didn't distinguish semantic ones from pragmatic ones. His failure to do so made a shambles of the philosophy of language for decades.'[418] Arguably, this was because of his HFA/ASP.

What is evident here is that Wittgenstein – in keeping with HFA/ASP – is only interested in original ideas, often with very limited practical applications. As noted above, Asperger commented on his patients' originality of thought and the frequency with which their interests were channelled into abstract and indeed obscure subjects with limited practical use. Clearly this is the case with Wittgenstein.

Wittgenstein had difficulty seeing the 'big picture', a concept which traditionally preoccupies the minds of philosophers past and present. His difficulty in conceptualising the big picture can also be seen with his rejection of a general theory of speech acts. However, it is possible to have a general theory of speech acts. This conceptualisation difficulty is also seen in his anti-theoretical stance. Consequently, his philosophy lacks coherence. As Happe points out, people with an autism spectrum of problems have difficulties in conceptualisation, reasoning and social judgement, and also difficulty in reasoning about other minds.[419] These were matters that Wittgenstein struggled with throughout his life and made considerable progress in overcoming. It is hardly surprising that he was interested in mathematics, engineering, and machines, where things happen in a predictable and logical fashion. In the end his philosophical theories were, I believe, excessively reductionistic and overly focused on very limited ideas. There is much more to philosophy than he allowed.

His work in focusing narrowly on language to the exclusion of the big picture has led to incredulity among other philosophers. Magee confesses 'I could never understand how anyone could take seriously the view that the subject matter of philosophy was linguistic'.[420] (1 agree, and the same happened to some extent in psychoanalysis with the theories of Lacan.) Wittgenstein's narrow focus has also ruled out by extension non-linguistic reality posing problems for philosophy, as Magee is correct in stating: 'anyone who truly believes that the real task of philosophy is to clarify utterance must believe that non-linguistic reality presents us with no philosophical problems and this is what the . . . older Wittgenstein did believe'.[421] Wittgenstein's later philosophy, Magee believes, amounted to a 'highly sophisticated form of intellectual frivolity'.[422]

The limited practical use of Wittgenstein's philosophy, reflecting as it does his autistic sensibility, has given rise to widespread disapproval.

Rather than providing the much-avowed clarity to philosophical problems, commentators have argued that Wittgenstein failed in his objective. Effectively, he presented a non-nourishing philosophy that leads to disillusionment, according to Fodor:

> There is a philosophy of philosophy that started with the later Wittgenstein and has been in the air ever since: namely, that it is a zero-sum game. Bad philosophy, we are told, presents itself in the guise of self-evident truths; good philosophy tears away the mask. You don't get nourished, for philosophy bakes no bread, but you can get disillusioned.[423]

In this respect, Wittgenstein's uncompromising search for truth results in a type of philosophy that offers little in the way of ethics or problem solving.[424] Essentially, it is an autistic philosophy.

Clarity is similarly lacking in the *Philosophical Investigations*, according to McGinn. She argues that very little sense is given of how Wittgenstein's texts work to diagnose and overcome philosophical confusion. The desire to command 'a clear view of the use of our words' at the expense of explanatory theory gives no satisfaction.[425]

So, too, with Caroline Moorehead's assessment of Wittgenstein as a philosopher. She famously remarked that Wittgenstein was to speak of great philosophy as showing 'the fly the way out of the fly-bottle'.[426] While acknowledging the extreme complexity of Wittgenstein's reasoning, being a most obscure and challenging modern philosopher, she was not surprised that certain individuals declared that 'far from showing anyone the way out of a bottle, Wittgenstein himself was trapped inside, unable to escape'. Of course, Wittgenstein was in an 'autistic bottle' himself, in a manner of speaking, but did partially find his way out. It is obvious that the limitations that HFA/ASP imposed on him made his philosophy difficult for people generally to understand.

What is clear is that Wittgenstein's work has spawned much research in philosophy, but whether the successive trends are nothing more than 'intellectual barbarism' is questioned by Hacker. Hacker describes what has happened to philosophy in the past 30 years as follows:

> in the mid 1970s, however, philosophy moved away from the connective analysis and Wittgensteinian thought. Post-positivism in the US came to dominate the scene. Quine's repudiation of the analytic–synthetic distinction, and with it any distinction between the *a priori* and the empirical, implied the demise of analytic philosophy, replacing it with a conception of philosophy as an extension of science, a cognitive discipline distinguished from science, if at all, only by its generality. Theory construction modelled on the empirical sciences displaced conceptual

analysis. During the 1980s 'cognitive science' inspired by Chomsky, and 'eliminative materialism', a form of scientism inspired by computer analogies for the mental and by speculative neurophysiology, came to displace analytic philosophy of mind. Whether these transformations represented an advance or a lapse into a new form of intellectual barbarism is debatable.[427]

Yet, for all the criticism levelled at him, Wittgenstein's philosophy remains as popular as ever. Self points out that Wittgenstein's legacy is still with us, and 'pulsating as I write'. He concludes that, arguably, the great shift from structuralism to post-structuralism as modes of enquiry into the human sciences and the arts reflects the two different phases of Wittgenstein's philosophic thinking.[428] Greenfield, in assessing Wittgenstein's contribution, points out that his later philosophy:

> informs debate at the interface between the philosophy of mind–language and the special sciences. In particular, the conclusions of his considerations on the nature of rule-following and the normativity of meanings are of some concern in much psychosemantic theory (the discipline concerned with the meaning or content of psychological states), especially the area of biosemantics, and it is a contemporary question whether his insights can be made to cohere with the basic tenets of Chomskyan theoretical linguistics.[429]

The sense of originality and genius that Wittgenstein's work inspires continues to this day. His uncompromising conviction is also a hallmark of his genius. Not surprisingly, his originality is difficult to categorise within trends and movements in philosophy. After all, Wittgenstein believed that 'the philosopher is not a citizen of any community of ideas. That is what makes him a philosopher.'[430] It certainly describes Wittgenstein's alienation and his sense of not belonging to any social community. Nagel claims that Wittgenstein was 'self-consciously out of step with the times . . . [yet he] remains for the most part unassimilated by contemporary philosophy, in spite of being conventionally venerated as one of the few great philosophers of the 20th century'.[431] In the light of his HFA/ASP, he was, not surprisingly, out of step with the times.

Criticism of the psychobiographical approach in relation to Wittgenstein

The idea of genius arising from a particular moment in history and as a product of a person's environment is strongly rejected by the present author. I disagree with Stephen Toulmin who places Wittgenstein's philosophy in the context of 'Viennese culture and the *fin de siècle* intellectual firmament'.[432] Indeed, I would take precisely the opposite view.

Personality is important and, in this respect, one cannot overestimate the role that nature played in the development of Wittgenstein's philosophy. The issue of what Wittgenstein essentially tried to hide from his peers throughout his life, namely his homosexuality, raises certain questions about how it influenced his philosophy. Monk related how the poet James Kirkup asked him what he thought Wittgenstein was up to in a public lavatory in Newcastle one night in the 1940s. Kirkup stated in his autobiography, *I, of All People*, that Wittgenstein was in the habit of picking up young men or 'rough trade' for the purpose of casual sex – contrary to what Monk had written about him in his biography, *Ludwig Wittgenstein – the Duty of Genius*. Monk relates Kirkup's version of events:

> 'Wittgenstein despised my passivism, but when I met him occasionally in town at the public toilet behind the YMCA in Eldon Place, a favourite haunt of cruisers, he was more friendly.' It seems pretty clear what Kirkup is implying here, but, to make sure, I wrote to him asking him to spell it out. In reply, he told me that he had not meant to imply that he and Wittgenstein had been sexual partners. If, he wrote, Wittgenstein was attracted by 'rough trade', then, 'I was certainly not his cup of tea' . . . Kirkup told me: 'at no time did I see him [Wittgenstein] indulging in any kind of sexual activity. Probably his presence in certain obscure places in the blackout was innocent, as part of his philosophic curiosity about human behaviour . . . I think associating Wittgenstein with 'rough trade' is a mistake. I sensed he was not that sort of homosexual.[433]

Nevertheless, there can be no doubt whatsoever about Wittgenstein's cottaging on the Prater in Vienna. His presence there was to serve his homosexual needs. Monk goes on to state:

> Hmm . . . Whatever one makes of that, I felt slightly resentful about finding myself involved in such an investigation. Does it really matter what Wittgenstein (or Kirkup, for that matter) was up to in Newcastle's public lavatories? No, of course it doesn't.

On the contrary, it does matter greatly, particularly when a philosopher writes about ethics. It made his writing on ethics deeply flawed. According to his theory, there were things that couldn't be spoken about. Because of his conflict over his homosexual behaviour, he was unable to think of these matters in a non-conflictual way, and this limited his theory. It was his homosexual behaviour that he was unable to speak about, and this limited the universality of his writings on ethics. Here is a clear example where biography is crucial.

None the less, critics might accuse the writer of a book such as this of prying unnecessarily into private lives. In Wittgenstein's case we have a philosopher writing about ethics picking up 'rough youths' in Vienna. It raises many questions, one of which is, what age were these youths? Kirkup's notion that Wittgenstein went to the public toilets to satisfy his philosophic curiosity about human behaviour defies belief. When Monk subtitled his biography of Wittgenstein 'The Duty of Genius', it provided only a partial explanation of what drove Wittgenstein. For Monk, the duty of Wittgenstein's genius was the duty to produce great works, in addition to cleansing himself of homosexual guilt and trying to understand people, especially himself.

Negative reaction to the exploration of Wittgenstein's private life has come from certain quarters, notably his literary executors. Indeed, the words of Elizabeth Anscombe indicate an extremely negative response: 'If by pressing a button it could have been secured that people would not concern themselves with [Wittgenstein's] personal life, I should have pressed the button'.[434] In addition, Rush Rhees wrote that 'there are certain stories (such as the ascription of homosexuality which it would be foul to relate or tell about somebody even if it were true. The word is foul).' He adds the word 'obscene' for good measure: 'obscene because of the kind of disrespect for the dead that it has. The terrible disrespect for the dead.'[435]

These are extreme attitudes, and would probably disqualify a great deal of biography. Furthermore, they are clearly expressions of censorship and anti-academic, and show an unwillingness to put the person's life and its meaning in context. Ian Brunskill points out that Wittgenstein's life and thoughts are inextricably intertwined to a far greater degree than is often acknowledged.[436] Sacks too states that:

> Hermelin, who studied (low-functioning) autistic savants for many years, feels that though they may have enormous talents, they are so lacking in subjectivity and inwardness that the major artistic creativity is beyond them. Christopher Gillberg, one of the finest clinical observers of autism, feels that autistic people of the Asperger type, in contrast, may be capable of major creativity and wonders whether indeed Bartok and Wittgenstein may have been autistic (many autistic people now like to think of Einstein as one of them).[437]

I agree with Gillberg, especially in reference to Bartók[438] and Wittgenstein.[439] Indeed, I am certain that Wittgenstein himself would support the approach of the current book, given that he said 'it is sometimes said that a man's philosophy is a matter of temperament, and there is something in this'.[440] Scharfstein stated quite rightly that most philosophers hide behind façades: 'their ideas are indeed constructions intended to make these façades more difficult to penetrate'.[441] Certainly, Bartley indicates that sometimes their ideas are the façade themselves.[442] I agree entirely with this viewpoint.

Conclusion

Wittgenstein is the most perfect example of an autistic philosopher. His autism has had a direct impact on the form of his thinking. It also put limitations on his philosophy. Moreover, his philosophy was therefore excessively narrow and reductionistic. For him, personally, it probably saved his life in a literal sense. Nevertheless, it was a hugely important influence because language is so critical in human interactions. Because so much personal data is available about him we can observe how massively stressful the course of his life was for a person with HFA/ASP. We can also see how important social relationships are – even if very impaired – for a person with HFA/ASP. He struggled tremendously in his effort to make relationships, to sustain them and to understand them. They were always a source of bafflement to him. For much of his life he suffered intense depression – so common in people with HFA/ASP – although in his case there was also a family history of depression. Indeed, he was a 'heroic creator'. One cannot examine the process of his creative work without being enormously impressed. What he achieved was almost unattainable by most people's standards. Without a doubt he ranks with Einstein, Freud, Turing, Yeats, Ramanujan and Russell as one of the intellectual giants of the twentieth century.

Chapter 5

Sir Keith Joseph

Keith Joseph was acknowledged by Margaret Thatcher as the founder of modern conservatism in Britain. Indeed, he was one of the most influential politicians of the late twentieth century. He served the Conservative Party for 40 years, became a government minister in 1959 and served in five departments before retiring from the front bench in 1986. He is best remembered for his desire to change the 'climate of opinion'.[1] John Gray identified his unique contribution to British politics:

> If any one person can be singled out as having set in motion the Conservative collapses, it is Keith Joseph. He was chiefly responsible for the party's abandonment of its traditional, pragmatic attitude to economic doctrines and for the increasing influence on it of the sectarian mentality of the right-wing think tanks. It is not unreasonable to credit him with being the main progenitor of the New Right in Britain. At the same time, by shifting the parameters of what was politically possible, he helped make the doctrinaire notions of the 1980s part of the common currency of mainstream politicians today. It may be hyperbolic to describe him as 'one of the godfathers of the Blair government', as Charles Leadbetter did in the *New Statesman* in May 1999, but there can be little doubt that Keith Joseph was the pivotal intellectual figure in British politics in the last quarter of the 20th century. Throughout his career, Joseph subscribed to the belief – shared with Enoch Powell and passed on to Margaret Thatcher – that the Tory party was first and foremost the party of capitalism. This was a caricature of Conservatism. It made no mention of the vital importance of maintained social cohesion – one of the abiding concerns of Conservatives from Disraeli to Macmillan.[2]

It is hardly surprising that a person with HFA/ASP would have problems with social cohesion. Born in 1918, Joseph was one of the most enigmatic figures in politics by the time of his death in 1994. However, his eccentricities and achievements can be understood in terms of the HFA/ASP he manifested.

Family background

Joseph's family were prominent members of the Anglo-Jewish business community in Britain. His father, Sir Samuel Joseph, became Mayor of London in 1943 and received much praise for his 'genius for organisation'.[3] A year later his obituary in the *City Press* paid tribute to his outstanding qualities. Indeed, they listed characteristics that his son Keith inherited, in particular his taste for public service:

> No one could say he was an easy man to serve, for all his life he had set before him a model of efficiency that was as exacting as it was his own. Everything he did had to be done not merely well but more than well; and with this he combined unquenchable energy surprising in a man who never really enjoyed perfect health. No detail was too small for Samuel Joseph.[4]

The entrepreneur, Samuel Joseph, was a partner in the Bovis construction company. Denham and Garnett note that in running the company, Keith Joseph's father was a stickler for detail. The unique billboards advertising the company were a case in point: 'He was particularly keen to see that the Bovis nameboards were cleaned'.[5] Besides such exacting traits, he was also an innovator and designed the commercially successful 'Compactom' wardrobe.[6] His decisive nature was not, however, inherited by his son. On the contrary, Joseph was never a person 'to make snap decisions, even on relatively trivial matters, and by the end of his career the furrowed brow had become his trademark'.[7] (Interestingly, the furrowed brow was also a trademark of Wittgenstein.)

Despite being an only child, Joseph admitted that his childhood had been happy, largely as a result of the material comfort and 'indulgence of his parents'.[8] By all accounts he was a sensitive and contemplative boy.[9] When he went to prep school and left the intense family environment behind, he felt an outsider.[10] In common with many people with HFA/ASP, Joseph was bullied at school.

Denham and Garnett suggest that Joseph yearned for friendship but had difficulty in forming relationships with his peers because of his reserved and diffident nature.[11] An indication of his discontent at school is shown by his poor academic performance, linked also to a 'psychosomatic disorder' according to Denham and Garnett.[12] His public school education continued at Harrow, where, like G.H. Hardy, he was obsessed with cricket. He was not a great athlete.[13] At cricket he bowled occasionally with an 'unorthodox' action.[14]

Speech and language

There is no evidence that Joseph had delayed language development. At school his linguistic skills were excellent and he specialised in modern languages.[15] Though Denham and Garnett remark that Joseph was almost the only senior cabinet minister of the 1980s not to have written a memoir,[16] this decision cannot be attributed to any language deficits he might have possessed. People with HFA/ASP have problems with auto-biographical memory.

There is some suggestion that Joseph had difficulty in sustaining conversations. Andrew Roth had frequent contact with him and observed the following:

> Whenever you are with him, although he is spasmodically very charming, you come away with the feeling that midway in the meeting, you 'lost' him because you were 'wasting' his time. This is a common experience of those who meet the redoubtable Sir Keith Joseph, Bt.[17]

Nevertheless, Joseph had a remarkable gift for oratory. Denham and Garnett point out that he had always been a 'connoisseur of oratory', and certainly by the end of his career could distinguish between a 'pregnant silence intended for dramatic effect' and one resulting from a frustrating search for the right words.[18] This was evidence of a reduction in his HFA/ASP.

In common with other geniuses, Joseph had difficulties with humour. There are countless episodes from his public life where he tried to rally crowds but failed hopelessly. A typical example was during the 1970 general election campaign when he attempted to warm up his audience with some humour. As Denham and Garnett note:

> Jokes do not come easily to him, and an expectant pause after the first one produced no results. 'I was Minister for Wales once,' he said. 'I was paid half what the present Minister is getting, but I built more houses and there were 50,000 more jobs here then.'[19]

Neither laughter nor applause met the end of his speech. Certainly problems with humour are common in people with HFA/ASP.

Social impairment

Joseph manifested severe communication problems and impairment in reciprocal social interaction. He was an 'intensely private man' and excessively modest.[20] Some describe him as 'an introverted young man',[21] while others say he was 'a shy, intense and rather guarded man'.[22] According to

Denham and Garnett, at interviews, rather than divulge anecdotes about his past, Joseph always preferred to discuss ideas:[23] 'He disliked speaking of himself; almost uniquely, he was very uneasy even when his name was mentioned in public. But if he was painfully shy he appeared to be remarkably candid on those occasions when he allowed himself to reminisce.'[24] This also demonstrates the honesty and openness of a person with HFA/ASP.

The lack of desire for social interaction was certainly evident during his time at Harrow. A story circulated that he paid the local barber five extra shillings per term for 'refraining from conversation while he was cutting his hair'.[25] Like Wittgenstein, Joseph had little capacity for small talk and generally would get straight down to work when dealing with people. According to Denham and Garnett, he was seen as prim and humourless but adopted 'an exaggerated style of self-deprecation' to counteract this.[26]

Joseph had no desire to interact with peers while studying jurisprudence at Magdalen College, Oxford. Denham and Garnett note that 'he did not partake in rowdy undergraduate parties, prevalent in pre-war days'.[27] The advent of the Second World War did little to mature his behaviour. During the war he served as captain with a regiment in Italy. Not surprisingly, he left the army having not 'imbibed the spirit of companionship which transformed the outlook and character of so many fellow-intellectuals'.[28] He himself acknowledged that the war 'didn't mature me as much as it matured many others'.[29] This bears a certain similarity to Wittgenstein's relations with his fellow soldiers during the First World War. Certainly, Joseph retained his immature autistic personality.

There is little information about his relationships with women. According to Denham and Garnett, 'no one remembered him having a girlfriend' at Oxford.[30] However, he did marry the equally serious Hellen Guggenheimer, with whom he had four children; their marriage was dissolved in 1985. He remarried 4 years prior to his death.

Joseph also showed a lack of appreciation of social cues because of his HFA/ASP. At Harrow his friend John Brocklehurst drew attention to it:

> At first he was thought to be rather 'priggish', and though he got over that, he never cured his greatest fault properly. This was that he would take everything far too seriously. Whenever he talked, he would talk seriously rather than listen to or try to make lighter conversation. Anything of this kind seemed to bore him all too soon. This is not to suggest that he was entirely lacking any sense of humour. It merely means that he preferred to be serious [rather] than frivolous. This caused him to be rather misunderstood by those who did not know him well, and who sometimes were embarrassed by his frankness and his apparent inability or unwillingness to discuss any topics other than intimate ones.[31]

Harold Macmillan, well accustomed to the *bonhomie* of his Jewish associates, claimed that Joseph was 'the only boring Jew I have met'.[32] Years later Simon Hoggart wrote a story based on Joseph's visit to a bird sanctuary.[33] 'How on earth do the birds know it is a sanctuary?', Joseph had asked. Denham and Garnett note that in fact this was an example of Joseph's sense of irony, but his image of 'other-worldly innocence was such that it was interpreted as a serious question'.[34] In fact it was really a sign of his HFA/ASP, showing an impairment of comprehension, where there was a misinterpretation of the literal/implied meaning.

A sense of detachment from reality pervaded Joseph. Indeed, emotional reciprocity was largely absent. In addition, Brocklehurst claimed that Joseph was little more than an actor, that he gave 'the impression that he was acting most of the time he was talking to one'.[35] Clearly, this was a sign of his identity diffusion.

Despite being a prominent member of a powerful political party, Joseph often looked as if he was disconnected from it. The *Sunday Express* described him as a 'loner, a mystery figure remote from the front-line troops in the Commons'.[36] Furthermore, Joseph showed, rather bizarrely, 'an unusual degree of detachment from political reality'.[37] This occurred many times. For a politician, he often showed an alarming naïvety in his dealings with people. During the 1960s, when the Race Relations Bill was going through the Houses of Parliament, Joseph was particularly naïve in his attitude towards racism. Like his father, he believed that the power of reason would win the day, as noted by Denham and Garnett: 'racist views should be contested by reasoning, patient but firm; confident that this would lead to the intellectual defeat of racism, his priority at this time was how to deal with the problem of those who tried to stir up unthinking prejudice'.[38] Similarly, Joseph failed in his attempt to have a well-meaning 'serious' conversation with a punk who constantly badgered him on his way to the shops near his home.[39] This demonstrates the naïvety that many people with HFA/ASP have, accompanied by a detachment from social reality.

Like many people with HFA/ASP, Joseph loved younger people and respected their views, regardless of their age. This demonstrated a naïvety and lack of empathy on his part. As Secretary of State in the Department of Education and Science he would 'slip away from his officials to quiz school children about the abilities of their teachers, and on one occasion he asked the class of astonished thirteen-year-olds for their considered opinion of "integrated humanities in the middle years"'.[40]

There are numerous examples of Joseph's socially inappropriate behaviour. Denham and Garnett note that during important committee meetings he would often disturb his colleagues by tearing out articles from the *Financial Times*.[41] In 1980 he reprimanded a Department of Industry receptionist 'for not smiling enough'.[42]

Joseph's socially inappropriate behaviour translated into poor political judgement. In May 1978, during the national steel strike, he exasperated colleagues by refusing to negotiate with the unions. Len Murray of the TUC informed him that 'talking to you is like trying to teach Chinese to a deaf mute'.[43] During an election campaign, instead of giving speeches 'to rally the faithful', he would deliver an analytical 'state of the nation' address. This is certainly in keeping with a person with HFA/ASP.[44] Similarly, a kind of autistic impulsiveness was evident in his habit of 'collecting ideas then speaking out before thinking through their implications'.[45] Not surprisingly, *The Spectator* described a speech of his as 'maladroit'.[46] Indeed he was often described as 'absent-minded'.[47]

Unwariness and a lack of empathy are evident in many of his speeches. The Edgbaston Speech following the Conservative defeat in 1974 is infamous for a quotation that highlights his lack of empathy and tactlessness, and was interpreted as racism: his statement that 'the balance of our population, our human stock is threatened' was to damage his political credibility severely.[48] In another speech he alluded to eugenics, with the words 'a high and rising proportion of children are being born to mothers least fitted to bring children into the world'.[49] He received a great deal of criticism – some critics accused him of hoping to create a 'master race'. The substance of the speech was later summarised as 'castrate or conform'.[50] This demonstrated a gross lack of empathy and signalled that he was out of touch with the modern world.

Further embarrassment to the Tories was brought by his numerous public gaffes. Speeches were made that reflected his self-doubt on many issues. In 1974 following the Birmingham pub bombings, Barbara Castle described Joseph's speech on the death penalty as a 'contribution of marvellous tortuousness and circumlocution'.[51] Roy Jenkins stated that it was 'both tortured and nonsensical'.[52]

Joseph's finest input in politics was that of ideologue, expressing the role that politics should play in society. Interestingly, Denham and Garnett claim that as a politician Joseph was not an original thinker. However, his love of ideas and reputation as an intellectual did not earn him much kudos among his colleagues.[53] Because of his inherent problems in social interaction and lacking the common touch, he was unsuitable as a politician. According to Denham and Garnett, Joseph gave the impression of a man 'searching for eternal truths who would prefer not to be diverted by the day-to-day problems'.[54] Indeed, this searching for eternal truths or fundamental ideas is typical of people with HFA/ASP. Ronald Butt pointed out that Joseph was 'a highly doctrinal non-interventionist' and a 'vocal believer in the platonic beauty and efficiency of the free and unimpeded market'.[55] This highlights the fascination for abstraction that people with HFA/ASP demonstrate.

Certainly, Joseph was regarded as a 'deeply impractical man' by his peers.[56] Lord Alport said to him, 'always remember, Keith, that you have no political judgement'.[57] Clearly Joseph was not aided by his distaste for tactics. He found 'tactical ploys . . . alien to his nature'.[58] *The Sunday Times* stated that he 'lacked the administrative skills and common touch needed to translate ideas into practical politics'.[59] Leo Abse identified him as Jung's 'introverted thinker', in that he was constantly 'searching for intellectual solutions for what are properly emotional problems'.[60] This is a classic feature of people with HFA/ASP, and was found in de Valera's case too. Furthermore, Denham and Garnett note that like most ideologues, Joseph was certain that his views were based on common sense.[61] Notwithstanding their good intentions, people with HFA/ASP tend to have very little common sense. In this light it is understandable that Professor Ted Wragg of Exeter University likened Joseph's approach to education to that 'of a Martian arriving in the middle of a rugby match'.[62] It is worth noting that people with HFA/ASP are often described as being from the planet Mars.

As expected, his detachment from reality made him a liability for the party he served. Lord Healy believed his political ideas were 'bizarre and damaging'.[63] Larry Lamb, editor of *The Sun*, told Margaret Thatcher that 'Keith's reputation as a cold intellectual, remote from the people, was a hindrance to the Tory campaign'.[64]

Nevertheless, Joseph had some insight into his deficiencies and for that reason did not seek the party leadership. Indeed, he had no regrets at not becoming prime minister. Denham and Garnett point out that though flattered when colleagues suggested it, he was aware that he lacked 'the breadth of judgement, let alone knowledge, to take on the task'.[65] Joseph himself admitted to Anthony Seldon before the 1987 general election that 'had I become Party Leader . . . it would have been a disaster for the party, country and me'.[66] Certainly, his autistic refusal to 'engage in general Cabinet dialogue' damaged his chances of ever becoming party leader, according to *The Times* in 1974.

Denham and Garnett note how Tony Benn likened Joseph to Enoch Powell, another Member of Parliament (MP). Many critics of Joseph's 1970 speech believed the Tories' new economic policies would lead to greater inequality. Benn described it as a 'pure and unadulterated nineteenth-century Powellite speech'.[67] Interestingly, Joseph and Powell shared eccentricities and 'a lack of media appeal'.[68] Indeed, Denham and Garnett state that, as with Powell's 'Rivers of Blood' speech in 1968, Joseph had 'underestimated the extent to which careless words could be taken as validation for the prejudices of the ignorant'.[69] Because of his autism it is hardly surprising that he was genuinely puzzled by the response to his speeches.[70] Indeed, Alan Watkins in the *New Statesman* called Joseph 'a saloon-bar Malthus'.[71]

Because of his poor social skills associated with HFA/ASP, Joseph learnt little about political or social relationships in his time in office. According to Denham and Garnett, for all his many virtues he still had an underdeveloped sense of politics as 'the art of the possible'.[72] In addition, they claim that:

> he never gained insights into the soul of the [Tory] Party by working inside the organisation. In many respects Joseph was an idiosyncratic Conservative, and perhaps the oddest thing about him was his evident conviction that his lack of real 'roots' in the party made no difference to his attractions as a candidate.[73]

His poor relationship with the media was not aided by his distaste for television. He would not allow television in his own house, thus depriving himself of insights into public opinion.

All-absorbing interests

Clearly as a politician Joseph had 'an obsessional outlook' and was a workaholic[74] (something that is very characteristic of people with HFA/ASP). After he entered politics he 'revealed an intensity which was unusual – if not unique'[75] (politicians with HFA/ASP are always described as 'unique'). A 1964 profile said that 'he drives himself without mercy and expects his aids to accept his merciless approach to work'.[76] He confessed that he was 'perturbed by things which I do not control'.[77] Placing such control and great demands on himself and others led to his being described as a 'masochistic politician'.[78]

Clearly, Joseph showed remarkable self-discipline, with all the traits of HFA/ASP that it entails. Denham and Garnett sum up his ability in this area: 'even if Joseph's performance can be attributed to relentless feeding on textbooks and relatively clear handwriting, it was a tribute to an excellent memory and notable self-discipline'.[79] In his approach to researching and gathering information Joseph showed a highly methodical and logical mind. Others remarked that he displayed 'the habit of mind of a first-class administrative civil servant'.[80] Certainly, he was obsessive about note taking. In fact he was rarely seen without a notebook and pencil, 'tools that accompanied him for the rest of his ministerial career and into retirement'.[81] The 'addiction' to notebooks is not uncommon in people with HFA/ASP, and was certainly evident in Wittgenstein's case. Joseph would record the most surprising details. Denham and Garnett note that when visiting a housing estate as Minister for Housing he would 'dart into the nearest house and flush the toilet in order to gauge the quality of the buildings' amenities. The habit stuck; even on social visits in later life he would comment on the facilities offered by his hosts.'[82] According to Denham and Garnett, Joseph's notebook and pencil could also appear on 'improbable occasions', for example while being interviewed on television.[83]

Denham and Garnett point out that Joseph was 'blessed with a formid-able memory, and he never lost his thirst for knowledge'.[84] Indeed, he possessed a remarkable ability to memorise facts and quotations.[85] Superb memory is common in people with HFA/ASP, certainly in remembering facts, particularly numbers. In Joseph's case, it extended to literary texts, where 'his ability to switch his thoughts rapidly from one language to another enabled him to absorb Italian by reading a translation of Shakespeare'.[86]

Not surprisingly, Joseph showed an all-encompassing interest in statis-tics, which amounted to an addiction.[87] Frequently he was described as a 'numbers man'.[88] In all likelihood the interest in statistics reveals his view of the world. Like Wittgenstein, he could only relate to facts about the world, believing them to contain fundamental truths. Denham and Garnett claim that in Joseph's eyes, 'statistical information was the only reliable guide to the existence of a problem'.[89] Consequently, rather than assessing the situation at the 'human' level, he based his views on statistics. This led to the obsession of conducting research into everything, which is almost a kind of autistic research in itself. All kinds of gatherings, family or political, were used as 'fact-finding opportunities'.

Like Lewis Carroll, Joseph took his correspondence seriously and was somewhat obsessed with it. Indeed, Denham and Garnett state that 'Joseph's correspondence was voluminous, and the time he allocated to non-essential tasks would have horrified the most slapdash civil servant'.[90] He responded diligently to all letters, time wasters or otherwise. Indeed, 'the views of people who would have been written off as cranks by any other MP were treated with unfailing respect'.[91] Certainly, this is autistic behaviour, where naïvety and lack of common-sense make one unable to differentiate between crucial and trivial issues.

Joseph was an avid reader and devoured books at a ferocious rate. Even in ministerial posts he managed to read 'about a book a week'.[92] Like Gladstone, with whom he shared more character traits than he did with Disraeli, Joseph snatched every spare moment for this 'recreation'. As well as political and historical works, he read Russian novels in translation and Proust in the original French.[93] Certainly, reading excluded time for other recreations.[94] Nevertheless, he was interested in music, which is often the case in people with HFA/ASP.

'Autistic aggression'

In his career as a politician, Joseph's views showed a sharp level of intoler-ance. Often they contained a measure of 'autistic aggression', obviously without any physical threat of violence in his case. Undoubtedly he had an abrasive and stubborn personality. Once he attacked the 'undeserving poor – the shirkers', whom he believed had enjoyed 'a field day' under the

Labour Government.[95] His speeches were highly critical of 'shirkers and scroungers'. Addressing a Maidstone Conservative Association meeting, he berated spongers and benefit cheats, and half jokingly stated that 'unfortunately, we cannot shoot them'.[96]

Like many people with HFA/ASP he had a temper. His fellow MP, Peggy Herbison, stated that 'each time that [Joseph] comes to the Dispatch Box he seems to be in a raging temper about something'.[97] School photographs show him to be 'both vulnerable and pugnacious'.[98] Clearly, Joseph did demonstrate some competitive and aggressive traits, which were certainly evident at school. Years later he remarked that failing to break into the first eleven at cricket 'makes one hate one's fellow boys'.[99]

Eccentric behaviour

Numerous anecdotes exist about Joseph's bizarre behaviour. By summing him up as 'rather an enigma', Denham and Garnett unwittingly express precisely how people with HFA/ASP are described, and Brocklehurst also described Joseph as 'rather an enigma' the whole time he was at Harrow.[100]

However, Joseph had insight into his eccentric behaviour. When reflecting on his performance as Secretary of State for Industry in Mrs Thatcher's first government, he admitted that his reputation for eccentricity had been useful; he had been 'a convenient madman' or 'I was a joke, a useful joke'.[101]

His speeches often contained bizarre references, signalling just how out of touch and misunderstood he was. Undeniably, his autistic traits were evident in the extraordinary speech he delivered at the opening of the Camping and Outdoor Life Exhibition and Motor Caravan Show at Olympia in 1975. *The Times* described it as follows:

> To get the full flavour, you have to picture it being delivered to the audience of apparently non-political campers, many with young children who were standing in front of a mock woodland area. In this incongruous setting, the speech Sir Keith chose to deliver amounted to an attack on the Soviet Union. While the campers and their young stood speechless, he spent several minutes pointing out that it was more difficult for the Russians to move about their country than it was for us. It was only when he came to the punch line that it was clear what he was on about. 'It does strike a chill', he said. 'Are we sure that we shall not eventually be subject to movement permits if socialism advances here? Don't be too sure.'[102]

This clearly is an 'autistic speech'. Oblivious to public opinion, Joseph described it as 'light-hearted'.[103] It was further proof that his sense of humour could be misunderstood. His habit of 'thinking aloud' was obviously perilous in political life.

Other bizarre remarks related by Denham and Garnett include Joseph's reference to illegitimacy among the underprivileged. When interviewed by the *Sunday Mirror* in March 1973 he stated 'one reason for the reluctance of such people to take advantage of family planning services was that they were ashamed to go out in dirty underclothes'.[104] Other examples include eyewitnesses claiming to have seen him 'banging his head against walls, obsessively tying and untying his shoelaces – even singing in a deserted railway compartment'.[105] Before one political meeting where Joseph as Secretary of State for Industry was a guest speaker, a local party member was told by his son that the chairman had appeared at his front door with 'a strange man wearing one slipper and one shoe and looking quite untidy'. Denham and Garnett report that the 'strange man' was none other than Joseph, who had been 'delayed in London and now wanted to make a telephone call to America'.[106]

Certainly, Joseph's reputation for eccentricity became newsworthy. According to Denham and Garnett, the press learnt that Joseph's obsession with unnecessary public expenditure 'had inspired him to write his departmental memos on scraps of used paper and the backs of envelopes'.[107] Not surprisingly, the political satire magazine, *Private Eye*, was keen to portray him as 'the unbalanced wild man of the right'.[108]

Non-verbal behaviour

Joseph had certain distinctive mannerisms. During a discussion with Joseph, Sir Nicholas Henderson, then British Ambassador to the USA, observed him hand flapping. Henderson described how Joseph had 'flung his hands in the air but revealed little'.[109] Clearly he had a 'nervous' disposition, certainly evident in his twisting body movements. Denham and Garnett cite the example of Joseph himself being a 'militant' anti-smoker who 'chewed his handkerchief rather than lighting up when particularly nervous'.[110] At another meeting Henderson recorded some interesting mannerisms after noticing that Joseph was tired: his 'explosive' laughter seemed at odds with his 'buttoned up' character, and his facial expressions clashed with his apparent thoughts, like 'an unsynchronised sound track in a film'.[111]

In this case Henderson's description of Joseph's face possibly relates to two different expressions appearing simultaneously on his face; this can occur in people with HFA/ASP and was noted in the case of Lewis Carroll. Others characterised him as 'taut of visage and fiery-eyed'.[112] Certainly, there is evidence to suggest he had a fixed stare. In a television appearance on ITV's *Weekend World* in 1981 he was observed to be 'staring transfixed either into the middle distance or down at his shoes'.[113] *Private Eye* claimed that officials at his department were referring to him as 'his Insanity'.[114]

In common with many geniuses with HFA/ASP, the image of the madman–magician–messiah is all-pervasive in Joseph's case. Like Wittgenstein, the effect that Joseph had on his peers and indeed the general public was often negative and destructive. Indeed, the nickname of 'the mad monk' coined by fellow MP Chris Patten was particularly apt.[115] On one occasion the academic critic, Ted Wragg, stated that 'he's very close to uttering sense'.[116] Denham and Garnett point out that by the end of 1975 'Joseph conjured a more dangerous image; he seemed like an untrained kamikaze pilot, who contrived to return from numerous missions but threatened one day to cause maximum destruction behind his own lines'.[117] The Labour leader, Michael Foot, likened him to 'a hapless magician–conjuror, who smashes a watch then forgets the rest of the trick'.[118] Similarly, James Callaghan described him as the 'Dr. Strangelove of the economic world'.[119] Not surprisingly, Joseph was variously described as Mrs Thatcher's 'mentor', 'policy guru', 'Svengali' and 'Rasputin'. For all his brilliance at being the 'guru of Thatcherism',[120] his colleagues, particularly Lord Hailsham, described him as an 'albatross', 'dotty' and 'Clever–silly, Attracts Barmies'.[121] On Joseph's retirement from politics, one relieved senior minister remarked that he was a 'marvellous man but a terrible politician'.[122] In fact, at Joseph's memorial service his son remembered that as a young boy he could never quite understand 'how such a clever man could get into so much trouble'.[123]

His extraordinary talents ensured that people treated him differently, making allowances and excuses for his eccentricities. He certainly enjoyed a special bond with Margaret Thatcher. Fellow politician Lord Young claimed that the Prime Minister gave him 'a dispensation from the rules of normal political behaviour'.[124]

Identity diffusion

It is highly likely that Joseph had problems with identity and identity diffusion. Denham and Garnett were impressed by the extent to which Joseph's quest for truth was associated with a search for 'an unambiguous sense of self – a settled *identity*'.[125] It is highly probable that his identity completely fused with that of Margaret Thatcher. Clearly, he imagined that she shared his motives for entering politics, i.e. 'to help the poor and downtrodden'.[126] Underpinning his search for identity was a search for certainty in the best tradition of philosophy:

> His psychological need for ideological certainty explains features of his life which would otherwise remain a puzzle: why this shy man forced himself to encounter derision and personal danger in an exhausting series of speeches; why a politician who thought that the need to feel 'loved' motivated most members of his profession found himself among

the best-hated people of his time and why this man of deep compassion
. . . never dissociated himself from policies which greatly increased the
poverty that he had set out to 'eliminate'.[127]

Joseph clearly had a 'harsh superego' visible to the general public. Commenting on a specific television appearance, Tony Benn stated that Joseph
'was an absolutely tortured soul – he was in agony, his face twisted in
anxiety, his stomach [seemed] all torn up, his head in his hands and he was
scribbling and worrying, he really is a sick man'.[128] Not surprisingly his
reputation for such 'agonised deliberation' led to the nickname of Mad
Monk, as we have seen.[129] This kind of stressed state is not untypical in
people with HFA/ASP. Moreover, it is typical of such people to possess a
severe superego resulting in harsh self-criticism, for example Wittgenstein.

Throughout his life Joseph was quite moralistic and self-critical. He
talked constantly about his lack of 'moral courage'.[130] Evidently, it was the
political quality he admired most. Denham and Garnett point out that
'from the outset Joseph regarded his political life as a moral calling'.[131] He
was obsessed with duty as Wittgenstein was, and with achieving 'certainty'
in whatever form it took.[132]

Certainly, he wanted to feel that he represented a cause rather than
merely a party.[133] For this reason he rarely allowed himself to become
constrained by narrow partisan interests.[134] His duty, as he perceived it,
resided in how to reconcile radical economic change with social stability.
However, because of his innate impairment in social interaction he could
not fulfil it. Denham and Garnett rightly point out that he was 'the
government's leading theoretician – and as someone whose fascination with
economics was matched by a deep interest in society – Joseph could have
been expected to address this difficulty but he never did'.[135] Furthermore,
they felt that his social vision was 'insular, blinkered and one-eyed' in terms
of reconciling party policies with public demands.[136] In one way he was an
autistic workaholic, who had never ceased political work in the 20 years
since first being elected to Parliament for Leeds North-East.[137] Moreover,
as Denham and Garnett point out, 'ideologues are driven by inner demons
which are inexplicable to normal mortals'.[138]

Clearly associated with his sense of duty were qualities of sincerity and
honesty, commonly found in those with HFA/ASP. Throughout his
political career he certainly was regarded as being honest, if somewhat
naïve. Denham and Garnett note that he always showed an 'unmistakable
sincerity'.[139] In effect, he was an extraordinary politician, described by
Patrick Cosgrave as 'the man who told the truth'.[140] Given that in the late
1970s he made public confessions of Tory errors, it is not surprising that
The Sunday Times too pointed out that 'honesty marked him out from most
of his contemporaries'.[141] For a politician this was exceptional behaviour
and somewhat incomprehensible, except in the light of HFA/ASP. Such was

his good standing that Woodrow Wyatt told readers of the *Sunday Mirror* that 'to think of him in connection with any vice would be an unpardonable offence'.[142] Dedication to his political duty was total. One pre-election profile of him spoke of a 'mind that operates like a high-powered search-light', and spoke of his 'radiation of a clear conviction that to waste time is a sin'.[143] Interestingly, Isaac Newton and Wittgenstein also considered wasting time as sinful. Denham and Garnett point out that 'few politicians have shown less inclination to rest on their laurels; none have accepted self-sacrifice more eagerly' than Joseph.[144] Linked to his self-sacrifice and sense of duty was a rare modesty, which might explain his desire not to write his memoirs. In reality, people with HFA/ASP have problems with auto-biographical memory and writing autobiographies. He also showed a slightly autistic attitude to money. Similarly to Wittgenstein after the war, he decided to live on as little money as possible.

Motor skills

There is some evidence to suggest that Joseph showed motor clumsiness. Denham and Garnett state that after graduation he set about learning the building trade at Bovis Construction Company, but was 'incompetent' at bricklaying.[145] He also described himself as hopelessly inept at skiing.[146]

Conclusion

Keith Joseph shows the strengths and weaknesses of the politician with HFA/ASP. He was a sincere person but lacked the ability to empathise with individuals, groups and society. As a consequence, he tried to understand society using a mathematical approach, i.e. through statistics and econ-omics. His 'autistic' workaholism, obsession with political ideas and fasci-nation with reading helped him in politics. Also, he was absolutely trustworthy and loyal, which helped his relations with the Prime Minister, Mrs Thatcher. None the less, his 'autistic lack of empathy' led him to make enormous errors in political speeches.

Keith Joseph also showed evidence of an obsessive compulsive person-ality disorder. He was preoccupied with details and perfectionistic. He was excessively devoted to work and was over-conscientious. He adopted a miserly spending style in his work. Of course, obsessive compulsive features are not uncommonly shown by people with HFA/ASP.

I believe that in the political arena Asperger's syndrome/eccentricity is no disadvantage in getting people to vote for one. The public at large like people with clear, narrow, definitive views. This is precisely what people with HFA/ASP present, and it is hardly surprising they are successful electorally. The relationship between a politician and an electorate of thousands or millions of people is not the kind of relationship we would understand as personal. Keith Joseph and de Valera are perfect examples of politicians with very poor personal relationships but who were, nevertheless, enormously influential politically.

Of course, people with HFA/ASP are generally not totally without friends. In the histories I often find (e.g. in the case of Ludwig Wittgenstein) that they do manage to have one friend in school.

Chapter 6

Eamon de Valera

Eamon de Valera is regarded as one of the great figures in Irish history. Born in 1882 in New York, he played a central role in the foundation of the Irish State, moving from revolutionary to Prime Minister to President. In fact, several world leaders and, indeed, a US intelligence agent have attested to his political genius. A gifted mathematician also, he is reputed to have been one of nine people in the world capable of understanding Einstein's theory of relativity during the scientist's lifetime.

However, de Valera's tenure generated as much rancour as tribute. Certainly, the ethos of the new Irish State under him was not always welcomed by leading figures. In fact his stature and inherent genius and its accompanying limitations can be explained within the context of HFA/ASP. Clearly, his political achievement was marked by its greater dedication to ideology than to people, which is certainly in keeping with HFA/ASP. None the less, his idealism was extraordinarily powerful, and with his enormous charisma he had a mesmerising effect on the Irish people. Moreover, his life demonstrates how a remarkable figure with a certain developmental psychopathology can affect the life of a nation. Indeed, he continues to affect it decades after his death through enduring legacies such as the Fianna Fáil political party, the Irish Constitution, and the regrowth of the Irish language.

Family background

Little is known about de Valera's family. His maternal grandfather was Patrick Coll, a farm labourer from Bruree, Co. Limerick, who died before de Valera was born. Coll never married but had nine children. De Valera's mother, Catherine Coll, was an Irish immigrant in New York in 1879. She married a Spaniard, Juan Vivion de Valera, and gave birth to Eamon. Juan died in 1884. When de Valera was 3 years old, for reasons unknown but most likely because of the poverty of the time, his mother sent him back to Ireland accompanied by an uncle, Ned Coll. He was later raised by his grandmother and uncle in Bruree, while his mother remained in New York.

De Valera's mother is described by Coogan as possessing 'determination and force'.[1] She was also noted for being bossy and 'having no frivolity about her'. In addition, she appears to have had a good memory, judging by the fact that she won a spelling competition in the USA.[2] That she banished her son to Ireland prompted Coogan to conclude that she had some 'coldness in her psychological make-up'.[3] Indeed, de Valera's upbringing was largely clerical; Desmond Ryan describes the long years spent in a 'semi-monastic atmosphere'.[4] Certainly, he lived in an isolated rural community and was raised within the strict confines of Catholicism. Coogan notes that as a child the young de Valera had the unusual pastime of 'digging for springs' and took up 'fowling', which perhaps reflects a certain eccentricity on his part.[5]

Speech and language problems

There is no record of de Valera showing delayed development in speech and language. However, there is evidence to suggest that he had superficially perfect expressive language consistent with HFA/ASP. When speaking he weighed his words carefully and, according to Ryan, with a 'slowness novel in an age of speed and slogans'.[6] Coogan, too, notes how he tended to read his speeches in a 'dull, halting manner'.[7] Furthermore, there was a lack of clarity in the speeches he delivered, with a distinct elusiveness in the rhetorical phrases used. Ryan observed that even after he spoke he 'left everyone in the dark'.[8] Clearly, de Valera had little ability to deliver speeches and, as Coogan points out, he 'showed failings as a public speaker'.[9] He was 'intensely verbose, wasting a great deal of time on elaborate explanations of the simplest points, with many repetitions, speaking in a tone of a schoolmaster to children' when speaking to adults.[10] Interestingly, language did preoccupy him and he devoted great time and effort to restoring the Irish language to the Irish people.

By all accounts de Valera was an excellent student, hard working and diligent; he won scholarships to prestigious colleges such as Blackrock College, Co. Dublin. There is no evidence that he had a poor school record like many with HFA/ASP. Clearly, he was an intellectual by nature and progressed to become a professor of mathematics at a relatively young age. He taught mathematics at some of the principal colleges in Dublin, such as Carysfort Teacher Training College and University College Dublin. According to Ryan, he was recognised as 'one of the greatest mathematicians in Ireland of his years'.[11] Ryan also notes how he was preoccupied with the 'science of abstractions' and studied 'spectroscopy, astrophysics and electro-optics'.[12] An interest in this area is frequently found in those with HFA/ASP.

De Valera had unusual voice characteristics that are commonly found in those with Asperger's syndrome. Certainly, from public recordings his voice was noted for its high-pitched quality. The writer, Sean O'Faolain, described it as a voice 'like a cracked or muffled bell', and the distinguished Irish civil servant, T.K. Whitaker, noted that he had an 'old gravelly voice'.[13]

De Valera did possess a sense of humour, but like that of many with HFA/ASP, it was peculiar. It was of a simple variety, lacking in subtlety; so much so that many of his peers considered him humourless. Ryan notes how many of his detractors cited him as a 'dull, pedantic, piqued professor . . . who lacked humour', but Ryan does not agree with this view.[14] Whitaker, who worked closely with de Valera, observed his sense of humour as follows:

> [De Valera] had a very strange sense of humour. I remember once I was over in the Dail [Irish parliament] . . . advising the Minister for Finance during a Budget debate. Suddenly Paddy Lynch appeared at my shoulder. He said that [de Valera] had sent him over to ask me did I know what an Epicycloid Circle was. Paddy said he did not know for the life of him what he meant. So I said I was no expert but I thought it was a circle enclosing a smaller circle which it touched tangentially. Paddy came back later . . . to say that Dev. was delighted. He was to tell me two things. Firstly that the Taoiseach said that it was reassuring to know there was someone in Finance who understood mathematics. Secondly that the tangential nature of the two circles touching contained about the same contact with truth as did the Opposition's attack on the Budget![15]

Coogan refers also to de Valera's 'grisly sense of humour'.[16] When lunching with his students at Blackrock College he described in great detail a corpse being eaten by worms, much to the students' disgust.

There is also evidence of the concrete thinking common in those with HFA/ASP. Coogan notes the occasion when de Valera was asked to write a school essay on 'Making Hay while the Sun Shines'. He could think of nothing to say except 'What other time would you make hay?'[17] This shows an impairment of comprehension, where there is a misinterpretation of the literal or implied meaning.

Impairment in social interaction

De Valera showed severe impairment in reciprocal social interaction. Certainly, his lack of empathy was pronounced at a political level. It was particularly evident during visits to the USA in the 1920s to gather support for the Irish political cause. He interfered in internal party politics, detrimentally affecting relations with Irish-Americans.[18] Ryan notes that at this time he was found to be devoid of 'political craft' and which showed an incapacity for leadership.[19] This took the form of 'temperamental outbreaks, snubs for life-long workers in the cause [of Ireland] and rejection of their advice'.[20] Coogan similarly records his arrogance and 'failure to consult with anyone', despite a poor knowledge of American politics and history.[21] By all accounts, in negotiations de Valera seemed an 'impossible person'.[22]

Lack of empathy was also manifest in his dealings with Protestants in Northern Ireland. According to Coogan, he was never capable of 'empathising very deeply' with Ulster Protestants and showed a 'consistently ungenerous spirit towards them'.[23] A remark that demonstrates the point came from Lady Craig, wife of the then Prime Minister of Northern Ireland, Sir James Craig. She described a letter sent to her husband in 1921 requesting a meeting with him (on the basis that he was a representative of a so-called 'minority group' in Ireland): 'as sheer impertinence it could hardly be beaten'.[24] Moreover, Coogan notes how de Valera's outlook was to have appalling consequences in terms of campaigns of terrorism and violence in Northern Ireland in the long term.[25]

Clearly, de Valera's inability to interact with peers made him less aware of the human consequences of his actions. Undoubtedly an 'ideologue' as described by Whitaker,[26] he was concerned with creating a perfect state as he envisioned one to be. Indeed, Coogan concludes that he 'did little that was useful and much that was harmful' during his time in office, especially on issues relating to emigration, partition and the economy.[27] Because of his inherent social impairment, the critical nature of these issues was not obvious to him. However, although his idealism was rigid, and, according to Ryan, was served by an often puzzling personality, it was 'never ignoble'.[28] There was a simplicity to de Valera, commonly found in those with HFA/ASP, which made him fail to see the complexities that life posed for others.

In the same way, Yeats expressed the view that de Valera was 'a living argument rather than a living man. All propaganda, no human life.'[29] Curiously, given the social impairment that Yeats displayed, he predicted the consequences of de Valera's outlook, remarking that 'he will fail through not having enough human life to judge the human life in others. He will ask too much of everyone and will ask it without charm.'[30] Undoubtedly, 'lacking in humanity' is a term commonly attributed to people manifesting the social impairment of HFA/ASP. Certainly it was so in Yeats's own case. T. Ryle Dwyer, too, refers to the lack of humanity in de Valera: 'if behind the cold, impersonal countenance of the subject of this biography, there seems to be no real humanity, possibly it's because there was none'.[31] Arguably, this lack of empathy resulted in the country being plunged into a horrific Civil War. Political reportage at the time cited it as 'a criminal attempt to divide the Irish nation'.[32]

A deep rivalry existed between de Valera and the other great Irish political and military leader of the time, Michael Collins. Their outlook and personality showed a marked difference. Indeed, Coogan makes the point that de Valera did not have the 'human qualities of Collins' because he was 'more reserved, a scholarly type' and regarded as being 'cold and controlled'.[33] Certainly, de Valera was capable of being 'tactless and abrasive' and 'aloof' according to Coogan.[34] In particular, during the uprising in 1916 against the British, there was 'little bonding' between him and other soldiers, who were largely working-class men.[35] Clearly, he distanced himself from his peers, expressing little desire for social interaction. As a student at Blackrock College, there is evidence of his isolating behaviour, given that he was 'something of an outsider' according to his peers.

There is also evidence to suggest that de Valera lacked social cues and showed socially inappropriate behaviour. According to Whittaker, de Valera had no 'social graces'.[36] Certainly, the above-mentioned lunch at Blackrock College, where he described in great detail to students a corpse being eaten by worms, indicates his socially inappropriate behaviour.[37] Time after time de Valera showed an 'indifference to the feelings of others', as noted by Coogan.[38] However, de Valera himself admitted to being 'too sensitive',[39] which is a common response from those with HFA/ASP, for example W.B. Yeats and Wittgenstein. Not surprisingly, for many with HFA/ASP, maintaining close friendships is difficult. In this respect, Coogan notes how de Valera's 'acquaintances were myriad, his near friends few'.[40] Certainly, he had minimal interest in women – although he married and had a family – and he never 'showed any disposition to improve their lot in society' according to Coogan.[41] More than likely he was a misogynist. That said, he was a typical male authoritarian figure of the time.

All-absorbing narrow interest

There is clear evidence that de Valera was obsessional about his interests and conducted them to the exclusion of other activities. Like many individuals with HFA/ASP, his focus was intense and he had absolute single-mindedness.[42] Coogan notes that he had an 'all-or-nothing attitude' and followed a 'fearsome work schedule'.[43] Ryan, too, remarks that he had an enormous capacity for industry and was described as a 'plugger'.[44]

His dominating interest was, of course, Irish nationalism; at various stages during his political career it bordered on the extreme. Moreover, in the pursuit of that goal he became more entrenched in the affairs of state, and likewise his struggle for power grew. This is not dissimilar to Newton's statecraft. Throughout his life he was obsessed with Ireland having 'no connection with England', according to Ryan.[45] When constitutional means to freedom failed, he resorted to violence. As Coogan states, de Valera took 'a road familiar to many an Irish idealist – forswearing the ballot box for the bomb and the bullet'.[46]

After the Treaty of Independence was signed by Ireland and Britain in

1921, extreme nationalism became apparent in de Valera's behaviour. His public rejection of the Treaty was fierce and he made what have been called 'the wading through blood speeches', as Coogan notes.[47] The purpose of what Coogan called these 'fiery and cold-blooded' speeches was ultimate power:

> [De Valera] decided to utilise extremist support – the IRA – for his purpose. Criticism made him desist from the use of such wild and swirling words, but not from his policy of making use of the IRA until he got into power and a break became inevitable.[48]

Thus, his thirst for power became all-embracing. As Coogan observes, he became a 'law-giver who helped to bring down a civil war on the heads of his people' and 'incited young men to hatred and violence'.[49]

Given the autistic traits that de Valera invariably demonstrated, it is not difficult to understand his detached idealism. In many respects, he corresponds to Kretchmer's detached idealist.[50] Ryan notes that he was obsessed with a 'self-contained isolated nationalism'.[51] His principal of 'ourselves alone' was to give rise to a government policy of neutrality.[52] Admittedly, it spared Ireland the horrors of the Second World War, and the policy of neutrality endures to this day. De Valera's policy of isolated nationalism, however, did not always best serve the needs of the Irish people. Many commentators, including Coogan, have remarked on the backward-looking, peasant, parochial society that he perpetuated:

> [He] chilled and frustrated by constant appeals to peasant fear, to peasant pietism, to the peasant's sense of self-preservation and all ending in a half-baked sort of civilisation which taken all over is of a tawdriness 100 miles from our day of vision.[53]

Furthermore, Coogan claims that de Valera certainly failed to modernise the state and did not 'enrich Irish culture or bring Ireland into the mainstream of western thought, never mind contributing to that intellectual development' and instead promoted an 'isolationist, parochial' culture.[54] In fact, it could be regarded as a kind of 'autistic' culture.

Under de Valera's stewardship, his all-encompassing desire to reduce links with Britain made him blind to the economic realities that such a scenario posed. According to Paddy Lynch, foremost economist in government during the Second World War, because of de Valera's obsession with nationalism he had absolutely 'no grasp of economics'.[55] He had no empathy for the thousands of Irish people forced to emigrate, nor any concept of the poor state of the country due to his 'totally unimaginative policies'.[56] Ryan claims that he engaged in an economic war with Britain that had a detrimental effect on the Irish economy.[57]

De Valera showed evidence of repetitive adherence to ideals and interests. With a limited vocabulary, he talked chiefly of ideals and, not surprisingly, constantly returned to the 'same few dominating notions'.[58] Indeed, his approach to political problems was grounded in reason and logic, and reflected his mathematical outlook. Like many people with HFA/ASP he had a mathematical frame of mind and sought mathematical solutions to problems. This is unsurprising since a logical mind-set is often found in people of genius with HFA/ASP, such as Wittgenstein, Lewis Carroll, Einstein[59] and Ramanujan.[60] Throughout his life de Valera was preoccupied with archiving material, and, according to Coogan, displayed a 'propensity for storing documents'.[61] This suggests that the collecting instinct, common to those with HFA/ASP, was present in de Valera too. In addition, it can also be viewed in terms of a striving for immortality inherent to people of genius with HFA/ASP.

De Valera had few interests outside politics, his only relaxations being chess and higher mathematics, according to Ryan.[62] Indeed, higher mathematics was a lifelong enthusiasm for de Valera. During breaks at political conferences he would ask for the 'latest work by some expert in . . . abstruse sciences'.[63] Reading was another interest evident from an early age. Ryan has described how in childhood de Valera spent his time 'between his books in solitude'.[64] Coogan too notes that he was an 'indefatigable reader'[65] who, not surprisingly, restricted his choice of reading material to non-fiction. One government secretary of the time, Maurice Moynihan, doubted that de Valera had ever read a serious novel in his life.[66]

Imposition of routines and control

There is evidence to suggest that de Valera continually imposed his interests and routines on others, arising from a need for control. In his case it was ultimately for political power, whether as a revolutionary in 1916, leader of Fianna Fáil or President of Ireland. So great was his controlling power that Coogan describes him as 'cunning', while the historian, Professor Joe Lee, claims that he showed 'ceaseless political calculation' and 'labyrinthine deviousness'.[67]

While serving in the Volunteer Army that instigated the 1916 Easter Rising, de Valera was, according to Coogan, a hierarchicalist who insisted on 'strict procedural behaviour'.[68] Moreover, he had a 'mania for uniforms and drill, orthodox, regular army organization and tactics' in addition to being a 'stickler for routine and procedures'.[69] Understandably, his behaviour did not endear him to soldiers who served under him, and who later concluded that he was 'a man we didn't care much about. He was very severe on drilling, giving orders in Irish and none of us knew Irish. He would never make free, was always grim, and we would make fun of him.'[70] In general there was a rigidity and strictness to his dealings with others.

Naturally, such traits were useful to him while imprisoned following the 1916 Rising. Coogan notes how de Valera admitted that 'there are few who can bear up against the prison life as I can'.[71] Certainly, Coogan describes him as 'unbending and unbreakable' during his time in prison.[72] Indeed, at this time de Valera attempted 'to control everything going on around him' as noted by Coogan.[73]

De Valera's imposition of control earned him an autocratic reputation. Coogan points out that later, as Prime Minister, he had total 'control of his Cabinet'.[74] Interestingly, Ryan chose the words 'Unique Dictator' as the title of his biography. In fact, Ryan claims that de Valera was most undemocratic in his behaviour, whereby he gave 'lip-service to democracy and used the ballot to seize power and transform a machinery he distrusted to further his original programme'.[75] Moreover, he highlights his 'dictatorial attitude and his obstinate insistence on his own way'.[76] Again, it was a feature that would dominate his political life. While in the USA during 1920 he changed his title from '*Príomh Áire*' (First Minister) to 'President' without first consulting his colleagues in Dublin.[77] When he failed to exercise total control, he was prepared to wreak havoc, judging from events that led to the Irish Civil War. Coogan asserts that at this time he 'wanted to take over the military as well as the political direction of events'. He was prepared for 'disruption without responsibility'.[78]

The historian, T. Ryle Dwyer, drew attention to how de Valera manipulated his representatives, Arthur Griffith and Michael Collins, by sending them to London in his stead to conclude the lengthy treaty negotiations with Britain, knowing full well that compromise was inevitable, and that he was unprepared to accept partition over a united Ireland. According to Ryle Dwyer, de Valera actually told the Cabinet 'we must have scapegoats'. He later explained that he had selected Griffith and Collins because he thought he could 'manipulate Griffith and Collins from Dublin and use them as "better bait" for the British'.[79]

Given de Valera's lack of empathy, the sense of betrayal and antipathy towards him during and after the Civil War was widespread. According to Ryan, one of de Valera's own comrades in 1916, Griffith, 'sick to the soul, cursed de Valera as the guns boomed on'.[80] So too the writer Sean O'Faolain. According to his daughter Julia, O'Faolain took de Valera's hard line in the Civil War and 'felt betrayed when de Valera reneged on his own principles'.[81]

Absolute conviction and belief in one's own ideals is commonly found in geniuses with HFA/ASP, and de Valera is no exception. According to Coogan, de Valera placed tremendous reliance on the soundness of his own judgement.[82] Ryan describes it as a continuous 'domineering self-righteousness'.[83] Indeed, de Valera's narcissism was such that he had a 'sense of infallibility' whereby 'he was right, everybody else was wrong, and he couldn't be wrong'.[84]

For all his political genius, many of de Valera's actions, such as those relating to economics and partition, were not well thought out. Ryan reasons that de Valera usurped 'the right to speak and act for Ireland'.[85] In fact, he showed little regard for democracy, instead having 'the whole alphabet of autocracy'.[86] Arguably, de Valera's arrogance and narcissism, in addition to his grandiosity, were seen in his inability to see things from other people's point of view, or even to respect their point of view. Both Coogan and Ryan attest to his breathtaking arrogance. Certainly, this was evident in his statement 'I had only to examine my own heart and it told me straight off what the Irish people wanted'.[87] He never questioned his powers of judgement, regarding himself as a good 'judging machine'.[88] Indeed, Ryan remarks that 'he would not accept the will of the people' when the people of Ireland voted to accept the treaty between Ireland and Britain.[89] Clearly, he believed that he knew better than the Irish people what was good for them and, according to Ryan, 'if individual freedom interfered with his sacred formulas' then it had to be sacrificed.[90] Unquestionably, de Valera felt he was a symbol of the republic.[91]

It is worth noting that de Valera's perception of reality was sometimes skewed. Effectively, he had difficulty differentiating between fact and fiction. This relates to the theory-of-mind deficit that can occur in HFA/ASP. Ryan notes how he had a remarkable tendency to 'regard something as either not having happened until he said it had, or, *per contra*, not having taken place at all if he so decided'.[92] Coogan, too, relates how de Valera dealt with the semantics of fact. He notes how there was a difference between 'a fact and a De Valera fact – that is, one that should be believed'.[93] Indeed, according to Ryan, de Valera spurned facts when it suited him.[94]

His sense of infallibility was evident in the way he conducted business. Coogan describes him as having a 'hard-headedness in business and a self-reliance bordering in the arrogant'.[95] Clearly, he was forceful towards his peers, as observed by one participant in the discussions between de Valera and Irish-Americans during the 1920s:

> [He has] an unconscious contempt or seem[s] to have such for the opinions of others. The Chief presides and does all the talking. Has a habit of getting on to side issues and shutting off people who wish to speak and thus makes a bad impression, if not sometimes enemies. Tends to force his own opinions without hearing from the other fellows and thus thinks he has co-operation when he only gets silent acquiescence.[96]

Among Irish-Americans his sanity was often questioned and indeed it was considered that he might be 'labouring under some psychopathic condition' or that he was 'crazy'.[97] Generally speaking, people with HFA/ASP are frequently likened to madmen by their peers or the public. Hans Asperger used the term 'autistic psychopathy' to describe them.

In exercising control, de Valera proved to be highly perfectionistic. Ryan described him as the 'implacable doctrinaire' with his 'logic-chopping' and 'quibblings'.[98] Coogan, too, describes his 'pedantry',[99] whereby he was 'very much a nit-picker'.[100] This was evident in his preoccupation with exactness. Ryan also notes how he showed 'a certain precision over commas, and the poetic shades of meaning'.[101] Moreover, Ryan describes him as 'formulistic . . . remote . . . niggling on details'.[102] In the 1920s, as Prime Minister, he supervised the 'minute details of the different departments' of government.[103] Coogan notes how he was forever drafting and re-drafting the answers to parliamentary questions.[104] His frequent interruptions to quibble over trivial points, whether during parliamentary business or in political negotiations, often impeded progress. According to Coogan, during the debate in the Dáil (Parliament) after the treaty was signed, he made '250 interruptions, relying on his prestige to ride roughshod over the procedures of the debate'.[105] Lloyd George stated that negotiating with him was like 'sitting on a merry-go-round and trying to catch up with the swing in front'.[106]

Another area where de Valera exerted ultimate control was the newspaper, *The Irish Press*, which was fund-aided by Irish-Americans. In discussing the setting-up of the paper, one crucial question de Valera asked, according to O'Brien, was 'How do you control it?'[107]

It was de Valera himself who drew up the company's carefully drafted articles of association, securing for himself the most powerful position on the board – that of controlling director – and allowing him to keep the post for as long as he saw fit. The position was not subject to re-election and on the death, resignation or incapacity of the controlling director, the director to whom he chose to transfer his powers automatically became controlling director. It was in this way that the de Valera stranglehold of the Press company was cast in stone. As the position of controlling director also incorporated the powerful positions of editor-in-chief and the managing director, it meant that de Valera had complete control of the editorial content of the paper as well as over the appointment of all staff. In effect, the controlling director had 'sole and absolute control of the public and political policy of the company and of the editorial management thereof and of all newspapers, pamphlets or other writings which may be from time to time owned, published, circulated or printed by the said company'. In addition, the controlling director could 'appoint and at his discretion, remove or suspend all editors, sub-editors, reporters, writers, contributors of news or information and all such other people as may be employed in or connected with the editorial department and may determine their duties and fix their salaries and or emoluments'.[108]

Clearly, in these circumstances, de Valera had wide-ranging control of the newspaper. Coogan claims that de Valera ran the newspaper in a highly parsimonious way.[109] However, it later emerged that he had amassed a considerable fortune from its operation. None the less, when called to account for his substantial shareholding, de Valera stated in the Dáil that 'I have no financial interest in *The Irish Press*'.[110] That he could simultaneously discredit the office of Taoiseach (Prime Minister) by such a conflict of interest shows once again that fact and fiction were not clearly delineated. Certainly, he showed some similarity with Newton in his thirst for power and prestige, but also in avoiding all ostentatious displays of wealth.

Nobody is exempt from a dishonest action and no human being has a complete monopoly on honesty. This goes for people with HFA/ASP as for every other human being. In terms of de Valera's own personal logic he was not dishonest. He couldn't see a difference, regarding conflict of interest, between a politician running a newspaper and anybody else running a newspaper. Of course Scragg and Shah[111] have shown that a small minority of people with Asperger's syndrome can be criminal. It is not an all-or-none situation, but my experience has been that people with HFA/ASP by and large tend to be more honest than the average population.

Co-morbidity

The level of co-morbidity in de Valera's life is worth noting, especially that relating to psychopathology. During the 1916 Rising it was claimed that he had a 'nervous breakdown'. Coogan relates how eyewitnesses recalled seeing 'a tall, gangling figure in green Volunteer uniform and red socks running around day and night, without sleep, getting trenches dug, giving contradictory orders and forgetting the password so that he nearly got himself shot'.[112] Coogan points out that he clearly was 'too far gone in anxiety and exhaustion' to evaluate the military situation.[113] Possibly, de Valera's condition in this case was induced by the stress and anxiety of the situation.

In addition, de Valera experienced sleep problems during his life, particularly recurrent sleepiness. Coogan notes how he had a tendency to fall asleep while studying.[114]

Non-verbal communication

There are many accounts of de Valera's enigmatic and eccentric behaviour, features commonly associated with HFA/ASP. Undoubtedly, he was an oddity, strange in appearance, manner and dress. For this reason his behaviour, especially when holding political office, tended to confuse and indeed anger many citizens. Ryan points out that it is 'difficult to label him' and he remains 'incalculable' and that he was a 'baffling figurehead'.[115] Coogan, too, notes that while growing up he was regarded as an 'odd bod'.[116]

De Valera's peers at Blackrock College remember him being 'idiosyncratic' as far as sport was concerned. On one occasion when he was captain of the rugby team, the team lost because he insisted in taking all the place kicks himself.[117] In 1916, while waiting to be executed, he took the news of his reprieve with a surprising calm. Before being told his death sentence had been commuted to imprisonment, he had been reading St Augustine's *Confessions*, and afterwards he thanked the gaoler for the news and went back to his reading.[118]

Arguably, one of his most bizarre and controversial actions was his response to Hitler's death. Following Hitler's suicide in 1945, he went to the German Embassy in Dublin to express his condolences to the ambassador. This event was highly bizarre. Even on the international stage, de Valera's enigmatic behaviour was puzzling. According to Coogan, following a meeting between de Valera and an official of the International Monetary Fund, Charles Merwin, de Valera was described as a 'strange man'.[119]

His style of dress was also unusual. Ryan stated that his clothes 'of rough home-spun also made him conspicuous; and he often wore a most unusual cap, with a prominent peak and flap folded across the top, rather like an airman's helmet'.[120] Coogan, too, notes how he was described as cutting a 'striking, rather eccentric figure'[121] with an 'austere manner and unusual appearance [that] set him apart'.[122]

There is evidence to suggest that de Valera displayed both limited facial expression and inappropriate expression, common in those with HFA/ASP. The impression of a stony-faced de Valera is given by Robert Kee. He quotes from O'Faolain, who likened de Valera to 'a Roman spear, with a voice like a cracked or muffled bell, and an ordered restraint in his looks, as if all lusciousness had been pared away by bitter experience'.[123] Certainly, many commentators have noted his seriousness; Ryan describes him as 'a very serious-looking man . . . with a long nose and spectacles, and a strangely foreign expression'.[124]

In all likelihood de Valera had an 'autistic charm' that captivated those around him. Noel Browne has pointed to the 'awesome charisma' of de Valera. Moreover, he had the 'air of an Archangel' and gave the impression that he never made a mistake in his entire political career. Undeniably, he had a profound effect on others, impressed as they were by his political genius and originality of thought. Certainly, his originality struck Lloyd George quite forcibly; he remarked that 'frankly, he had never seen anything quite like him . . . Mr de Valera was perfectly unique, and the poor distracted world had a good right to be profoundly thankful that he was unique'. Indeed, such was the effect on his peers that de Valera, like Wittgenstein and other geniuses, was surrounded by utterly devoted followers.

Ryan notes how communication with him was conducted through intermediaries: 'it was only possible through worshipful and eloquent acolytes who cultivated the art of saying nothing at length and handed out typewritten answers to questions borne reverently' to him.[125] Moreover, the awe that de Valera engendered helped him control his Cabinet 'through parallel reins of awe and comradeship'.[126]

The one-time republican leader, Ernie O'Malley, also described de Valera's powerful effect on others: 'any intelligent person coming into de Valera's enormous force field, encountering his extraordinary facility for demonstrating that black was white and vice versa, could be led to a denial of reality'.[127] Interestingly, Wittgenstein also had enormous 'force fields'; this effect is associated with autism.

Clearly, de Valera too had an extraordinary effect on the nation as a whole, ensuring he served in high office for the greater part of his life. The extent to which the nation held de Valera in high esteem and beyond reproach is illustrated in a civil case that he brought against Oliver St John Gogarty. The case went against Gogarty. A. Norman Jeffares noted that Gogarty:

> must also have been depressed by the way the jurors had voted in the libel action. J.B. Lyons records how it was said that a juryman had insisted, 'Whatever about the Jewman, he must be made to pay for what he said about de Valera'.[128]

De Valera's success as a political leader, despite his shortsightedness in foreign and economic affairs, was without doubt impressive. The source of his commanding power is attributed to various elements, as observed by Whitaker: 'he had leadership qualities. He wasn't Irish in his manner. He had the strange name, 1916, the mathematics. It all inspired awe.'[129] His awe-inspiring nature and the inevitable power he wielded also had religious connotations. He was variously described as a sort of 'lay cardinal'[130] and a 'lay pontiff'.[131] The clerical association is not surprising. Certainly, it could be said that de Valera had a religious disposition, evident from his staunch Catholic upbringing. Indeed, he considered joining the priesthood as a young adult.[132] Certainly, it could be argued that there was never a closer alliance of Church and State in Ireland than during de Valera's tenure. Archbishop Lefebvre described de Valera as 'the ideal Christian statesman'.[133]

Ryan notes the appearance of the 'alert, tall, spare, well-knit figure, dark, clear, thoughtful eyes, gracious and aloof manner suggest rather the monkish recluse than the fighter'.[134] Moreover, Ryan claims that in personality de Valera showed a strong 'asceticism and rigidity',[135] in addition to 'the quality of stoicism'.[136] These features are certainly in keeping with the attraction for the supernatural and the spiritual manifested in those with HFA/ASP. Certainly, the austerity is prominent; Ryan describes him as 'austere' with 'more than a hint of force in reserve'. During the 1916 Rising his bravery inspired many of his fellow soldiers. According to Ryan, he showed an 'indifference to his own personal fate, made the most lasting impression on all who met him at this time [and] he cared not whether the roof collapsed over his head'.[137] An alternative view is presented above. He was an enigmatic dictator – a man with HFA/ASP. This gives a new perspective on his behaviour during the course of his life.

Conclusion

De Valera's HFA/ASP seriously limited his political contribution. His narrow autistic outlook seriously damaged the development of Ireland. He lived 'in his head', and showed lack of empathy with the underprivileged. He devoted his life to personal power and control.

De Valera would also meet the criteria for narcissistic personality disorder. He had a grandiose sense of his own self-importance, was arrogant, believed that he was special and unique, and had a tremendous sense of entitlement. He was interpersonally exploitive and lacked empathy. Nevertheless, HFA/ASP is the preferred diagnosis.

Chapter 7

William Butler Yeats

The genius of the poet and playwright William Butler Yeats, who was awarded the Nobel Prize for Literature in 1923, is well recognised. Indeed, he has been described as the dominant poet of our time by biographer Richard Ellmann. His work is renowned for its sheer beauty and symbolism, and for its Irish nationalism, with a deep love of Irish myth and landscape. Born in 1865 in Dublin, Yeats had an unconventional upbringing and demonstrated evidence of HFA/ASP. Many biographers, notably Ellmann, have drawn attention to Yeats' tendency to construct myths, earning him a reputation as 'the Poet of Shadows'.[1] Keith Alldritt claims that Yeats was a master craftsman, and that one of his most skilful constructs was his own image. He distinguished himself in many fields; in the arts as poet, playwright, painter, theatre director and occultist, and as a political figure serving the newly established Irish state as senator during the 1920s.

Family background

Yeats inherited many family characteristics that shaped his genius as a poet. There appear to be strong indications that his relatives also displayed autistic-like behaviour. Yeats' paternal grandfather, William Butler Yeats, was a deeply orthodox rector of the Church of Ireland and Yeats' father was a complete sceptic. As a result Yeats developed, according to Ellmann, 'an eccentric faith somewhere between his grandfather's orthodox belief and his father's unorthodox disbelief'.[2] His grandfather was described as 'a remarkable man',[3] but his vanity was extreme: Ellmann notes that he was 'so dandiacal that he ripped three pairs of riding breeches in a day because he insisted upon wearing them so tight'.[4] Moreover, Ellmann claims that he was an 'unusual clergyman'.[5] It is possible that he showed signs of Asperger's syndrome. On one occasion he boxed his son's (Yeats' father's) ears and afterwards 'shook hands with him and hoped he was not offended'.[6] Evidently he believed in harsh discipline; he sent Yeats' father to a school run by a Scotsman whose 'floggings were famous'.[7]

Yeats' maternal grandfather, William Pollexfen, showed signs of severe social impairment. He was a man with whom 'no one, even his wife, became intimate'.[8] There is also evidence of an autistic aggression. He kept a hatchet beside his bed 'in readiness for burglars'.[9] Yeats' maternal grandmother was deeply religious and superstitious. According to Yeats in his *Autobiographies*, childhood memories of Sligo were filled with the 'silent grandfather, inspiring fear and deference, of the quiet religious grandmother interested in nature cures, of visits of the strange melancholic uncles, and of nearly wild dogs roaming the spacious lands about Merville [home of the Pollexfens]'.[10]

There is much evidence to suggest that Yeats' father, John Butler Yeats, had autistic traits. Despite his family's expectation of a legal career, he switched to painting. He gained a considerable reputation as a painter but led a somewhat Bohemian lifestyle. Yet his constant search for an individual style of painting left him unsatisfied, as Ellmann notes 'he could never be satisfied, was constantly searching for the individual style as if for the Philosopher's Stone, yet it eluded him always'.[11] Furthermore, Ellmann claims that he was 'too exacting'.[12] This is indeed consistent with the perfectionist traits of those with high-functioning autism.[13] It was possibly also an autistic search for perfection in creativity.

Certainly, Yeats' father was a strange and eccentric man. He had little sense of financial responsibility, and this impacted on his family. His grandson, Michael Butler Yeats, notes how John Butler Yeats was 'incapable of making money' although a good portrait painter.[14] Alldritt states that John B. Yeats often did portraits of people 'whose faces interested him, knowing full well his sitter could not afford to buy the finished painting'.[15] Consequently, John Butler Yeats often disrupted any thread of family life by shunting the Yeats household between London, Dublin and Sligo, depending on the prevailing fortunes. Ellmann, too, claims that he had 'no mind for business. He always felt financial salvation was just around the corner',[16] also possibly indicating a naïvety associated with HFA/ASP.[17] Furthermore, 'he had an irresponsible eccentricity in his indifference to money, in his lack of success, and in his search for an intangible goal'.[18] The controlling element of his personality was also evident. Ellmann points to his stubborn nature,[19] while the writer John McGahern claims that Yeats' father took an active part in the education of his sons: 'he commenced the education of his eldest son, which became a long battle of minds and formidable wills that was to last his lifetime'.[20] In addition, McGahern notes how individual and independent he was: 'he disliked being forced to do what other people planned'.[21] This again centres on the issue of control.

John Butler Yeats also demonstrated an all-absorbing interest in his work, accompanied by self-imposed social isolation. According to Ellmann he 'worked feverishly' and in reality was 'a solitary man'.[22] Indeed, John

Butler Yeats believed that a work of art was the social act of a solitary man.[23] As mentioned above, he was a sceptic who believed that 'revealed religion was myth and fable'.[24] As a result he pursued truth, which was reflected in his work, both in painting and poetry. According to Ellmann, Yeats' father 'unable to rest easy with his scepticism, yet opposed to faith, exalted poetry as a form of knowledge which was independent of both'.[25] Additionally, McGahern notes that John Butler Yeats turned from the 'romantic pre-Raphaelite influences of his early work to paint and draw what he saw in front of him'.

In terms of language, it appears that John Butler Yeats was an accomplished debater and 'controversialist', who took delight in expressing extreme views in order to get a rousing response from his opponents, as noted by Ellmann.[26]

Many biographers have remarked on the withdrawn nature of Yeats' mother. Ellmann has described Susan Pollexfen as being 'so silent, so instinctive, so deep-feeling' that she couldn't have been more unlike her husband, who had 'sought the opposite to his own affable, argumentative, opinionated mind'.[27] Commenting on the deep, instinctive nature of the Pollexfens, Ellmann notes that they would have 'nothing to do with theorizing',[28] a feature replicated in both her famous sons and common in those with HFA/ASP. She is described as 'taciturn, withdrawn and gloomy like all the Pollexfens'[29] and 'sensitive . . . but undemonstrative'.[30] By all accounts the lack of desire to interact with peers was acute in her case. Brown describes her as an 'uncommunicative, apparently emotionless companion' to Yeats' father, and quotes Yeats' own words about his mother: 'she was not sympathetic. The feelings of people around her did not concern her. She was not aware of them. She was always in an island of her own.'[31] Certainly, as Yeats grew up his mother remained a shadowy figure.

Thus it would appear her genetic input was significant in Yeats. Brown states that Yeats was 'most a Pollexfen in his refusal or inability to confront in his writings in any direct way the pain of his childhood'.[32] However, this is largely untrue as the difficulties in understanding and writing about his childhood resulted from autism. Equally, the assertion that lack of maternal love gave rise to his inadequacies is erroneous. Harry McGee, in a review of *Georgie's Ghosts: A New Life of W.B. Yeats* by Brenda Maddox, quotes Maddox: 'the secret of Yeats is that his mother did not love him'.[33] I disagree with this view. I believe the secret of Yeats was the impact of autism on his life and work.

A large measure of eccentricity is evident in Yeats' relatives, notably the Pollexfens. Hilary Pyle elaborates on this point in reference to Yeats' uncles: '[Uncle George] had a tongue of leather fitted over the keyhole of his door in order to keep the draught out; and another, who designed the Sligo quays, gradually went mad, seeking to invent a warship that could not be sunk because of its hull of solid wood'.[34] According to Pyle, there also appears to have been a strong mystical trait evident in Uncle George's interest in the occult. This feature clearly was replicated in Yeats. Indeed, it is quite possible there were a number of relatives with autistic-like traits. Certainly, autistic traits were also evident in his brother, the painter Jack Butler Yeats.

Speech and language

Yeats showed evidence of delayed speech and language development. His language difficulties and peculiarities are well documented. In fact his mother's family believed him to be mentally as well as physically defective, having failed to teach him how to read. This phenomenon is not uncommon in people with HFA/ASP. Alldritt notes that he was 'slow in mastering his alphabet and learning to read'.[35] Similarly, Yeats' son, Michael, recorded that his grandfather, having noticed that Yeats could not read by the age of 9 years, considered him a difficult pupil, 'boxed his ears' and set about teaching him himself.[36] He also recalls that Yeats had 'a total inability to spell even simple words correctly ("gas" would be spelt "gass"). His punctuation also was peculiar.'[37] Alldritt notes that Yeats showed a 'conspicuous inability to spell and punctuate'.[38] This inability persisted throughout his life.

As with many people with HFA/ASP, Yeats' sense of humour was simple and juvenile. According to Ellmann it took the form of 'prankishness'.[39]

Yeats also displayed unusual voice characteristics typical of individuals with HFA/ASP. There are many accounts of his beautiful speaking voice, earning him the reputation of speaking in an 'affected voice' according to his son, who preferred to call it a 'Sligo accent' with a 'strong voice'.[40] The poet John Masefield was struck by Yeats' poetic delivery:

> I often heard Yeats's method. It is not easy to describe; it would not be easy to imitate; probably it influenced all who heard it either for or against. It put a great (many thought too great) yet always a subtle insistence upon the rhythm; it dwelt upon the vowels and the beat. In Lyric, it tended ever towards what seemed like Indian singing; in other measures towards an almost fierce recitativo. When reading or reciting verse to a friend, he was frequently dissatisfied with the rendering of a line. He would then say, 'no, no' and would repeat the faulty line with a more delicate rhythm, helping it to perfection with the gestures of his (most strangely beautiful) hands.[41]

Ellmann claims that Yeats had a 'curiously rhythmical manner of speaking' that others found hard to reproduce.[42] Equally, Anthony Cronin, in a review of Maddox, described Yeats as 'studied in manner and speech, unremittingly poetic'.[43] Certainly, this is classic HFA/ASP speech often characterised by unusual prosody. The slow, mannered way of speaking is consistent with HFA/ASP.

Yeats' schooling was erratic because of his family's frequent change of address. However, his home was largely in Sligo for the first 10 years of his life. Not surprisingly, Yeats was a poor student, as is often the case in HFA/ASP. Indeed, very few geniuses have anything good to say about their experience of school, and Yeats was no exception. According to Ellmann, Yeats found school 'pedestrian and demoralizing'.[44] Alldritt remarks that Yeats remembered his time at school as 'one of failure, misery and humiliation'.[45] He showed a clear lack of interest in many of the subjects taught, particularly history. According to Alldritt, Yeats said 'What could I, who never worked when I was not interested, do with a history lesson that was but a column of dates?'[46] He certainly failed to distinguish himself and was poor in classics but good, however, at science. The family wish for him to be educated at Trinity College Dublin was unrealised when he failed to meet the entrance requirements in classics and mathematics.[47] Ellmann notes how one headmaster was sure 'he would never amount to anything'.[48] By all accounts he was difficult to handle. Instead he became a keen chess player and was responsible for introducing a way to play chess secretly in class, a skill that spread rapidly throughout the school.

Like many others with HFA/ASP, he was bullied at school. Clearly, from an early age his eccentricities – collecting butterflies and moths and incessant daydreaming – made him a figure of fun. At school in England, where he was with boys of his own age, he was called the 'Mad Irishman'.[49] Ellmann notes how 'they laughed at his awkwardness and bullied him because he was weak'.[50]

Despite his poor performance at school Yeats was autodidactic, like many people with HFA/ASP such as Wittgenstein, Ramanujan and Lewis Carroll.[51] Certainly, as his life progressed Yeats educated himself in many subjects, particularly philosophy and the occult.

Social impairment

It is hardly surprising that Yeats had major difficulties in social relationships because of his autism. There is evidence to suggest that he showed severe impairment in social interaction. Certainly, during his formative years and early adulthood there was a desire for isolation and lack of interaction with peers. However, he did overcome this problem to a certain extent, becoming somewhat gregarious in later life. Many people, including his wife, tell of Yeats being 'shy' and timid.[52] Unquestionably at school Yeats was a loner; he 'felt himself set apart'.[53] Ellmann attests to Yeats' isolation due to a feeling of loneliness and powerlessness during his adolescence.[54] Moreover, Ellmann notes that Yeats remembered little from his childhood but its 'pain'.[55] According to Alldritt he took 'intense pleasure in being alone' and engaged in 'solitary wanderings'.[56] These wanderings took place in particular in the hill country around Howth, Co. Dublin, where the Yeats family had located following their return to Ireland, as described by Alldritt:

> He would pass the hours and eat and sleep in total isolation, on the excuse of catching moths. Sometimes, to his father's dismay, he would go and sleep at night among the rhododendrons and rocks in the wilder part of the grounds of Howth Castle.[57]

Evidently, Yeats was regarded as somewhat delicate and foreign looking and inadequate at games, which also set him apart from his peers. Ellmann claims that to cope with the Pollexfens' disapproval of his awkwardness and from a keen awareness of his own physical inadequacies, Yeats retreated into 'reverie and solitude'.[58] Nevertheless, this was an autistic trait. The reverie was indicative of a highly active imagination. Alldritt notes how he 'was a highly strung, imaginative child'.[59] In addition, his passion for poetry emerged, judging from a description of him by a schoolmate:

> [He was a] dreamy fellow, lackadaisical too, didn't go in for games . . . was a good talker. He would argue and discuss matters with the master . . . he used to spout reams of poetry to us, which none of us could comprehend as his delivery was so fast . . . rather fond of attitudin-ising.[60]

References to Yeats being aloof and remote dominate many accounts of him. McGahern describes him as 'aloof and imperious'.[61] Ellmann, too, highlights a peculiar remoteness in Yeats' autobiography, *Reveries over Childhood and Youth*. Yeats' old friend George Russell (Æ) attests to the lack of a personal tone of the recollections:

> His memories of his childhood are the most vacant things man ever wrote, pure externalities, well written in a dead kind of way, but quite dull except for the odd flashes. The boy in the book might have become a grocer as well as a poet.[62]

Brown, too, points to the autobiography as having a 'curious remoteness of tone'.[63] Certainly, this is an autobiography typical of a person with HFA/ ASP.

Yeats' aloofness and remoteness were often read as a sign of his inhumanity, which is commonly assumed about people with autism. Indeed, Brown refers to Yeats' effect on people – not always positive – with much mention of his 'unsettling cold nature, his distance from quotidian human warmth despite the passion of his poetry'.[64] Brown quotes one acquaintance of Yeats who was struck by 'a certain malicious vein in his nature' and thought his 'worst personal fault' was 'a lack of ordinary good nature'.[65] It was a subject that preoccupied Yeats himself. Responding to his friend, the poet Katharine Tynan's, rebuke about his bookishness, he explained that the reason he buried his head in books was that he was anxious about other aspects of life:

> I am a much more human person than you think. I cannot help being 'inhuman' as you call it . . . On the rare occasions when I go to see anyone I am not quite easy in my mind, for I keep thinking I ought to be at home trying to solve my problems – I feel as if I had run away from school. So you see my life is not altogether ink and paper.[66]

Furthermore, Yeats provides an explanation for his lack of desire to interact with peers: 'sometimes the barrier between myself and other people filled me with terror'.[67] Indeed, in 1909 when writing an unsent letter to Robert, the son of his friend Lady Gregory, he drew attention to his lack of social instincts. 'I have no instincts in personal life. I have reasoned them all away & reason acts very slowly & with difficulty & has to exhaust every side of the subject'.[68] Ellmann notes how he attempted to build bridges to 'connect himself with humanity',[69] which naturally were not always successful. Indeed, it is a typical Asperger aspiration. Rather tellingly, Yeats' wife always maintained that he 'had no interest in people as such, only in what they said or did'.[70] This certainly is common to many geniuses with autism, most notably Wittgenstein. In this respect Alldritt is correct in claiming that Yeats was interested in 'literary anthropology', especially as he visited peasant homes around the communities of Gort, Co. Galway to collect folklore. Certainly, this is similar to the activities of Bartók, who travelled about the Hungarian countryside collecting folk music and who also had HFA/ASP.[71]

Interacting with Yeats was not without its own difficulties for his peers. Brown quotes the Ulster writer, St John Ervine, who spoke about conversations held with Yeats during the 1920s:

> it is not easy to talk to him in a familiar fashion, and I imagine he has difficulty in talking easily on common topics. I soon discovered that he is not comfortable with individuals: he needs an audience to which he can discourse in a pontifical manner . . . I doubt very much whether he takes any intimate interest in any human being.[72]

This behaviour was typical of Wittgenstein and Kinsey too, where conversation consisted more of monologues than an exchange of views.[73] Certainly, people with HFA/ASP make poor listeners and are incapable of meaningful dialogue. Furthermore, Ellmann notes how Yeats admitted that 'I do not listen enough'.[74] When Yeats met Eoin O'Duffy (future leader of the Irish fascist party, the Blueshirts) in the early twentieth century, O'Duffy's wife noticed that 'they spoke on different lines and neither listened to the other'.[75]

Friendships

Yeats showed an ability to form and maintain a number of friendships throughout his life. However, the nature of many of those friendships was autistic. In general, he formed friendships only with those who shared his interests closely such as poets and writers, e.g. Æ, Katherine Tynan and Lady Gregory. According to Alldritt he shared an interest in cultural matters with Lady Gregory, a friendship that ultimately led to an Irish literary renaissance and the establishment of a national theatre, the Abbey Theatre. The lifelong friendship between himself and Æ was formed from their first meeting at Art College in Dublin, where the two were 'rebels against the actual, and, wildly hopeful, were intimate at once'.[76] Tynan, who met him in 1885, said he seemed to her 'all dreams and all gentleness'.[77]

Certainly, as he grew older Yeats admitted that he overcame his shyness somewhat. This shyness often made him hide behind masks, whereby he became the creator of multiple identities. Undoubtedly, it led to huge complexities in his dealings with people. In this respect, Frank O'Connor has described Yeats' relations with other men as 'a circuitous and brilliant strategy performing complicated manoeuvres about non-existent armies'.[78] In fact this is typical of people with HFA/ASP.

One of Yeats' most defining relationships was with the revolutionary Maud Gonne. His unrequited love for her was a much-recognised focus of his poetry. Certainly, his courtship of Maud Gonne was quite naïve and its failure depressed him. Naturally much of the depression stemmed from disappointed love; however, the naïvety and propensity for unrequited love is typical of people with HFA/ASP. For example, Wittgenstein similarly showed an extraordinary naïvety in his marriage proposal to Marguerite Respinger, which occurred a few hours before her marriage to someone else, she having had no knowledge of the depth of his feelings towards her.

Yeats' obsession with Maud Gonne meant that liaisons with other women were often idealised, resulting in a lack of appreciation of social cues, and inevitably doomed to failure.[79] Ellmann describes how he conducted his liaison with the woman he referred to as 'Diana Vernon':

> In 1895 and 1896, when a beautiful married woman fell in love with him, he spent the first year in idealized chastity, meeting her only in museums and railway carriages; and then, when they finally went to

bed together, he kept expecting love to end until finally it did, and he returned to his former hopeless adoration of Maude Gonne and to his twilit state between chastity and unchastity.[80]

By all accounts, Yeats had little involvement with women during his adolescence and early adulthood. His difficulties in social relationships were apparent in his affair with Diana Vernon. Ellmann notes that Yeats at the age of 30 years 'did not know how to conduct the affair, for since childhood he had never touched a woman's lips'.[81]

Marriage

Having reached middle age Yeats had an urgent need to marry. Lisa Jardine, in a review of Maddox, points out that in October 1917, at the age of 52 years, Yeats finally married. His decision was influenced more by astrology than emotion, which certainly would not be considered unusual in a person with HFA/ASP:

> For almost 30 years he had pursued the impossible dream of a lasting liaison with Maud Gonne . . . Time was running out for Yeats if he wanted to start a family to carry on his name. Besides, the occult sources he assiduously consulted had informed him that the autumn of that year was a propitious time for him to produce a son and heir. Casting around on the rebound for a suitable bride, he settled on an unprepossessing young woman just turned 25, Bertha Georgie Hyde-Lees, who was a member of the circle of psychics he frequented in London.[82]

In the conduct of his affairs Yeats often displayed socially inappropriate behaviour. On the occasion of his marriage to Georgie he thought it unnecessary to inform his two sisters of his nuptials, despite being on good terms with them both.[83] Indeed, Georgie had not been his first choice of bride. He had tried to woo Maud Gonne for many years, and then her daughter Iseult, all to no effect. This is another example of autistic inappropriateness. Furthermore, in a review of Brown, McGahern points to the 'doubts and hesitations' that accompanied Yeats' marriage to Georgie Hyde-Lees.[84] McGahern quotes Brown on the socially inappropriate nature of his behaviour:

> It was Lady Gregory who managed to bring the reluctant but lonely prospective husband to the sticking point, having first been persuaded that Yeats' intentions were in fact honourable, if ill-expressed. Some home truths must have been spoken. The mistress of Coole was

particularly scathing about Yeats intending to marry Hyde-Lees in the clothes he had purchased to woo Iseult (daughter of Maud Gonne).[85]

Yeats' misgivings were confirmed on the wedding night. According to Jardine, Yeats told his young wife that 'he could summon up no desire for her'.[86] How his wife coped with this information became a defining moment in their marriage. She introduced 'automatic writing', whereby, trance-like, she wrote down occult messages for the benefit of Yeats. It saved their marriage because the poet believed that his wife was his female inspiration or muse. Brown elaborates on this point:

> [automatic writing] was a gift she [Georgie] was to explore to remarkable effect in the early years of a marriage which might otherwise have foundered. For it quickly made her a daily focus of the poet's almost insatiable curiosity about the paranormal, about the possibility of a spirit communication, and gave her the means by which she might direct, without obviously appearing to do so, a conjoint exploration of their relationship.[87]

The question of whether or not Georgie faked the occult messages has been the subject of much debate.[88] Given that Yeats displayed such remarkable naïvety consistent with HFA/ASP, it would not have been difficult for her to deceive him. In this respect Yeats was little more than a puppet on a string. By all accounts Georgie was an extraordinarily mature, clever, sensitive woman, who loved Yeats deeply, and who was willing to save her marriage at all costs.

Without a doubt Yeats had the good fortune to marry her, as it turned out. She was the perfect mother figure for him, aside from being his muse. Moreover, the issue of supporting Yeats was a primary concern. According to Alldritt, Yeats 'was incapable of fending for himself'.[89] As is often the case in geniuses with HFA/ASP, their spouses or partners provide enormous support, nurture and security. Clearly Yeats' marriage was enormously important and successful, as his wife organised him and devoted herself to helping him express his creativity. Indeed, Ellmann notes that she partly helped him to emerge from his 'isolation and eccentricity'.[90] Jardine points out that Lady Gregory 'reveals him openly treating the liaison with Georgie as therapeutic, a restorative and remedy for his failing faculties'.[91] Equally he settled for 'a companionate emotion-free relationship' that clearly had a stabilising effect on him. Interestingly, Jardine points out that a poem from this period, 'On Woman', confirms this 'thoughtlessly patronising attitude to such a partner. The merit of a good woman is her capacity to obliterate herself in the interests of the well-being of the man.'[92]

This feature often occurs in the spouses or partners of geniuses with HFA/ASP, and is not necessarily restricted to women. Examples include the submissive partners of Wittgenstein, and the respective wives of Kinsey, Bartók, etc. Following his marriage Yeats, interestingly, chose to call his wife 'George', evidently more comfortable with the masculine form of her name. This bears some similarity to Wittgenstein and his close friend, Elizabeth Anscombe, whom he addressed affectionately as 'old man'.[93]

Father figure

Yeats' social impairment was most acute in his dealings with his children. Whereas Yeats saw his own father as being 'affectionate but intellectually dominating',[94] Michael Butler Yeats regarded his father as a 'remote figure'.[95] When Yeats died in 1939, Michael did not feel any deep sense of personal loss, as Yeats had always been to him a 'formidable, towering figure' and living with him was like 'living with a national monument'.[96]

In a review of Michael Butler Yeats' memoirs, Martin Mansergh comments that Yeats comes across as a 'distant and dysfunctional father'.[97] Yeats junior claims that he himself has no notion of what a 'normal' father is, i.e. someone who is 'young and energetic, plays with the children, goes on picnics with them, takes an active part in family discipline'.[98] Clearly his father did none of these things. Though Yeats was pleased to have a family, he had 'absolutely no idea how to talk to children' according to Michael.[99] On one occasion Yeats' wife tried to get him to talk seriously to his daughter Anne when she was 14 years old, but instead he embarked on an hour-long monologue with her. The attempt was a total failure. Michael also remembers that only once in all their childhood did his father get involved in family discipline. This took the form of reading aloud a poem, which left the children 'bemused'.[100]

As a father, Yeats was renowned for his socially inappropriate behaviour. On one occasion he accompanied his wife on a visit to St Columba's College, Dublin, where they were considering sending their son. Rather than enquire about entry requirements and facilities, he asked the warden for a detailed explanation of the state of the college drains. In doing so he thought that he was behaving like a normal father, but failed to think of any other subject to discuss with the warden.[101] Clearly, he was extraordinarily out of touch; nonetheless, it is an endearing and amusing story.

All-absorbing interests

Throughout Yeats' life his interests were varied but always pursued narrowly and obsessively. It is worth noting that as he approached his seventieth birthday his 'literary energy and creativity lost none of their power'.[102] This certainly is in keeping with many other geniuses with HFA/ASP, such as Wittgenstein, who have been highly creative right to the end of their lives. Similarly, Ellmann notes the frenzied period of activity from 1889 to 1903, when Yeats 'had so many interests and activities during this time, with so little obvious relation between them, that a strictly chronological account would give the impression of a man in frenzy, beating on every door in the hotel in an attempt to find his own room'.[103] Geniuses have an acute sense of death, and they need to produce before they die.

An affinity for animals is a common feature of the autistic person. Certainly it was evident in Yeats' case. Ellmann notes that as a child he became preoccupied with two dogs and followed them everywhere.[104] This affinity extended to many creatures, e.g. cats, dogs, horses, and, most interestingly, insects. The collecting instinct, so characteristic of the autistic person, is to be found in Yeats too. Like Kinsey and Bartók, Yeats collected insects. Particularly from 1888, when his family moved back to Ireland and lived at Howth, he took an especial interest in the work of the evolutionary biologists, Darwin and Wallace. He went on frequent entomological field trips and, according to Alldritt, collected 'insects and moths, in which he took a serious scientific interest'.[105] However, after a time, 'growing tired of collecting butterflies and other specimens, he roamed Howth still carrying his green net, but beginning to play at being a sage, a magician, or a poet'.[106]

Details on the all-absorbing nature of Yeats' interests are well recorded. By all accounts he had an extraordinary ability to immerse himself in his interests with an intensity of concentration. Frequently he lapsed into reverie as a child. It was a practice that continued throughout his life, becoming a necessary part of his creative process. The fanciful, wildly imaginative side of his character was apparent in Sligo, where his mind was full of heroism and mythology. It later became the basis for much of his early poetry. Alldritt notes the occasion when Yeats 'imagined himself dying a hero's death fighting the Fenians . . . He saw his first "fay" or fairy; it descended down a moonbeam towards him.'[107] He also imagined himself one of the heroes from the works of the Romantic poets, such as Byron and Shelley: 'I was now Manfred on his glacier, and now Prince Athanase with his solitary lamp'.[108]

Ellmann, too, attests to Yeats' daydreaming, an activity not without purpose. Yeats would have liked 'to dream the days away, but he also wanted to be a success in the world'.[109] He buried himself in dreams and in books.[110] In his youth, according to Ellmann, Yeats' mind was too 'addicted to reverie' for him to do well at lessons and games, where he was hopelessly inadequate.[111] Moreover, his dilemma was that he was 'naturally dreamy, poetic, and self-conscious, and therefore unable to act with the spontaneity of the man of action'.[112]

According to his son, Yeats was afflicted 'by extreme absent-mindedness'.[113] On one occasion at the Arts Club in Dublin he was so distracted that 'when told he had not yet eaten he believed this, and went in and had a second dinner'.[114] Michael Butler Yeats claims that at dinner parties his father became so readily absorbed in conversation that he wouldn't know what he was eating. On one occasion after eating parsnips – a vegetable he much disliked – he turned to his wife and said 'that wasn't a very nice pudding'.[115] His family were attuned to all signs of their father lapsing into creative mode:

> One afternoon my sister Anne got on a bus on her way home to find the poet already sitting in a front seat, obviously deep in the throes of composition. So she left him alone and took a seat near the back. In due course they both got off the bus at the family gate and, as they went in, he looked at her vaguely and asked, Who is it you are looking for?[116]

Indeed, Yeats' absent-mindedness was legendary. It was succinctly captured in a cartoon in the journal *Dublin Opinion* in 1925. In a classic 'Asperger pose', Yeats has his head in the air, oblivious to his old friend Æ passing him by on the street.[117]

Yeats' repetitive interest in certain topics formed the basis of his poetry. It is also consistent with the repetitive adherence to ideas and practices found in those with HFA/ASP. Certainly, his work is characterised by frequent questioning of the nature of human existence. According to Ellmann, Yeats 'keeps asking the same questions over and over again until they become profound: what is truth? what is reality? what is man?'[118] In this respect he also showed an imposition of control. Clearly, he was highly motivated, driven and obsessional in his writing. Furthermore, Ellmann says that 'few poets have found mastery of themselves and of their craft so difficult or have sought such mastery, through conflict and struggle, so unflinchingly' as Yeats.[119]

The character of Yeats' work was also influenced by his genetic make-up. His work *A Vision* outlines the spiritual and visionary dimension of reality, drawing from the occult and philosophy, and full of symbolism. *A Vision* reflects a logical mind-set and a taste for abstraction commonly found in those with HFA/ASP, characterised by an attempt to structure life into categories and cycles, which are largely repetitive in nature. Indeed, Ellmann points out that *A Vision* contains a lot of 'abstract schematizing'.[120] However, like Wittgenstein, Yeats did not attempt to impose a rigid, scientific system on his work. Ellmann adds that the system evolved in *A Vision* was one that had 'a sort of anti-system built into it'.[121] According to Pat Boran, Yeats had 'an obsession with symbols and symbolism [which] even led him to claim that "poetry and religion are the same thing"'.[122] Yeats' poetry is remarkable for its simplicity too. This feature he shared with many geniuses, such as Wittgenstein and Bartók, who made fundamental simplicity the core of their work.

Clearly, Yeats' imagination was predominantly visual. As a poet he had an extraordinary visual ingenuity. Moreover, the use of concrete images in his work is consistent with HFA/ASP, something akin to Wittgenstein's picture theory of reality. This is borne out in references to Yeats' autobiography, *Reveries over Childhood and Youth*. Ellmann quotes from Æ, who claimed that it was far from an autobiography but a 'chronological arrangement of pictures'.[123] In fact, this is typical of 'autistic biographies'.

The obsession with a higher order of reality meant that Yeat's poetry tended to discount material life. John Carey points out that his poems, 'like nearly all his great poetical statements, disparage earthly life'.[124] Of course, dealing with 'earthly life' is highly difficult for a person with HFA/ASP. However, Yeats is somewhat atypical. His attitude to money was unusual, and was quite unlike that of others with HFA/ASP such as Wittgenstein, Bartók and Ramanujan. According to Alldritt, when Yeats won the Nobel Prize for Literature he asked the journalist, Bertie Smyllie 'How much, Smyllie, how much is it? The answer was £7,000.'[125] That Yeats presented an atypical picture of HFA/ASP on this point can perhaps be best explained by the lasting legacy of his father. The poverty and hardship that the Yeats family endured through their father's Bohemian years had affected them greatly. Alldritt points out that Yeats was a 'dedicated careerist, a man of determined self-interest, a man preoccupied with money, a seeker after social standing'.[126] Moreover, Yeats was quite good at advancing his work, getting good reviews by using people for his benefit,[127] particularly in the 1890s with the poets of the Rhymers Club in London. It can be well argued that Yeats was quite narcissistic and, as stated by Alldritt, 'always eager to promote himself'.[128] Yeats was not unlike Newton in this respect.

Non-verbal behaviour

Yeats displayed several non-verbal communication problems consistent with HFA/ASP. His eyes were distinctive and the focus of much attention. Tynan described them as 'eager, dark eyes'.[129] A.L. Rowse observed the older Yeats as having 'a puckered look of a small child; weak eyes, visionary and estranged from the world'.[130] St John Ervine remembered him as follows:

> A tall man, with dark hanging hair that is now turning grey, and he has a queer way of focusing when he looks at you. I do not know what is the defective sight from which he suffers, but it makes his way of regarding you somewhat disturbing. He has a poetic appearance, entirely physical, and owing nothing to any eccentricity of dress; for, apart from his necktie, there is nothing odd about his clothes.[131]

Reference has also been made to Yeats' limited facial expression. According to Brown, Yeats as public man seemed to many – 'cold, aloof, curiously without evident affect'.[132]

There is evidence to suggest that Yeats had stereotypies commonly found in autistic people. First, he displayed repetitive motor mannerisms. These stereotyped or ritualised movements were accompanied by a dissociated or trance-like state that usually occurred when he was composing poetry. Indeed, this is a classic autistic state. Alldritt describes how he roamed 'the streets of Dublin . . . sometimes flapping his arms about as he recited or composed poems aloud'.[133] Tynan described their long walks around Dublin, where Yeats would 'flail his arms around in a violent way that . . . intrigued policemen'.[134] Second, the stereotypy involved a speech element that is highly unusual. Alldritt quotes from John Butler Yeats' recollection of the times when Yeats would compose poetry at home:

> oblivious to everyone else, [he] would start to murmur, developing lines of poetry. Then he would speak them louder and louder. And louder. Then, still utterly preoccupied, he would chant and declaim. Finally, as John Yeats remembered, 'his sisters would call out to him, "Now, Willie, stop composing!"'.[135]

The chanting and ritualised movements generally occurred at the beginning of a period of composition, which was likely to happen at any time, as Michael Butler Yeats pointed out:

> All the family knew the signs, we were careful to do nothing that might interrupt the flow of thought. Without warning he would begin to make a low, tuneless humming sound, and his right hand would wave vaguely as if beating time. This could happen at the dinner table, while playing croquet, or sitting in a bus, and he would become totally oblivious to what was going on around him.[136]

Clearly, Yeats had an extraordinary effect on people in much the same way that geniuses with great originality generally have on their followers. The brilliance of his work gave rise to his frequently being described as a deity. John Carey points out that Yeats 'wrote like God. He could put words together with such certainty that they seemed to have been graven on tablets of stone from the beginning of time.'[137] He was also described as behaving like a 'demi-god' during a quarrel over the editorial policy of the family printing business, Dun Emer Press.[138] Undoubtedly, in the twentieth century his stature as a poet was monolithic. And his other-worldly effect on people became widespread. When working on *Blake's Prophetic Books* with Edwin Ellis, Yeats unnerved Ellis' German wife to a bizarre degree:

she became alarmed by the shabbily dressed mystical poet who would throw his arms about rhythmically in her drawing-room, as though conducting an orchestra . . . On one occasion she threw him out of the house for, said Yeats, she was entirely convinced that he had thrown a spell on her.[139]

Certainly, his presence was profoundly affecting, not merely in regard to his mannerisms. Alldritt relates how a classmate stated that he was a 'queer chap' and that 'there was something quietly repellent in his manner which affected even his relations with his masters'.[140] Indeed, Yeats was aware of the effect he had on others, and 'acknowledged that people were put off by his posing and by his artificial manner'.[141]

Imposition of control

Imposition of control over his interests and those of others was marked in Yeats. Certainly, the issue of control was hugely important to him. It was central to his genius, as Alldritt remarks 'for an important part of Yeats' genius was his keen and often manipulative relationship with the turbulent life around him as well as with the turbulent life within'.[142]

In addition, Alldritt points out that Yeats had extraordinary 'determination and perseverance',[143] and notes his 'pushy single-mindedness'.[144] This was evident from an early age, when his autodidactic nature became apparent – a feature common in people with HFA/ASP. In later life Yeats' striving for perfection led him to rewrite his previously published works in prose and verse 'indefatigably'.[145] Undoubtedly his force of absolute conviction led to fiercely held beliefs. In fact this is typical of geniuses with HFA/ASP who force others to revise their opinions in line with their own, e.g. Wittgenstein and de Valera. Indeed, Yeats' wife remarked that 'everything had to be either geese or swans to him'.[146]

Similarly, Ellmann points to Yeats' controlling nature: he became 'a terrible man in combat, who could compel by sheer force of personality, or, as he would put it, by power of his mask, a jeering crowd into silence'.[147]

He was extremely controlling in relation, not only to his own work but also to that of friends and family. According to Alldritt he tried to control Tynan's life by planning her career: 'ever the shrewd, tireless planner of his own literary career, he also sought to organize hers'.[148] Alldritt notes how at times Yeats would 'seek energetically, even aggressively, to impose his will on others; at times he permitted others to compel him'.[149]

The frequent exertion of control made him extremely powerful. Mary Colum recalls one notorious event. At a riotous debate during the performance of J.M. Synge's play, *The Playboy of the Western World*, at the Abbey Theatre, Yeats dominated the audience:

who remembering that passionately patriotic play [Yeats' *Cathleen Ni Houlihan*] forgot its antagonism for a few moments and Yeats got his cheers . . . I never witnessed a human being fight as Yeats fought that night, nor knew another with so many weapons in his armoury.[150]

Preservation of sameness is also evident in Yeats, particularly in his dress style. According to his son, Michael Butler Yeats, as a young man Yeats would dress in an unusual fashion with 'a long black cloak, dropping from his shoulders, a soft black sombrero on his head, a voluminous black silk tie flowing from his collar, long black trousers dragging untidily over his long, heavy feet'.[151] His friend, the poet Lionel Johnson, described Yeats 'with his long, lank hair . . . a brown velveteen coat, a loose tie and a very old Inverness cape, discarded by my father 20 years before'.[152]

'Autistic aggression'

There are many accounts of Yeats' violent temper and aggressive behaviour, especially towards family members. This leads one to suggest that he possibly had 'autistic aggression'. Certainly, it is associated with his controlling nature. Alldritt points out that Yeats was 'a combative man with a violent temper that sustained him in many nasty quarrels . . . a brawler and scrapper. The arrogant, bullying, aggressive Yeats that "Lollie" [sister], and some others, provoked was, to be sure, not the only Yeats'.[153]

In geniuses with HFA/ASP, aggression often arises from a striving for perfection with a perceived lack of success and resulting hypersensitivity. Ellmann notes how Yeats, certainly in his youth, was highly sensitive – the 'over-sensitive young man who had built in his imagination the perfect love, the Castle of the Heroes, an Ireland made spiritual'.[154] Moreover, Ellmann remarks that Yeats went into long sieges of self-criticism from 1908 to 1910. In 1908 he began to keep a diary recording dissatisfaction with his life and his attempts at reformation.[155] This has echoes of Wittgenstein and Lewis Carroll, who displayed an 'autistic superego'. Whether or not guilt was the basis for such dissatisfaction is subject to debate. Clearly, Yeats' widespread use of masks to hide behind gave rise to a sense of deception. Ellmann notes that:

> in 1933 [Yeats] admitted that, though he had overcome his shyness a little, 'I am still struggling with it and cannot free myself from the belief that it comes from a lack of courage, that the problem is not artistic but moral'. Although of late years he had spoken more directly, he was still unsatisfied and felt that he had played his inner being false by dressing it in costume and metaphor instead of expressing it directly . . . Sometimes he was content to think his real self was in his verse. 'My character is so little myself', he put in a manuscript book, that all my

life it has thwarted me. It has affected my poems, my true self, no more than the character of a dancer affects the movements of a dance.'[156]

Identity diffusion

Yeats manifested the problem of identity diffusion to an extraordinary extent. Identity diffusion is common to many with HFA/ASP. Certainly, to the general public he presented several distinct personae: the poet, the dramatist, the nationalist, the politician, whereas Yeats the painter and occultist were less well known. Clearly, identity diffusion was central to his genius, and it was no surprise that Ellmann titled his biography of the poet *Yeats – The Man and the Masks*. Similarly, Desmond McCarthy highlighted the issue of identity in 1934 with his reference to Yeats' 'Mask or Anti-self'.[157] I believe that the mask or anti-self is a manifestation of his autistic persona. It is clear that from early adolescence Yeats showed significant dissatisfaction with his 'self'. According to Alldritt, as a young man Yeats spoke 'only of the terrible inner turmoil, the churning sense of inadequacy within. As he approached his twentieth birthday his sense of self was unformed, still volatile and a mass of contradictions.'[158] The multiple personae were arguably the outcome of a restless mind, rooted in an insecurity over personal identity.

Yeats' insecurity over personal identity led to an interest in the occult and astrology, whereby his belief in the transmutation of the soul could facilitate the self being remade again and again. In this regard, Ellmann notes how Yeats believed that 'the human mind had power to control the universe, to make and unmake reality.'[159] Certainly, justification for the use of masks by Yeats indicates the cognitive intellectual approach typical in ASP/HFA.

Yeats presented multiple faces to those he met, depending on the occasion, and not always flattering. Michael Butler Yeats remarked that his father was 'a man of many masks, and could project totally different images, depending on the person he was meeting or the circumstances of the time'.[160] The critic, Anthony Cronin, comments on the widely varying views of Yeats, himself describing Yeats as 'aloof, withdrawn, studied in manner and speech, unremittingly poetic'.[161] It is a view that contrasts sharply with that of Maddox. According to Cronin, her view is of a Yeats preoccupied with sex well into his old age: 'he is a rather cold-hearted philanderer, not to say womaniser or dirty old man'.[162] The issue of conscience is central to Maddox's portrayal. She claims that his conscience required him at the end of his life 'to reveal himself as he was, as a confused, vulgar, sometimes generous but often selfish old lecher'.[163]

Certainly, the issue of identity preoccupied Yeats when he first met Maud Gonne. Ellmann writes that when Yeats met her he 'immediately fell in love', and the question was 'which of his two selves should he show her? He had to show her his inmost heart, so with her he was John Sherman, the wild yet timid dreamer.'[164]

In later life Yeats showed a certain dissatisfaction with masks and the multiple personae he presented. Ellmann compares him to 'Melville's Ahab', whereby he sometimes wanted 'to break through all masks'.[165] This could be interpreted as an attempt by someone with HFA/ASP to make real contact with other people. Yeats did change, as people with HFA/ASP certainly can do. By his own admission as he grew older he confessed that 'he was not the same timid clumsy boy who twenty-five years before had put on a pose so he could face the world'.[166]

Poet

However, the outcome of Yeats' inner turmoil and adoption of masks was the refinement of his poetry. Ellmann explains the ambiguity in Yeats' work as the result of a divided mind:

> Given his sense of a divided mind, Yeats had to try to achieve in his verse what Coleridge called the 'balance or reconcilement of opposite or discordant qualities' . . . His shortcoming in the 'nineties was that he conceived of his art . . . as a see-saw sometimes between scepticism and belief, sometimes between natural and supernatural love, sometimes between action and the dream, sometimes between the peasant and aristocratic traditions.[167]

His marriage facilitated the greater use of masks through his wife's support and encouragement.[168] Had he remained a bachelor, it is unlikely that he would have become the Nobel Laureate poet celebrated today. Ellmann notes that 'had he not married but lived on in bachelorhood, he would probably have continued his indefatigable attendance at spiritualist séances and made minor elaborations in his rather confusing theories of the mask and of life after death'.[169] Thus it is clear that people with HFA/ASP can grow and develop.

Many commentators claim that by immersing himself in masks and creeds – often of an esoteric nature – Yeats distanced himself from reality, or more specifically, common-sense. Certainly Carey holds this view. He points out that 'as time went on, [Yeats] accumulated a bizarre panoply of creeds that could liberate him from the prison of common sense – Rosicrucianism, reincarnation, cyclical patterns of history based on the phases of the moon'.[170] I disagree that Yeats wanted to be liberated from common-sense. Indeed, he lacked common-sense and therefore could not be liberated from it. Moreover, with marked social impairment, lacking empathy and understanding, he was incapable of common-sense.

Thus, Carey points to a problem which I believe Yeats' autism can answer. The question of why Yeats should have recourse to disciplines lacking in scientific rigour that peddled nonsense is highly relevant: 'Why one of our supreme poetic masters should have needed the help of beliefs that would disgrace a fairground fortune-teller is a question that takes us to the heart of the modern poets' predicament'.[171] Like Wittgenstein and his mystical-laden philosophy, some of Yeats' verse, such as 'Sailing to Byzantium', is described by Carey as 'senselessness'. As Yeats got older, Carey notes that the poet 'longed to get out of his body and become an artificial golden bird, singing to the lords and ladies of Byzantium, and scorning/in glory of changeless metal/Common bird or petal'. In some of his poems it can be argued that the autistic-like feeling is indicative of a lack a central coherence in the poet (or, indeed, what Brown refers to as 'the absence of communicable meaning').[172] Certainly, it can be argued that Yeats was attracted to fundamental issues, in much the same way that Wittgenstein and many other geniuses are. However, Carey claims that Yeats' poetry has moved beyond rationality:

> his poetry is like music – not because it sounds beautiful, though it does, but because it conquers rationality. Listening to a Beethoven symphony, you do not ask 'Does it make sense?' because it has got beyond that. So with Yeats.[173]

Arguably, Yeats' poetic instincts rather than rationality were integral to his creative process. Certainly, I believe that what Yeats' poetry partially conquers is the autistic world in which he lived.

Painter, politician, theatre director

Given the family talent for painting, Yeats not surprisingly took an active interest in this pursuit. At one time he considered becoming a painter and embarked on a course of training. In his recollections of the poet, John Masefield remembers that he:

> trained for a time as a painter, spoke always of painting as a painter speaks, and from time to time worked for his amusement with paints and pastels . . . From an early age he was deeply moved by the beauty and mystery of the Sligo coast.[174]

It is worth noting that Wittgenstein, too, was fascinated by the Irish landscape, particularly along the west coast.

Following the foundation of the Irish State, Yeats became a distinguished senator and held progressive ideas on education and equality. He was also involved in drafting a new Copyright Act and helped develop a new Irish coinage (not unlike Newton's work in the Royal Mint), although he had little knowledge of 'economic questions' and 'practical politics'.[175] However, his verbal skills had improved over the years – he had gradually acquired great skill as a public speaker during the 1890s, according to Ellmann.[176]

In common with many people with features of HFA/ASP who are attracted to fundamentalist forms of governance, Yeats' political leanings were controversial. During the 1930s he was attracted to Mussolini's elitist government and got involved with an Irish political group, the Blueshirts, known for its fascist persuasions. Ellmann notes that Yeats also advocated eugenics and individualism during this time.[177] He refers to the period as his 'flirtation with authoritarianism'.[178] However, it can be argued that Yeats' 'hostility to democracy' was because of his political naïvety.[179] Indeed, political naïvety is not surprising in people with HFA/ASP as they lack empathy and show little reciprocal social interaction, as with de Valera and Keith Joseph. That said, Yeats later became aware of the dangers of political fanaticism.[180]

Another aspect of Yeats' character was shown in the establishment of a national theatre. He showed considerable skill in running the Abbey Theatre along with his associates, often dogged in their defence of the national institution. Alldritt highlights a famous incident where the Government incurred Yeats' wrath. In 1933 the then ruling party, Fianna Fáil, had a group based in New York that passed a motion deploring the Abbey Theatre's American tour the previous year.[181] The Irish Government threatened to withhold funding until the plays were made more acceptable to the public, i.e. with fewer scenes involving bad language, drunkenness, murder and prostitution. Yeats refused to change the programme. Alldritt quotes him: 'We refuse such a demand; your Minister may have it in his power to bring our theatre to an end, but as long as it exists it will retain its freedom'.[182] De Valera arranged a meeting with Yeats, and the matter was later resolved peacefully. Alldritt describes the two starkly different men thus 'the tall, gaunt Catholic zealot and the plump, white-haired mystic of Anglican origins whose life had been dedicated to spiritual unorthodoxies; the insistently logical mathematics teacher and the poet of passions and . . . the irrational'.[183]

Religious disposition and esotericism

An attraction to the supernatural and esoteric subjects is frequently seen in people with HFA/ASP. Newton had a considerable interest in occultism. Not surprisingly, the quasi-mystical origin of Yeats' work has made him a 'difficult subject' according to many critics, such as Boran.[184] Clearly, the spiritual–mystical dimension of his poetry can be attributed to his interest in the occult. Judging by biographies of him, he displayed a religious disposition from an early age. Ellmann relates how Yeats, as a young boy, would ask questions like 'What religion do the ants have?'[185] Moreover, he claims that Yeats as a youth was 'full of thoughts about God and intensely religious by nature'.[186] Similarly, Alldritt described him as a 'young introvert and dreamer who brooded on the mystical works of Mohini Chatterji'.[187] As an adult he joined an occult group called the Order of the Golden Dawn, which Alldritt maintained was one of the most important moments in his career as a mystic.[188]

Yeats' interest specifically in 'psychical research and mystical philosophy'[189] grew out of dissatisfaction with himself and an awareness of his own 'imperfections', according to Ellmann.[190] More significantly, it became the key inspiration for his poetry that was to intensify during his lifetime. As he grew to maturity, Ellmann notes that 'he wanted not merely to protect the inviolability of his own mind, but to ferret out more and deeper secrets which were withheld from logicians and literalists'.[191] Certainly, his obsessive need for the esoteric and the ambiguity that it entailed was central to his autism and genius.[192]

The spirit world was also a manifestation of Yeats' autism, wherein the cosmic logic he espoused did not perceive the threats that authoritarianism, fascism or eugenics posed for humanity. Arguably, the practices and beliefs associated with occultism facilitated his social naïvety. Consequently, many critics and commentators have raised the issue of Yeats' gullibility, given that occultism has a reputation for drawing people not always of rational mind. According to Alldritt, Yeats discovered that spiritualism had a special attraction for 'crackpots and charlatans'.[193] Certainly, Alldritt believes that Yeats' venture into occultism was bizarre in so far as it was 'theologically and socially perverse'. Undoubtedly, the ritual, magic and mystery associated with the Golden Dawn held particular appeal for the poet, according to Boran:

> for the poet who felt called towards mystery – as 'The Stolen Child' is called towards the wild – religion was a stew of folklore, oriental and occidental mythology, and a fair smattering of the mumbo-jumbo fancy-dress magic of the Order of the Golden Dawn, an organisation in which he crossed swords with the lunatic clown Aleister Crowley, and in which his own initiation involved, among other things, being bound to a cross.[194]

Maddox judges Yeats to be gullible for certain, but only because 'he believed in faith'.[195] The fact that he was interested in metaphor, which is natural for a poet, inclined him more than most. According to Maddox, metaphor 'predisposed him to believing in the spiritual and the mystic'. In regard to the automatic writing during his marriage, Yeats was fully confident that the source was supernatural. As Ellmann points out, Yeats believed in the 'communicators of the automatic writing as being spirits beyond space and time'.[196] Quite the opposite view is held by Maddox, who believes that both Yeats and his wife were involved in some deception: 'I think that they both believed they were talking to spirits but I also believe there was a bit of mutual conning going on and it's up to the reader to decide where the truth of the matter actually lies'.[197] I would not agree with this view. Certainly, I have no doubt that Georgie was deceiving Yeats, but it could be argued that Yeats was without guile as a result of his HFA/ASP. None the less, because of his wife's extraordinary intuition and ability to bring out the best in him, I agree with Maddox that the automatic writing 'moved [him] from being a good poet to a great one'.[198]

Yeats' interest in the occult led to many eccentricities. Ellmann refers to his 'eccentricity',[199] and Alldritt cites an occasion when he tried to hypnotise hens in a farmyard at Clondalkin, near Dublin city.[200]

Co-morbidity

Ellmann notes that Yeats talked about his 'dreadful despondent moods',[201] leading one to believe that he may have suffered from a recurring depression. Certainly, this is typical of the depressions associated with HFA/ASP.

Motor clumsiness

There is evidence to suggest that Yeats showed signs of motor clumsiness. His awkwardness and physical weakness as a child kept him from being a favourite of his mother's family, who were excellent athletes. It is possible that he showed motor clumsiness. Ellmann notes that it upset Yeats' father that he 'did not learn to ride well', nor had he the 'physical courage' to make up for his 'lack of horsemanship'.[202]

Conclusion

William Butler Yeats meets the criteria for HFA/ASP and resembles the other people described in this book in terms of his problems in social relations, problems with empathy and very eccentric interests. It is necessary now for literary critics to examine the effect of Yeats' psychopathology on his poetry and other writings.

Chapter 8

Lewis Carroll

The phenomenal success of the children's classic stories, *Alice's Adventures in Wonderland* and *Through the Looking Glass*, ensured that the author, Lewis Carroll, became a household name. According to his biographer, Morton Cohen, these classics – along with the Bible and Shakespeare's works – are among the most widely quoted books in the world today.[1]

Lewis Carroll was the pen-name of the Reverend Charles Lutwidge Dodgson, a deeply religious Victorian mathematics don whose life was mainly spent at Christ Church, Oxford. Yet, Lewis Carroll remains an enigma. From the many accounts of his life he clearly displayed significant features of HFA/ASP. Cohen considers him to be:

> a puzzle, on the surface a tall, straight figure dressed in black, formal, precise, exacting and proper in every detail of behaviour but his severe exterior concealed a soaring imagination, a fountain of wit, a wide-ranging and far-reaching appreciation of the human condition, and the knowledge of how to touch others, how to move them, and how to make them laugh.[2]

Like Newton, Carroll, as a man of science, had no difficulty in combining the scientific with the supernatural. His library contained many books on occult subjects and, indeed, he wrote widely about fairies. Undeniably, his genius rested in the primacy of his imagination and, as Will Self notes, 'a conviction that the fantastic is anterior to the naturalistic'.[3] Cohen attributes Carroll's creative genius to a combination of his 'stern self-discipline, his determination to control thought and action, his deep commitment to the child, his friendship with the Liddell sisters, his suppressed emotional life, and his font of endless energy'.[4]

Family background

Born on 27 January 1832 in Daresbury, Cheshire, Lewis Carroll was the third child in a family of eleven. His father was a formidable high church curate who was described as 'a pillar of righteousness and accomplishment'.[5] Carroll's nephew, D.S. Collingswood, recorded that he was a man of deep piety with a rather 'reserved and grave disposition'.[6] Not surprisingly, the household was dominated by an 'Evangelical orderliness and rule of denial' where the churchman ruled imperiously.[7] Despite the restrictive and punitive environment, Carroll respected and revered his father and became a 'faithful and dutiful' son, according to Cohen.[8] Nevertheless, he was torn between 'filial devotion and filial rebellion'.[9] Certainly, 'the grumbling-father theme' noted by Cohen was a regular feature of Carroll's work as he grew older.[10]

From the information available it would appear that Mrs Dodgson was devoted to her eldest son; he was her 'special pet'.[11] Indeed, in her role as wife and mother she has been described as saintly. Certainly, her son 'worshipped her above all others', while she was sensitive to his 'uncommon nature'.[12] Indeed, his first 11 years were lived in 'complete seclusion from the world'.[13] It was a veritable 'Wonderland'. According to Cohen, as a child Carroll had the strangest pastimes and 'numbered certain snails and toads among his intimate friends'. He also tried to encourage 'civilised warfare among earthworms'.[14] In childhood he was often seen 'sitting or lying full length on the lawn under the noble acacia tree in the rectory garden, writing'.[15] As she had provided such a sheltered upbringing, his mother's death brought considerable grief to Carroll at the age of 19 years.

Speech and language problems

Cohen notes that Carroll was an extraordinarily gifted man who 'in spite of a deaf right ear and an incurable stammer, lived a busy and productive life'.[16] Indeed, there was a strong family history of stammering, affecting both Carroll and his siblings. His stammer persisted throughout his life despite receiving long-term therapy from James Hunt, 'a foremost speech correctionist', according to Cohen.[17] There is no evidence that he had language difficulties or delayed development, in fact quite the reverse. He took great pleasure in playing with words:

> [His] early compositions in prose and poetry and his artwork showed that his handwriting was already remarkably adult, strong, confident; his vocabulary and allusions prove him well ahead of his years; and if his drawings are crude, they do not lack force or humour. So mature does he appear so early that one wonders whether he moved from childhood directly into adulthood, somehow skipping boyhood.[18]

Carroll was very much an autodidact; this was certainly evident during his time at Oxford. Indeed, as a small boy he was 'very precocious in learning' and insisted that his father explain a book of logarithms; at the age of seven he set about reading *The Pilgrim's Progress*.[19] Far from having a poor school record, Carroll excelled at school, particularly at mathematics. His genius was recognised early. The headmaster at Richmond described him as having 'a very uncommon share of genius':

> he is capable of acquirements and knowledge far beyond his years, while his reason is so clear and so jealous of error, that he will not rest satisfied without the most exact solution of whatever appears to him obscure. He has passed an excellent examination just now in mathematics, exhibiting at times an illustration of that love of precise argument, which seems to him natural.[20]

However, opinions differ on Carroll's style of conversation according to the Oxford don, Lionel A. Tollemache. Some claimed that there could be no doubt about its brilliance, yet it was very difficult to 'define or focus'.[21] Others claimed the opposite:

> Dodgson was not a brilliant talker; he was too peculiar and paradoxical, and the topics on which he loved to dwell were such as would bore many persons; while, on the other hand, when he himself was not interested, he occasionally stopped the flow of serious discussion with the intrusion of a discerning epigram.[22]

Like Newton, Carroll was serious in person and laughed infrequently, despite the celebrated humour of his writings. An Oxford colleague, Frederick York Powell, recalled 'the quiet humour of his voice, the occasional laugh . . . He was not a man that laughed, though there was often a smile playing about his sensitive mouth.'[23]

Impairment in reciprocal social interaction

Carroll showed impairment in reciprocal social interaction. However, despite his shy and sensitive nature, he did form friendships and during the 1860s led an active social life, with a particular fondness for the theatre and art exhibitions. Though his interests filled every minute of the day and kept him busy, Carroll's life was lonely and isolated. Even after his ordination as deacon he was the odd man out.[24] Cohen notes that H.A.L. Fisher, Warden of New College, observed that Carroll's 'intense shyness and morbid dislike of publicity made him a figure apart'.[25] Indeed, Carroll confessed:

> My constant aim is to remain, *personally*, unknown to the world; consequently I have always refused applications for photographs or autographs, as my features and handwriting belong to me as a private

individual . . . I so much hate the idea of strangers being able to know me by sight that I refuse to give my photo.[26]

At school he sought 'solitude and privacy'.[27] When sent to public school at Rugby he showed little interest in sports, was not athletic and consequently was bullied.[28] He was described as 'by many accounts unassertive, by some accounts, a recluse'.[29] The dramatist, A.W. Dubourg, described him as a 'quiet, retiring, scholar-like person, full of interesting and pleasant conversation, oftentimes with an undercurrent of humour, and certainly with a sense of great sensitiveness with regard to the serious side of life'.[30]

Cohen claims that he could be insensitive in some social situations, e.g. 'rude, rigid, and off-putting'. His niece, Violet Dodgson, reported that in dealing with his peers, many found him 'difficult, exacting, and uncompromising in business matters and in college life'.[31] He also showed a lack of appreciation of social cues and socially inappropriate behaviour. Indeed, he was rather like Wittgenstein in his manner of abruptly leaving a gathering. For example, Violet reports that:

> [He] had undoubtedly his foibles. For instance . . . he had a disconcerting way (on becoming aware that the informal tea which he was settling down to enjoy was a real *party*, with people invited to meet him) of rising and departing with polite but abrupt excuses, leaving an embarrassed hostess and a niece murmuring scared apologies.[32]

He also showed a lack of empathy whereby his severe morals and principles took precedence over the concerns of others. On many occasions he walked out of theatres in protest at what he believed were sacrilegious performances. According to Cohen, he surely knew that his 'uncompromising approach pained others, despite his effusive apologies, disclaimers and sympathetic language. But he had to turn a blind eye to the hurt he caused . . . his obdurate principles had to prevail at all costs.'[33]

Carroll had no personal interest in small talk of any description, and was often silent in adult company. In general he later 'shunned groups of people and came to prefer individuals'.[34] Not surprisingly, he was a poor lecturer and an unsatisfactory tutor. His lectures were described as 'dull as ditchwater'.[35] In common with many geniuses with autism, he was unable to communicate in a manner appropriate for students. Cohen notes that he had a 'singularly dry and perfunctory manner in which he imparted instruction . . . never betraying the slightest personal interest in matters that were of deep concern to students'.[36]

Cohen describes Carroll as a bachelor living a cloistered life within college walls.[37] Undoubtedly, it was a suppressed emotional life, with no desire for close personal interaction. Many of the 'dull and doleful verses' that he wrote, though not autobiographical, reflect some of his 'inner fears', according to Cohen.[38] The themes of 'unsatisfactory love affairs and frustrated emotional states' figure highly. This can be seen in one of his poems, 'Only a Woman's Hair', which was inspired by the single lock of a woman's hair found among Jonathan Swift's effects.[39]

Children

In common with many geniuses with HFA/ASP, such as Wittgenstein, Carroll related better to children than to adults. Indeed, he was very much at ease in the company of younger people. According to Cohen, people testified over and over again that 'when they were children, he was as completely at ease with them as they were with him, that they found him fluent, kind, open-minded, and open-hearted'.[40] Furthermore, Cohen claims that he was obsessed with 'child nature', in which he saw 'the primitive and pure, the noble and divine . . . he yearned for their favour and friendship'.[41] He preferred girls to boys and insisted that he did not like 'boys as a breed', but nonetheless made friends with individual boys. Collingwood states that Alice Liddell (the model for Alice in his books, and daughter of the college dean) was unquestionably his pet, and it was his 'intense love for her (although a child), which pulled the trigger and released his genius'.[42] Though he never married, speculation exists that he 'proposed marriage' to Alice, then aged 11 years, possibly resulting in the subsequent rift between him and the Liddell family. Instead, he chose a life pursuing child friendships and devoted himself 'to searching out the Elysium of childhood'.

Clearly, he was obsessed with relationships with children and when new ones were formed he 'clung to them tenaciously'.[43] Indeed, he heaped gifts on his child friends. Cohen points out that 'his child friends were more than a source of pleasure – they were his mainstay, as essential as the air he breathed'.[44]

His interest in children has sparked huge controversy. Photographs of them scantily clad and his later nude studies (albeit with permission from parents and chaperoned) have raised questions about possible scopophilia and latent paedophilia, and have led some to believe that his devotion was 'an obsession, a manifestation of some inadequacy, a maladjustment, even a perversion'.[45] There can be no doubt that indulging his scopophilic instincts in such a fashion was clearly a perversion. That said, Cohen attempts to put Carroll's actions in perspective:

> None of his child friends seemed to have suffered any scars from his attentions, and he certainly boosted their morale, flattered their vanities, helped them achieve the courage of their convictions, and in sum, did for them what their elders had neither the time nor the inclination to do.[46]

Undeniably, Carroll was aware that his relationships with children were out of the ordinary. For this reason he took precautions so that he 'compromised neither the child nor his own stern conscience'.[47] Of course, his conscience was continuously compromised and he suffered a great deal of guilt. Nevertheless, he only liked children who were 'loveable'.[48] Cohen quotes from Isabel Standen that not all children 'endured the torture' of the photographic process. Of particular concern here is that he 'put enormous energy and time into finding appropriate child sitters, then to cultivating their friendship while photographing them and amassing his pictorial oeuvres'.[49] He disliked children who were self-conscious or unsettled in his company. Cohen claims that Carroll had an 'arrested development', whereby he remained a child all his life.[50] Undoubtedly this was the case. Commonly, those with HFA/ASP retain a childlike outlook, which makes being in the company of children more satisfying. However, his cultivation of children had echoes of the behaviour of a paedophile.

Imposition of routines and interests

Carroll had 'a compulsive orderliness' and was systematic in his approach to organising his work and activities.[51] Undoubtedly a severe disciplinarian, he was 'a master of regulating his life, and superhuman in today's terms, in controlling his impulses during waking hours'.[52] Moreover, his imposition of routines and order affected those around him. According to Cohen, his 'devotion to the rigid laws of logic led to a rigid, uncompromising set of rules that governed his life and spilled over into the lives of others'.[53]

One of the most extraordinary things about Carroll was that he was an 'indefatigable record keeper'.[54] Apart from his diary, letter register, photograph register, and the register of correspondence when he was Curator of Common Room at Christ Church, there were lists recording meals he served guests, birthdays, offers of hospitality, where everything was done systematically and tidily. The most remarkable one was the letter register he began halfway through his life, which showed that in his last 35 years he had sent and received 98,721 letters.[55] He was fastidious in both mind and body. Cohen quotes from one observer who recalled that 'he always appeared to have emerged from a hot bath and a band box'.[56]

Clearly, Carroll was an extremely controlled man for whom 'ritual was all'.[57] This extended to his reading habits. He was a prodigious reader and read systematically, believing that 'thoroughness must be the rule of all this reading'.[58]

Carroll had many eccentricities that formed the basis of many routines, chief among which was the belief that 'Tuesdays were his lucky days'. He also had an affinity for the number 42, which he repeated in his works and letters over and over again.[59] Other eccentricities included his method of making tea. One of Carroll's child friends, Isa Bowman, recalls him 'walking up and down his sitting room swaying the teapot to and fro for precisely 10 minutes in order to achieve the desired brew'.[60] He also had sensory hypersensitivity. A horror of draughts led him to place thermometers near oil stoves in his room to check that the temperature was equalised.[61]

All-absorbing narrow interests

Carroll was quite obsessional and focused intensely on his interests, particularly writing, mathematics and photography. His colleague, T.B. Strong, observed that:

> [He] was a laborious worker, always disliking to break off from the pursuit of any subject which interested him; apt to forget his meals and toil on for the best part of the night, rather than stop short of the object which he had in view.[62]

This lifestyle, of course, is similar to that of many geniuses. Not unlike other geniuses discussed here, Carroll was a perfectionist in terms of the publication of his work. He frequently made 'insistent and uncompromising demands' on publishers.[63] Cohen notes that even in his late fifties Carroll worked 'obdurately, frantically'.[64] He drove himself relentlessly in order to write 'purposeful, serious works which he hoped would have lasting value'.[65]

The level of focus and concentration that Carroll gave his letter-writing was remarkable:

> The inventive powers that drove Charles in so many directions and enabled him to reach such exceptional heights were evident in his letter writing as well. Writing letters was a ritual for him; he thought carefully about them and executed them with the greatest care and enthusiasm. He often composed letters lying awake during the night, and for those sleepless hours he invented a device, the Nyctograph, that enabled him to take notes under the covers in the dark.[66]

Carroll also demonstrated preservation of sameness. At Oxford he always wore black clergyman's clothes except when boating on the river, when he would swap them for white flannel trousers and a white straw hat.[67]

Cohen notes how Carroll was an inveterate collector of gadgets, toys, games, puzzles, etc.[68] Moreover, he produced a vast amount of puzzles, acrostics, stories, and nonsense verse. In this respect his work can be viewed as a challenge to meaning. Cohen claims that Carroll's poem, *The Hunting of the Snark*, in common with the Alice books, is 'anti-meaning': 'It is more about *being* than *meaning*, listening than seeing, feeling than thinking'.[69] This bears a similarity to Wittgenstein's anti-theoretical, anti-meaning stance. As we have seen, people with HFA/ASP are often atheoretical. Furthermore, as Cohen points out, the Alice book has no moral; Carroll himself 'was fed up with the moral baggage that burdened children, that perhaps he himself had struggled with when a boy, and he was not purveying any more'.[70] In fact, the Alice books can be seen as 'antidotes to the child's degradation', where equal time is given to the child's point of view.[71] However, the absence of a moral makes the text incomprehensible. The effect of such textual confusion is explained by Will Self:

> All significant texts are distinguished by the preponderance of a single word. In *Alice's Adventures in Wonderland* the word is 'curious'. The word 'curious' appears so frequently in Lewis Carroll's text that it becomes a kind of toxin awakening us from our reverie. But it isn't the strangeness of Alice's Wonderland that reminds us of – it's the bizarre incomprehensibility of our own.[72]

If the world is incomprehensible for those without HFA/ASP, then it is even more so for those with it. At a certain level such works illustrate or highlight for us the incomprehensibility of the world.

Visuo-spatial ability

Carroll demonstrated the good visuo-spatial ability common in those with HFA/ASP. He could draw reasonably well from an early age, and many of his manuscripts were littered with illustrations and drawings. From his prolific output of photographs, he was clearly a first-rate photographer. Indeed, Cohen claims that he was the finest photographer of children of the 19th century.[73] In common with Wittgenstein and Newton, Carroll also showed an early interest in devices and machines, particularly trains. According to Cohen, as a child Carroll constructed a miniature replica of a passenger railway line in the rectory garden. He also devised a timetable and rules governing its operation. Cohen points out that as a child he 'proved supple in matters mechanical, creative in art, and a responsible leader and instructor of the other Dodgson children. With a carpenter's help, he built a marionette theatre, composed plays and learned to manipulate the marionettes for the presentation.'[74] Clearly, Carroll showed no evidence of motor clumsiness in these activities.

His railway interests continued throughout his life, and he became obsessed with 'the complexity of the problem of fixing time relatively'.[75] This has echoes of Einstein. He was also fascinated by novelty gadgets, particularly those showing mechanical and technological advances, and invented a chessboard for use when travelling. Undoubtedly, he was an inventor, which reflected his logical mind-set. Carroll had a first-rate mathematical mind and produced first-class creative mathematics. Cohen notes that he had a particular gift for 'ordering masses of information into intelligible categories'.[76] His great contribution to mathematics was recognised by Bartley, who regarded him as a good logician.[77] Bartley also confirms that Bertrand Russell and Eric Bell shared the view that Carroll had in him 'the stuff of a great mathematical logician'.

Non-verbal problems

Carroll's face had a certain peculiarity common among those with HFA/ASP. According to Cohen 'his face presented a peculiarity of having two very different profiles; the shape of the eyes, and the corners of the mouth did not tally'.[78] It is not unusual for someone with HFA/ASP to have two different emotions simultaneously on the face. He was also described as being highly strung. As an adult his child friend, Isa Bowman, thought him 'almost old-maidenishly prim'.[79] Others described him as a pensive, attractive young man.

There is evidence of clumsy body language, as observed by Alice Liddell. His gait was particularly marked. Her biographer records how, years after their rift, Alice would often catch a glimpse of Carroll walking about Oxford 'with that stiff and curiously jerky gait'.[80] Others noted that he walked upright and 'held himself stiffly, one shoulder slightly higher than the other; in his almost over-emphasised erectness there was an old-fashioned seriousness, an air of punctiliousness'.[81]

Carroll had a strong impact on his peers. Tollemache emphasises his brilliancy, whereby words could sway his peers: 'all he said, all his oddities and clever things, arose out of conversation [and had] an odd logical sequence, almost impelling your assent to most unexpected conclusions'.[82] His friend, the artist Gertrude Thompson, described the extraordinarily attractive quality so commonly associated with people of genius:

> I always had a mysterious feeling, when looking at him and hearing him speak, that he was not exactly an ordinary human being of flesh and blood. Rather did he seem as some delicate, ethereal spirit, enveloped for the moment in a semblance of common humanity . . . His head was small, and beautifully formed; the brow rather low, broad, white, and finely modelled. Dreamy grey eyes, a sensitive mouth, slightly compressed when in repose, but softening into the most beautiful smile when he spoke. He had a slight hesitancy sometimes, when speaking, but though [he] deplored it himself, it added a certain piquancy, especially if he was uttering any whimsicality.[83]

Mark Twain, on meeting Carroll for the first time, found him 'only interesting to look at, for he was the stillest and shyest full-grown man I have ever met except "Uncle Ramos"'.[84]

'Austistic superego'

Like Wittgenstein, Carroll had an 'autistic superego'. Cohen describes it as 'a brooding guilt'.[85] From his twenties onwards Carroll chastised himself for 'unfulfilled resolves, bad habits, inconsistency'.[86] Nearing his thirty-first birthday, his diary reflects his harsh conscience: 'here at the close of another year how much of neglect, carelessness and sin have I to remember! Oh God . . . take me vile and worthless as I am'.[87] Similarly, he wrote 'I do trust most sincerely to amend myself in those respects in which the past year has exhibited the most grievous shortcomings and I trust and pray that the most merciful God may aid me in this and all other good undertakings'.[88] Indeed, avoiding temptation became a constant concern during his mature years, which he hoped would be overcome through self-discipline: 'self-discipline must be my chief work for a long while to come'.[89]

According to Cohen, his diary contains endless self-chastisements with fresh determination to live a holier life:

> [His diary was] a steady flow of self-criticism, importunities, fresh resolves, pleas and prayers, largely adhering to the traditional pattern of Christian self-examination and resolution of other diarists. As the flow increases, however, a gnawing, deep-seated guilt emerges, accompanied by spiritual weariness and gloom: they are the cries of a man keenly dissatisfied with himself.[90]

His mind was preoccupied with guilt, and the idea that every aspect of his life had the potential to damn him. He believed that 'a stray thought, a light-hearted indulgence, a careless pleasure could instantly damn an unrepentant soul'.[91] Nevertheless, Carroll's diary suggests that his sins went beyond 'ordinary failings like idleness or indolence'.[92] It would appear then that considerable guilt arose from indulging his perverse instincts. It is possible that he used the pen-name of Lewis Carroll to hide his scopophilia and latent paedophilia. Certainly, in 1883 he wrote 'I use the name of Lewis Carroll in order to avoid all *personal* publicity'.[93] It is clear that while he wanted to give up his scopophilac activities he was unable to do so.

Nevertheless, Carroll maintained that his reasons for photographing children were entirely aesthetic. This is clearly absurd. The mother of his most famous sitter, Alice, regarded his attentions as over-zealous and judged him to be 'excessive, intrusive, improper and perhaps impure'. It is quite clear that she was absolutely accurate and perceptive in her view. According to Cohen, Carroll's strong and virile imagination must also have bred sexual fantasies. Certainly, he used all manner of dress for his sitters, which included:

> ragged garments, party frocks, fancy costumes – he also took them with no dress at all. Not right away, to be sure. In a sense he worked

his way slowly towards the nude child model. First he took a number, besides Alice Liddell, costumed as beggar children, with bare feet; he also took photographs of children in bed, lying in their nightdresses, propped up on settees.[94]

The guilt associated with taking nude photographs most likely led him to destroy them at a later stage. According to Cohen, most of the negatives and prints were destroyed and any remaining ones he asked his executors to destroy. By all accounts they complied with his wishes.[95] Clearly, he was aware of the perversity of his actions. It is hardly surprising that a 'current of whispers' about the nude photography ran through Oxford at the time.[96] However, with the advent of the dry plate process in 1880, Carroll stopped taking photographs and switched to sketching children without clothes.[97] Possibly, with his rigidity of routine he had no wish to change to another photographic format.

Religious disposition

In common with many geniuses discussed in this book, Carroll showed a distinct religious disposition. He was ordained a deacon in the Church of England by Bishop Wilberforce in 1861. According to Cohen, he had 'a fiercely religious cast of mind, a faith worked out by his own stern rules of logic'.[98] Moreover, his logical mind-set belonged to an age of Scholasticism, a view held by Canon Henry Scott Holland:

> [Lewis Carroll] ought to have lived in the Middle Ages in the balmy days of Scholasticism. His peculiar gifts of mind would . . . have enabled him to rout all other schoolmen, and to produce subtleties and dialectical terms which would have beaten and confounded the whole of Europe.[99]

Any levity on the subject of religion displeased him. His child friend, Ethel Arnold, recalled that 'the patriarchs, the prophets, major and minor, were as sacrosanct in his eyes as any of the great figures of the New Testament; and a disrespectful allusion to Noah . . . or Nebuchadnezzar . . . would have shocked and displeased him'.[100] Similarly, he showed gravity in matters of social injustice and conflict, springing from his sincere humility and generosity. Indeed, his great concern was with 'rules, natural, social, religious'.[101]

Not surprisingly, these traits made others uncomfortable. Cohen notes that his 'uncompromising moral stance, his harsh judgement of others, his occasional priggishness would be even more objectionable were they not leavened by sincere and abject humility and extraordinary generosity'.[102] His social conscience was acute, perhaps influenced by his father's sense of

Christian charity and the social reform of the time. It is hardly surprising that all conflict depressed him. Furthermore, Cohen points out that 'he opposed sham and greed', though politically conservative.[103] When he uncovered 'ugliness or injustice' he had no hesitation in putting pen to paper; he wrote 'scathing attacks and proposed reasonable remedies'.

Carroll, in common with many other geniuses, had no concern for wealth or pomp. His humility extended to his own funeral arrangements. He left instructions for his funeral to be 'simple and inexpensive, avoiding all things which are merely done for show, and retaining, only what is, in the judgement of those who arrange my funeral, requisite for its decent and reverent performance'.[104]

Conclusion

Lewis Carroll shows that a person with HFA/ASP has a capacity for enormous imagination, even if of an immature kind. His HFA/ASP and his immature personality – part of the condition – attuned him to children and helped him to be one of the greatest writers of children's stories of all time. He had a mechanical–mathematical mind, which is highly characteristic of people with HFA/ASP. Other features of the condition that helped him be successful included his workaholism and extreme self-control.

Chapter 9

Ramanujan

Srinivasa Ramanujan, born in 1887, was India's greatest mathematician. Despite a lifetime of poor health and poverty, he was a genius who independently changed the face of mathematics in the early twentieth century. His legacies in the field of analytical theory of numbers, elliptic functions, continued fractions and infinite series have reinvented modern mathematics. Despite his early death, recognition of his genius did come in his lifetime after he was invited to Cambridge University by the eminent mathematician, G.H. Hardy. He was subsequently elected a Fellow of the Royal Society in 1918 at the age of 30 years. Yet, from an early age he showed clear signs of autism.[1]

Family background

The genetic component of both his autism and his genius is evident. It appears likely that he inherited his talent from his mother's side of the family, which could claim a line of Sanskrit scholars. Her intense and obsessive nature was often the driving force behind Ramanujan and raises questions about her own autistic traits. In his distinguished biography of Ramanujan, Robert Kanigel noted that the games she played with her young son demanded 'logic, strategy, and fierce chess-like concentration',[2] which were similar to features which Ramanujan later showed.

His father, who received a tiny income from his work as a clerk, was a quiet figure whose presence in the house went largely unnoticed. He took little interest in the upbringing of his family, although this would have been customary among the devout Brahmin caste in southern India. None the less, when Ramanujan married, his father was not invited to the wedding ceremony. By the time Ramanujan had reached his seventh birthday, the household had lived through three sibling deaths. Yet the environment had little effect on the young Ramanujan. From an early age he showed signs of autism and was, according to Kanigel, a 'sensitive, stubborn, and eccentric child'.[3]

Speech and language problems

For the first 3 years of his life, Ramanujan scarcely spoke. The language delay led to a great deal of anxiety on his mother's part over what she considered his 'muteness'. It is worth noting that Einstein's parents were equally concerned at the language delay observed in the young Einstein. Nevertheless, with help from his maternal grandfather, Ramanujan quickly learned 12 vowels and 18 consonants as well as 216 combined consonant–vowel forms of the Tamil alphabet by 1892, dispelling fears about his 'dumbness'. Indeed, Kanigel points out that Ramanujan was a self-directed child who appeared to be quiet and contemplative, fond of asking probing questions such as 'Who is the first man in the world?'[4] These are the kind of childlike questions that, if adults are able to remain in touch with them, can lead to great discoveries. In fact, Einstein put great emphasis on this in relation to his own discoveries.

At school Ramanujan was far from being an exemplary student despite his aptitude for mathematics. He was not well rounded, 'flunked physiology', and, with the exception of mathematics, had a poor record in most subjects.[5] He showed no interest in studying and on one occasion scored very low points in an examination: 10 per cent in physiology, 20 per cent in Greek, 20 per cent in Roman history and 25 per cent in English. This was partly attributed to his narrow focus on mathematics and partly to boredom with other subjects. It is worth noting that recognised geniuses have done badly at school, particularly in non-mathematical subjects, and indeed this is a recurring feature of genius. Ramanujan's poor school record was verified by a classmate, Srinivasa Raghavacharya, who noted that he was often so absent-minded and heavily engrossed in mathematical research that many thought he was 'brain-sick'.[6]

When Ramanujan sat exams in mathematics he would finish them in half the allotted time. Kanigel notes that by the age of 14 years, the young genius was regarded by classmates as 'someone off in the clouds with whom they could scarcely hope to communicate'.[7] Certainly, Wittgenstein experienced much the same type of isolation at a similar age. None the less, Ramanujan's talents did come to the attention of his school in Madras, which had a 'respectful awe of him' despite teachers rarely understanding him.[8]

Throughout his life, Ramanujan maintained adequate speech but showed a marked impairment in the ability to initiate or sustain conversation with others. He was attentive to what other people said but in conversation would remain silent and spoke briefly when asked a question. Ranganathan notes how, on the rare occasions when he joined in any general conversation, 'he would speak frankly, but briefly'.[9] This brevity was also characteristic of Wittgenstein.

For all Ramanujan's towering intellectual genius, the kind of humour he enjoyed was rather childish. In people with autism, humour is generally of an immature, 'slapstick' variety, lacking in subtlety and often inappropriate. A flavour of his humour is provided by his wife, Janaki. On his deathbed, she recalls, he was 'full of wit and humour. Even while mortally ill he used to crack jokes.'[10]

Social impairment

From an early age Ramanujan showed signs of social impairment, characteristic of those with autism. Disagreement exists as to whether or not his parents encouraged his isolation and self-absorption. Certainly, there is evidence that Ramanujan liked to be by himself, which as Kanigel suggests was 'a tendency abetted by parents who, when friends called, discouraged him from going out to play; so he'd talk to them from the window overlooking the street'.[11] He expressed no interest in team sports and indeed had no desire to share enjoyment, interests or achievements with others.

Throughout his life he had a tendency to vanish abruptly and run away. This generally happened when things went badly for him. At school he was once 'punished by having to sit with his arms folded in front of him, and one finger turned up to his lips in silence . . . he would at times stalk out of class in a huff', according to Kanigel. Kanigel also points out that he would often simply vanish because he had 'an enormous pathological sensitivity to the slightest breath of public humiliation',[12] especially when he was refused scholarships or failed in school. On one occasion in Cambridge, he cooked a meal for a group and because a woman declined to have a third helping of sole he disappeared for 4 days and felt very rejected.[13]

Ramanujan clearly lacked empathy. Kanigel describes him as not 'particularly attuned to interpersonal nuance'.[14] A classmate, N. Hari Rao, recalls how, when he visited Ramanujan, he 'would open his notebooks and explain to me intricate theorems and formulae without the least suspecting that they were beyond my understanding or knowledge'. Lack of social or emotional reciprocity is indicative of autism. Kanigel points out that 'once Ramanujan was lost in mathematics, the other person was as good as gone'.[15] He lacked all appreciation of social cues and had little desire to interact with peers. The social sensitivity he lacked made him appear innocent and simple. Despite Ramanujan appearing like a 'simple soul', Ranganathan could never imagine anyone being unfriendly towards him. Indeed, it was Ramanujan's contemplative air that made forming close relationships difficult. 'He had always a contemplative look and somehow I could not imagine anyone getting very intimate with him'.[16]

Despite Hardy being Ramanujan's mentor at Cambridge and responsible for bringing him to England, they were not intimate friends.[17] None the less, there appears to have been a mutual attraction between them, as is often the case among people of genius. Indeed, those with HFA/ASP are often attracted to people with similar disorders. It is likely that Hardy also had HFA/ASP, which obviously made it more difficult for him to help Ramanujan in a social capacity. Mathematicians need social support if they are likely to be successful in the long run, as in the case of David Hilbert. Therefore, the communication impairment among the two mathematicians was not conducive to forming a close friendship. R.A. Rankin of the Indian Academy of Science draws Hardy in a light not dissimilar to Ramanujan:

> [Hardy] was a shy man in the sense that he would rather say nothing than indulge in small talk or the trivia of polite conversation. In mixed company he tended to ignore members of the other sex, unless they happened to be mathematicians. He had distaste for ceremonies and formal occasions of all kinds, not only religious ones, and, for example, rarely attended college fests. This dislike extended even to such mundane matters as shaking hands on first acquaintance.[18]

In terms of interpersonal relationships, Ramanujan did marry when quite young, but this was perhaps more indicative of the pressure to conform to social custom than of his ability to form attachments. At the age of 21 years, his devout mother arranged his marriage to a girl called Janaki, then aged 9 years. He waited 3 years until she reached puberty and then married her. When he went to Cambridge in 1913 she remained behind in India, his fears that she might interfere with his work outweighing any consideration of his personal welfare. Given that he looked after himself so poorly and cooked so sporadically, she might have prevented him succumbing to tuberculosis by giving him a proper diet and care.

Further evidence of his lack of social connectedness was that his wife slept at different times to him and he never spoke about sexual matters.[19] They had no children, and indeed Ramanujan comes across as asexual. A fellow student, R. Randhakrishna Ayyar, described him as 'fair and plumpy' and 'his build reminded one of a woman since his palms were smooth having nothing of the rough characteristics of a man'.[20] The description of being woman-like brings to mind many people with HFA/ASP that have identity diffusion without clear gender identities. Indeed, people with autism spectrum disorders may be androgynous.

All-absorbing narrow interest

It was in mathematics that Ramanujan showed his extraordinarily intense focus, with an all-absorbing narrow interest in the subject. He was like someone transported to another world when in the midst of original mathematical work. Kanigel records that he gradually settled into 'an unsettling realm of intellectual passion and fierce, unbending intensity that would rule the rest of his life'.[21] He engaged in 'fiercely single-minded intellectual activity'.[22] Indeed, Kanigel points out that once he was 'ensnared' by pure mathematics, he lost interest in everything else 'He was all math. He couldn't get enough of it.'[23] Interestingly, the mathematician, Paul Erdös, demonstrated precisely the same behaviour. The English mathematician, Neville, claimed that Ramanujan was 'the slave of his genius'.[24]

A close neighbour, Mr Govindarajan, recalled how classmates came to Ramanujan's house to observe him solve mathematics problems, where Buddha-like he sat, oblivious to all spectators and discomfort:

> Ramanujan used to sit in the upper pial [verandah seat] and he would be surrounded by his school mates and others who turned to him to solve their mathematical problems. Ramanujan would sit right on the pial floor with his legs folded vertically up and very many of the school mates used to amuse themselves by filling his underwear with small pebbles that Ramanujan would not notice; it was a measure of the extent to which he would lose contact with the world without, when under the spell of his beloved science.[25]

He became even more absorbed in mathematics, to the point where finding a job to help ease his family's financial burden was neglected. A friend, Mr K. Gopalachary, remarked that he was always 'engaged in doing something of mathematics', much to his parents' disapproval as he was 'without doing anything by way of earning', and took to hiding himself under a cot whenever he wished to do his mathematics.[26]

Strict adherence to routines

From Kanigel we learn that Ramanujan's earliest childhood game consisted of lining up household utensils,[27] a form of play which today is one of the diagnostic features of autism. Throughout his life, Ramanujan demonstrated a rigid need for routine in order to facilitate his mathematical work. There is also evidence of preservation of sameness in his dietary and work habits. In this respect, Ranganathan considered that 'Ramanujan happened to be a no-changer'.[28] Ramanujan's work in the pursuit of truth was unrelenting, according to Ranganathan:

> To read through the dry-as-dust collection of formulae in Carr's Synopsis (Mathematics) required not only intellectual capacity but also abundant industry. Ramanujan had it even when he was at school. After he left college, he was incessantly working – not to earn money, but to find out the truth and the beauty of mathematics. He worked most of the day and night. He worked even when Death was knocking at his door.[29]

In Ramanujan's case, routines to facilitate his mathematical work involved curtailing his sleep. He would ask his mother or grandmother to wake him up after midnight so that he could continue his work in the silent and cooler hours of the after-night.

Intimacy with numbers

Intimacy with numbers is a characteristic feature of mathematicians of genius who also have autism. This effectively is a substitute for intimacy with human beings, which involves enormous difficulty for them. Numbers formed the cornerstone of Ramanujan's work, and Kanigel points to him 'building an intimacy with numbers, for the same reason that the painter lingers over the mixing of his paints, or the musician endlessly practises his scales'.[30] Ranganathan records that at the age of 12 years, it was evident that Ramanujan showed a special interest in numbers. He asked 'is zero divided by zero also unity? If no fruits are divided among nobody, will each get one?'[31] This was perhaps the first indication of his unusual insight into the behaviour of numbers. In the same year he is said to have worked out the properties of arithmetical, geometrical and harmonic progression. At the age of 13 years he had solved all the problems in *Loney's Trigonometry*, borrowed from a student in the degree class of the government college, Kumbakonam. His next year saw him deriving Euler's expansions of the circular functions in infinite series unaided.

The world of mathematics was so comfortable to him that Ranganathan noted that 'every integer [was] a friend of Ramanujan'.[32] He also reports that according to Hardy, Ramanujan could remember the idiosyncrasies of numbers in an almost uncanny way. On one occasion when Ramanujan was ill with tuberculosis in England, Hardy paid him a visit in hospital and informed him that his taxicab number was 1729. Hardy had remarked that it was a rather dull number and feared it to be an unfavourable omen. Ramanujan replied to the contrary; 'No, it is a very interesting number. It is the smallest number expressible as the sum of two cubes in two ways.'[33] In addition, Kanigel notes that he was bewitched in particular by prime numbers: 3, 5, 7, etc.[34]

The intimacy with numbers continued during Ramanujan's sleeping hours, and he experienced dreams that aided his mathematical discoveries. T. Rajagopaln recounts a dream told to him by Ramanujan in 1911:

> While asleep I had an unusual experience. There was a red screen formed by flowing blood as it were. I was observing it. Suddenly a hand began to write on the screen. I became all attention. That hand wrote a number of results in elliptic integrals. They stuck to my mind. As soon as I woke up, I committed them to writing.[35]

Non-verbal communication

Certainly the non-verbal behaviour of Ramanujan was peculiar and affected people around him profoundly. His peculiar stiff gaze, which was particularly captivating, is a trait commonly associated with people with HFA/ASP:

> all his physical features escaped our attention, whenever we were face to face with him, conversing with him or listening to a talk by him. It was the eyes alone that would engage our mind. The glow in them would captivate us.[36]

At school Randhakrishna observed that when Ramanujan concentrated hard 'the pupils in the eyes would vanish making it appear that he had a squint or something like that'.[37] Similarly, Ramachandra Rao, secretary of the Indian Mathematical Society, found him 'a short, uncouth figure, stout, unshaven, not overly clean, with one conspicuous feature – shining eyes'.[38]

People with HFA/ASP can have a unique 'autistic charm'. The kind of charm exuded is not one found in good social relationships but a unique compelling kind mediated through gestures or non-verbal behaviour. On one occasion Ramanujan began a talk on God, zero and infinity with Gopalachary, K.S. Patrachariar – a lecturer in mathematics – and a number of other students, which lasted 6 hours. Gopalachary remarked to Patrachariar the next day that he personally found it hard to follow Ramanujan's train of thought. Patrachariar replied that 'while listening to him, I thought I was following him. But now it is all like a dream. I am not able to recall anything coherently.'[39] The charm concealed what was essentially incoherent analysis from Ramanujan's audience. This explains why people with autism are often confused with those with schizophrenia and are misdiagnosed as having thought disorder. The conversation also highlights the enormous impact that Ramanujan had on people, not unlike Wittgenstein. People with HFA/ASP with an ability of genius often have a mesmeric effect on people. It perhaps comes from the absolute conviction of their ideas. Certainly, there is a potency to their absolute certainty.

Naïvety and lack of common-sense

There are many accounts of Ramanujan's innocent and unselfconscious disposition. A devotee, K. Chengalvarayan, stated that 'innocence and absence of self-consciousness were his other qualities. He was unconscious of his abilities and attainments.'[40] Indeed, it was Hardy and his colleagues at Cambridge who discovered Ramanujan's genius, as he had little awareness of his own talent, according to Chengalvarayan. 'I may not be wrong when I say that other eminent mathematicians discovered Ramanujan for him.'[41] It is clear that his genius was not a product of his environment. Moreover, there never was more clear evidence of a hugely genetic component in producing a mathematician of genius.

Ramanujan's innocence could not be overestimated. The accountant general of Madras, W. Graham, suggested that Ramanujan's brains were akin 'to those of the calculating boy'. Graham was obviously referring to what today would be called 'savants', those who possess the peculiar ability to perform extremely rapid calculations without any real understanding of higher mathematics.[42] The comparison to the calculating boy is erroneous as these boys are incapable of highly original mathematics.

Ramanujan also demonstrated a certain naïvety in terms of his academic responsibilities. Geniuses often make bad teachers, and Ramanujan was no exception. He displayed no common-sense or capacity for mathematical empathy with his students. The failure to provide them with careful expositions of mathematical problems or proofs was a case in point. When awarded scholarships he often lost them, having spent all his time doing mathematics and not attending to the full academic curriculum. This again shows a lack of capacity to empathise with the institution, and a lack of common-sense about the requirements for a scholarship. Simply put, he went his own way. One of his students, Mr Govindarajan, recalled why he abandoned all tuition by Ramanujan:

> He was my tutor for a few days – say a fortnight; but in almost all those days, he would talk only of infinity and infinitesimal and I felt that his tuition might not be of real use to me in the examination and so I gave it up – certainly not the first incidence of the world finding one of its geniuses unfit for its day-to-day commercial necessities!'[43]

Adapting to life at Cambridge was not without difficulty, and commonplace activities such as bed making were a source of mystery to Ramanujan. A fellow student at Cambridge, P.C. Mahalanobis, describes how he went to Ramanujan's room to investigate why he was so cold at night. 'He did not know that he should turn back the blankets and get into the bed . . . The bedcover was loose; he was sleeping under that linen cover with his overcoat and shawl. I showed him how to get under the blankets.'[44] This bears some similarity to the famous mathematician with HFA/ASP described by Baron-Cohen and colleagues, who ran everywhere and had to be told, for example, to walk along corridors.[45]

Kanigel noted the childlike simplicity that Ramanujan displayed: 'there was something so direct, so unassuming, so transparent about him that it melted distrust of him'.[46] This childlike disposition was also a feature of Einstein. The general picture painted of Ramanujan is of a shy and quiet man with 'a dignified bearing and pleasant manners'.[47] Those features continued to dominate in England, where he remained 'the same childish man, with no style in dress or affectations of manner'.[48]

Idiosyncrasies and eccentricities

Like Wittgenstein and Erdös, Ramanujan kept notebooks faithfully recording his work. The use of notebooks is a common feature of autistic people of genius: they are carried at all times and constantly filled with notes. This reflects the level of their obsession. From his earliest schooldays Ramanujan filled notebooks with theorems even when not in contact with other mathematicians:

> Notebooks, crammed with theorems, that each day, each week, bulged wider . . . Mathematical jottings piled up, now in a more impetuous hand, with some of it struck out, and sometimes with script marching up and down the page rather than across it.[49]

According to Kanigel these notebooks formed 'a distinctly idiosyncratic record' where even widely standardised terms sometimes acquired new meaning.[50] Ramanujan's mode of expression was unusual: Kanigel remarks that the notebooks were 'flurries of thought transmuted into paper and ink', and while there was nothing 'wrong' in what Ramanujan did, it was just 'weird'.[51]

When he failed to find fresh paper for writing, he would use a slate wiped clean over and over again. In conversation with Sandow, Ramanujan stated 'my elbow has become rough and black in making a genius of me! Night and day I do my calculation on slate. It is too slow to look for a rag to wipe it out with. I wipe out the slate almost every few minutes with my elbow.' Sandow replied 'so, you are a mountain of industry. Why use a slate when you have to do so much calculation! Why not use paper!' To which Ramanujan replied, 'when food itself is a problem, how can I find money for paper? I may require four reams of paper every month.'[52]

Ranganathan reports that a classmate met Ramanujan picking up bits of paper in Madras Harbour, and asked what he was doing. Ramanujan replied 'I am picking up pieces of plain unwritten paper used for packing. For, I am in want of paper to write mathematical problems.'[53] Indeed, so much was Ramanujan's need to express his formulae that sometimes he would write notes and problems in red ink across already written paper when no plain paper was available.

Genius and creativity

Professional recognition of Ramanujan's genius came in January 1913 when Hardy received a letter from Ramanujan in India:

I beg to introduce myself to you as a clerk in the Accounts Department
of the Port Trust Office at Madras on a salary of only £20 per annum. I
am now but 23 years of age . . . I would request you to go through the
enclosed papers.[54]

After poring over the enclosed papers for a number of hours with his
colleague, Littlewood, Hardy recognised that they were clearly produced by
a man with mathematical genius. He noticed 'wild theorems' and 'theorems
such as he had never seen before or imagined'.[55] Equally, Littlewood
described him as a prodigy.

The creative urge to discover new mathematical formulae drove
Ramanujan. Kanigel points out that he was 'completely original' and
'ensnared by pure mathematics, he lost interest in everything else'.[56] In this
respect, Ramanujan met the conditions of creativity – isolation and self-
direction. He put colossal mental effort into his work and worked alone.
This suggests that genetic factors far outweighed any environmental ones or
teaching in the development of his mathematical career:

> For five solid years, Ramanujan was left alone to pursue mathematics.
> He received no guidance, no stimulation, no money beyond the few
> rupees he made from tutoring . . . [He] had found a home in mathe-
> matics, one so thoroughly comfortable that he scarcely ever wished to
> leave it. It satisfied him intellectually, aesthetically, emotionally.[57]

So impressive was his genius that Hardy gave Ramanujan a score of 100
out of 100 for natural mathematical ability while he gave himself a humble
score of 25.[58] Ramanujan had extraordinary mathematical intuition and 'a
knack for manipulating formulas, a delight in mathematical form for its
own sake'.[59] Kanigel quotes Hardy's recognition of Ramanujan's originality: he combined the power of generalisation, a feeling for form, and a
capacity for rapid modification of his hypotheses, that were often really
startling, and made him, in his own peculiar field, without rival in his day'
and also 'a profound and invincible originality'.[60]

Ramanujan's mathematical discoveries were distinctly intuitive but
lacked rigour. For all his mastery, Ramanujan's knowledge of the funda-
mentals of mathematics was startlingly limited, according to Hardy. He had
grasped the complexities of modular equations and theorems of complex
multiplications to unheard-of orders, yet had never heard of such basics as
doubly periodic function or Cauchy's theorems and had only 'the vaguest
notion of what the function of a complex variable was'.[61] In the crucial
letter to Hardy in 1913, Ramanujan acknowledged that he 'had not trodden
through the conventional regular course'.[62] This is typical of autistic
geniuses.

None the less, unconventional methods often produce astonishing results, and mathematics has been most advanced by those renowned for intuition rather than rigorous methods of proof. L.J. Mordell, who succeeded Hardy in his chair at Cambridge, supported the German mathematician Felix Klein's evaluation of Ramanujan by emphasising the novelty and importance of his original work. The 'secret of gifted productivity will always be that of finding new questions and new points of view, and without these mathematics would stagnate'.[63]

Very often great mathematicians are unable to explain how they have conducted their calculations. Indeed, Hardy points out that Ramanujan's results 'new or old, right or wrong, had been arrived at by a process of mingled argument, intuition, and induction of which he was entirely unable to give any coherent account'.[64] It comes as no surprise then that he failed to make reference to standard theorems in his work, because he had worked them out in a fashion best known to himself. To overcome Ramanujan's ignorance of certain basic mathematical facts, Hardy attempted to work with him in a 'participative way, involving reciprocal learning'.[65] As Kanigel puts it 'Ramanujan's Intuition Incarnate had run smack into Hardy, the Apostle of Proof'.[66]

The view that Ramanujan was not concerned with proof is supported by Cambridge colleagues. Littlewood claims that Ramanujan had no 'clear-cut conception of proof':

> If a significant piece of reasoning occurred somewhere and the total mixture of evidence and intuition gave him certainty, he looked no further. In this case any 'real' proof was inevitably beyond his grasp, and the significant pieces of reasoning which are indicated in the notebooks and reports though we shall find them curious and interesting, are quite inadequate as proof . . . His method, however, was not the normal one in which the theorem arises out of the proof; no proof, no theorem.[67]

The kind of intuition mentioned here would fit what Baron-Cohen called 'folk physics', that which relates to the understanding of the physical world.[68] Indeed, later mathematicians did come to prove Ramanujan's mathematical statements. This is not unlike Wittgenstein, who made assertions without adding proofs. Certainly, Wittgenstein held proofs in his head but refused to write them down. It is not surprising then that many people with HFA/ASP and of genius are only interested in absolutely new ideas and leave the mechanical and tedious job of supplying proof to technicians. Ranganathan quotes Littlewood, who saw it as fitting that Ramanujan should be exclusively an innovator:

the proper use of Ramanujan would be to leave him to his intuition and to his startling, penetrating conjectures, since such persons are few and far between. The proof and the verification is the work for a technician in mathematics . . . It would have been bad economy, as Hardy said, to have tamed and trained Ramanujan in that way and make a technician of him. Intuition characterised Ramanujan not only as a mathematician but also as a man.[69]

Ramanujan's unusual style of doing mathematics is often characteristic of great mathematicians. Hence the imparting of new ideas in mathematics often brings more confusion than clarity. He was well known to 'jump around the problem, working out key steps in his head but omitting them from his exposition – leaving his classmates thoroughly confused'.[70] In fact, this is not unlike the mathematician with Asperger's syndrome who received a Fields Medal for mathematics, as described by Baron-Cohen and colleagues and outlined above.[71] It certainly raises questions about the nature of genius. The mathematician, Bruce Berndt, after working through Ramanujan's notebooks, concluded that 'the enigma of Ramanujan's creative process is still covered by a curtain that has barely been drawn'.[72] Eighty years on, molecular genetics is probably only now beginning to unravel the enigma left by Ramanujan. According to Kanigel, he appeared to have some anonymous mathematical intelligence:

this had to come from somewhere, had to be seen before it could be proved. But where did it come from? That was the mystery, the source of all the circular, empty, ultimately unsatisfying explanations that have always beset students of the creative process.[73]

Kanigel gets to the heart of the matter here and approaches what I have been trying to elucidate in terms of people of genius having HFA/ASP. Indeed, Kanigel used what could be regarded as a good description of people of genius with HFA/ASP when he surmised that Ramanujan was 'like a species that had branched off from the main evolutionary line and, like an Australian echidna or Galápagos tortoise, had come to occupy a biological niche all his own'.[74] In Hardy's estimation, Ramanujan was unrivalled as a mathematician in his time and had an exceptional approach to his work:

It was his insight into algebraical formulae, transformation of infinite series, and so forth that was most amazing. On this side, most certainly I have never met his equal, and I can compare him only with Euler . . . It is possible that the great days of formulae are finished, and that Ramanujan ought to have been born a hundred years ago; but he was by far the greatest formalist of his time. There have been a good many more important, and I suppose one must say greater, mathematicians than Ramanujan during the last 50 years, but not one who could stand up to him on his own ground. Playing the game of which he knew the rules, he could give any mathematician in the world 15.[75]

Esotericism

Ramanujan's theory of reality was a combination of mathematics and Hindu philosophy. Religion was very important to him, as Ranganathan notes:

> Ramanujan and his family were ardent devotees of the god Narasimha (the lion-faced incarnation (*avasara*) of God), the sign of whose grace consisted in drops of blood seen during dreams. Ramanujan stated that after seeing such drops, scrolls containing the most complicated mathematics used to unfold before him and that after waking, he could set down on paper only a fraction of what was shown to him.[76]

His spiritual status did not go unnoticed by the Indian mathematician, Srinivasan, who considered him 'a true mystic in the full significance of the term'.[77] Indeed, the picture painted of Ramanujan before he went to England was of the detached serenity of the mystic. Sitting bow legged on the *pial* or verandah seat of his house, almost Buddha-like, scribbling furiously on a large slate spread over his lap, oblivious to the noisy activity in the street and life going on around him, he 'inhabited an island of serenity'.[78] Even Ramanujan's insight into how he got started in mathematics has quasi-religious overtones:

> One night, I had the following dream. I heard a peddler's voice in the street. He was selling pills. The price of each pill was less than one anna (presently six Paise or two American Cents) but the price of one was only 50 Paise. I asked him what its special use was. He said he did not know about it. I bought it immediately. The next day the ideas about Arithmetic Progression, Geometric Progression, and Harmonic Progression began to develop in my mind.[79]

Evidence for the association of God with mathematics is provided by Ramanujan. As a teenager, Ramanujan remarked to his father 'Sir, an equation has no meaning for me unless it expresses a thought of God'. His father was surprised by the remark but believed it came to encapsulate the essence of truth about God, man and the universe: 'In that statement I saw the real Ramanujan, the philosopher–mystic–mathematician'.[80]

Ramanujan's attitude to mathematics was not unlike that of Einstein or Erdös. He believed that mathematical reality existed independently of mathematicians and was 'discovered' by them. He believed that 'each new theorem was one more piece of the Infinite unfathomed',[81] whereby zero is represented as the absolute reality. This suggests the idea that mathematics is discovered, not created. Indeed, Ramanujan was obsessed with the concept of infinity and would often talk only of infinity and infinitesimals. According to Kanigel, he had a fascination for theta functions and felt they could be represented as infinite series, which encapsulated his theory of reality.[82] Likewise, Dr P. Mathalanopis argues that:

> he was eager to work out a theory of reality which would be based on the fundamental concepts of zero, infinity and the set of finite numbers. I used to follow in a general way, but I never clearly understood what he had in mind. He sometimes spoke of zero as the symbol of the Absolute (*Nirguna–Brahmam*) of the extreme monistic school of Hindu philosophy that is, the reality to which no qualities can be attributed, which cannot be defined or described by words, and which is completely beyond the reach of the human mind. According to Ramanujan, the appropriate symbol was the number zero, which is the absolute negation of all attributes. He looked on the number infinity as the totality of all possibilities, which was capable of becoming manifest in reality and which was inexhaustible. According to Ramanujan, the product of infinity and zero would supply the whole set of finite numbers. Each product of creation, as far as I could understand, could be symbolised as a particular product of infinity and zero, and from each such product would emerge a particular individual of which the appropriate symbol was a particular finite number.[83]

This kind of reasoning, displaying an apparent absence of logic or reason, gets to the heart of Ramanujan's view of the world through mathematics. It is also the kind of idea frequently developed by people with HFA/ASP and may explain why Wittgenstein's philosophy is so complex. Clearly, the way of thinking is often mystical in nature, culminating in the identification of zero with an absolute being, e.g. God in Ramanujan's case. In fact, Ramanujan had reached a level of mathematics that is indeterminate, that goes beyond proof. People with HFA/ASP often have an interest in philosophy and/or religion, e.g. Wittgenstein, Spinoza and Einstein, which is promoted by a sheer intellectual urge to understand the origin or what lies beyond the physical world. Indeed, Wittgenstein declared that he could not help but see everything from a religious point of view, leading others to conclude that he was a mystic.

Ramanujan displayed a capacity for astrology as well as for metaphysics. He was deeply interested in the occult, particularly life after death, astrology and psychic phenomena. According to Janaki, many of his relatives and friends would often come to 'consult him about their future and particularly for fixing auspicious hours for different festive or religious functions'.[84] Indeed, Ramanujan's occult explanations of the planets, stars, colour blindness, etc., gave him an almost prophet-like status.

The greater Ramanujan's engagement was with the non-physical world, the less it was with the material world. He had a similar attitude to wealth as had Wittgenstein, basically seeing it as an encumbrance. Despite the straitened circumstances that Ramanujan found himself in for the first 26 years of his life, he considered it 'undignified' to accept a gift of money. Afterwards, when he had sufficient income to live in comfort, he believed that 'any money which comes to one's share beyond the actual needs . . . should be used only for the benefit of those that were in need'.[85] This is extraordinarily close to Wittgenstein, who gave away all his money except that needed for basic living.

Co-morbidity

It would appear that certain aspects of Ramanujan's HFA/ASP indirectly precipitated his death, certainly in terms of alternating food fads and fasting. Food fads and eating disorders are commonly found in people with HFA/ASP. For the most part, eating took second place to Ramanujan's mathematical work. However, his case was complicated by the eating rituals of Hinduism. On many occasions he would simply forget to eat, being engrossed in his work, particularly at Cambridge. Indeed, when he lived in India his mother or grandmother would serve food in his hand 'made of cooked rice mixed with sambhar, rasam, and curd successively' to minimise the distractions while he worked.[86]

This contrasts with the times when he did eat, but was careful to observe Hindu customs. He was a strict vegetarian and superstitious about food. According to Srinivasan, he would not take food unless it was prepared correctly or cooked by 'people he approved'.[87]

In Cambridge he would often work for up 30 hours at a stretch and sometimes cooked for himself 'only once a day, or sometimes only once every other day, and then, at weird hours in the early morning'.[88] When Ramanujan lived in India, Randhakrishna remembers him as 'obstinate and would not drink hot water and insisted on eating grapes which were sour and were bad for him'.[89]

While at Trinity College, Ramanujan never dined in hall according to Rankin, nor ate any food prepared by the college kitchen since 'he suspected that even vegetarian food ordered from the college kitchen would be polluted by undetectable animal fats'.[90] On one occasion while staying in

London in 1915 he was given a drink of ovaltine. According to Dr C.D. Deshmakh, this had shocking consequences:

> He was horrified to find from the legend on the tin that the contents included a little powdered egg. This so upset him that he immediately packed his bags and left the place for Liverpool Street station on his way back to Cambridge. Later the landlady received a letter from him to inform her that as he approached the station there was heavy bombing of the neighbourhood and that it was with great difficulty he could get a train for Cambridge and get away from London. He had added that he was convinced that the raid was a punishment meted out to him by God for having partaken of anything non-vegetarian.[91]

Therefore, the possibility exists that Ramanujan's food fads were due more to his religious beliefs than HFA/ASP. However, his all-absorbing interest in mathematics clearly contributed to his erratic eating habits. Ranganathan makes the point that Ramanujan's 'social practices and religious practices get blended and become undistinguishable'.[92]

Undoubtedly, his tuberculosis was hastened by poor eating habits and personal neglect. Rankin points out that 'there is ample evidence that as a patient his recovery was retarded by his obstinacy in dietary and other matters'.[93] His failure to allow his wife to reside with him in England clearly signalled that he had little regard for his personal welfare, given that he looked after himself so poorly and wasn't attuned to his need for food. Perhaps, if it had been otherwise, he might not have developed tuberculosis so quickly and been forced to return home, where he died at the age of 32 years at Chetped, Madras.

It is interesting to note that when ill in the United Kingdom, Ramanujan was described by Kanigel as difficult to manage and extremely self-willed to the point of being pigheaded. At Cambridge he was taunted and teased by students because of his shyness,[94] which could also have led to some anxiety. On one occasion in 1918 when suffering from tuberculosis Ramanujan threw himself in front of a train but was rescued. Certainly, he was in great psychological pain and one can only speculate that he was depressed at the time. Yet, for all his failing health, Ramanujan's obsession with mathematics sustained him to the day he died. His wife, Janaki, helped maintain that interest right to the end:

> He returned from England only to die. He was only skin and bones . . . He often complained of severe pain. In spite of it he was always busy doing his Mathematics. That evidently helped him to forget the pain. I used to gather the sheets of paper which he filled up. I would also give him the slate whenever he asked for it.[95]

Conclusion

There is no doubt that Ramanujan met the criteria for HFA/ASP. He had major difficulties in social relationships and an all-absorbing narrow interest, was a man of routine and imposed enormous control on himself. In his early life his mother was worried about his 'muteness'. He had a peculiar stiff gaze. The condition of HFA/ASP can be helpful for mathematicians because their work requires extraordinary levels of concentration, and if the person has little interest in human relationships this allows increased concentration and precludes distractions. Unfortunately, it also meant that he was unable to look after himself properly when away from home, precipitating his death from tuberculosis while still a relatively young man.

Ramanujan would also meet the criteria for schizoid personality disorder. He almost always chose solitary activities, and had little interest in having sexual experiences with another person. He lacked close friends or confidants and wasn't interested in personal relationships. He was detached from people.

Chapter 10

Conclusion

This book set out to examine the relationship between HFA/ASP and creativity of genius proportions. The author believes this has been demonstrated in the individuals described herein. Since HFA/ASP is a highly genetic condition, the explanation favoured by this book is a largely innate explanation of creativity in certain circumstances, i.e. in those individuals with both HFA/ASP and the creativity of genius. While environmental factors do play a role, this is small in comparison to the genetic component. This still fits the gene-environment interaction explanation of the phenomenon, which is so popular today. A small proportion of persons with HFA/ASP have the capacity for enormous creativity, as described in this book. Indeed, their psychopathology is critical to their creativity.

Evolutionary psychology

Arguably, this book could be seen as attempting to support the evolutionary psychology project. People with HFA/ASP behave in a creative way that benefits themselves and humankind – one might even speculate that the wheel would not have been discovered had it not been for people with an HFA/ASP configuration of genes. (Some support for this contention comes from Baron-Cohen and colleagues, who state that 'it is a tautology that without highly developed folk physics (e.g. engineering), *Homo sapiens* would still be pre-industrial'.[1]) Nevertheless, the environmental contribution of HFA/ASP is probably about 10 per cent, whereas hereditable factors account for about 90 per cent of the aetiological variance. The concept of the 'selfish gene' is not appropriate, since by and large the contributions of geniuses with HFA/ASP have been enormously valuable to society.

R.T. Abed states that the core idea of evolutionary psychology is 'the assumption that the human mind has a species-specific architecture that contains a degree of variability and plasticity depending upon environmental influences, but is not infinitely malleable, as the standard social science model would have us believe'.[2] Indeed, Stephen R.L. Clarke has stated in relation to 'genetic drift' that 'neutral variations automatically accumulate, to stand revealed (perhaps) when some sudden environmental change, or some other minor mutation, enables their expression'.[3] Certainly in HFA/ASP, the 'species-specific architecture', this 'variability and plasticity' is greatly reduced as compared to other conditions because genetic factors are so high.

Maggie Gee points out that Darwin described the human species 'as evolving, like other animals, through natural selection (what Herbert Spencer called "the survival of the fittest")'.[4] Clearly, humans with mechanical minds would be particularly suited to the invention of tools, which give an advantage over other humans in the survival stakes – in cultivation, faction fighting, and war activities which all seem to be part of being a member of the human race.

There are many severe critics of the evolutionary psychology project. Though Darwinian in outlook, the author is not an evolutionary fundamentalist, but is aware that Stephen Rose has stated that 'what is at stake is the autonomy of the social sciences as research fields from the imperialistic claims of an overly reductive biology at the hands of the new evolutionary fundamentalists'.[5]

Certainly, Rose's claim of 'overly reductive biology' needs to be qualified. In relation to this book, the author is mindful that Rose has stated that 'what currently passes for evolutionary psychology is little more than an untestable bunch of anecdotes'.[6] However, the biographies and various accounts of individuals cannot be viewed simply as an 'untestable bunch of anecdotes'. Rose describes evolutionary psychology as 'transparently part of a right-wing libertarian attack on collectivity, above all the welfare state'.[7] This seems to me to be absurd as it ignores the vast amount of research done on the phenotype and genotype of psychiatric disorders over the past 15 years. Indeed, it appears that ideology and political correctness are more associated with the social sciences. The social sciences have been far removed from a hypothesis-driven scientific discipline (although some effort is being made to correct this now). The most serious weakness of the social sciences is their 'blind spot' and lack of understanding of psychopathology and genetics. The social sciences have been full of assertions without scientific proof. On balance, Jerry Coyne claims that the dispute over evolutionary psychology rests not on whether this can happen, but on the degree to which it can happen: 'the truth lies somewhere between the rigid genetic determinism of reductionists and the nay-saying holists'.[8]

Many of the individuals with HFA/ASP described in this book came from an average expectable environment. The environment played a very small role in their creative genius. I have diagnosed approximately eight young persons with autistic-like conditions who came from orphanages in Eastern Europe where they suffered extreme physical and emotional deprivation in their early years. The clinical picture was quite similar to people with autism, but appeared to be environmentally induced. The best phrase to describe them would be 'autistic-like'. In the most severely traumatised young people, reversal of the autistic-like process proved to be impossible or only partially successful. They reminded the author of so-called feral children. It is clear that no child can develop its brain without minimally acceptable physical, emotional and sensory stimulation. Nevertheless, a child born with HFA/ASP will not be able to lose that diagnosis no matter how good the environment is. This is not to say that good early intervention cannot improve their capacity for social relationships. Certainly, intervention could have helped many of the persons described in this book.

Creativity studies

The term 'autism' or 'Asperger's syndrome' is not found in the index to the *Encyclopaedia of Creativity*. This shows how far creativity studies are from a fundamental association with the creativity that is associated with HFA/ASP. The most creative individual of the past 1,000 years was Isaac Newton, and he had HFA/ASP. Arguably, creativity studies in the past have failed to come to terms with one of the most creative and influential individuals of the past millennium. The most serious flaw of creativity studies to date is their excessive reliance on simplistic environmental theories. These environmental theories offer very little explanation of people of creativity at the level of genius. The environmental theories do offer some help in understanding the kind of creativity for which every individual has a certain capacity. However, creative theorists have confused everyday creativity with the creativity of genius.

The autism spectrum

Another important point emerging from this book is that the autism spectrum is very wide, and this book widens it still further. What we saw in the early years after the diagnosis was originally made in 1943 were classic cases. It then took many years to identify the milder forms of HFA/ASP. Indeed, as Dr Robert Spitzer, Chief of Biometric Research at the New York State Psychiatric Institute, Columbia College of Physicians and Surgeons, noted:

> Mental disorders exist on a continuum, like blood pressure and cholesterol levels. It is somewhat arbitrary as to where we make a cut off between health and disease. Throughout the history of medicine, first the more severe forms of a disorder have been recognised, then the milder forms.[9]

Many of the people described in this book would be described as having milder forms of autism. The author disagrees with the word 'mild', as these people suffered major social emotional problems in their lives with co-morbid depression, suicidal ideas, and occasionally psychosis. Nevertheless, this book is a celebration of their creativity.

Notes

1 Introduction

1 J. Rossman, *Industrial Creativity*, New York: University Books, 1964, p. 1.
2 R.C. Atkinson, 'The origins and development of high ability', *Ciba Foundation Symposium*, 178, Chichester: Wiley, 1993, pp. 1–2.
3 R. Porter, 'Foreword', in A. Steptoe (ed.) *Genius and the Mind*, Oxford: Oxford University Press, 1998, p. v.
4 R. Gregory, *Oxford Companion to the Mind*, Oxford: Oxford University Press, 1987, p. 286.
5 M.A. Howe, *Genius Explained*, Cambridge: Cambridge University Press, 1999, p. 11.
6 Mark Twain, in D. Lykken, 'The genetics of genius', in Steptoe, op. cit., p. 22.
7 Howe, op. cit., p. 1.
8 P. Murray (ed.) *Genius: The History of An Idea*, Oxford: Basil Blackwell, 1989, p. 2.
9 Quoted in Atkinson, op. cit., p. 1.
10 Quoted in A. Storr, *The School of Genius*, London: 1988, André Deutsch, p. 169.
11 Quoted in Murray, op. cit., p. 202.
12 Thomas Roscoe (ed.) *Thoughts on Various Subjects in the Works of Jonathan Swift*, vol. 2, London, 1841, p. 304.
13 The term 'HFA/ASP' is used in this book because it is not possible scientifically to separate high-functioning autism accurately from Asperger's syndrome.
14 H. Grossman, *Manual on Terminology and Classification in Mental Retardation*, Washington, DC: American Association on Mental Deficiency, 1977, p. 143.
15 C. Gillberg, *A Guide to Asperger's Syndrome*, Cambridge: Cambridge University Press, 2002, p. 66.
16 I.B. Hermelin, *Bright Splinters of the Mind: A Personal Story of Research with Autistic Savants*, London: Jessica Kingsley, 2001, p. 176.
17 Ibid., p. 177.
18 Ibid.
19 Oliver Sacks, 'Foreword', in Temple Grandin, *Thinking in Pictures – And Other Reports from My Life with Autism*, New York: Doubleday, 1995, pp. 11–12.
20 Oliver Sacks, *An Anthropologist on Mars: Seven Paradoxical Tales*, London: Picador, 1995, p. 281.
21 Ibid.
22 Ami Klin, Robert Schulz and Donald Cohen, 'Theory of mind in action: developmental perspectives on social neuroscience', in S. Baron-Cohen, H.

Tager-Flusberg and D.J. Cohen (eds) *Understanding Other Minds*, Oxford: Oxford University Press, 2000, p. 357.

23 Ibid., p. 383.
24 H. Asperger, 'Die "Autistischen Psychopathen" im Kindesalter', *Archives fur Psychiatrie und Nervenkrankheiten*, 1944/1991, 117: 76–136. Translated in U. Frith (ed.) *Autism and Asperger's Syndrome*, Cambridge: Cambridge University Press, 1991, pp. 37–92.
25 Grandin, op. cit., pp. 178–9.
26 Ibid., p. 124.
27 S. Ozonoff and E. McMahon Griffith, 'Neuropsychological function and external validity of Asperger's syndrome', in A. Klin, F. Volkmar and S. Sparrow, *Asperger's Syndrome*, New York: Guilford Press, 2000, pp. 72–96; Baron-Cohen *et al.*, op. cit.
28 Grandin, op. cit., p. 125.
29 Gregory, op. cit., p. 171.
30 Liam Hudson, 'Creativity', in Gregory, op. cit., pp. 171–2.
31 Despite the paucity of sources, there is certain evidence to suggest that both Socrates and Michelangelo displayed significant features of HFA/ASP. Alain de Botton in *The Consolations of Philosophy* notes that Socrates believed 'the product of thought is superior to the product of intuition' (p. 25). Certainly, in common with many individuals with HFA/ASP, such as Wittgenstein, he placed logic and the intellect at the highest level. Socrates' logical disposition, spawning centuries of philosophical discourse, is undisputed, whereby Socratic dialogue became synonymous with logic and reason. The courage and fearless obsession with 'truth' (which culminated in him being put to death), and the moral and ethical outlook so common among those with HFA/ASP, occur in Socrates too. The lack of appreciation of social cues and emotional empathy is evident from the way in which he harassed the citizens of Athens about their common-sense beliefs. According to de Botton, 'his most curious feature was a habit of approaching Athenians of every class, age and occupation and bluntly asking them, without worrying whether they would think him eccentric or infuriating, to explain with precision why they had held certain common-sense beliefs and what they took to be the meaning of life' (pp. 14–15). Socrates realised that people took things for granted and didn't think very clearly, a claim that was echoed by Wittgenstein in the twentieth century. Certainly, Socrates was teased and the subject of public ridicule, notably by Aristophanes in his play, *The Clouds*, performed in 423 BC. Preservation of sameness is demonstrated in the way in which 'he wore the same cloak throughout the year and almost always walked barefoot' (p. 14). His all-absorbing interest in logic and reason and analysing common-sense beliefs ensured little time for eating, bathing or sleeping; 'he had been up at dawn for most of his life talking to Athenians' (p. 36). The utter disregard for money is evident too. De Botton notes how 'he did not charge for his lessons and so slid into poverty . . . he had little concern for material possessions' (p. 14). In terms of non-verbal behaviour, he demonstrated 'prominent swollen eyes' and a 'curious rolling gait' (p. 14). Clearly he had an extraordinary effect on young people (as Wittgenstein had many centuries later), so much so that one of the charges levied against him was of 'corrupting the young men of Athens' (p. 4). (See Alain de Botton, 'Consolation for unpopularity', in *The Consolations of Philosophy*, London: Hamish Hamilton, 2000.)
    According to Davies in *Michelangelo*, the celebrated sculptor born in 1475 showed a 'single-minded devotion to his art' whereby he accomplished the work of two or three ordinary men in his lifetime. Imposition of control is evident and

'his life . . . showed a strong sense of control, and [he] asked for no special pleas such as genius is apt to put forward for itself'. His desire for perfection was clearly seen in his delaying the commissioned work of patrons, in one case for 50 years. Autistic aggression also features in his social interaction. Certainly in temper and speech he was often uncontrolled. The obsession with truth and certitude is apparent and he treated in a high-handed fashion 'all opinion contrary to his own; the impatience with all opposition even from men whose attainments qualified them to oppose'. This was especially so with his rivals; he 'can be needlessly fierce and rude with speech when he thinks he is being made sport of by Leonardo da Vinci'. In common with many with HFA/ASP Michelangelo was a poor teacher, imparting little knowledge to his pupils. 'He sought no proselytes; he issued no propaganda; he left no school; it may almost be said to have trained no pupils.' In terms of co-morbidity he did suffer from long bouts of depression. Clearly he was a man of religious disposition that lived simply, as is often the case with geniuses with HFA/ASP. 'His private life was pure in an age when laxity of morals brought little reproach.' Davies notes how he had lived from the beginning the simplest of lives, in which comfort, as other men counted comfort, had no place. 'His fare was that of his workmen'. His genius was undisputed. Davies states that 'the perplexities of heredity have no more striking illustration than is here to be found – brain power, nervous energy, strength of purpose, capacities of the highest quality in several directions, bestowed by Nature in their fullest bounty upon this one son; with complete contradiction of all these qualities in the case of the other sons'. See Gerald Davies, *Michelangelo*, London: Methuen, 1909.

32 David Joseph Weekes with Kate Ward, *Eccentrics: the Scientific Investigation*, Stirling: Stirling University Press, 1988, p. 27.
33 R. Mathews and W. Wacker, *The Deviant's Advantage*, New York: Crown Business, 2002.
34 Weekes and Ward, op. cit., p. 2.
35 Ibid., p. 3.
36 Ibid.
37 Howard Gardner, *Extraordinary Minds*, New York: Basic Books, 1997, p. 175.
38 Howe, op. cit., p. viii.
39 Storr, op. cit., p. 64.
40 Ibid., p. 67.
41 Gregory, op. cit., p. 172.
42 S. Dehaene, *The Numbers Sense: How the Mind Creates Mathematics*, New York: Oxford University Press, 1997, p. 6.
43 M. Fitzgerald, 'Did Isaac Newton have Asperger's Syndrome?', *European Child and Adolescent Psychiatry*, 1999: 204.
44 M. Fitzgerald, 'Einstein: Brain and Behaviour', *Journal of Autism and Developmental Disorders*, 2000, 30: 620–1.
45 Dehaene, op. cit., p. 7.
46 Ibid., p. 8.
47 R. Porter, *The Social History of Madness*, London: Weidenfeld and Nicolson, 1987, p. 63.
48 Quoted in Murray, op. cit., p. 7.
49 A. Steptoe, 'Artistic temperament in the Italian Renaissance: a study of Georgio Vasari's lives', in Steptoe, op. cit., p. 255.
50 J.H. Broad, in Gordon Claridge (ed.) *Schizotypy*, Oxford: Oxford University Press, 1997, p. 277.
51 Ibid., p. 284.

52 John Dryden, *Absalom and Achitophel*, in D.K. Simonton, *Greatness: Who Makes History and Why*, New York: Guilford Press, 1994, p. 284.
53 Cesare Lombroso, in Murray, op. cit., p. 200.
54 Cesare Lombroso, in P. Ostwald and L. Zegans, *The Pleasures and Perils of Genius*, Madison, WI: International University Press, 1993, p. 171.
55 Simonton, op. cit., p. 314.
56 See S. Freud, 'Introductory lectures on psychoanalysis' (English version in standard edition), in James Stratechy (ed.) *Complete Psychological Works of Sigmund Freud*, London, 1963, vol. XIV, p. 376.
57 Havelock Ellis, *A Study of British Genius*, London, 1904, p. 195.
58 Gregory, op. cit., p. 171.
59 Simonton, op. cit., p. 33.
60 S. Baron-Cohen and J. Hammer, 'Parents of children with Asperger's syndrome; what is the cognitive phenotype?', *Journal of Cognitive Neuroscience*, 2001, 9: 548–54.
61 Quoted in M. Fitzgerald, 'Did Isaac Newton have Asperger's Syndrome?', *European Child and Adolescent Psychiatry*, 1999, 8: 204. See also S. Baron-Cohen, *Understanding Other Minds*, 2nd edn, Oxford: Oxford University Press, 2001, p. 78.
62 Paul Moebius, in Ostwald and Zegans, op. cit., p. 175.
63 Simonton, op. cit., p. 6.
64 U. Frith and R. Houston, *Autism in History*, Oxford: Blackwell, 2000; Sula Wolff, *Loners*, London: Routledge, 1995; C. Gillberg and M. Coleman, *The Biology of Autistic Syndromes*, Cambridge: MacKeith Press, 2000.
65 Frith and Houston, op. cit., pp. 5–9.
66 R. Hyman, *The Pan Dictionary of Famous Quotations*, London: Grange Books, 1993, p. 137.
67 D. Edmonds and J. Eidinow, *Wittgenstein's Poker*, London: Faber and Faber, 2001, p. 10.
68 American Psychiatric Association, *Diagnostic and Statistical Manual of Mental Disorders* (DSM-IV), Washington, DC: APA, 1994.
69 C. Gillberg, 'Clinical and neurobiological aspects of Asperger's syndrome in six family studies', in U. Frith (ed.) *Autism and Asperger's Syndrome*, Cambridge: Cambridge University Press, 1991, pp. 122–46.
70 Frith and Houston, op. cit., p. 114.
71 E. Eloma, *Nature*, 1991, 351: 179.
72 O. Sacks, *An Anthropologist on Mars*, London: Picador, 1995, p. 254.
73 E.T. Rakitzis, *Nature*, 1991, 351: 179.
74 R. Monk, 'Private lives', *The Times* magazine, 30 November 1996, 37.
75 Ibid.
76 M. Kuehn, *Kant*, Cambridge: Cambridge University Press, 2001, p. 22.
77 Ibid.
78 Monk, op. cit., p. 37.
79 Ibid.
80 K. Hughes-Hallet, 'How best to disturb silence', *New Statesman*, 14 May 2001, 39.
81 D. Ellis, *Literary Lives: Biography and the Search for Understanding*, London: Routledge. Quotation in H. Lee, 'Tracking the untrackable', *New York Review of Books*, 12 April 2002, p. 55.
82 Lee, op. cit., p. 55.
83 G. Alper, *Portrait of the Artist as a Young Patient*, San Francisco: International Scholars Publication, 1998, p. 160. See also S. Freud, *Leonardo da Vinci and a Memory of his Childhood*, Standard Edition, vol. 9, London: Hogarth Press, 1957.

84 A. Steptoe, 'Exceptional creativity and the psychological sciences', in Steptoe, op. cit., p. 2.
85 Jerry Fodor, 'Wotan's law and Tristan's love', *Times Literary Supplement*, 17 November 2000, 6.
86 Monk, op. cit., p. 35.
87 M. Fitzgerald, 'Wittgenstein and autism', *Times Literary Supplement*, August 2002, 15.
88 Rush Rhees, 'Wittgenstein', *The Human World*, no. 14, February 1974, 71.
89 Christopher Gehrke, *Philosophers' Magazine*, 2002, p. 65.
90 Albert W. Levi, 'Wittgenstein once more: a response to critics', *Telos*, 1979, 40: 165–73.
91 Stephen Logan, 'Critique of practical reasons', *The Independent*, 15 December 2001, 12.
92 Levi, op. cit., p. 173.
93 Ludwig Wittgenstein, *Culture and Value* (ed. G.H. von Wright) Oxford: Basil Blackwell, 1980, p. 20.
94 J. Bouveresse, 'Wittgenstein and the modern world', in A.B. Griffiths (ed.) *Wittgenstein: Centenary Essays*, Cambridge: Cambridge University Press, 1991.
95 Kuehn, op. cit.
96 J.C. Klagge, 'Wittgenstein's community', in *Metaphysics in the Post-metaphysical Age, Proceedings of the 22nd International Wittgenstein Symposium*, Kirchberg am Wechsel, 1999, p. 336.
97 Ben Ami Scharfstein, *The Philosophers: their Lives and the Nature of their Thought*, New York: Oxford University Press, 1980, p. 334. See also Karl Popper, *Objective Knowledge*, Oxford. Oxford University Press, 1972, pp. 146–7.
98 W.W. Bartley, *Wittgenstein*, La Salle, IL: Open Court, 1985, p. 171.
99 Scharfstein, op. cit., p. 334.
100 Bartley, op. cit., p. 32.
101 Quoted in ibid., p. 169.
102 Ibid.
103 C. Gillberg, *A Guide to Asperger's Syndrome*, Cambridge: Cambridge University Press, 2002, p. 134.

2 Diagnostic Issues

1 L. Kanner, 'Autistic disturbances of affective contact', *The Nervous Child*, 1943, 2: 217.
2 L. Kanner, 'The conception of wholes to parts in early infantile autism', *American Journal of Psychiatry*, 1951, 108: 23–9.
3 L. Kanner and L. Lesser, 'Early infantile autism', *Psychiatric Clinics of North America*, 1958, 5: 711–30.
4 L. Eisenberg, 'The fathers of autistic children', *American Journal of Orthopsychiatry*, 1957, 7: 723.
5 L. Wing, 'Diagnosis, clinical description, and prognosis', in L. Wing (ed.) *Early Childhood Autism: Clinical, Educational and Social Aspects*, 2nd edn, Oxford: Pergamon, 1976, pp. 15–64.
6 H. Asperger, 'Problems of infantile autism', *Communication*, 1979, 13: 45–52.
7 A.D. van Krevelen, 'The psychopathology of autistic psychopathy', *Acta Paedopsychiatrica*, 1962, 24: 22–31.
8 L. Wing, 'Asperger's syndrome – a clinical account', *Psychological Medicine*, 1981, 11(47): 115–29.
9 H. Asperger, 'Die "Autistischen Psychopathen" im Kindesalter, *Archives fur*

Psychiatrie und Nervenkrankheiten, 1944, 117: 76–136. Translated in U. Frith (ed.) *Autism and Asperger's Syndrome*, Cambridge: Cambridge University Press, 1991, pp. 37–92. This is reviewed in S. Mayes, S. Calhoun and D. Crites, 'Does DSM-IV Asperger's disorder exist?', *Journal of Abnormal Child Psychology*, 2001, 29(3): 263–71, which selects Uta Frith's quotations on Asperger's work.

10 Ibid.
11 Ibid.
12 R.P. Ebstein, J. Benjamin and R. Belimaker, 'Genetics of personality dimensions', *Current Opinion in Psychiatry*, 2000, 13: 617.
13 Ibid.
14 Ibid.
15 L. Wing, 'Letter: Clarification on Asperger's syndrome', *Journal of Autism and Development Disorders*, 1986, 16: 513–15.
16 Checkley, in T. Millon and R. Davis, *Personality Disorders in Modern Life*, New York: Wiley, 2000, pp. 114–15.
17 Ibid., p. 115.
18 Ibid.
19 Ibid.
20 Ibid.
21 Ibid., p. 117.
22 Ibid.
23 Ibid.
24 American Psychiatric Association, *Diagnostic and Statistical Manual IV*, Washington, DC: American Psychiatric Association, 1994.
25 B. Dolan and J. Coid, *Psychopathic and Antisocial Personality Disorders*, London: Gaskell, 1993, p. 2.
26 J. Gunn, 'The treatment of psychopaths', in R. Gaind (ed.) *Current Themes in Psychiatry*, London: Macmillan, 1978, p. 38.
27 Dolan and Coid, op. cit., p. 269.
28 I. Kershaw, *Hitler 1889–1936: Hubris*, London: Allen Lane, 1998, p. 46.
29 Ibid., p. 84.
30 Ibid., p. 93.
31 Ibid., p. 281.
32 Ibid., p. 343.
33 W.C. Langer, *The Mind of Adolf Hitler*, New York: Basic Books, 1972, p. 86.
34 Ibid., p. 353.
35 Kershaw, op. cit., p. 342.
36 Ibid., p. xii.
37 Ibid., p. xxviii.
38 Langer, op. cit., p. 71.
39 Kershaw, op. cit., p. 293.
40 Deutsche Arbeiter Partei – German Workers' Party.
41 Anton Drexler, in Kershaw, op. cit., p. 107.
42 Langer, op. cit., p. 45.
43 Ibid., p. 83.
44 Ibid., p. 187.
45 Ibid., p. 188.
46 Langer, op. cit., p. 43.
47 Herman Rauschning, in Kershaw, op. cit., p. 99.
48 Ibid., p. 187.
49 Langer, op. cit., p. 93.
50 Asperger (1944), op. cit.

51 Kershaw, op. cit., p. xx.
52 Wing (1981), op. cit., pp. 115–29.
53 G. Mesibov, V. Shea and L. Adams, *Understanding Asperger's Syndrome or High Functioning Autism*, London: Plenum Press, 2001, p. 17.
54 Hans Asperger, in Frith, op. cit., pp. 87–9.
55 A. Van Krevelen and C. Kuipers, 'The psychopathology of autistic psychopathy', *Acta Paedopsychiatrica*, 1962, 29: 22–31.
56 Ibid.
57 Ibid.
58 Ibid.
59 D. Tantam, 'Asperger's syndrome in adulthood', in Frith, op. cit., p. 161.
60 L. Wing, 'The history of Asperger's syndrome', in E. Schopler, G. Mesibov and L. Kunce (eds) *Asperger's Syndrome or High Functioning Autism?*, London: Plenum Press, 1998, pp. 12–28.
61 C. Gillberg, 'Clinical and neurobiological aspects of Asperger's syndrome', in Frith, op. cit., p. 123.
62 American Psychiatric Association, *Diagnostic and Statistical Manual III*, Washington, DC: American Psychiatric Association, 1987.
63 Mesibov *et al.*, op. cit., p. 31.
64 Ibid.
65 M. Fitzgerald, 'Criteria for Asperger's syndrome', *Journal of the American Academy of Child and Adolescent Psychiatry*, 1999, 28(9): 1071.
66 American Psychiatric Association, *Diagnostic Criteria from DSM-IV-TR*, Washington, DC: American Psychiatric Association, 2000, p. 64.
67 L. Wing and J. Gould, 'Severe impairments of social interaction and associated abnormalities in children: epidemiology and classification', *Journal of Autism and Childhood Schizophrenia*, 1979, 9: 11–29.
68 World Health Organisation, *The ICD-10 Classification of Mental and Behavioural Disorders*, Geneva: WHO, 1992, pp. 255–9.
69 van Krevelen, op. cit., pp. 84–5.
70 Ibid.
71 L. Tsai, 'From autism to Asperger's disorder', *American Academy of Child and Adolescent Psychiatry Conference*, Hawaii, October 2001, pp. 5–6.
72 Asperger (1979) op. cit.
73 H. Asperger, 'Formen des Autismus bei Kindern', *Deutsches Arzteblatt*, 1974, 14(4): 49.
74 Ibid., p. 48.
75 Ibid., p. 49.
76 Ibid.
77 G. Bosch, *Early Infantile Autism*, New York: Springer-Verlag, 1970.
78 Mesibov *et al.*, op. cit., p. 17.
79 B. Kugler, 'The differentiation between autism and Asperger's syndrome', *Autism*, 1998, 2(1): 11–32.
80 M. Ghaziuddin, E. Butler, L. Tsai and N. Ghaziuddin, 'Is clumsiness a marker for Asperger's syndrome?', *Journal of Intellectual Disability Research*, 1994, 38: 519.
81 S. Mayes, S. Calhoun and D. Crites, 'Does DSM-IV Asperger's disorder exist?', *Journal of Abnormal Child Psychology*, 2001, 29(3): 63.
82 L. Wing, 'Asperger's syndrome and Kanner's autism', in Frith, op. cit., p. 111.
83 Ibid.
84 L.Y. Tsai, 'Diagnostic issues in high-functioning autism', in E. Schopler and G.B. Mesibov (eds) *High Functioning Individuals with Autism*, New York: Plenum, 1992, p. 16.

85 L. Wing and D. Potter, 'The epidemiology of autistic spectrum disorders: is the prevalence rising?', *Mental Retardation and Developmental Disabilities Research Reviews*, 2002, 8: 151–61.
86 Wing, 'Asperger's syndrome and Kanner's autism', in Frith, op. cit., p. 111.
87 Ibid.
88 Ibid.
89 E. Schopler, 'Convergence of learning disability, higher-level autism, and Asperger's syndrome', *Journal of Autism and Developmental Disorders*, 1985, 15(4): 359.
90 Ibid.
91 J. Miller and S. Ozonoff, 'Did Asperger's cases have Asperger's disorder? A research note', *Journal of Child Psychology and Psychiatry*, 1997, 38: 247–51.
92 National Autistic Society (United Kingdom) Fact Sheet on Autism, London, 2001, p. 2.
93 M. Fitzgerald and A. Corvin, 'Diagnosis and differential diagnosis of Asperger's syndrome', *Advances in Psychiatric Treatment*, 2001, 7: 310–18.
94 American Psychiatric Association (2000) op. cit., pp. 65–7.
95 Ibid., p. 217.
96 S. Baron-Cohen, 'Do autistic children have obsessions and compulsions?', *British Journal of Clinical Psychology*, 1989, 28: 193–200.
97 American Psychiatric Association (2000), op. cit., p. 217.
98 S. Wolff, 'Schizoid personality in childhood: the links with schizophrenia spectrum disorders, Asperger's syndrome and elective mutism', in Schopler *et al.*, op. cit., p. 138.
99 D. Tantam, 'Lifelong eccentricity and social isolation: Asperger's syndrome or schizoid personality disorder?', *British Journal of Psychiatry*, 1988, 153: 783.
100 Ibid.
101 American Psychiatric Association (2000), op. cit., p. 292.
102 Ibid., pp. 153–65.
103 M. Fitzgerald, 'Antecedents to Asperger's syndrome', *Autism International Journal of Research and Practice*, 1998, 2(4): 427–9.
104 American Psychiatric Association (2000), op. cit., p. 290.
105 P. Szatmari, 'Differential diagnosis of Asperger disorder', in Schopler *et al.*, op. cit., p. 69.
106 S. Kumra, 'Multidimensionally impaired disorder', *Journal of the American Academy of Child and Adolescent Psychiatry*, 1998, 37(11): 1125–6.
107 M. Fitzgerald, 'Multidimensionally impaired disorder', *Journal of the American Academy of Child and Adolescent Psychiatry*, 1998, 37(11): 1125.
108 K. Towbin, 'Pervasive developmental disorder not otherwise specified', in D. Cohen and F. Volkmar (eds) *Handbook of Autism and Developmental Disorders*, New York: Wiley, 1997.
109 M. Fitzgerald, 'Pervasive developmental disorder not otherwise specified', *Journal of the American Academy of Child and Adolescent Psychiatry*, 1999, 3(8): 229.
110 D.R. Jordan, *Dyslexia in the Classroom*, Columbus, OH: Merrill, 1972, p. 87.
111 M. Fitzgerald, 'Cycles and epicycles of autism', *Journal of Autism and Developmental Disorders*, 1999, 29(2): 183.
112 M. Kinsbourne and P.J. Caplan, *Children's Learning and Attention Problems*, Boston: Little, Brown and Company, 1979, pp. 276–7.
113 R. Yeung-Courchesne and E. Courchesne, 'From impasse to insight in autism research', *Development and Psychopathology*, 1997, 9: 394.
114 American Psychiatric Association (1994), op. cit.

115 S. Wolff and A. Barlow, 'Schizoid personality in childhood: a comparative study of schizoid, autistic and normal children', *Journal of Child Psychology and Psychiatry*, 1979, 19: 175–80.

116 C. Gillberg, *Clinical Child Neuropsychiatry*, Cambridge: Cambridge University Press, 1995, pp. 146–7.

117 I. Rapin and D. Allen, 'Developmental language disorder', in V. Kirk (ed.) *Neuropsychology and Language Reading and Spelling*, New York: Academic Press, 1983, pp. 155–84.

118 D.R. Jordan, *Dyslexia in the Classroom*, Columbus, OH: Merrill, 1972.

119 M.B. Denckla, 'The neuropsychology of socio-emotional learning disability', *Archives of Neurology*, 1983, 40: 461–2.

120 B.P. Rourke, 'The syndrome of non-verbal learning disabilities: developmental manifestations in neurological disease, disorder and dysfunction', *The Clinical Neuropsychologist*, 1988, 2: 293–330.

121 D.J. Cohen, K. Paul and F.R. Volkmar, 'Issues in the classification of pervasive developmental disorders: towards DSM-IV', *Journal of the American Academy of Child Psychiatry*, 1986, 25: 213–29.

122 K. McKenna, C.T. Gordon, M. Lenane, D. Kaysen, K. Faitey and J.L. Rapoport, 'Looking for childhood onset schizophrenia. The first 71 cases screened', *Journal of the American Academy of Child and Adolescent Psychiatry*, 1994, 33: 636–44.

123 American Psychiatric Association (2000), op. cit., p. 217.

124 Ibid., p. 296.

125 Ibid., p. 65.

126 Ibid., p. 290.

127 Ibid., p. 78.

128 Ibid., p. 153.

129 Ibid., p. 295.

130 Ibid., p. 215.

131 J.D. Schmahmann and J.C. Sherman, 'The cerebellar cognitive affective syndrome', *Brain*, 121: 561–79.

132 Kinsbourne and Caplan, op. cit., pp. 276–8.

3 Psychology of high-functioning autism/Asperger's syndrome

1 S. Baron-Cohen, 'Theory of mind and autism: a fifteen year review', in S. Baron-Cohen, H. Tager-Flusberg and D.C. Cohen (eds) *Understanding Other Minds*, Oxford: Oxford University Press, 2000, p. 3.

2 D. Tantam, 'Adolescence and adulthood of individuals with Asperger's syndrome', in A. Klin, F. Volkmar and S. Sparrow (eds) *Asperger's Syndrome*, New York: Guilford Press, 2000, p. 382.

3 V. Cummine, J. Leach and G. Stephenson, *Asperger's Syndrome*, London: David Fulton Publishers, 2001, pp. 21–2.

4 C.J. Gomez, 'Do concepts of intersubjectivity apply to non-human primates?', in S. Braten (ed.) *Intersubjective Communication and Emotion in Early Ontogeny*, Cambridge: Cambridge University Press, 1998, pp. 246–9.

5 Ibid., p. 247.

6 O. Sacks, *An Anthropologist on Mars*, London: Picador, 1995, p. 113.

7 S. Baron-Cohen, in S. Braten, 'Intersubjective communication and understanding', in Braten, op. cit., p. 380.

8 S. Baron-Cohen, *Mind Blindness: An Essay on Autism and Theory of Mind*, Cambridge, MA: MIT Press, 1995, p. 41.

9 M. Fitzgerald, 'Did Ludwig Wittgenstein have Asperger's syndrome?', *European Child and Adolescent Psychiatry Journal*, 2000, 9: 61–5.

10 M. Sigman and L. Capps, *Children with Autism*, Cambridge, MA: Harvard University Press, 1997, pp. 157–8.

11 Gomez, op. cit., pp. 247–8.

12 S. Baron-Cohen, 'Autism: deficits in folk psychology exist along with superiority in folk physics', in Baron-Cohen *et al.*, op. cit., pp. 73–4.

13 J.-P. Dupuy, *The Mechanization of the Mind*, Princeton, NJ: Princeton University Press, 1994, pp. 3–4.

14 S. Baron-Cohen, 'Theory of mind and autism', in Baron-Cohen *et al.*, op. cit., p. 13.

15 Tantam, op. cit., p. 379.

16 J. de Villiers, 'Language and theory of mind: what are the developmental relationships?', in Baron-Cohen *et al.*, op. cit., p. 129.

17 J. Quigley, *The Grammar of Autobiography*, London: Lawrence Erlbaum, 2000.

18 J.S. Bruner, *Acts of Meaning*, Cambridge, MA: Harvard University Press, 1990.

19 P. Miller, J. Mintz, L. Hoogstra, H. Fong and R. Potts (1992) 'The narrated self: young children's construction of self in relation to others in conversational stories of personal experience', *Merill Palmer Quarterly*, 1992, 38: 45–67.

20 E. Ochs and L. Capps, 'Narrating the self', p. 20, *Annual Review of Anthropology*, 1996, 25: 19–43.

21 Quigley, op. cit., pp. 185–6.

22 J. Quigley, personal communication, 22 September 2002.

23 R. Jordan and S. Powell, *Understanding and Teaching Children with Autism*, Chichester: Wiley, 1995, p. 8.

24 M. Prior and S. Ozonoff, 'Psychological factors in autism', in F. Volkmar (ed.) *Autism and Pervasive Development Disorders*, Cambridge: Cambridge University Press, 1998, p. 67.

25 T. Shapiro and M.E. Hertzig, 'Social deviance in autism: a central integrative failure as a model for social non-engagement', *Psychiatric Clinics of North America*, 1991, 14: xi, 19.

26 D. Siegel, 'Memory: an overview, with emphasis on developmental, interpersonal, and neurobiological aspects', *Journal of the American Academy of Child and Adolescent Psychiatry*, 2001, 40: 9.

27 Ibid.

28 F. Happe, 'Autism: cognitive deficit or cognitive style?', *Trends in Cognitive Science*, 1999, 3(6): 216–22.

29 Baron-Cohen, 'Autism: deficits in folk psychology', in Baron-Cohen *et al.*, op. cit., p. 78.

30 S. Baron-Cohen, S. Wheelwright, V. Stone and M. Rutherford, 'A mathematician, a physicist, and a computer scientist with Asperger's syndrome', *Neurocase*, 1999, 5: 475–83.

31 Happe, op. cit.

32 Ibid.

33 R. Monk, *Ludwig Wittgenstein – the Duty of Genius*, London: Jonathan Cape, 1990, p. 502.

34 Sigman and Capps, op. cit., p. 155.

35 Cummine et al., op. cit., p. 26.

36 Baron-Cohen, 'Autism: deficits in folk psychology', in Baron-Cohen *et al.* (2000), op. cit., p. 79.

37 F. Happe, 'Parts and wholes, meaning and minds', in Baron-Cohen *et al.* (2000), op. cit., p. 207.

38 Ibid.

39 J. Radford, *Child Prodigies and Exceptional Early Achievers*, Hemel Hempstead: Harvester Wheatsheaf, 1990, p. 140.

40 Sacks, op. cit.

41 S. Baron-Cohen, H.A. Ring, S. Wheelwright, E.T. Bullmore, M.J. Brammer, A. Simmons and S.C.R. Williams, 'Social intelligence in the normal and autistic brain: an fMRI study', *European Journal of Neuroscience*, 1999, 11: 1891.

42 V. Stone, 'The role of the frontal lobe and amygdala in theory of mind', in Baron-Cohen *et al.* (2000), op. cit., p. 254.

43 R.E. Schultz, E. Romanski and K. Tsatsanis, 'Neurofunctional models of autistic disorder and Asperger's syndrome', in Klin *et al.*, op. cit., p. 190.

44 U. Frith, 'The neurocognitive basis of autism', *Trends in Cognitive Science*, 1997, 1(2): 75.

45 J. Ratey, *A User's Guide to the Brain*, London: Little, Brown & Co., 2001, p. 24.

46 Ibid.

47 Schultz *et al.*, op. cit.

48 Frith, op. cit.

49 T. West, *In the Mind's Eye*, Buffalo, NY: Prometheus Books, 1991, p. 14.

50 Sigman and Capps, op. cit., pp. 164–5.

51 West, op. cit.

52 R. Gregory, *Oxford Companion to the Mind*, Oxford: Oxford University Press, 1987, p. 530.

53 West, op. cit., p. 14.

54 Baron-Cohen *et al.* (2000), op. cit., p. 78.

55 Baron-Cohen, S. and Hammer, J. (1997) 'Parents of children with Asperger's syndrome: what is the cognitive phenotype?', *Journal of Cognitive Neuroscience*, 9: 548–54.

56 R. Jordan, *Autistic Spectrum Disorders*, London: David Fulton, 2001, p. 53.

57 K. Schmidt, 'It was my genes guv', *New Scientist*, 8 November 1997, 44–50.

58 Jordan, op. cit., p. 53.

59 T. Attwood, *Asperger's Syndrome*, London: Jessica Kingsley Press, 1995, p. 152.

60 C. Gillberg, *A Guide to Asperger's Syndrome*, Cambridge: Cambridge University Press, 2002, pp. 71–2.

61 Ibid., p. 22.

62 Ibid.

63 Ibid., p. 78.

64 Ibid., p. 41.

65 C. Gillberg, *Clinical Child Neuropsychiatry*, Cambridge: Cambridge University Press, 1995, p. 69.

66 U. Frith, *Autism and Asperger's Syndrome*, Cambridge: Cambridge University Press, 1991, p. 85.

67 L. Obler and D. Fine, *Exceptional Brain*, Guilford Press, New York, 1988, p. 272.

68 Schultz *et al.*, op. cit., pp. 182–3.

69 Ibid.

70 S. Baron-Cohen and J. Hammer, 'Parents of children with Asperger syndrome: what is the cognitive phenotype?', *Journal of Cognitive Neuroscience*, 1997, 9: 548–54.

71 Schultz *et al.*, op. cit., p. 183.

72 P. Wells, *Times Literary Supplement*, 30 September 1994, 13.

73 Happe (1999), op. cit., p. 222.
74 L.L. Cohen, 'An artificial neural network analogue of learning in autism', *Biological Psychiatry*, 1994, 36: 5.
75 Happe (1999), op. cit., p. 222.

4 Ludwig Wittgenstein

1 He claimed that the glory of the intellectual and cultural life of the Austro-Hungarian Empire had an evil 'shadow-side' or 'apocalyptic kitsch' to which he swiftly succumbed and from which he never fully freed himself. See J.C. Marshall, 'The meaning of Wittgenstein', *Nature*, 1990, 348: 384.
2 According to Paul Wijdeveld, the principle developed by Wittgenstein was of a jet engine that formed a whole with the propeller it drove, which was put to use in the Second World War by the Austrian engineer von Doblhoff in the rotor of a helicopter, and was later adapted by an American aircraft factory. See P. Wijdeveld, *Ludwig Wittgenstein, Architect*, London: Thames and Hudson, 1994, p. 26.
3 R. Monk, *Ludwig Wittgenstein – the Duty of Genius*, London: Jonathan Cape, 1990, p. 579.
4 M. Fitzgerald and D. Berman, 'Of sound mind', *Nature*, 1994, 368: 92.
5 B.F. McGuinness, *Wittgenstein, A Life – Young Ludwig (1889–1921)*, London: Penguin, 1988, and Monk, op. cit.
6 M. Fitzgerald, 'Did Ludwig Wittgenstein have Asperger's syndrome?', *European Child and Adolescent Psychiatry*, 2000, 9(6): 61–5.
7 McGuinness, op. cit., p. 5.
8 Ibid., p. 19.
9 Ibid., p. 9.
10 Ibid., p. 5.
11 Ibid., p. 12.
12 Ibid., p. 10.
13 Ibid., p. 18.
14 Ibid., p. 26.
15 Ibid., p. 11.
16 Ibid., p. 9.
17 Ibid., p. 20.
18 Ibid., p. 47.
19 Wijdeveld, op. cit., p. 63.
20 Ibid., p. 65.
21 Ibid., p. 67.
22 Anna Maija Hintikka, 'Dialogues with inner pictures: Ludwig Wittgenstein as dyslexic', paper presented at the *25th Ludwig Wittgenstein Society Meeting*, Kirchberg-am-Wechsel, 2002, p. 4.
23 McGuinness, op. cit., p. 52.
24 Ibid.
25 N. Malcolm, *Ludwig Wittgenstein: a Memoir* (with a biographical sketch by G.H. von Wright), 2nd edn, Oxford: Oxford University Press, 1984.
26 McGuinness, op. cit., p. 51.
27 Monk, op. cit., p. 15.
28 I agree entirely with Marie McGinn's assessment of Wittgenstein's non-relations with Hitler. In her review of Lawrence Goldstein's book *Clear and Queer Thinking* (London: Duckworth, 1999), she states that Goldstein describes as 'overwhelmingly probable' the completely unfounded claim in *The Jew of Linz*

(Kimberly Cornish, London: Century, 1988) that Wittgenstein, as a schoolboy in Austria, met Hitler and became the source of the latter's anti-semitism. It was, Goldstein suggests, because Wittgenstein appeared as a 'stammering, precocious, precious, aristocratic upstart who . . . disdainfully flaunted his wealth and superiority' that Hitler formed the idea of 'the filthy Jew'. Ignoring the absurd knowingness of Goldstein's description of the young Wittgenstein, one is amazed at the sheer looseness of thought that allows him to assert that 'at certain points in *Mein Kampf* where Hitler seems to be raging against Jews in general it is the individual young Ludwig Wittgenstein whom he has in mind', and to suggest that Wittgenstein 'may have inspired . . . the hatred of Jews which led, ultimately to the Holocaust'. According to McGinn, it is 'exactly this sort of sloppy, irresponsible, but "plausible" style of thought that Wittgenstein's philosophy, by its careful attention to the particular and to not saying more or less than is warranted, is directed against. Goldstein's susceptibility to the charms of such obvious myths makes his hubristic claim that his "understanding of Wittgenstein's work has improved immeasurably as a result of developing an empathy for the man" offensive as well as risible.' See M. McGinn, 'Hi Ludwig!', *Times Literary Supplement*, 26 May 2000, 24.

29 Hintikka, op. cit., p. 3.
30 Ibid.
31 Malcolm, op. cit., p. 78.
32 Monk, op. cit., p. 526.
33 Ben-Ami Scharfstein, *The Philosophers: Their Lives and the Nature of Their Thought*, Oxford: Blackwell, 1980, p. 327.
34 Ibid., p. 328.
35 B. McGuinness (ed.) *Letters from Ludwig Wittgenstein with a Memoir by Paul Engelmann*, Oxford: Blackwell, 1967, p. 19.
36 Scharfstein, op. cit., p. 329.
37 A. Ambrose and M. Lazerowitz, *Ludwig Wittgenstein: Philosophy and Language*, London: Allen & Unwin, 1972, p. 13.
38 Gasking and Jackson, quoted in K.T. Fann (ed.) *Ludwig Wittgenstein: The Man and his Philosophy*, New York: Dell, 1967, p. 50.
39 F. Ramsey, 'Letter to his mother, 20 September 1923', quoted in Scharfstein, op. cit., p. 463.
40 L. Wittgenstein, Vermischte Bemerkungen, Frankfurt am Main/Oxford: Suhrkamp/Blackwell, 1977–1978, pp. 124–9.
41 H.J. Glock, 'Second thoughts', *Times Literary Supplement*, 23 June 1995, 9.
42 J. Mahon, 'The great philosopher who came to Ireland', in F.A. Flowers (ed.) *Portraits of Wittgenstein*, vol. 4, Bristol: Thoemmes Press, 1999, p. 6.
43 Scharfstein (op. cit., pp. 326–7) points out that Wittgenstein expressed the beautiful and good 'with literally nonsensical and yet impressive language' and that 'perhaps this was a reason that he pre-occupied himself with the nature and limits and language and with, as he saw it the related problems of solipsism (and idealism)'.
44 Monk, op. cit., p. 16.
45 Ibid., p. 48.
46 Ibid., p. 49.
47 C. Moorehead, *Bertrand Russell*, London: Sinclair-Stephenson, 1992, p. 338.
48 D. Edmonds and J. Eidinow, *Wittgenstein's Poker*, London: Faber and Faber, 2001, p. 159.
49 Malcolm, op. cit., p. 529.
50 Ibid., p. 74.

51 Ibid.
52 George Kreisel, in Edmonds and Eidinow, op. cit., p. 12.
53 Monk, op. cit., p. 267.
54 Ibid., p. 266.
55 Ibid., p. 256.
56 Peter Gray-Lucas, in Edmonds and Eidinow, op. cit., p. 19.
57 L. Wittgenstein, in G.H. von Wright with Heikki Nyman (eds) *Culture and Value*, Oxford: Blackwell, 1980, p. 78.
58 Monk, op. cit., p. 530.
59 Ibid.
60 McGuinness (1988), op. cit., p. 36.
61 Ibid., p. 51.
62 Ibid., p. 35.
63 R. Wall, *Wittgenstein in Ireland*, London: Reaktion Books, 2000, pp. 32–3.
64 L. Wing, 'Syndromes of autism and atypical development', in D. Cohen and F. Volkmar (eds) *Handbook of Autism and Pervasive Developmental Disorders*, New York: Wiley, 1997, pp. 93–7.
65 A.J. Ayer, *Ludwig Wittgenstein*, London: Penguin, 1985, p. 11, quoting from Malcolm, op. cit., p. 34.
66 Moorehead, op. cit., p. 171.
67 M. Fitzgerald, 'Did the "man who loved only numbers", Paul Erdös, have Asperger's syndrome?', *Nordic Journal of Psychiatry*, 1999, 536: 465.
68 Monk, op. cit., p. 271.
69 Personal communication between Eileen Drury, David Berman (Professor of Philosophy, Trinity College Dublin) and the author, 13 November 1995.
70 Monk, op. cit., p. 65.
71 Bertrand Russell, in ibid., p. 42.
72 Ibid., p. 88.
73 McGuinness (1988), op. cit., p. 123.
74 Monk, op. cit., p. 255.
75 Scharfstein (op. cit., p. 330) accounts for Wittgenstein's often wilful misunderstanding as follows. 'This characterisation like the previous one implies the ambivalence everywhere evident in both his person and thought. It was his pleasure and need to teach with fierce intensity, yet he was immediately disgusted with what he had taught and with himself as a teacher. It appears to me that he used his teaching to establish some connection with people interested in his philosophically-expressed problems and therefore in himself; but to establish the connection he had to risk revealing himself; and he was sure in advance that, whatever he said, the others would not really understand him; and if they did understand him, they would value him for his ideas, and not for himself. In effect, he was frightened, repelled, and disgusted by the closeness that his intellectual and emotional intensity did succeed in establishing, and he immediately tried to wipe out consciousness of this trying experience with the help of the impersonal excitements of a film.'
76 M. Fitzgerald and D. Berman, *Taped Interview with Norman Moore*, Dublin, 12 November 1993.
77 Monk, op. cit., pp. 390–1.
78 Ibid., p. 119.
79 Ibid., p. 181.
80 Ibid.
81 A. Kenny, *Wittgenstein*, London: Penguin, 1973, p. 13.
82 Monk, op. cit., p. 119.

83 McGuinness (1988), op. cit., p. 250.
84 B. Rogers, *A.J. Ayer*, London: Chatto & Windus, 1999, p. 85.
85 McGuinness (1988), op. cit., p. 271.
86 L. Wittgenstein (1980), op. cit., p. 49, quoted in Monk, op. cit., p. 492.
87 Monk, op. cit., p. 493.
88 McGuinness (1988), op. cit., p. 498.
89 G.H. von Wright quoted in Edmonds and Eidinow, op. cit., p. 149.
90 Scharfstein, op. cit., p. 325.
91 Edmonds and Eidinow, op. cit., p. 27.
92 Ibid., p. 28.
93 Monk, op. cit., p. 251.
94 Edmonds and Eidinow, op. cit.
95 Ibid., p. 33.
96 Edmonds and Eidinow (op. cit.) relate how, having decided during a bicycle ride that he no longer loved his first wife, Alys, Russell broke the news to her immediately on returning home. Though he had divorced her, she never stopped loving him. Moreover, his granddaughter claimed that he slept with his daughter-in-law, resulting in the break up of his son John's marriage. Also, he has been charged with driving John to madness, and of 'causing two of his wives to attempt suicide'.
97 Russell emphasised the similarities between Wittgenstein and himself as follows: 'I have the most perfect intellectual sympathy with him – the same passion and vehemence, the same feeling that one must understand or die, the sudden jokes break down the frightful tension of thought' (Monk, op. cit., p. 43).
98 Ibid., p. 80.
99 Ibid., p. 491.
100 Ibid., p. 586.
101 Ibid., p. 376.
102 Ibid., p. 492.
103 Personal communication, 13 November 1995.
104 McGuinness (1988), op. cit., p. 59.
105 Monk, op. cit., p. 258.
106 Ibid., p. 239.
107 McGuinness (1988), op. cit., p. 149.
108 Obituary of Elizabeth Anscombe, *The Irish Times*, 27 January 2001.
109 Monk, op. cit., p. 498.
110 M. Warnock, *A Memoir*, London: Duckworth, 2000, p. 75.
111 Ibid., p. 73.
112 Obituary in *The Irish Times*, 27 January 2001. According to the obituary, Anscombe later stopped regarding Wittgenstein as a 'Christ-figure' and 'partly at least, dropped his mannerisms'. She was against contraception and condemned homosexuality despite Wittgenstein being homosexual. The obituary described her as follows: 'outspoken, often rude, she was sometimes dubbed "dragon lady". For a time she sported a monocle . . . she was notorious for a forthright foulmouthedness . . . On entering a smart Boston restaurant, she was told that ladies were not admitted in trousers (she always wore trousers except when pregnant) so she simply took them off.'
113 Monk, op. cit., p. 212.
114 Ibid.
115 Ayer, op. cit., p. 5.
116 Gretl Wittgenstein, in McGuinness (1988), op. cit., p. 27.

117 W.W. Bartley, *Wittgenstein*, London: Quartet Books, 1973, p. 70.
118 R. Rhees (ed.) *Recollections of Wittgenstein*, Oxford: Oxford University Press, 1984.
119 Ibid.
120 Monk, op. cit., p. 154.
121 Bartley, op. cit., p. 65.
122 Wall, op. cit., p. 93.
123 B. McGuinness and G.H. von Wright (eds) *Letters to Russell, Keynes and Moore*, Oxford: Blackwell, 1974, p. 43.
124 David Pinsent, in Monk, op. cit., p. 80.
125 Maud Kingston, in Wall, op. cit.
126 Ibid., p. 11.
127 Ibid., p. 178.
128 Fr Fechim O'Doherty, in G. Hetherington, 'Wittgenstein in Ireland: an account of his various visits from 1934 to 1949', in Flowers, op. cit., p. 14.
129 *Liveline*, RTÉ Radio 1, 27 December 2001.
130 H. Browne, 'What Wittgenstein did in Wicklow' (RTÉ Radio 1, 27 December 2001), *The Irish Times*, 30 December 2000, p. 7.
131 E. Skidelsky, *Times Literary Supplement*, 18 August 2001, 27.
132 D. Pinsent, in G.H. von Wright (ed.), *A Portrait of Wittgenstein as a Young Man – from the diary of David Pinsent, 1912–1914*, Oxford: Basil Blackwell, 1990, pp. 79–80.
133 Bartley, op. cit., 1977, p. 72.
134 Iris Murdoch, in Edmonds and Eidinow, op. cit., p. 47.
135 Monk, op. cit., p. 171.
136 Ayer, op. cit., p. 11.
137 Oscar Fuchs, in Frau Luise Haussmann, *Wittgenstein als Volksschullehrer*. See also version published in *Club Vultair*, vol. 4, Hamburg: Rohalt Verlag, 1970, pp. 391–6.
138 K. Johannessen, R. Larson and K Amas, *Wittgenstein and Norway*, Sullum: Forlag, 1994.
139 J. Klagg, *Metaphysics in the Post-metaphysical Age: Proceedings of the 22nd International Wittgenstein Symposium*, Kirchberg-an-Wechsel, 1999, pp. 333–4. Also, Edmonds and Eidinow state that with his students Wittgenstein was 'brutally intolerant of any remark he considered sloppy or portentous'. Similarly, Stephen Toulmin is quoted as stating 'for our part, we struck him as intolerably stupid. He would denounce us to our faces as unteachable' (Edmonds and Eidinow, op. cit., p. 149).
140 Johannessen *et al.*, op. cit., p. 30.
141 Rhees, op. cit., p. 140.
142 Monk, op. cit., pp. 97–8.
143 Ibid., pp. 99–100.
144 Ibid., p. 100.
145 Moorehead, op. cit., p. 172.
146 Malcolm, op. cit., p. 61.
147 W.A. Hijab, 'Wittgenstein on the future of philosophy', *Proceedings of the 24th International Wittgenstein Symposium*, Kirchberg-am-Wechsel, 2001, p. 313.
148 Warnock, op. cit., p. 71.
149 G.H. von Wright, in Malcolm, op. cit., pp. 18–19.
150 Hetherington, op. cit., p. 14.
151 Edmonds and Eidinow, op. cit., p. 148.
152 G.H. von Wright, in Ibid., p. 24.

153 B. Leitner, *The Architecture of Ludwig Wittgenstein*, London: Studio Publications, 1973, p. 20.
154 Wijdeveld, op. cit., p. 50.
155 Scharfstein, op. cit., pp. 303–33.
156 Paul Engelmann, in Edmonds and Eidinow, op. cit., p. 157.
157 McGuinness (1988), op. cit., p. 82.
158 Monk, op. cit., p. 536.
159 Ibid., p. 522.
160 Ibid., p. 577.
161 Malcolm, op. cit., p. 24.
162 Bartley, op. cit., p. 73.
163 Monk, op. cit., p. 49.
164 O. Sacks, *An Anthropologist on Mars: Seven Paradoxical Tales*, New York: Knopf, 1995, p. 281.
165 Malcolm, op. cit., p. 27.
166 Bertrand Russell, in Monk, op. cit., p. 43.
167 Ibid., p. 80.
168 Ibid., p. 284.
169 McGuinness (1988), op. cit., p. 70.
170 M. O'C. Drury, in Rhees, op. cit., p. 156.
171 Bertrand Russell, in Monk, op. cit., p. 240.
172 Bertrand Russell, in Moorehead, op. cit., p. 175.
173 W. Self, 'Oh no, not another silly title', *New Statesman*, 9 April 2001, 50–51.
174 McGuinness (1988), op. cit., pp. 44–5.
175 N. Malcolm, quoted in Scharfstein, op. cit., p. 325.
176 Malcolm, op. cit., p. 31.
177 David Pinsent, in McGuinness (1988), op. cit., p. 181; Monk, op. cit., p. 61.
178 Obituary of Margaret Louden, a surgeon who worked with Wittgenstein, *Daily Telegraph*, 19 February 1999, 29.
179 E.G. Bywaters, in Monk, op. cit., pp. 456–7.
180 Sir John Vinelott, in Edmonds and Eidinow, op. cit., p. 149.
181 Monk, op. cit., p. 548.
182 Monk (ibid.) notes that this idea is summed up in one of Wittgenstein's most striking aphorisms: 'if a lion could talk, we would not understand him' (Wittgenstein, in G. Anscombe, R. Rhees and G.H. von Wright (eds) *Philosophical Investigations*, Oxford: Basil Blackwell, 1953, p. 223).
183 Monk, op. cit., pp. 548–9.
184 Wittgenstein (1953), op. cit., p. 227.
185 Monk, op. cit, p. 549.
186 S. Baron-Cohen, 'Autism: deficits in folk psychology exist along with superiority in folk physics', in S. Baron-Cohen, H. Tager-Flusberg and D.C. Cohen (eds) *Understanding Other Minds*, Oxford: Oxford University Press, 2000, pp. 73–4.
187 Monk, op. cit, p. 549.
188 Ibid.
189 M.O'C. Drury, in Rhees, op. cit, p. 112.
190 Wijdeveld, op. cit, pp. 69–70.
191 G.E. Moore, *Philosophical Papers*, London: Allen & Unwin, 1959, p. 256.
192 A student named Hijab, in Edmonds and Eidinow, op. cit., p. 9.
193 Karl Popper, in ibid., p. 19.
194 Ibid., p. 2.
195 B. Morton, 'Heat in the embers', *Sunday Tribune*, 29 April 2001, 9.

196 Sir John Vinelott, in Edmonds and Eidinow, op. cit., p. 149.
197 J.R. Smythies, 'Wittgenstein's paranoia', *Nature*, 1991, 9: 350.
198 Quoted in Rogers, op. cit., p. 94.
199 Edmonds and Eidinow, op. cit., p. 121.
200 Fann, op. cit. Quoted in Monk, op. cit., p. 244.
201 Self, op. cit.
202 J.C. Marshall, 'Unscientific postscript', *Nature*, 1990, 347: 435.
203 Wall, op. cit., pp. 27–8.
204 McGuinness (1988), op. cit., p. 272.
205 According to Tallis, Lacan's doctrines were 'a magpie muddle of often unacknowledged expropriations from writers whose disciplines were alien to him, cast in borrowed jargon and opaque neologism – were Rorschach ink-blots into which anything could be read. Lacan's ideas were insulated against critical evaluation by his writing style, in which according to Roudinesco 'a dialectic between the presence and absence alternated with a logic of space and motion'. See R. Tallis, 'The shrink from hell', *Times Higher Educational Supplement*, 31 October 1997, 20.
206 Ibid.
207 Elizabeth Roudinesco, in her biography of Lacan (*Jacques Lacan*, Cambridge: Polity Press, 1999), states that '[Lacan was not only] a womaniser and a libertine, moody and impossible to satisfy, but he was also possessed by the idea that he was a genius who would produce great works and by an immense desire to be recognised and famous. All he thought about was himself and his work. His hunger for fame and knowledge made him insatiably curious, assailing with question after question anyone whose learning he might hope to absorb. He looked at people so intently that they often took him for some sort of diabolical being, possessed himself and trying to possess them.' Furthermore, 'he was at once tyrannical and attractive, inquisitorial and anxious, a show-off and a man haunted by the truth'. Lacan was expelled from the International Psychoanalytic Association. It is interesting that Anthony Easthope ('Theory of authority, *Times Higher Educational Supplement*, 7 November 1997, 13) pointed out that 'I am sure Raymond Tallis is right that as a moral individual Jacques Lacan was a monster'.
208 Monk, op. cit., p. 194.
209 Wall, op. cit., p. 70.
210 Monk, op. cit., p. 526.
211 Moorehead, op. cit., p. 307.
212 Edmonds and Eidinow, op. cit., p. 17.
213 M. Baghramian, 'Ireland in the life of Ludwig Wittgenstein', in Flowers, op. cit., p. 30.
214 Edmonds and Eidinow, op. cit., p. 18.
215 N. Malcolm, *Wittgenstein: a Religious Point of View*, London: Routledge, 1993, p. 22.
216 McGuinness (1988), op. cit., p. 294.
217 Bartley, op. cit., p. 94.
218 Wijdeveld, op. cit., p. 189.
219 Monk, op. cit., p. 94.
220 Rhees, op. cit., p. 184.
221 J. Klagg and A. Nordman (eds) *Philosophical Occasions*, Indianapolis: Hackett Publishing Co., 1993, p. 11.
222 Rhees, op. cit., p. 153.
223 Ibid., p. 175.

224 Wittgenstein (1953), op. cit., p. ix.
225 A. Giddens, 'A matter of truth', *Times Literary Supplement*, 29 March 1996, 10.
226 Malcolm (1953), op. cit., p. 97.
227 Rhees, op. cit., p. 50.
228 Wittgenstein, *Vermischte Bemerkungen*, p. 56.
229 L. Wolff, *The Journey not the Arrival Matters*, London: Hogarth Press, 1969, p. 48.
230 Edmonds and Eidinow, op. cit., p. 138.
231 Ibid., p. 161.
232 Monk, op. cit., pp. 195–6.
233 Ibid., p. 232.
234 F. Piribauer, interview with Adolf Hubner, 10 April 1975, quoted in ibid., p. 233.
235 Bartley, op. cit., p. 90.
236 Personal communication, 14 September 1997.
237 Edmonds and Eidinow, op. cit., p. 2.
238 Morton, op. cit., p. 9.
239 Self, op. cit., p. 51.
240 American Psychiatric Association, *Diagnostic and Statistical Manual IV*, Washington, DC: APA, 1994, p. 176.
241 Monk, op. cit., p. 5.
242 McGuinness (1988), op. cit., p. 10.
243 Ibid., p. 48.
244 Ibid., p. 50.
245 A. Klin and F. Volkmar, 'Asperger's syndrome', in Cohen and Volkmar, op. cit, p. 114.
246 McGuinness (1988), op. cit., p. 27.
247 Ibid., p. 155.
248 B. Russell, *Autobiography*, vol. II, London: Allen & Unwin, 1968, p. 99.
249 McGuinness (1988), op. cit., p. 193.
250 Wittgenstein (1980), op. cit. Wittgenstein could also be flippant about his prospects of insanity. Monk noted that at philosophical gatherings he demanded, 'from the participants a degree of absorption and attentive rigour to which they were unaccustomed. After one such discussion Bouwsma asked Wittgenstein whether such evenings robbed him of sleep. He said they did not, but then, recalls Bouwsma, he added in all seriousness and with the kind of smile Dostoyevsky would suggest in such circumstances, 'no but do you know, I think I may go nuts' (Monk, op. cit., p. 544).
251 Monk, op. cit., p. 422.
252 Ibid., p. 526.
253 McGuinness (1988), op. cit, p. 154.
254 Edwards and Eidinow, op. cit, p. 147.
255 Monk, op. cit., p. 187.
256 McGuinness (1988), op. cit, p. 157.
257 Ibid., p. 158.
258 Smythies, op. cit., p. 9.
259 R. Matthews, 'The baffling genius of philosophy was more sad than bad', *Sunday Telegraph*, 13 March 1994, 22.
260 E. Eloma, in E. Rakitzis, *Nature*, 1991, 351: 179. Rakitzis states that 'the metaphorical, or the highly suggestive use of language, described as "schizo-phreneze" by Smythies, has met with a happier treatment by Pascal: "we recognise truth not only through reason but also through the heart". See Blaise

Pascal, *Pensées*, Nouveaux, Paris: Classique la rousse, 1965. Again, such an extreme rationalist philosopher as Spinoza acknowledges intuition as the highest form of knowledge – the intuitive knowledge of God. See B. Spinoza, *Ethica*, 5, Prop. XXV, The Hague: van Vloten and Land, 1914, p. 73.'

261 Fitzgerald and Berman (1994), op. cit., p. 92.
262 Matthews, op. cit., p. 22.
263 Wittgenstein (1977/1978), op. cit., pp. 124–9.
264 Rhees, op. cit., p. 40.
265 A. Storr, *The Art of Psychotherapy*, London: Secker & Warburg, 1979, p. 107.
266 A.T. Beck, A.J. Rush and P.F. Shaw, *Cognitive Therapy of Depression*, Chichester: Wiley, 1979.
267 H. Meisner, 'Phenomenology of the self', in A. Goldberg (ed.) *Self Psychology and the Future of Psychoanalysis*, New York: International Universities Press, 1983, p. 75.
268 D. Berman, M. Fitzgerald and J. Hayes, *Danger of Words*, Bristol: Thoemmes Press, 1996, p. 136.
269 Monk, op. cit., p. 388.
270 Rhees, op. cit., p. 154.
271 W.R. Bion, 'Attacks on linking', in *Second Thoughts*, London: Heinemann, 1959, p. 67.
272 J. Grotstein, 'Perspectives on self psychology', in Goldberg, op. cit., p. 179.
273 Storr, op. cit., p. 95.
274 Monk, op. cit., p. 442.
275 Ibid., pp. 518–19.
276 P. Coulthard and M. Fitzgerald, 'In God we trust? A discussion of organised religion and personal beliefs as resources and coping strategies and their implications for health in parents with a child on the autistic spectrum', *Mental Health, Religion and Culture Journal*, 1999, 2(1): 19–33.
277 Wijdeveld, op. cit., p. 40.
278 Monk, op. cit., p. 523.
279 It is interesting that his disciple, Yorick Smythies, was prescribed amphetamines for depression, but became addicted to them and developed a paranoid psychosis. See J.R. Smythies, 'Alas, poor Yorick', *Nature*, 1994, 371: 470.
280 McGuinness (1988), op. cit., pp. 25–9.
281 Ibid., p. 28.
282 Ibid., p. 33.
283 J. Laplanche and J.D. Pontalis, *The Language of Psychoanalysis*, London: Hogarth Press, 1973, p. 159.
284 S. Freud, *On Narcissism, An Introduction*, Standard Edition, 14, London: Hogarth Press, 1914, p. 160.
285 H. Nunberg, *Principles of Psychoanalysis*, New York: International Universities Press, 1955, p. 161.
286 McGuinness (1988), op. cit., p. 8.
287 A. Levi, 'Wittgenstein once more: a response to critics', *Telos*, 1979, 40: 169.
288 Cyril Barrett (ed.) *Lectures and Conversations*, Oxford, 1970, p. 51.
289 O. Weininger, *Sex and Character*, Heinemann, 1906, p. 41.
290 McGuinness (1988), op. cit., p. 41.
291 Malcolm, *A Religious Point of View*, op. cit., p. 8.
292 McGuinness (1967), op. cit., p. 8.
293 McGuinness (1988), op. cit., p. 240.
294 R. Monk, 'Private lives', *The Times Magazine*, 30 November 1996, p. 39.
295 McGuinness (1988), op. cit., p. 156.

296 Monk (1990), op. cit., p. 367.
297 Sacks, op. cit., p. 281. Sacks refers to Grandin's badness in the following way: 'Temple had spoken earlier of being mischievous, or naughty, saying she enjoyed this at times, and she had been pleased at having smuggled me successfully into the slaughterhouse. She likes to commit small infractions on occasion – "I sometimes walk two feet outside the line at the airport, a little act of defiance" – but all this is in a totally different category from "real badness". That could have terrifying, instantly lethal consequences. "I have a feeling that if I do anything really bad, God will punish me, the steering linkage will go out on the way to the airport", she said as we were driving back. I was startled by the association of divine retribution with a broken steering linkage.'
298 Ibid.
299 Monk (1990), op. cit., pp. 64–5.
300 Wittgenstein (1977/1978), op. cit., p. 45.
301 Monk (1990), op. cit., p. 376.
302 Levi, op. cit., p. 166.
303 Malcolm (1984), op. cit., p. 59.
304 Rhees, op. cit., p. 94.
305 McGuinness (1998), op. cit., p. 220.
306 B. Magee, *The Great Philosophers*, London: BBC Books, 1987, p. 344.
307 Monk (1990), op. cit., p. 138.
308 McGuinness (1988), op. cit., p. 239.
309 Coulthard and Fitzgerald, op. cit., pp. 19–33.
310 McGuinness (1988), op. cit., p. 43.
311 Ibid., p. 45.
312 Ibid.
313 Monk (1990), op. cit., p. 453.
314 Ibid., p. 237.
315 I.B. Whyte, 'The perfect light bulb', *Times Literary Supplement*, 11 November 1994, 6.
316 Monk (1990), op. cit., p. 237.
317 Leitner, op. cit., p. 23.
318 Monk (1990), op. cit., p. 237.
319 Whyte, op. cit., p. 6.
320 Ibid.
321 Wijdeveld, op. cit.
322 U. Frith, *Autism and Asperger's Syndrome*, Cambridge: Cambridge University Press, 1979, p. 97.
323 Ibid., p. 110.
324 Monk (1990), op. cit., p. 75.
325 Ibid., p. 270.
326 Ibid., p. 43.
327 Moorehead, op. cit., p. 172.
328 Monk (1990), op. cit., p. 46.
329 Wijdeveld, op. cit., jacket cover.
330 McGuinness (1998), op. cit., p. 47.
331 Alper points out that Wittgenstein appeared to be seduced by his own genius: 'a fairly commonplace, intellectualising, paranoid suspiciousness and craving for certainty, joined and elevated by genius, repeatedly leads to findings of philosophical beauty'. See G. Alper, *Portraits of an Artist as a Young Patient*, San Francisco: International Scholars Publications, 1998, pp. 167 70.
332 Ibid., p. 170. Alper also points out (p. 172) that Wittgenstein 'because of his

need to bar the world and especially affect and deep personal meaning from his writing is accordingly blocked and because of it has a greater need to release his powerful inner conflicts, which emerge in his famous, enigmatic style . . . never did a man expend so much feeling about so much abstraction.'

333 Edmonds and Eidinow, op. cit., p. 150.
334 McGuinness (1988), op. cit., p. 153.
335 Rudolph Carnap, in Fann, op. cit., pp. 33–9.
336 Monk (1990), op. cit., p. 258.
337 Fann, op. cit.
338 Monk (1990), op. cit., p. 243.
339 Hetherington, op. cit., p. 185.
340 Wing, op. cit., pp. 157–8.
341 Ibid., p. 158.
342 Ibid., p. 157.
343 Ibid., p. 158.
344 Ibid.
345 Ibid.
346 Ibid., p. 159.
347 Fitzgerald (1999), op. cit., p. 465.
348 Bartley, op. cit., p. 26, quoting from McGuinness (1967), op. cit., p. 57.
349 Bertrand Russell, in ibid., p. 54.
350 B.F. McGuinness and G.H. von Wright (eds) *Briefe, Briefwechsel mit B. Russell, G.E. Moore, J.M. Keynes, F.P. Ramsey, W. Eccles, P. Engelmann, und L. von Ficker*, Frankfurt: Suhrkamp, 1980, p. 215.
351 Monk (1990), op. cit., p. 314.
352 Walter Kaufman, in Bartley, op. cit., p. i.
353 Glock, op. cit., p. 9.
354 G.E. Moore, 'Wittgenstein's Lectures' in Klagg and Nordman, op. cit., p. 51.
355 Monk (1990), op. cit., p. 286.
356 Rogers, op. cit., p. 85.
357 Alper, op. cit., p. 168.
358 P.M. Hacker, 'Thought, language and reality', *Times Literary Supplement*, 17 February 1997, 8.
359 G. Alper, op. cit., p. 168.
360 Monk (1990), op. cit., p. 13.
361 Wijdeveld, op. cit., pp. 185–6.
362 Ibid., p. 184.
363 Edmonds and Eidinow, op. cit.
364 C.D. Broad, quoted in Ayer, op. cit., p. 4.
365 Wijdeveld, op. cit., p. 194.
366 Ibid., p. 130.
367 Anthony Kenny demonstrates the pictorial element in spatial relationships in the following way. 'Take the sentence "my fork is to the left of my knife". This sentence says something different from another sentence containing exactly the same words, namely, "My knife is to the left of my fork". What makes the first sentence, but not the second, mean that the fork is to the left of the knife? It is the fact that the words "my fork" accord to the left of the words "my knife" in the context of the first sentence but not in that of the second. So here we have a spatial relationship between things.' See Kenny, op. cit., pp. 4–5.
368 P. Giovacchine, *A Clinician's Guide to Reading Freud*, New York: Jason Aronson, 1982, p. 2.
369 Wittgenstein, L., *Tractatus Logico-Philosophicus*, Chapter 7, London:

Routledge & Kegan Paul, 1955. J. Loizzo points out that in the *Tractatus* 'the view of language as "picturing . . . simple objects" was his means to the Kantian end of limiting empirical language to allow for silence respecting the subject. After a silent period come the transitional studies meant to correct "grave mistakes" in the early work: to find a post-Kantian way to solve the problem of inner–outer dualism. Here Wittgenstein arrives at what I call his "grammatical method" which "dissolved" his residual dualism by treating "inner" and "outer" as fictions "projected" by grammar, not language – independent realities.' According to Loizzo this was an 'anthropocentric' method. See J. Loizzo, 'Intersubjectivity in Wittgenstein and Freud: other minds and the foundations of psychiatry', *Theoretical Medicine*, 1997, 18: 379–400.

370 Wijdeveld, op. cit., p. 194.
371 Levi, op. cit., p. 171.
372 Wittgenstein (1955), op. cit., vi.
373 Ibid., ix.
374 Levi, op. cit., p. 167.
375 Ibid.
376 Malcolm (1993), op. cit., p. 8.
377 Monk (1990), op. cit., p. 261.
378 Wittgenstein (1953), op. cit., p. 40.
379 Monk (1990), op. cit., p. 261.
380 Sacks, op. cit., p. 233.
381 Bartley, op. cit., p. 115.
382 Monk (1990), op. cit., p. 261.
383 W. A. Hijab, 'Wittgenstein's missing map', *Proceedings of the 24th International Wittgenstein Symposium*, Kirchberg-am-Wechsel, 2001, p. 315.
384 Wittgenstein (1953), op. cit., p. 199.
385 Ibid., p. 145.
386 J. Klagg, 'Wittgenstein's community', op. cit., p. 333.
387 Ibid, p. 334. It is also surprising that Wittgenstein was not able to recognise a fellow person with HFA/ASP, when he declared: 'reading the Socratic dialogues one has the feeling: what a frightful waste of time!' (Edmonds and Eidinow, op. cit., p. 22). The paradox was that he himself was very similar to Socrates. Interestingly, Wittgenstein did not immerse himself in the works of other philosophers, and his regard for them was rather autistic. Lucy Hughes-Hallett, in a review of Adam Phillips' book *The Beast in the Nursery*, describes Wittgenstein's inspiration as follows: 'disarmingly, Wittgenstein confides to his interlocutor that though he reads Kierkegaard he prefers not to read very much of him. He did not want another man's thought all chewed, and anyway he had been far more profoundly moved by a banal line from the third-rate play.' (*The Spectator*, 28 February 1998, 31).
388 Klagg, 'Wittgenstein's community', op. cit., p. 334.
389 Wijdeveld (op. cit., p. 195) remarks that in the *Philosophical Investigations*, 'Wittgenstein introduced the language game by the example of an activity of erecting a building, in which it should be noted that the actual game seems to spell out the abridged syntax of a classical column . . . A calls out words; B brings the stone which he has learned to bring at each particular call – conceive this as a complete primitive language.'
390 P. Hobson, 'The intersubjective foundations of thoughts', in S. Braten (ed.) *Intersubjective Communication and Emotion in Early Ontogeny*, Cambridge: Cambridge, Cambridge University Press, 1998, p. 290.
391 Wittgenstein (1953), op. cit., p. 193.

392 Wall, op. cit., p. 102.

393 John Searle, in Magee, op. cit., p. 239.

394 Kenny, op. cit., p. 18. Wittgenstein's quotes translated by N. Malcolm, *The Philosophical Review*, 1973, LXXVI: 229.

395 John Searle, in Magee, op. cit., p. 327.

396 Monk (1990), op. cit., p. 523.

397 McGinn, op. cit.

398 Thomas Nagel points out that 'demonstrations of the limits of thought are an important element in philosophy, and Wittgenstein tried to turn philosophy into a method of showing that most of it consists of doomed attempts to violate these limits'. See T. Nagel, 'What is it about lemons?', *London Review of Books*, 20 September 2001, 26.

399 Scharfstein, op. cit., p. 334. Similarly, Glock (op. cit., p. 9) points out that Wittgenstein often struggled to find 'the redeeming word which would break the hold of the captivating pictures which he held responsible for many philosophical confusions'.

400 McGinn, op. cit.

401 Hacker, op. cit.

402 Edmonds and Eidinow, op. cit., p. 82.

403 Monk (1990), op. cit., p. 404.

404 As Edmonds and Eidinow (op. cit., p. 118) point out, 'Wittgenstein discussed contradictions in mathematical logic with Alan Turing, who thought Wittgenstein's idea that contradictions were not significant, utterly wrong-headed'. Turing also had HFA/ASP (and was homosexual); however, in this case I am sure he is correct about the issue of contradictions.

405 Magee, op. cit., p. 336.

406 Kenny states that 'Wittgenstein showed . . . that even when we think our most private and spiritual thoughts we are employing the medium of a language which is essentially tied to its public and bodily expression. But it is a measure of the enormous influence of Descartes that even those who most admire the genius of Wittgenstein think that his greatest achievement was the overthrow of Descartes' philosophy of mind' (A. Kenny, *A Life in Oxford*, London: John Murray, 1999).

407 Rogers, op. cit., pp. 253–4.

408 Monk (1990), op. cit., p. 95.

409 Rogers, op. cit., p. 253. Searle similarly believes that Wittgenstein's argument against this is a *reductio ad absurdum* argument. 'If we try to think of a sensation language on this model we wouldn't be able to make the distinction between actually using the word right and just thinking we are using it right. But if there isn't a distinction between really getting it right and just thinking we have got it right, then we can't talk about right at all. So the idea that we could have a private sensation language reduces to absurdity. His solution to this puzzle, the puzzle of how we can ever use words to refer to inner sensations, is the same as his solution to the general problem about rule following. The rules for using sensation words are public social rules. They are learned and applied in a social setting. And these external criteria are socially sanctioned and socially applied. It is because we are members of a linguistic community that we can have linguistic rules at all, and it is because we have public social criteria for our inner experiences that we can have a language referring to our inner experiences. He summarises this point by saying "an inner process" stands in need of outer criteria' (Magee, op. cit., p. 338).

410 In a discussion of Wittgenstein's view of philosophy, Ayer stated that 'the task

of the philosopher, as Wittgenstein came to see it, is not to devise theories to deal with these problems but to "dissolve" them by calling attention to the way language works – a job which involved all the practice, patience and dexterity that goes into the untangling and mending of fishing nets. This method was well illustrated by Wittgenstein's treatment of "mental psychology", where he sought to show how the empiricist belief in an inner self, made up of sense-data and mental images, arises from neglect of the way we actually use the phrase like "it hurts", "it seems to me" or "I remember".' See Rogers, op. cit., pp. 253–4.

411 Kenny, op. cit., p. 16.

412 A.J. Greenfield, 'The meaning of Wittgenstein', *Nature*, 1990, 348: 384.

413 Strawson does admit to a difficulty here, 'in that it would clearly be intolerable to deny sentience in non-human animals. They too, for example, surely feel pain. But they are not conceptualising rational creatures' (P.F. Strawson, 'At home in the "space of reasons"', *Times Literary Supplement*, 25 November 1994, 12).

414 Loizzo, op. cit., pp. 379–400.

415 Ibid., p. 395.

416 Ibid., p. 379.

417 Marshall (1990), 'The meaning of Wittgenstein', op. cit., p. 384.

418 According to Fodor, Wittgenstein encourages us to 'conflate the use of an expression with its meaning; more specifically, to conflate the meaning of an expression with what it can do, or be used to do, in virtue of what it means (ditto, *mutatis mutandis*, for the contents of statements and thoughts)' (J. Fodor, 'Dicing with shadows', *Times Literary Supplement*, 6 July 2001, 7).

419 F. Happe, *Autism*, London: UCL Press, 1994, pp. 34–66.

420 B. Magee, *Confessions of a Philosopher*, London: Weidenfeld & Nicholson, 1997, p. 35.

421 Ibid., p. 117.

422 Ibid., p. 215. Magee also notes the significant influence of Schopenhauer on Wittgenstein's work.

423 Fodor (2001), op. cit.

424 According to Will Self, the 'current, ruckled relativism of our moral and political thinking can be directly traced to the limitation [Wittgenstein] identified in the powers of reason to resolve our ethical dilemmas. And when it comes to philosophy the puzzlers have won hands down over the problem-solvers. You would be hard put nowadays to find an academic philosopher who would seriously contend that work on their subjects – given the necessary fiscal apportionment – will eventually turn up the solution to such questions as the nature of certain knowledge, or the status of reality, or the purpose of humanity' (Self, op. cit., p. 51).

425 McGinn, op. cit., p. 24.

426 Moorehead, op. cit., p. 308.

427 Hacker, op. cit., p. 9.

428 Self, op. cit., p. 51.

429 Greenfield, op. cit., p. 384.

430 Kenny, op. cit., p. 4.

431 Nagel, op. cit., p. 25.

432 Stephen Toulmin, in Edmonds and Eidinow, op. cit.

433 Monk (1996), op. cit., p. 35.

434 Quoted in the preface to McGuinness (1967), op. cit., p. xiv.

435 R. Rhees, 'Wittgenstein', *The Human World*, no. 14, February 1974, 71.

436 Ian Brunskill, *The Times*, 25 April 2001, 4–5.
437 Sacks, op. cit., p. 281.
438 M. Fitzgerald, 'Did Bartók have HFA/ASP?', *Autism Europe Link*, 2000, 29: 21.
439 Fitzgerald (2000), 'Did Ludwig Wittgenstein have Asperger's syndrome?', op. cit.
440 Wittgenstein (1980), op. cit., p. 20.
441 Scharfstein, op. cit., p. 334.
442 Bartley, op. cit., p. 169.

5 Sir Keith Joseph

1 Andrew Denham and Mark Garnett, *Keith Joseph*, London: Acumen, 2001, p. xii.
2 John Gray, 'The mad monk', *New Statesman*, 23 Aprril 2001, 54.
3 Denham and Garnett, op. cit., p. 39.
4 Ibid., p. 40.
5 Ibid., p. 11.
6 Ibid.
7 Ibid., p. 12.
8 Ibid., p. 11.
9 Ibid., p. 17.
10 Ibid., p. 14.
11 Ibid., p. 15.
12 Ibid., p. 17.
13 Ibid., p. 21.
14 Ibid., p. 18.
15 Ibid., p. 20.
16 Ibid., p. xi.
17 *City Press* obituary, in ibid., p. 184.
18 Ibid., p. 76.
19 Ibid., pp. 190–1.
20 Ibid., p. xi.
21 Ibid., p. 24.
22 Ibid., p. 210.
23 Ibid., p. xvi.
24 Ibid., p. xi.
25 Ibid., p. 24.
26 Ibid., p. 24.
27 Ibid., p. 31.
28 Ibid., p. 36.
29 Ibid.
30 Ibid., p. 50.
31 Ibid., p. 23.
32 Ibid., p. 121.
33 Simon Hoggart, *On the House*, London: Robson Books, 1981, pp. 25, 108–10, 140; interview with Alan Watkins, p. 354.
34 Denham and Garnett, op. cit., p. 354.
35 Ibid., p. 23.
36 Ibid., p. 302.
37 Ibid., p. 318.
38 Ibid., p. 169.

39 Ibid., p. 354.
40 Ibid., p. 387.
41 Ibid., p. 344.
42 Ibid., p. 339.
43 Ibid., p. 347.
44 Ibid., p. 261.
45 Ibid., p. 306.
46 Ibid., p. 310.
47 Ibid., p. 308.
48 Ibid., p. 265.
49 Ibid., p. 267.
50 Ibid., p. 268. .
51 Ibid., p. 283.
52 Ibid.
53 Returning to power in late 1966, Joseph showed signs that his 'love of ideas might present a problem to his [Conservative] colleagues' (ibid., p. xiv). Clearly he was an intellectual and alienated from a significant proportion of his colleagues. Denham and Garnett point out that in Britain, 'where promotion depends on a broad conformity with "the rules of the game", the odds are stacked against those who earn an "intellectual" reputation (ibid.).
54 Ibid., p. 353.
55 Ronald Butt, *The Times*, 6 May 1971. (Quoted in Denham and Garnett, op. cit., p. 10.)
56 Denham and Garnett, op. cit., p. xiii.
57 Ibid., p. 84.
58 Ibid., p. 60.
59 Ibid., p. 426.
60 Ibid., p. 333.
61 Ibid., p. 289.
62 Ibid , p. 405.
63 Ibid., p. 425.
64 Ibid., p. 326.
65 Ibid., p. 277.
66 Ibid., p. xi.
67 Ibid., p. 185.
68 Ibid., p. 163.
69 Ibid., p. 269.
70 Ibid.
71 Ibid., p. 270.
72 Ibid., p. 109.
73 Ibid., p. 56.
74 Ibid., p. 49.
75 Ibid., p. 55.
76 Ibid., p. 40.
77 Ibid., p. 398.
78 Ibid., p. 132.
79 Ibid., p. 33.
80 Ibid., p. 43.
81 Ibid., p. 97.
82 Ibid.
83 Ibid., p. 197.
84 Ibid., p. xiv.

85 Ibid., p. 432.
86 Ibid., p. 36.
87 Ibid., p. 81.
88 Ibid., p. 341.
89 Ibid., p. 78.
90 Ibid., p. 312.
91 Ibid.
92 Ibid., p. 183.
93 Ibid., p. 183.
94 He didn't list any recreations in *Who's Who*. Anthony King asked him 'is there a blank there because you don't give any?', then quickly corrected himself saying 'clearly you do – you read' (ibid., p. 183).
95 Ibid., p. 191.
96 Ibid., p. 219.
97 Ibid., p. 148.
98 Ibid., p. 236.
99 Ibid., p. 200.
100 John Brocklehurst, in ibid., p. 23.
101 Ibid., p. 280.
102 *The Times*, 2 January 1975, text of a speech given at Olympia, 1 January 1975; see Denham and Garnett, op. cit., p. 282.
103 Denham and Garnett, op. cit.
104 Ibid., p. 270.
105 Ibid., p. 354.
106 Ibid., p. 355.
107 Ibid., p. 336.
108 According to Denham and Garnett, '*Private Eye* was told that to accompany his reading list, "Sir Sheath" (or the "Mad Mullah" as the *Eye* now called him) had drawn up a feeding list, which was sent ahead of the Secretary of State whenever an engagement included an invitation to eat. Unnamed officials were said to be alarmed by his dietary habits, and by the fact that the list of acceptable foodstuffs had allegedly been registered as "classified information". The reason for this precaution was Joseph's chronic digestive condition, but mischief-making journalists preferred to connect the symptoms with his image as the unbalanced wild man of the right. Tales soon emerged of Joseph ordering single boiled eggs and lavish business lunches' (ibid., pp. 336–7).
109 Ibid., p. 354.
110 Ibid., p. 218.
111 Ibid., p. 354.
112 Ibid., p. 132.
113 Ibid., p. 353.
114 Ibid.
115 Ibid., p. 304.
116 Ibid., p. 388.
117 Ibid., p. 302.
118 Ibid., p. 363. Denham and Garnett note that 'Michael Foot had been right all along: Joseph was indeed a conjuror who had forgotten the second half of his trick after smashing the wrist-watch. More exactly, his lifelong weakness for "utopian" thinking had deluded him into the belief that the watch would miraculously rebuild itself without any further intervention' (ibid., p. 437).
119 Ibid., p. 365.
120 Ibid., p. 186.

121 Ibid., p. 301.
122 Ibid., p. 405.
123 Ibid., p. 365.
124 Ibid., p. 350.
125 Ibid., p. xv.
126 Ibid., p. 416.
127 Ibid., p. xv.
128 Ibid., p. 291.
129 Ibid., p. xii.
130 Ibid., p. 207.
131 Ibid., p. 134.
132 Ibid., p. 135.
133 Ibid., p. xv.
134 Ibid., p. xiii.
135 Ibid., p. xvi.
136 Ibid., p. 313.
137 Ibid., p. 318.
138 Ibid.
139 Ibid., p. 56.
140 Patrick Cosgrave, 'The man who told the truth', *The Spectator*, September 1974.
141 Denham and Garnett, op. cit., p. 426.
142 Ibid., p. 185.
143 Ibid., p. 132.
144 Ibid., p. xvi.
145 Ibid., p. 44.
146 Ibid., p. 32.

6 Eamon de Valera

1 T.P. Coogan, *De Valera – Long Fellow, Long Shadow*, London: Hutchinson, 1993, p. 14.
2 Ibid., p. 14.
3 Ibid., p. 6.
4 D. Ryan, *Unique Dictator – a Study of Eamon de Valera*, London: Arthur Barker, 1936, p. 28.
5 Coogan, op. cit., p. 16.
6 Ryan, op. cit., p. 254.
7 Coogan, op. cit., p. 146.
8 Ryan, op. cit., p. 81.
9 Coogan, op. cit., p. 146.
10 Ibid., pp. 96–7.
11 Ryan, op. cit., p. 25.
12 Ibid., pp. 26.
13 Coogan, op. cit., p. 703.
14 Ryan, op. cit., p. 15.
15 T.K. Whitaker, in Coogan, op. cit., pp. 703–4.
16 Ibid., p. 25.
17 Ibid., p. 18.
18 Ryan, op. cit., p. 125.
19 Ibid., p. 126.
20 Ibid., p. 127.

21 Coogan, op. cit., p. 173
22 Ryan, op. cit., p. 125.
23 Coogan, op. cit., p. 695.
24 Ibid., p. 227.
25 Ibid., p. 695.
26 T.K. Whitaker, in ibid., p. 703.
27 Ibid., p. 693.
28 Ryan, op. cit., p. 13.
29 W.B. Yeats, in Coogan, op. cit., p. 191.
30 Ibid.
31 T. Ryle Dwyer, in ibid., p. 10.
32 Ibid., p. 296.
33 Ibid., p. 204.
34 Ibid., p. 703.
35 Ibid., p. 74.
36 Ibid., p. 703.
37 Ibid., p. 25.
38 Ibid., p. 26.
39 Ibid.
40 Ibid., p. 684.
41 Ibid., p. 17.
42 Ibid., p. 117.
43 Ibid., p. 28.
44 Ryan, op. cit., p. 128.
45 Ibid., p. 78.
46 Coogan, op. cit., p. 21.
47 Ibid., p. 696.
48 Ibid.
49 Ibid., p. 1.
50 E. Kretchmer, *Physique and Character: An Investigation of Nature and Constitution and Theory of Temperament* (trans. W.J. Sprott), London: Kegan Paul, 1925.
51 Ryan, op. cit., p. 265.
52 Ibid.
53 Coogan, op. cit., p. 6.
54 Ibid., p. 697.
55 Ibid., p. 699.
56 Ibid.
57 The negative aspects of life in de Valera's Ireland are depicted by Ultan Cowley: 'We had people and we exported them faster than cattle and like cattle, and while fathers, sons and daughters cried all the way to the train and the bus and the ship'. Another feature was a 'de-lousing' procedure carried out 'with the consent of the Irish Government to ensure that Irish emigrants were not carriers of infection'. J. Duffy, in a personal communication to Ultan Cowley, noted the anger towards the Irish Government following this de-lousing precedent: 'Anger was expressed among the twenty or so migrants, not only against the perfidious English but to a greater degree against the Irish Government who allowed such debasement to be practised against its own citizens' (Ultan Cowley, *The Men Who Built Britain*, Dublin: Wolfhound, 2001, pp. 111–16).
58 Coogan, op. cit., p. 235.
59 M. Fitzgerald, 'Einstein: brain and behaviour', *Journal of Autism and Developmental Disorders*, 2000, 3: 620–1.

60 M. Fitzgerald, 'Did Ramanujan have Asperger's syndrome?', *Journal of Medical Biography*, 2002, 10: 167.
61 Coogan, op. cit., p. 22.
62 Ryan, op. cit., p. 14.
63 Ibid., pp. 25–6.
64 Ibid., p. 14.
65 Coogan, op. cit., p. 254.
66 Ibid., p. 698.
67 Ibid., p. 704.
68 Ibid., 121.
69 Ibid., p. 122.
70 Ibid., p. 54.
71 Ibid., p. 117.
72 Ibid.
73 Ibid., p. 109.
74 Ibid., p. 685.
75 Ryan, op. cit., p. 10.
76 Ibid., p. 109.
77 Coogan, op. cit., p. 680.
78 Ibid., p. 201.
79 T. Ryle Dwyer, 'Treaty split blighted politics for most of last century', *Irish Examiner*, 6 December 2001, 23.
80 Ryan, op. cit., p. 208.
81 Julia O'Faolain, 'A snug and weedy place', *Times Literary Supplement*, 24 March 2000, 16.
82 Coogan, op. cit., p. 699.
83 Ryan, op. cit., p. 227.
84 Coogan, op. cit., p. 138.
85 Ryan, op. cit., p. 111.
86 Ibid., p. 119.
87 Coogan, op. cit., p. 296; Ryan, op. cit., p. 12.
88 Coogan, op. cit., p. 698.
89 Ryan, op. cit., p. 162.
90 Ibid., p. 10.
91 Coogan, op. cit., p. 248.
92 Ryan, op. cit., p. 203.
93 Coogan, op. cit., p. 254.
94 Ryan, op. cit., p. 186.
95 Coogan, op. cit., p. 25.
96 Ibid., p. 187.
97 Ibid., p. 175.
98 Ryan, op. cit., p. 227.
99 Coogan, op. cit., p. 167.
100 Ibid., p. 257.
101 Ryan, op. cit., p. 127.
102 Ibid., p. 162.
103 Ibid., p. 134.
104 Coogan, op. cit., p. 257.
105 Ibid., p. 289.
106 Ryan, op. cit., p. 137.
107 Mark O'Brien, *De Valera, Fianna Fáil and the Irish Press*, Dublin: Irish Academic Press, 2001, 26.

108 Ibid., p. 236, from Frank Gallagher's papers, NLI MS 18361, Irish Press Articles of Association, Article 77.
109 Coogan, op. cit., p. 693.
110 Ibid., p. 674. Events that led to de Valera's public denial of a vested interest in the *Irish Press* are described in *Against the Tide*, the autobiography of Noel Browne, a former Minister for Health. Browne believed that the Press newspapers 'influenced a substantial number of the Irish people and created and kept unchallenged the awesome charisma of Eamon de Valera'. Browne recalled that in 1957 while examining the records of the *Irish Press*, as he slowly 'turned the pages of the great volume of listed shareholders and transfers, it became clear that de Valera had systematically over a period of years become a majority shareholder of Irish Press Newspapers. Although he was controlling director of the newspapers, the share prices were not quoted publicly. The price paid by the de Valera family to shareholders was nominal. It was clear that he was now a very wealthy newspaper tycoon.' Browne framed a motion for debate in the Dáil, which took place a year later in 1958. According to O'Brien, Browne succeeded in moving a private member's motion which stated that by continuing to hold the post of controlling director of the Press Group while acting as Taoiseach, de Valera held 'a position which could be reasonably regarded as interfering or being incompatible with the full and proper discharge by him of the duties of his office'. Moreover, according to Browne, the company was worth nearly £1 million and reeked of corruption and nepotism. De Valera had abused his dual role of Taoiseach and controlling director to create 'a very solid nest egg' and turn the company into a family concern by bringing his son Vivion and Vivion's brother-in-law onto the board. See O'Brien, op. cit., p. 38 and Noel Browne, *Against the Tide*, Dublin: Gill and Macmillan, 1986, p. 234. Indeed, Oliver J. Flanagan of Fine Gael – in opposition at the time – is on record as saying that 'there is no family made more out of this country than the de Valera family'. See *Dáil Éireann Record*, 14 January 1959, 590.
111 P. Scragg and A. Shah, 'Prevalence of Asperger's syndrome in a secure hospital', *British Journal of Psychiatry*, 1994, 165: 679.
112 Coogan, op. cit., p. 69.
113 Ibid., p. 72.
114 Ibid., p. 34.
115 Ryan, op. cit., p. 13.
116 Coogan, op. cit., p. 34.
117 Ibid., p. 26.
118 Ryan, op. cit., p. 15.
119 Coogan, op. cit., p. 703.
120 Ryan, op. cit., pp. 26-7.
121 Coogan, op. cit., p. 53.
122 Ibid., p. 54.
123 R. Kee, 'The lay cardinal', *Times Literary Supplement*, December 1993, 4.
124 Ryan, op. cit., pp. 26–7.
125 Ibid., p. 254.
126 Coogan, op. cit., p. 685.
127 Ibid., p. 254.
128 A. Norman Jeffares, *Oliver St John Gogarty*, Gerrards Cross, Buckinghamshire: Colin Smythe, 2001, p. 26.
129 Coogan, op. cit., p. 703.
130 Ibid., p. 36.

131 Ibid., p. 1.
132 Ibid., p. 36.
133 Ibid., p. 698.
134 Ryan, op. cit., p. 13.
135 Ibid., p. 256.
136 Ibid., p. 257.
137 Ibid., p. 45.

7 William Butler Yeats

 1 R. Ellmann, *Yeats: The Man and the Masks*, London: Penguin, 1979, p. 2.
 2 Ibid., p. 7.
 3 Ibid.
 4 Ibid., p. 8.
 5 Ibid.
 6 Ibid., p. 9.
 7 Ibid.
 8 Hilary Pyle, *Jack B. Yeats – A Biography*, 2nd edn, London: André Deutsch, 1989, p. 5.
 9 Ellmann, op. cit., p. 13.
10 Ibid., p. 13.
11 Ibid.
12 Ibid.
13 There are many accounts of John B. Yeats' failure to complete paintings. According to Ellmann (ibid.), 'instead of finishing a picture one square inch at a time, he kept all fluid, every detail dependent upon every other, and remained a poor man to the end of his life, because the more anxious he was to succeed, the more did his pictures sink through innumerable sittings into final confusion'. Similarly, the writer John McGahern notes that 'temperamentally, he was incapable of finishing a painting. He would work and rework one canvas until it was ruined. Yeats recollected in *Reveries over Childhood and Youth* how he became known as the son of the painter who scraped out each day the work he had done the day before.' Moreover, McGahern notes that 'his career made little progress. This was almost entirely due to his own character.' Lady Gregory's opinion of the painter is also quoted by McGahern: 'Space and time mean nothing to him, he goes his own way, spoiling portraits as hopefully as he begins them, and always on the verge of a great future.' See J. McGahern, 'Introduction', in Joseph Hone (ed.) *John Butler Yeats: Letters to his Son W.B. Yeats and Others, 1869–1922*, London: Faber and Faber, 1999, pp. 6–10.
14 M.B. Yeats, *Cast a Cold Eye – Memories of a Poet's Son and Politician*, Dublin: Blackwater Press, 1999, p. 34.
15 K. Alldritt, *W.B. Yeats – The Man and the Milieu*, London: John Murray, 1997, p. 8.
16 Ellmann, op. cit., pp. 23–4.
17 The critic Penelope Fitzgerald, in a review of Hone, op. cit. (*Times Literary Supplement*, 19 November 1999, p. 31), states that John Butler Yeats never acquired 'any kind of business sense' and although he had commissions for portraits, he 'took an obsessively long time to carry them out, and could not bring himself to charge enough for them'. McGahern states that Yeats' father took no interest in his properties, 'passing the collection of rents and management of the estate to others, until he was to lose it all'. He spent his time 'sketching at the law courts instead of looking for remunerative legal work'.

18 Ellmann, op. cit., p. 25.
19 Ibid., p. xxvii.
20 McGahern, op. cit., p. 6.
21 Ibid.
22 Ellmann, op. cit., pp. 11–12.
23 Ibid., p. 17.
24 Ibid., p. 10.
25 Ibid., p. 19.
26 Ibid., pp. 15–16.
27 Ibid., p. 10.
28 Ibid., p. 17.
29 McGahern, op. cit., p. 4.
30 Ellmann, op. cit., p. 24.
31 Terence Brown, *The Life of W.B. Yeats – a Critical Biography*, Dublin: Gill and Macmillan, 1999, p. 15.
32 Ibid., p. 17.
33 Harry McGee, 'Romantic Yeats is dead and gone', *Sunday Tribune*, 30 May 1999, 8. See also Brenda Maddox, *George's Ghosts: A New Life of W.B. Yeats*, London: Picador, 1999.
34 Pyle, op. cit., p. 7.
35 Alldritt, op. cit., p. 15.
36 Michael B. Yeats, in Ellmann, op. cit., p. 26.
37 Yeats, op. cit., p. 35.
38 Alldritt, op. cit., p. 33.
39 Ellmann, op. cit., p. xxi.
40 Yeats, op. cit., p. 29.
41 John Masefield, *So Long to Learn: Chapters of an Autobiography*, London: Heinemann, 1952, p. 130. Quoted in Ellmann, op. cit., p. 182. Yeats's distinctive voice also caught the imagination of other writers. At a prize-giving ceremony for James Stephens in Dublin, another writer (most likely Richard Aldington) described Yeats' contribution to the event: '[He] explained with Dublin Theatre gestures and parsonic elocution that he had no manuscript to read from. He had given his to the press. He smiled benignly, and recited his memorised speech perfectly. He spoke in his beautiful voice; he expressed Celtic love with his more beautiful face; he elevated and waved his yet more beautiful hands. He blessed us with his presence. He spoke of spirits and Phantasmagoria. He spoke of finding two boots in the middle of a field and the owner of the boots listening for earth spirits under a bush.' See Ezra Pound and Dorothy Shakespeare, *New Free Woman*, 15 December 1913, 282.
42 Ellmann, op. cit., p. 27.
43 Anthony Cronin, 'Down from Olympus', *Sunday Independent*, 29 August 1999, 9.
44 Ellmann, op. cit., p. 26.
45 Alldritt, op. cit., p. 27.
46 Ibid., p. 26.
47 Ellmann, op. cit., p. 32.
48 Ibid., p. 27.
49 Alldritt, op. cit., p. 16.
50 Ellmann, op. cit., p. 27.
51 M. Fitzgerald, 'Did Ramanujan have Asperger's Syndrome?', *Journal of Medical Biography*, 2002, 10: 167.
52 Ellmann, op. cit., p. xxii.

53 Alldritt, op. cit., p. 15.
54 Ellmann, op. cit., p. 29.
55 Ibid., p. 25.
56 Alldritt, op. cit., p. 29.
57 Ibid., p. 30.
58 Ellmann, op. cit., p. 25.
59 Alldritt, op. cit., p. 15.
60 Ibid., p. 28.
61 McGahern, op. cit., p. 19.
62 Ellmann, op. cit., p. 22.
63 Brown, op. cit., p. 14.
64 Ibid., p. 14.
65 E.H. Mikhail, *W.B. Yeats: Interviews and Recollections*, vol. 1, London: Macmillan, 1977, p. 33. Quoted in Brown, op. cit., p. 14.
66 Ellmann, op. cit., p. 80.
67 Ibid., p. 81.
68 Ibid., p. 177.
69 Ibid., p. 179.
70 Yeats, op. cit., p. 28
71 M. Fitzgerald, 'Did Bartók have high-functioning autism/Asperger's syndrome?', *Autism – Europe Link*, 2000, 29: 21.
72 Mikhail, op. cit., p. 103. Quoted in Brown, op. cit., pp. 14–15.
73 M. Fitzgerald, 'Alfred Kinsey's Aperger Disorder', *Journal of Autism and Developmental Disorders*, 1999, 29, 4: 346–7, and M. Fitzgerald, 'Did Ludwig Wittgenstein have Asperger's syndrome?', *European Child and Adolescent Psychiatry*, 2000, 9, 6: 61–5.
74 Ellmann, op. cit., p. 193.
75 Ibid., p. xxi.
76 Ibid., p. 33.
77 Ibid., p. 41.
78 Frank O'Connor, in ibid., p. 277.
79 John Burns writes that 'Yeats said "all the trouble of my life began" after he met Gonne in 1889 and his long unfulfilled obsession with the Aldershot-born daughter of an army officer began'. See J. Burns, 'Yeats love story is turned into a musical', *The Sunday Times*, 7 May 2000, 3.
80 Ellmann, op. cit., p. 85.
81 Ibid., p. 159.
82 Lisa Jardine, 'Female muse', *New Statesman*, 21 June 1999, 48.
83 Alldritt, op. cit., p. 258.
84 John McGahern, *The Irish Times*, 27 November 1999, 12. See also Brown, op. cit., p. 247.
85 Brown, op. cit., p. 247.
86 Jardine, op. cit., 48.
87 Brown, op. cit., p. 252.
88 In a review of Brown (op. cit.), Boran discusses Yeats' marriage: 'on the second night of their honeymoon, what Brown calls their "occult marriage", a nightly meeting of the minds of William and George, in the presence of a grand cast of guides, facilitators and otherworldly Communicators. In the beginning George admitted to faking the automatic writing that quickly had William in thrall, but later claimed to feel herself "seized by a superior power".' Pat Boran, 'The mysterious inward journey of a nation's communicator', *The Sunday Business Post*, 21 November 1999, 40. See also Brown, op. cit., p. 252.

89 Alldritt, op. cit., p. 176.
90 Ellmann, op. cit., p. 224.
91 Jardine, op. cit., p. 49.
92 Ibid.
93 R. Monk, *Ludwig Wittgenstein – the Duty of Genius*, London: Jonathan Cape, 1990, p. 498.
94 Ellmann, op. cit, p. 23.
95 Yeats, op. cit., p. 29.
96 Ibid., p. 28.
97 Martin Mansergh, 'Journey back into Yeats's country', *Irish Independent*, 13 March 1999, 11.
98 Yeats, op. cit., p. 1.
99 Ibid., p. 30.
100 Ibid., p. 31.
101 Ibid., p. 16.
102 Alldritt, op. cit., p. 335.
103 Ellmann, op. cit., p. 73.
104 Ibid., p. 25.
105 Alldritt, op. cit., pp. 29–30.
106 Ibid., p. 30.
107 Ibid., p. 13.
108 Ibid., p. 30.
109 Ellmann, op. cit., p. 77.
110 Ibid., p. 80.
111 Ibid., p. 27.
112 Ibid., p. 83.
113 Yeats, op. cit., p. 33.
114 Ibid., p. 34.
115 Ibid.
116 Ibid., p. 35.
117 Michael B. Yeats (op. cit., p. 34) describes the event as follows: 'On one occasion in the 1920s our house in Merrion Square was briefly in the public eye. We lived at No. 82 and my father's great friend George Russell ('Æ'), the poet and mystic, lived at No. 84. They were both very absent-minded, and one afternoon they set off simultaneously to visit each other. Russell as usual walked with his hands behind his back and his head down, my father with his hands behind his back and his head in the air. By chance a well-known cartoonist of the day, Isa McNee, was just across the street at this moment, and the humorous journal *Dublin Opinion* appeared the following week with a cartoon by her illustrating this event'.
118 Ellmann, op. cit., p. 298.
119 Ibid.
120 Ibid., p. xix.
121 Ibid., p. xxviii.
122 Boran, op. cit., 40.
123 Ellmann, op. cit., p. 22.
124 John Carey, 'Collected poems by Yeats', *The Sunday Times*, 18 June 1999, 7.
125 Alldritt, op. cit., p. 287.
126 Ibid., p. xiii.
127 Ibid., p. 101.
128 Ibid., p. 194.
129 Katharine Tynan, in Ellmann, op. cit., p. 47.

130 Richard Ollard, *A Man of Contradictions – a Life of A.L. Rowse*, London: Allen Lane Penguin Press, 1999, pp. 125–6.
131 St John Ervine, in Mikhail, op. cit., p. 103. Quoted in Brown, op. cit., p. 14.
132 Brown, op. cit., p. 15.
133 Alldritt, op. cit., p. 33.
134 Ibid., p. 48.
135 Ibid., p. 37.
136 Yeats, op. cit., p. 35.
137 Carey, op. cit., 7.
138 Alldritt, op. cit., p. 209.
139 Ibid., p. 105.
140 Ibid., p. 28.
141 Ibid.
142 Ibid., p. xiii.
143 Ibid., p. 50.
144 Ibid., p. 207.
145 Ellmann, op. cit., p. 189.
146 Ibid., p. 182.
147 Ibid., p. 179.
148 Alldritt, op. cit., p. 88.
149 Ibid., p. xiii.
150 Mary Colum, 'Memories of Yeats', *The Saturday Review of Literature*, vol. XIX, 25 February 1939, 4.
151 Yeats, op. cit., p. 29.
152 Alldritt, op. cit., p. 97.
153 Ibid., p. xiii.
154 Ellmann, op. cit., p. 219.
155 Ibid., pp. 192–3.
156 Ibid., pp. 277–8.
157 Referring to the predicament of a poet in the modern world, Desmond McCarthy in *The Sunday Times*, 4 February 1934, notes that 'the theory of the Mask or Anti-self which the poet must impose on his natural self' is continually found in Yeats' prose. Quoted in *The Sunday Times*, 18 June 1999, 7.
158 Alldritt, op. cit., p. 46.
159 Ellmann, op. cit, p. 290.
160 Yeats, op. cit., p. 29.
161 Cronin, op. cit., 9. See also Maddox, op. cit.
162 Cronin, op. cit., 9.
163 Ibid.
164 Ellman, op. cit., p. 83.
165 Ibid., p. 277.
166 Ibid., p. 219.
167 Ibid., p. 164.
168 Commenting on the way Yeats' wife promoted séances and occult events in their marriage, Boran (op. cit., p. 40) says that 'among the many dangers of being the conduit for such wisdom and occult learning in a world in which "the centre cannot hold", however, is the conclusion that one is irreplaceable, a member of a long dreamt-of intellectual elite, rather than, for instance, a person with "an insecure hold on personal identity"'.
169 Ellmann, op. cit., p. 223.
170 Carey, op. cit., p. 7.
171 Ibid.

172 Terence Brown, in Boran, op. cit., 40.
173 Carey, op. cit.
174 John Masefield, *Some Memories of W.B. Yeats*, New York: Macmillan, 1940; quoted in Ellmann, op. cit., p. 1.
175 Ellmann, op. cit., p. 114.
176 Ibid., p. 111.
177 Ibid., p. 282.
178 Ibid., p. 248.
179 Commenting on Yeats' fascist leanings and the dangerous naïvety of his politics, Boran (op. cit., p. 40) writes that 'from such an elevated, even Promethean position, the journey to Fascism was not long. Indeed, the advent of war in Europe in 1914 found Yeats "almost indifferent" according to Brown.'
180 Ruth Dudley Edwards (op. cit., p. 7) writes that 'it is hard to better Yeats' definition of political fanaticism as "a bitter acid that destroyed the soul", or such of his timeless truths as that "no people hate as we do in whom (the) past is always alive", or that "A powerful class by terror, rhetoric, and organised sentimentality may drive their people to war, but the day draws near when they cannot keep them there".'
181 Alldritt, op. cit., p. 326.
182 Ibid., p. 327.
183 Ibid.
184 Boran, op. cit., 40.
185 Ellmann, op. cit., p. 26.
186 Ibid.
187 Alldritt, op. cit., p. 54.
188 Ibid., p. 103.
189 Ellmann, op. cit., p. 42.
190 Ibid., p. 56.
191 Ibid., p. 57.
192 Boran (op. cit., p. 40) outlines how Brown, in his biography of the poet, recognises Yeats' ambiguity towards the occult: 'Brown identifies Yeats' obsessive relationship with the spirit world as simultaneously a threat to his very humanity and as a source for his work neatly and convincingly . . . he enables the reader to take the magic as seriously as did Yeats himself, and even to feel how the poet's peculiar brand of cosmic logic drew him on to the Fascism of his later years.'
193 Alldritt, op. cit., p. 102.
194 Boran, op. cit., p. 40.
195 In an interview with Tim Brannigan, 'Removing the ghosts from Yeats' cupboard', *The Irish News*, 12 June 1999, 10.
196 Ellmann, op. cit, p. 239.
197 Maddox, op. cit.
198 Ibid.
199 Ellmann, op. cit, p. 73.
200 Alldritt, op. cit., p. 47.
201 Ellmann, op. cit, p. 80.
202 Ibid., p. 25.

8 Lewis Carroll

1 M.N. Cohen, *Lewis Carroll: A Biography*, London: Papermac, 1995, p. xxi.
2 Ibid.

3 It is interesting that Will Self in *The Independent* states that 'when people ask me which books have influenced me the most as a writer I almost always detail the same three: Swift's *Gulliver's Travels*, Kafka's *Metamorphosis* and Carroll's *Alice's Adventures in Wonderland*. What these three share is a marvellous confidence in the primacy of the imagination and a conviction that the fantastic is anterior to the naturalistic. Swift's masterpiece is a declaration of the polymorphous character of human society, Kafka's of human biology, and Carroll's of reality itself' (Will Self, 'Weekend review', *The Independent*, 11 August 2001, 1). Undeniably all three authors had major difficulties in interpersonal relationships, and certainly could be described as loners, with Swift and Carroll being the most closely allied. Kafka was more a schizoid personality. Clearly, Carroll had major intimacy anxieties. Cohen (op. cit., p. 225) suggests that the Alice tale is 'an autobiographical allegory, that Alice is Charles in disguise'.

4 Cohen, op. cit., p. 123.

5 Ibid., p. 194.

6 Stewart Dodgson Collingwood, *The Life and Letters of Lewis Carroll*, London: T. Fisher Unwin, 1898, pp. 6–8.

7 Cohen, op. cit., p. 10.

8 Ibid., p. 324.

9 Ibid., p. 329.

10 Ibid., p. 334.

11 Ibid., p. 7.

12 Ibid.

13 Ibid., p. 6.

14 Ibid., p. 5.

15 Ibid., p. 10.

16 Ibid., p. xx.

17 Ibid., p. 76.

18 Ibid., p. 12.

19 Ibid., p. 7.

20 Ibid., pp. 24–25.

21 Ibid., p. 285.

22 Ibid., p. 286.

23 Ibid., p. 285.

24 Ibid., p. 365.

25 Ibid., p. 295.

26 Ibid., p. 296. See also Morton N. Cohen (ed., with the assistance of Roger Lancelyn Green) *The Letters of Lewis Carroll*, 2 vols, London: Macmillan, 1979, p. 446.

27 Cohen, 1995, op. cit., p. 338.

28 Ibid., p. 21.

29 Ibid., p. 340.

30 Ibid., p. 284.

31 Ibid., p. 301.

32 Ibid., p. 301.

33 Ibid., p. 306.

34 Ibid., p. 299.

35 Ibid., p. 84.

36 Ibid.

37 Ibid., p. xx.

38 Ibid., p. 222.

39 According to Cohen (ibid., p. 223), 'Jonathan Swift's love affair with Stella

echoes [Lewis Carroll's] own frustrations, and he responds feelingly . . . Other
similarities appear when we look at the Swift–Dodgson histories. Swift often
wrote letters to Stella in baby language.'

40 Ibid., p. 290.
41 Ibid., p. 107.
42 Ibid., p. 342.
43 Ibid., p. 174.
44 Ibid., p. 181.
45 Ibid., p. 105.
46 Ibid., p. 189.
47 Ibid., p. 182.
48 Ibid., p. 183.
49 Ibid., p. 160.
50 Ibid., p. 191.
51 Ibid., p. 291.
52 Ibid., p. xxi.
53 Ibid., p. 306.
54 Ibid., p. 290.
55 Ibid., p. xx.
56 Ibid., p. 290.
57 Ibid., p. 197.
58 Ibid., p. 60.
59 Ibid., p. 314.
60 Ibid., p. 291.
61 Ibid., p. 293.
62 Ibid., p. 290.
63 Ibid., p. 304.
64 Ibid., p. 479.
65 Ibid., p. xxii.
66 Ibid., p. 261.
67 Ibid., p. 284.
68 Cohen (ibid., p. 288) also points out that Carroll collected fountain pens and
    pencil sharpeners, and 'ordered five different sizes of notepaper so as to have the
    right size for each letter'.
69 Ibid., p. 409.
70 Ibid., p. 142.
71 Ibid., p. 145. According to Cohen, Carroll's prose is also unconventional: 'He
    uses big, polysyllabic words, sophisticated concepts, notions that a child cannot
    possibly be expected to grasp . . . He was a genius at double meanings, at playing
    games with words, and he challenges every child who picks up the book to play
    the game with him' (ibid., pp. 142–3). Cohen also notes that Carroll's early
    nonsense verse contained subversive elements that persisted in his later work:
    'beneath the banter run a dark strain of complaint, a smarting resentment, even
    gratuitous violence' (ibid., p. 14).
72 Self, op. cit., pp. 1–2.
73 Cohen, 1995, op. cit., p. xx.
74 Ibid., p. 12.
75 Ibid., p. 27.
76 Ibid., p. 255.
77 W.W. Bartley, 'Lewis Carroll as a logician', *Times Literary Supplement*, 15 June
    1973, 665. Bartley also notes that 'symbolic logic was one of his interests and [he]
    was by profession a geometer and Oxford don who lectured on mathematics'.

78 Cohen, 1995, op. cit., p. 284.
79 Ibid., p. 289.
80 Ibid., p. 505.
81 Ibid., p. 284.
82 Ibid., p. 285.
83 Ibid., p. 284.
84 Ibid., p. 295.
85 Ibid., p. xxi.
86 Ibid., p. 200.
87 Ibid.
88 Ibid., p. 201.
89 Ibid., p. 200.
90 Ibid., p. 202.
91 Ibid., p. 120.
92 Ibid., p. xxi.
93 Ibid., p. 191.
94 Ibid., p. 165.
95 Ibid.
96 Ibid., p. 171.
97 Ibid., p. 172.
98 Ibid., p. 306.
99 Ibid., p. 83.
100 Ibid., p. 305.
101 Ibid., p. 410.
102 Ibid., p. 308.
103 Ibid., p. xx.
104 Ibid., p. 526.

9   Ramanujan

1 M. Fitzgerald, 'Did Ramanujan have Asperger's Syndrome?', *Journal of Medical Biography*, 2002, 10: 167.
2 Robert Kanigel, *The Man who Knew Infinity – A Life of the Genius Ramanujan*, New York: Charles Scribner and Sons, 1991, p. 18.
3 Ibid., p. 13.
4 Ibid.
5 Ibid., p. 47.
6 S.R. Ranganathan, *Ramanujan: the Man and the Mathematician*, London: Asia Publishing House, 1967, p. 75.
7 Kanigel, op. cit., p. 27.
8 Ibid.
9 Ranganathan, op. cit., p. 196.
10 Ibid., p. 91.
11 Kanigel, op. cit., p. 13.
12 Ibid., p. 50.
13 Ibid., p. 238.
14 Ibid., p. 76.
15 Ibid.
16 Ranganathan, op. cit., p. 61.
17 Kanigel, op. cit., p. 276.
18 R.A. Rankin, 'Ramanujan as a patient', *Proceedings of the Indian Academy of Science*, 1984, 93(2, 3): 79–100. Clearly, Hardy demonstrated many features of

Asperger's syndrome too. Ramanujan's physician, Dr P.S. Chandrasckhar, described him as 'shy, reserved and endowed with an infinite capacity to bare the agonies of the mind and spirit with fortitude'.

19 Ranganathan, op. cit., p. 87.
20 Ibid., p. 72.
21 Kanigel, op. cit., p. 28.
22 Ibid., p. 46.
23 Ibid.
24 Ibid.
25 Ranganathan, op. cit., p. 62.
26 Ibid., pp. 86–7.
27 Kanigel, op. cit., p. 13.
28 Ranganathan, op. cit., p. 101.
29 Ibid., p. 95.
30 Kanigel, op. cit., p. 63.
31 Ranganathan, op. cit., p. 105.
32 Ibid., p. 113.
33 Kanigel, op. cit., p. 312.
34 Ibid., p. 216.
35 Ranganathan, op. cit., p. 87. This reminds one of the dream that the German chemist Kekulé had which helped him to discover the structure of the benzene ring. His discovery had a major impact on developments in organic chemistry. Kekulé himself describes what happened. He was writing a textbook on chemistry 'but it did not go well; my spirit was with other things. I turned the chair to the fireplace and sank into a half sleep. The atoms flitted before my eyes. Long rows, variously, more closely, united; all in movements wriggling and turning like snakes. And see, what was that? One of the snakes seized its own tail and the image whirled scornfully before my eyes. As though from a flash of lightning I awoke; I occupied the rest of the night in working out the consequences of the hypothesis' (quoted in E.N. Beardmore, *The Art of Scientific Investigation*, New York: WW Norton, 1957. Republished by Vintage, Random House, New York, 1990). Thomas West takes up the story, stating that 'Kekulé somehow came to see that if the structure of benzene was six carbon atoms arranged in a ring, then the pieces of the puzzle would fall into place and all the apparently contradictory evidence finally make sense' (T. West, *In the Mind's Eye*, Buffalo, NY: Prometheus Books, 1991).
36 Ranganathan, op. cit., p. 92.
37 Ibid., p. 72.
38 Kanigel, op. cit., p. 24.
39 Ranganathan, op. cit., pp. 83–4.
40 Ibid., p. 63
41 Ibid.
42 Kanigel, op. cit., p. 104.
43 Ranganathan, op. cit., p. 63.
44 Ibid., p. 81.
45 S. Baron-Cohen, S. Wheelwright, V. Stone and M. Rutherford (1999) 'A mathematician, a physicist and a computer scientist with Asperger's syndrome: performance on folk psychology and folk physics tests', *Neurocase*, 5: 475–83. The subject, a male mathematician of genius, married another mathematician (not uncommon for mathematicians) and showed his brilliance by winning the Fields Medal in mathematics, equivalent to the Nobel Prize. He didn't realise how strange his behaviour was: for example, running everywhere and not

walking. He had difficulty judging what was normal behaviour because of his autism spectrum disorder. He had an excellent knowledge of the physical world (what Baron-Cohen called 'folk physics'), but was extremely poor at folk psychology, which is about how the social world operates.

46 Kanigel, op. cit., p. 76.
47 Ranganathan, op. cit., p. 83.
48 Kanigel, op. cit., p. 334.
49 Ibid., pp. 56–7.
50 Ibid., p. 60.
51 Ibid., pp. 58–61.
52 Ranganathan, op. cit., p. 26.
53 Ibid., p. 76.
54 Bela Bollobas, 'Ramanujan – a glimpse of his life and his mathematics', *The Cambridge Review*, June 1988, 36.
55 Kanigel, op. cit., p. 162.
56 Ibid., pp. 45–6.
57 Ibid., p. 65.
58 Ibid., p. 226.
59 Ibid., p. 205.
60 Ibid., p. 207.
61 Ranganathan, op. cit., p. 41.
62 Kanigel, op. cit., p. 159.
63 L.J. Mordell, 'Ramanujan', *Nature*, 141: 647.
64 Kanigel, op. cit., p. 216.
65 Ranganathan, op. cit., p. 41.
66 Kanigel, op. cit., p. 224.
67 John Littlewood, in Ranganathan, op. cit., pp. 116–7.
68 S. Baron-Cohen, 'Are children with autism superior at folk physics?', in H. Wellman and K. Inagki (eds) *Children's Theories*, New Direction for Child Development Series, San Francisco: Jossey-Bass, 1997.
69 Ranganathan, op. cit., p. 99.
70 Kanigel, op. cit., p. 53.
71 Baron-Cohen *et al.*, op. cit. This mathematician was so single-minded that he had no hobbies and spent all his time on mathematics.
72 Bruce Berndt, in Kanigel, op. cit., p. 280.
73 Ibid., p. 226.
74 Ibid., p. 61.
75 G.H. Hardy, in Ranganathan, op. cit., pp. 114–5.
76 Ibid., p. 87.
77 Srinivasan, in ibid., p. 85.
78 Kanigel, op. cit., p. 67.
79 Ranganathan, op. cit., p. 82.
80 Ibid., p. 88.
81 Kanigel, op. cit., p. 66.
82 Ibid., p. 323.
83 Dr P. Mathalanopis, in Ranganathan, op. cit., pp. 82–3.
84 Ibid., p. 90.
85 Ibid., p. 103.
86 Ibid., p. 90.
87 Srinivasan, in ibid., p. 88.
88 Kanigel, op. cit., p. 256.
89 Raudhakrishna, in Ranganathan, op. cit., p. 74.

90 R.A. Rankin, in ibid., pp. 82–3.
91 Dr C.D. Deshmakh, in ibid., p. 79.
92 Ibid., p. 103.
93 R.A. Rankin, in ibid., p. 83.
94 Kanigel, op. cit., p. 230.
95 Ranganathan, op. cit., p. 91.

10 Conclusion

1 S. Baron-Cohen, H. Tager-Flusberg and D.J. Cohen, *Understanding Other Minds*, 2nd edn, Oxford: Oxford University Press, 2000.
2 R.T. Abed, 'A defence of evolutionary psychology', *British Journal of Psychiatry*, 2001, 179: 267.
3 Stephen R.L. Clarke, 'Perfect pidgin', *Times Literary Supplement*, 30 September 1994, 11.
4 M. Gee, 'Genomania', *Daily Telegraph*, 1 July 2000, 2.
5 Quoted in A. Ayton, 'A defence of evolutionary psychology', *British Journal of Psychiatry*, 2001, 179: 267.
6 Ibid.
7 Quoted in Gee, op. cit., 2.
8 Jerry Coyne, 'Between fear and worship', *Times Literary Supplement*, 11 January 2002, 9.
9 Jane Brody, 'Quirks and oddities may be mild forms of psychiatric illness', *New York Times*, 4 February 1997, p. 4.

Bibliography

Abed, R.T. 'A defence of evolutionary psychology', *British Journal of Psychiatry*, 2001, 179: 267.

Alldritt, K. *W.B. Yeats – the Man and the Milieu*, London: John Murray, 1997.

Alper, G. *Portraits of an Artist as a Young Patient*, San Francisco: International Scholars Publications, 1998.

Ambrose, A. and Lazerowitz, M. *Ludwig Wittgenstein: Philosophy and Language*, London: Allen & Unwin, 1972.

American Psychiatric Association, *Diagnostic and Statistical Manual III*, Washington, DC: APA, 1987.

American Psychiatric Association, *Diagnostic and Statistical Manual IV*, Washington, DC: APA, 1994.

American Psychiatric Association, *Diagnostic Criteria from DSM-IV-TR*, Washington, DC: APA, 2000.

Arnold, B. *Jack Yeats*, Yale: Yale University Press, 1998.

Asperger, H. 'Formen des Autismus bei Kindern', *Deutsches Arzteblatt*, 1974, 14: 4.

Asperger, H. 'Problems of infantile autism', *Communication*, 1979, 13: 45–52.

Asperger, H. 'Die "Autistischen Psychopathen" im Kindesalter', *Archives fur Psychiatrie und Nervenkrankheiten*, 1944/1991, 117: 76–136. Translated in U. Frith (ed.) *Autism and Asperger's Syndrome*, Cambridge: Cambridge University Press, 1991, pp. 37–92.

Atkinson, R.C. *The Origins and Development of High Ability*, Ciba Foundation Symposium 178, Chichester: Wiley, 1993.

Ayer, A.J. *Ludwig Wittgenstein*, London: Penguin, 1985.

Ayton, A. 'A defence of evolutionary psychology', *British Journal of Psychiatry*, 2001, 179: 267.

Baghramian, M. 'Ireland in the life of Ludwig Wittgenstein', in F.A. Flowers (ed.) *Portraits of Wittgenstein*, vol. 4, Bristol: Thoemmes Press, 1999.

Baron-Cohen, S. 'Do autistic children have obsessions and compulsions?', *British Journal of Clinical Psychology*, 1989, 28: 193–200.

Baron-Cohen, S. *Mind Blindness: An Essay on Autism and Theory of Mind*, Cambridge, MA: MIT Press, 1995.

Baron-Cohen, S. 'Are children with autism superior at folk physics?', in H. Wellman and K. Inagki (eds) *Children's Theories, New Directions for Child Development*, San Francisco: Jossey-Bass, 1997.

Baron-Cohen, S. 'Autism: deficits in folk psychology exist along superiority in folk physics', in S. Baron-Cohen, H. Tager-Flusberg and D. Cohen (eds) *Understanding Other Minds*, Oxford: Oxford University Press, 2000, pp. 73–4.

Baron-Cohen, S. 'Theory of mind and autism: a fifteen year review', in S. Baron-Cohen, H. Tager-Flusberg and D.C. Cohen (eds) *Understanding Other Minds*, Oxford: Oxford University Press, 2000.

Baron-Cohen, S. and Hammer, J. 'Parents of children with Asperger's syndrome; what is the cognitive phenotype?', *Journal of Cognitive Neuroscience*, 2001, 9: 548–54.

Baron-Cohen, S., Ring, H., Moriarty, J. and Ell, P. 'Recognition of mental state terms: clinical findings in children with autism and a functional neuroimaging study of normal adults', *British Journal of Psychiatry*, 1994, 165: 640–49.

Baron-Cohen, S., Wheelwright, S., Stone, V. and Rutherford, M. 'A mathematician, a physicist, and a computer scientist with Asperger's syndrome', *Neurocase*, 1999, 5: 475–83.

Barrett, C. (ed.) *Lectures and Conversations on Aesthetics, Psychology and Religious Belief (by L. Wittgenstein)*, Oxford: Blackwell, 1970.

Bartley, W.W. 'Lewis Carroll as a logician', *Times Literary Supplement*, 15 June 1973, 665.

Bartley, W.W. *Wittgenstein*, London: Quartet Books, 1973.

Beck, A.J., Rush, A.J. and Shaw, P.F. *Cognitive Therapy of Depression*, Chichester: Wiley, 1979.

Berg, M. (ed.) *Narrative Developments: Six Approaches*, Mahwah, NJ: Lawrence Erlbaum Associates, 1997, pp. viii–xi.

Berman, D. and Fitzgerald, M. (eds) and introduced by J. Hayes, *The Danger of Words*, Bristol: M.O.C. Drury, Thoemmes Press, 1996.

Berney, T. 'Current developments in autism', *Learning Disabilities in Psychiatry*, 2002, 4(2): 1.

Bion, W.R. 'Attacks on linking', in *Second Thoughts*, London: Heinemann, 1959.

Bollobas, B. 'Ramanujan – a glimpse of his life and his mathematics', *The Cambridge Review*, June 1988, 36.

Bouvveresse, J. 'Wittgenstein and the modern world', in A.B. Griffiths (ed.) *Wittgenstein: Centenary Essays*, Cambridge: Cambridge University Press, 1991.

Bragg, M. *On Giants' Shoulders*, London: Hodder & Stoughton, 1998.

Braten, S. 'Intersubjective communication and understanding', in S. Braten (ed.) *Intersubjective Communication and Emotion in Early Ontogeny*, Cambridge: Cambridge University Press, 1998, p. 380.

Braten, S. (ed.) *Intersubjective Communication and Emotion in Early Ontogeny*, Cambridge: Cambridge University Press, 1998.

Brewster, D. *Memories of the Life, Writings, and Discoveries of Sir Isaac Newton*, vol. II, Edinburgh, 1855.

Broad, J.H. *Schizotypy* (ed. Gordon Claridge), Oxford: Oxford University Press, 1977.

Brown, T. *The Life of W.B. Yeats – a Critical Biography*, Dublin: Gill & Macmillan, 1999.

Browne, N. *Against the Tide*, Dublin: Gill & Macmillan, 1986.

Butler, S. *The Notebook of Samuel Butler* (ed. H.F. Jones), London, 1918.

Carey, J. 'Collected poems of W.B. Yeats', *The Sunday Times*, 18 June 1999, 7.

Chalmers, K. *Béla Bartók*, London: Phaidon Press, 1995.

Clarke, S.R.L. 'Perfect pidgin', *Times Literary Supplement*, 30 September 1994, 11.

Cohen, D.J., Paul, K. and Volkmar, F.R. 'Issues in the classification of pervasive developmental disorders: towards DSM-IV', *Journal of the American Academy of Child Psychiatry*, 1986, 25: 213–29.

Cohen, I.L. 'An artificial neural network analogue of learning in autism', *Biological Psychiatry*, 1994, 36: 5–20.

Cohen, M.N. *Lewis Carroll: a Biography*, London: Papermac, 1995.

Cohen, M.N. *The Letters of Lewis Carroll*, 2 vols (ed. Morton N. Cohen with the assistance of Roger Lancelyn Green), London: Macmillan, 1979.

Coid, J. 'DSM-III diagnosis of criminal psychopaths: a way forward', *Criminal Behaviour and Mental Health*, 1992, 2: 78.

Collingwood, S.D. *The Life and Letters of Lewis Carroll*, London: F. Fisher Unwin, 1898.

Colum, M. 'Memories of Yeats', *The Saturday Review of Literature*, vol. XIX, 25 February 1939, 4.

Coogan, T.P. *De Valera – Long Fellow, Long Shadow*, London: Arrow, 1993.

Cosgrave, P. 'The man who told the truth', *The Spectator*, September 1974.

Coulthard, P. and Fitzgerald, M. 'In God we trust? Organised religion and personal beliefs as resources and coping strategies, and their implications for health in parents with a child on the autistic spectrum', *Mental Health, Religion, and Culture Journal*, 1999, 2(1): 19–33.

Cowley, U. *The Men Who Built Britain*, Dublin: Wolfhound, 2001.

Coyne, J. 'Between fear and worship', *Times Literary Supplement*, 11 January 2002, 9.

Cummine, V., Leach, J. and Stevenson, G *Asperger's Syndrome*, London: David Fulton, 2001.

Davies, G. *Michelangelo*, London: Methuen, 1909.

de Botton, A. *The Consolations of Philosophy*, London: Hamish Hamilton, 2000.

de J. Villiers, 'Language and theory of mind: what are the developmental relationships?', in S. Baron-Cohen, H. Tager-Flusberg and D. Cohen (eds) *Understanding Other Minds*, Oxford: Oxford University Press, 2000, p. 129.

Dehaene, S. *The Number Sense: How the Mind Creates Mathematics*, New York, Oxford: Oxford University Press, 1997.

Denckla, M.B. 'The neuropsychology of socio-emotional learning disability', *Archives of Neurology*, 1983, 40: 461–2.

Denham, A. and Garnett, M. *Keith Joseph*, Chesham, UK: Acumen, 2001.

Desmond, A. and Moore, J. *Darwin*, London: Penguin Books, 2001.

Dodgson Collingwood, S. *The Life and Letters of Lewis Carroll*, London: T. Fisher Unwin, 1898.

Dolan, B. and Coid, J. *Psychopathic and Antisocial Personality Disorders*, London: Gaskell, 1993.

Dupuy, J.P. *The Mechanization of the Mind*, Princeton: Princeton University Press, 1994.

Easthope, A. 'Theory and authority', *Times Higher Educational Supplement*, 7 November 1997, p. 13.

Ebstein, R.P., Benjamin, J. and Belimaker, R. 'Genetics of personality dimensions', *Current Opinion in Psychiatry*, 2000, 13: 617.

Edmonds, D. and Eidinow, J. *Wittgenstein's Poker*, London: Faber and Faber, 2001.

Eglington, J. *A Memoir of Æ: John William Russell*, London: Macmillan, 1937.

Eisenberg, L. 'The fathers of autistic children', *American Journal of Orthopsychiatry*, 1957, 7: 723.

Ellis, D. *Literary Lives: Biography and the Search for Understanding*, London: Routledge, 1904.

Ellis, H. *A Study of British Genius*, London: Hurst and Blackwell, 1904.

Ellmann, R. *Yeats: the Man and the Masks*, London: Penguin, 1979.

Fann, K.T. (ed.) *Ludwig Wittgenstein: The Man and His Philosophy*, New York: Harvester, Dell, 1967.

Fitzgerald, M. 'Antecedents to Asperger's syndrome', *Autism International Journal of Research and Practice*, 1988, 2(4): 427–9.

Fitzgerald, M. 'Multidimensionally impaired disorder', *Journal of the American Academy of Child and Adolescent Psychiatry*, 1988, 37(11): 1125.

Fitzgerald, M. 'Alfred Kinsey's Asperger's disorder', *Journal of Autism and Developmental Disorders*, 1999, 29(4): 346–7.

Fitzgerald, M. 'Criteria for Asperger's syndrome', *Journal of the American Academy of Child and Adolescent Psychiatry*, 1999, 28(9): 1071.

Fitzgerald, M. 'Cycles and epicycles of autism', *Journal of Autism and Developmental Disorders*, 1999, 29(2): 183.

Fitzgerald, M. 'Did Isaac Newton have Asperger's syndrome?', *European Child and Adolescent Adult Psychiatry*, 1999, 8: 204.

Fitzgerald, M. 'Did the "man who loved only numbers", Paul Erdös, have Asperger's syndrome?', *Nordic Journal of Psychiatry*, 1999, 536: 765.

Fitzgerald, M. 'Pervasive Developmental Disorder Not Otherwise Specified', *Journal of the American Academy of Child and Adolescent Psychiatry*, 1999, 3(8): 229.

Fitzgerald, M. 'Did Bartók have high functioning autism/Asperger's syndrome?', *Autism Europe Link*, 2000, 29: 21.

Fitzgerald, M. 'Did Ludwig Wittgenstein have Asperger's syndrome?', *European Child and Adolescent Psychiatry*, 2000, 9: 61–5.

Fitzgerald, M. 'Einstein: brain and behaviour', *Journal of Autism and Developmental Disorders*, 2000, 30: 620–21.

Fitzgerald, M. 'Autistic psychopathy', *Journal of the American Academy of Child and Adolescent Psychiatry*, 2001, 40(8): 870.

Fitzgerald, M. 'Did Ramanujan have Asperger's syndrome?', *Journal of Medical Biography*, 2002, 10: 167.

Fitzgerald, M. 'Wittgenstein and autism', *Times Literary Supplement*, 2 August 2002, 15.

Fitzgerald, M. and Berman, D. 'Of sound mind', *Nature*, 1994, 368: 92.

Fitzgerald, M. and Corvin, A. 'Diagnosis and differential diagnosis of Asperger's syndrome', *Advances in Psychiatric Treatment*, 2001, 7: 310–18.

Fitzgerald, P. 'A bind tied to a string', *Times Literary Supplement*, 19 November 1999, 31.

Flamsted, J. *Self-Inspections of J.F.*, vol. 32, vols 78–82, Archives of the Royal Greenwich Observatory at Herstmonceux.

Fodor, J. 'Wotan's law and Tristan's love', *Times Literary Supplement*, 17 November 2000, 6.

Fodor, J. 'Dicing with shadows', *Times Literary Supplement*, 6 July 2001, 6.

Fombone, E. 'The epidemiology of autism: a review', *Psychological Medicine*, 1999, 29: 769.

Freud, S. *On Narcissism, an Introduction*, Standard Edition, 14, London: Hogarth Press, 1914.

Freud, S. *Leonardo da Vinci and a Memory of his Childhood*, Standard Edition, 9, London: Hogarth Press, 1957.

Freud, S. 'Introductory lectures on psychoanalysis', in J. Strachey (ed.) *Complete Works of S. Freud*, London: Hogarth Press, 1963, vol. XIV.

Frith, U. *Autism: Explaining the Enigma*, Oxford: Blackwell, 1989.

Frith, U. *Autism and Asperger's Syndrome*, Cambridge: Cambridge University Press, 1991.

Frith, U. 'The neurocognitive basis of autism', *Trends in Cognitive Sciences*, 1997, 1(2): 75.

Frith, U. and Houston, R. *Autism in History*, Oxford: Blackwell, 2000.

Gardner, H. *Extraordinary Minds*, New York: Basic Books, 1997.

Gerchwind, N. and Galaburda, M. *Cerebral Lateralisation*, Cambridge, MA: The MIT Press, 1987.

Ghaziuddin, M., Butler, E., Tsai, L. and Ghaziuddin, N. 'Is clumsiness a marker for Asperger's syndrome?', *Journal of Intellectual Disability Research*, 1994, 38: 519.

Giddens, A. 'A matter of truth', *Times Literary Supplement*, 29 March 1996, 10.

Gillberg, C. 'Clinical and neurobiological aspects of Asperger's syndrome', in U. Frith (ed.) *Autism and Asperger's Syndrome*, Cambridge: Cambridge University Press, 1991, p. 123.

Gillberg, C. 'The Emmanuel Miller Memorial Lecture, 1991. Autism and autistic-like conditions: subclasses among disorders of empathy', *Journal of Child Psychology and Psychiatry*, 1992, 33: 818–42.

Gillberg, C. *Clinical Child Neuropsychiatry*, Cambridge: Cambridge University Press, 1995.

Gillberg, C. and Coleman, M. *The Biological Basis of Autism*, Cambridge: MacKeith Press, 2000.

Gillberg, C. 'Asperger's syndrome and high functioning autism', Blake Marsh Lecture, *Quarterly Meeting of the Royal College of Psychiatrists*, Stratford-upon-Avon, 1996.

Giovacchine, P. *A Clinician's Guide to Reading Freud*, New York: Jason Aronson, 1982.

Glock, H.J. 'Second thoughts', *Times Literary Supplement*, 23 June 1995, 9.

Gomez, C.J. 'Do concepts of intersubjectivity apply to non-human primates?', in S. Braten (ed.) *Intersubjective Communication and Emotion in Early Ontogeny*, Cambridge: Cambridge University Press, 1998.

Grandin, T. *Thinking in Pictures – and Other Reports from My Life with Autism*, New York: Doubleday, 1995.

Gray, J. 'The mad monk', *New Statesman*, 23 April 2001, 54.

Greenfield, A.J. 'The meaning of Wittgenstein', *Nature*, 1990, 348: 384.

Gregory, R. *Oxford Companion to the Mind*, Oxford: Oxford University Press, 1987.

Grotstein, J. 'Perspectives on self psychology', in A. Goldberg (ed.) *Self Psychology and the Future of Psychoanalysis*, New York: International Universities Press, 1983.

Gunn, J. 'The treatment of psychopaths', in R. Gaind (ed.) *Current Themes in Psychiatry*, London: Macmillan, 1978.

Hacker, P.M. 'Thought, language and reality', *Times Literary Supplement*, 17 February 1997, 8.

Hall, A.R. *Isaac Newton: Adventure in Thought*, Cambridge: Cambridge University Press, 1996.

Happe, F. *Autism*, London: University College London Press, 1994, 34–66.

Happe, F. 'Study in Greek central coherence at low levels', *Journal of Child Psychology and Psychiatry*, 1996, 37: 873–7.

Happe, F. 'Autism: cognitive deficit or cognitive style?', *Trends in Cognitive Sciences*, 1999, 3(6): 216–22.

Happe, F. 'Parts and wholes, meaning and minds', in S. Baron-Cohen, H. Tager-Flusberg and D. Cohen (eds) *Understanding Other Minds*, Oxford: Oxford University Press, 2000.

Hare, R.D. *Manual for the Hare Psychopathy Checklist – Revised*, Toronto: Multi-Health Systems, 1991.

Hart, M. *The 100*, London: Simon and Schuster, 1993.

Haussmann, L. *Wittgenstein als Volksschullehrer*. See also version published in *Club Vultair*, vol. 4, Hamburg: Rohalt Verlag, 1970, 391-6.

Hetherington, G. 'Wittgenstein in Ireland: an account of his various visits from 1934 to 1949', in F.A. Flowers (ed.) *Portraits of Wittgenstein*, vol. 4, Bristol: Thoemmes Press, 1999.

Hijab, W.A. 'Wittgenstein on the future of philosophy', *Proceedings of the 24th International Wittgenstein Symposium*, Kirchberg-am-Wechsel, 2001, p. 313.

Hijab, W.A. 'Wittgenstein's Missing Map', *Proceedings of the 24th International Wittgenstein Symposium*, Kirchberg-am-Wechsel, 2001, p. 315.

Hill, A.L. 'Idiots savants: rate of incidence', *Perceptual and Motor Skills*, 1977, 44: 161–2.

Hintikka, A.M. 'Dialogues with inner pictures: Ludwig Wittgenstein as dyslexic', paper presented at the *Ludwig Wittgenstein Society Meeting*, Kirchberg-am-Wechsel, 2002, p. 4.

Hobson, P. 'The intersubjective foundations of thoughts', in S. Braten (ed.) *Intersubjective Communication and Emotion in Early Ontogeny*, Cambridge: Cambridge University Press, 1998.

Hollander, E., Cartwright, C., Wong, C., De Caria, C., Delgiudice-Asch, G., Ruchsbaum, M. and Aronowitz, B. 'A dimensional approach to the autism spectrum', *CNS Spectrums*, 1988, 3(3): 22–39.

Howe, M.A. *Genius Explained*, Cambridge: Cambridge University Press, 1999.

Hudson, L. 'Creativity', in *Oxford Companion to the Mind*, Oxford: Oxford University Press, 1987, 171–2.

Hughes-Hallet, K. 'How best to disturb silence', *New Statesman*, 14 May 2001, 39.

Hyman, R. *The Pan Dictionary of Famous Quotations*, London: Grange Books, 1993.

Jardine, L. 'Female muse', *New Statesman*, 21 June 1999, 48.

Jeffares, A.M. (coll., ed., ann.) *Oliver St John Gogarty*, Gerrards Cross, Buckinghamshire: Colin Smythe CTD, 2001.

Johannessen, K., Larson, R. and Amas, K. *Wittgenstein and Norway*, Sullum: Forlag, 1994.

Jones, James H., *A.C. Kinsey, A Public/Private Life*, New York: Norton, 1997.

Jordan, D.R. *Dyslexia in the Classroom*, Columbus, OH: Merrill, 1972.

Jordan, R. and Powell, S. *Understanding and Teaching Children with Autism*, Chichester: Wiley, 1995.

Kanigel, R. *The Man Who Knew Infinity – A Life of the Genius Ramanujan*, New York: Charles Scribner's Sons, 1991.

Kanner, L. 'Autistic disturbances of affective contact', *The Nervous Child*, 1943, 2: 217.

Kanner, L. 'The conception of wholes to parts in early infantile autism', *American Journal of Psychiatry*, 1951, 108: 23–9.

Kanner, L. and Lesser, L. 'Early infantile autism', *Psychiatric Clinics of North America*, 1958, 5: 711–30.

Kasari, C., Chamberlain, B. and Bauminger, N. 'Social emotions and social relationships: can children with autism compensate?', in J. Burack, T. Charman, N. Yirmiya and P. Zelazo (eds) *The Development of Autism*, New Jersey: Lawrence Erlbaum, 2001.

Kaufman, W. 'Preface', in W.W. Bartley *Wittgenstein*, London: Quartet Books, 1977.

Kee, R. 'The lay cardinal', *Times Literary Supplement*, December 1993, 4.

Kendell, R. 'The distinction between personality disorder and mental illness', *British Journal of Psychiatry*, 2002, 180: 110–114.

Kenny, A. *Wittgenstein*, London: Penguin, 1973.

Kenny, A. *A Life in Oxford*, London: John Murray, 1999.

Kershaw, I. *Hitler 1889–1936: Hubris*, London: Allen Lane, 1998.

Keynes, J.M. *Newton the Man*, Royal Society, Cambridge: Cambridge University Press, 1947.

Kinsbourne, M. and Caplan, P. *Children's Learning and Attention Problems*, New York: Little Brown and Company, 1979.

Kinsey, A.C. *Sexual Behaviour in the Human Male*, Philadelphia: Sanders, 1948.

Klagge, J.C. 'Wittgenstein's community', in *Metaphysics in the Post-metaphysical Age: Proceedings of the 22nd International Wittgenstein Symposium*, Kirchberg-am-Wechsel, 1999, p. 336.

Klagge, J.C. 'Metaphysics in the post-metaphysical age', *Proceedings of the 22nd International Wittgenstein Symposium*, Kirchberg-am-Wechsel, 1999, p. 333.

Klagge, J.C. and Nordman, A. (eds) *Philosophical Occasions*, Indianapolis: Hackett Publishing Company, 1993.

Klin, A. and Volkmar, F. 'Asperger's syndrome', in D.J. Cohen and F. Volkmar (eds) *Handbook of Autism and Pervasive Developmental Disorders*, New York: Wiley, 1997.

Klin, A., Schulz, R. and Cohen, D. 'Theory of mind in action: developmental perspectives on social neuroscience', in S. Baron-Cohen, H. Tager-Flusberg and D. Cohen (eds) *Understanding Other Minds*, Oxford: Oxford University Press, 2000.

Koenig, K., Tsatsanis, K. and Volkmar, F. 'Neurobiology and genetics of autism', in J. Burack, T. Charman, N. Yirmiya and P. Zelazo (eds) *The Development of Autism*, New Jersey: Lawrence Erlbaum, 2001.

Kretschmer, E. *Physique and Character* (trans. W.J. Sprott), London: Kegan Paul Trench and Trubner, 1925.

Kuehn, M. *Kant*, Cambridge: Cambridge University Press, 2001.

Kugler, B. 'The differentiation between autism and Asperger's syndrome', *Autism*, 1998, 2(1): 11–32.

Kumra, S. 'Multidimensionally impaired disorder', *Journal of the American Academy of Child and Adolescent Psychiatry*, 1998, 37(11): 1125–6.

Langer, W.C. *The Mind of Adolf Hitler*, New York: Basic Books, 1972.

Laplanche, J. and Pontalis, J.D. *The Language of Psychoanalysis*, London: Hogarth Press, 1973.

Lee, H. 'Tracking the untrackable', *New York Review of Books*, 12 April 2002, 55.

Leitner, B. *The Architecture of Ludwig Wittgenstein*, London: Studio Publications, 1973.

Leitner, B. *The Architecture of Ludwig Wittgenstein: a Documentation*, New York: New York Universities Press, 1976.

Levi, A.W. 'Wittgenstein once more: a response to critics', *Telos*, 1979, 40: 165–73.

Lewes, K. 'Catalyst for a cultural change', *Science*, 1997, 578: 2068–9.

Loizzo, J. 'Intersubjectivity in Wittgenstein and Freud: other minds and the foundations of psychiatry', *Theoretical Medicine*, 1997, 18: 379–400.

Lombroso, C. *The Man of Genius*, London: Walter Scott, 1891.

Lykken, D. 'The genetics of genius', in A. Steptoe (ed.) *Genius and the Mind*, Oxford: Oxford University Press, 1998.

McGahern, J. review of T. Brown *The Life of W.B. Yeats – a Critical Biography*, Dublin: Gill and Macmillan, 1999, *The Irish Times*, 27 November 1999, 12.

McGinn, M. 'Hi Ludwig!', *Times Literary Supplement*, 26 May 2000, 24.

McGuinness, B. (ed.) *Letters from Ludwig Wittgenstein with a Memoir by Paul Engelmann*, Oxford: Blackwell, 1967.

McGuinness, B.F. *Wittgenstein A Life – Young Ludwig (1889–1921)*, London: Penguin, 1988.

McGuinness, B. and von Wright, G.H. (eds) *Letters to Russell, Keynes and Moore*, Oxford: Blackwell, 1974.

McGuinness, B.F. and von Wright, G.H. (eds) *Briefe, Briefwechsel mit B. Russell, G.E. Moore, J.M. Keynes, F.P. Ramsey, W. Eccles, P. Engelmann, und L. von Ficker*, Frankfurt: Suhrkamp, 1980.

McKenna, K., Gordon, C.T., Lenane, M., Kaysen, D., Faitey, K. and Rapoport, J.L. 'Looking for childhood onset schizophrenia. The first 71 cases screened', *Journal of the American Academy of Child and Adolescent Psychiatry*, 1994, 33: 636–44.

Maddox, B. *George's Ghosts: A New Life of W.B. Yeats*, London: Picador, 1999.

Magee, B. *The Great Philosophers*, London: BBC Books, 1987.

Magee, B. *Confessions of a Philosopher*, London: Weidenfeld & Nicolson, 1997.

Mahon, J. 'The great philosopher who came to Ireland', in F.A. Flowers (ed.) *Portraits of Wittgenstein*, Bristol: Thoemmes Press, 1999, vol. 4.

Malcolm, N. *Ludwig Wittgenstein: a Memoir (with a biographical sketch by G.H. von Wright)*, 2nd edn, Oxford: Oxford University Press, 1984.

Malcolm, N. *Wittgenstein: A Religious Point of View*, London: Routledge, 1993.

Marshall, J.C. 'The meaning of Wittgenstein', *Nature*, 1990, 348: 384.

Marshall, J.C. 'Unscientific postscript', *Nature*, 1990, 347: 435.

Masefield, J. *Some Memories of W.B. Yeats*, New York: Macmillan, 1940.

Masefield, J. *So Long to Learn: Chapters of an Autobiography*, London: Heinemann, 1952.

Matthews, S. and Walker, W. *The Deviant's Advantage*, New York: Crown Business, 2002.

Mayes, S., Calhoun, S. and Crites, D. 'Does DSM-IV Asperger's disorder exist?', *Journal of Abnormal Child Psychology*, 2001, 29(3): 63.

Meisner, H. 'Phenomenology of the self', in A. Goldberg (ed.) *Self Psychology and the Future of Psychoanalysis*, New York: International Universities Press, 1983.

Mesibov, G., Shea, V. and Adam, L. *Understanding Asperger's Syndrome and High Functioning Autism*, Lancaster: Kluwer Academic/Plenum Publishers, 2001.

Mikhail, E.H. *W.B. Yeats: Interviews and Recollections*, vol. 1, London: Macmillan, 1977.

Miller, J. and Ozonoff, S. 'Did Asperger's cases have Asperger's disorder? A research note', *Journal of Child Psychology and Psychiatry*, 1997, 38: 247–51.

Millon, T., Davis, R., Millon, C., Escovar, L. and Meagher, S. *Personality Disorders in Modern Life*, New York: Wiley, 2000.

Monk, T. *Ludwig Wittgenstein – the Duty of Genius*, London: Jonathan Cape, 1990.

Moore, G.E. *Philosophical Papers*, London: Allen & Unwin, 1959.

Moore, G.E. 'Wittgenstein's lectures', in J.C. Klagge and A. Nordman (eds) *Philosophical Occasions 51*, Indianapolis: Hackett Publishing Company, 1993.

Moorehead, C. *Bertrand Russell*, London: Sinclair-Stephenson, 1992, p. 338.

Mordell, L.J. 'Ramanujan', *Nature*, 1941, 141: 647.

Murphy, W. *The Prodigal Father: the Life of John Butler Yeats*, Ithaca, NY: Cornell University Press, 1978.

Murphy, W.M. *Family Secrets: William Butler Yeats and his Relatives*, Syracuse: Syracuse University Press, 1995.

Murphy, W.M. *Irish Arts Review*, 1999, 15: 204–5.

Murray P. (ed.) *Genius: the History of an Idea*, Oxford: Basil Blackwell, 1989.

Nagel, T. 'What is it about lemons?', *London Review of Books*, 2001, 23: 25–6.

National Autistic Society (United Kingdom) Fact Sheet on Autism. London: National Autistic Society, 2001, 2, reprint.

Nunberg, H. *Principles of Psychoanalysis*, New York: International University Press, 1955.

O'Brien, M. *De Valera, Fianna Fáil and the Irish Press*, Dublin: Irish Academic Press, 2001.

Ochs, S. and Capps, L. 'Narrating the self', *Annual Review of Anthropology*, 1996, 25: 19–43.

O'Faolain, J. 'A snug and needy place', *Times Literary Supplement*, 24 March 2000, 16.

Ollard, R. *A Man of Contradictions – a Life of A.L. Rowse*, London: Allen Lane, Penguin Press, 1999.

Ostwald, P. and Zegans, L. *The Pleasures and Perils of Genius*, Madison: International University Press, 1973.

Pilgrim, D. 'Personality disorder', *British Journal of Psychiatry*, 2002, 183: 77.

Pinsent, D. in G.H. von Wright (ed.) *A Portrait of Wittgenstein as a Young Man – from the Diary of David Pinsent, 1912–1914*, Oxford: Basil Blackwell, 1990.

Pirito, J. *Education Forum*, 1995, 59: 362–70.

Popper, K. *Objective Knowledge*, Oxford: Oxford University Press, 1972.

Porter, R. *The Social History of Madness*, London: Weidenfeld & Nicolson, 1987.

Porter, R. in A. Steptoe (ed.) *Forward Genius and the Mind*, Oxford: Oxford University Press, 1998.

Pound, E. and Shakespeare, D. *New Free Woman*, 15 December 1913, 282.

Pyle, H. *Jack B. Yeats – a Biography*, 2nd edn, London: André Deutsch, 1989.

Quigley, J. *The Grammar of Autobiography*, London: Lawrence Erlbaum, 2000.

Radford, J. *Child Prodigies and Exceptional Early Achievers*, New York: Harvester Wheatsheaf, 1990.

Rakitzis, E.T. *Nature*, 1991, 351: 179.

Ramsey, F. 'Letter to his mother, 20th September 1923', quoted in B.A. Scharfstein *The Philosophers: Their Lives and the Nature of their Thought*, New York: Oxford University Press, 1980, p. 463.

Ranganathan, S.R. *Ramanujan: the Man and the Mathematician*, London: Asia Publishing House, 1967.

Rankin, R.A. 'Ramanujan as a patient', *Proceedings of the Indian Academy of Science*, 1984, 93(2, 3): 79–100.

Rapin, I. and Allen, D. 'Developmental language disorder', in V. Kirk (ed.) *Neuropsychology and Language Reading and Spelling*, New York: Academic Press, 1983, pp. 155–84.

Ratey, J. *A User's Guide to the Brain*, London: Little Brown and Company, 2001.

Rhees, R. 'Wittgenstein', *The Human World*, 1974, 14: 71.

Rhees, R. (ed.) *Ludwig Wittgenstein: Personal Recollections*, Oxford: Blackwell, 1981, 140.

Rhees, R. *Recollections of Wittgenstein*, Oxford: Oxford University Press, 1984.

Rimland, B. and Fein, D. 'Special talents of autistic savants', in L. Obler and D. Fein (eds) *Exceptional Brains*, New York: Guilford Press, 1988.

Rogers, B. *A.J. Ayer*, London: Chatto & Windus, 1999.

Roscoe, T. (ed.) *Thoughts on Various Subjects in the Works of Jonathan Swift*, London, 1841, vol. 2.

Rossman, J. *Industrial Creativity*, New York: University Books, 1964, p. 2.

Roudinesco, E. *Jacques Lacan*, Cambridge: Polity Press, 1999.

Rourke, B.P. 'The syndrome of non-verbal learning disabilities: developmental manifestations in neurological disease, disorder and dysfunction', *The Clinical Neuropsychologist*, 1988, 2: 293–330.

Russell, B. *Autobiography*, vol. II, London: Allen & Unwin, 1968.

Ryan, D. *Unique Dictator – A Study of Eamon de Valera*, London: Barker, 1936.

Sacks, O. *An Anthropologist on Mars: Seven Paradoxical Tales*, London: Picador, 1995.

Sacks, O. 'Foreword', Temple Grandin, *Thinking in Pictures, and Other Reports from My Life with Autism*, New York: Doubleday, 1995.

Scharfstein, R.A. *The Philosophers: Their Lives and the Nature of their Thought*, New York: Oxford University Press, 1980.

Schmahmann, J.D. and Sherman, J.C. 'The cerebellar cognitive affective syndrome', *Brain*, 1998, 121: 561–79.

Schopler, E. 'Convergence of learning disability, higher-level autism, and Asperger's syndrome', *Journal of Autism and Developmental Disorders*, 1985, 15(4): 359.

Schopler, E. 'Premature popularisation of Asperger's syndrome', in E. Schopler, G.

Mesibov and L. Kunce (eds), *Asperger's Syndrome or High Functioning Autism*, New York: Plenum Press, 1998.

Schultz, R.E., Romanski, E. and Tsatsanis, K. 'Neurofunctional models of autistic disorder and Asperger's syndrome', in A. Klin, F. Volkmar and S. Sparrow (eds), *Asperger's Syndrome*, New York: Guilford Press, 2000.

Schwarzschild, S. 'Wittgenstein as alienated Jew', *Telos*, 1979, 40: 160–65.

Self, W. 'Oh no, not another silly title', *New Statesman*, 9 April 2001, 51–2.

Siegel, D. 'Memory: an overview, with emphasis on developmental, interpersonal, and neurobiological aspects', *Journal of the American Academy of Child and Adolescent Psychiatry*, 2001, 40(9): 997–1010.

Sigman, M. and Capps, L. *Children with Autism*, Cambridge, MA: Harvard University Press, 1997.

Simonton, D.K. *Greatness: Who Makes History and Why*, New York: Guilford Press, 1994.

Slater-Walker, G.C. *An Asperger Marriage*, London: Jessica Kingsley, 2002.

Smythies, J.R. 'Wittgenstein's paranoia', *Nature*, 1991, 9: 350.

Smythies, J.R. 'Alas poor Yorick', *Nature*, 1994, 9: 371.

Spinoza, B. *Ethica*, 5, Prop XXV, The Hague: van Vloten and Land, 1914.

Ssucharewa, G.E. 'Die schizoiden Psychopathien im Kindesalter', *Monatschrift fur Psychiatrie und Neurologie*, 1926, 60: 235–61.

Steiner, G. *After Babel*, Oxford: Oxford University Press, 1998.

Steptoe A. (ed.) *Genius and the Mind*, Oxford: Oxford University Press, 1988.

Stevens, H. *The Life and Music of Béla Bartók*, 3rd edn, prepared by Malcolm Gillies, Oxford: Clarendon Press, 1993.

Stone, V. 'The role of the frontal lobe and amygdala in theory of mind', in S. Baron-Cohen, H. Tager-Flusberg and D. Cohen (eds) *Understanding Other Minds*, Oxford: Oxford University Press, 2000, p. 254.

Storr, A. *Solitude*, New York: The Free Press, 1988.

Storr, A. *The School of Genius*, London: André Deutsch, 1988.

Strawson, P.F. 'At home in the "space of reasons"', *Times Literary Supplement*, 25 November 1994, 12.

Stuckley, W. in A. Hastings White (ed.) *Memories of Sir Isaac Newton's Life*, London: Taylor & Francis, 1936.

Tantam, D. 'Lifelong eccentricity and social isolation: Asperger's syndrome or schizoid personality disorder', *British Journal of Psychiatry*, 1988, 153: 783.

Tantam, D. 'Adolescence and adulthood of individuals with Asperger's syndrome', in A. Klin, F. Volkmar and S. Sparrow (eds) *Asperger's Syndrome*, New York: Guilford Press, 2000.

Tantam, D. 'Asperger's syndrome in adulthood', in U. Frith (ed.) *Autism and Asperger's Syndrome*, Cambridge: Cambridge University Press, 1991.

Towbin, K. 'Pervasive Developmental Disorder Not Otherwise Specified', in D. Cohen and F. Volkmar (eds) *Handbook of Autism and Developmental Disorders*, New York: Wiley, 1997.

Tsai, L. 'From autism to Asperger's disorder', *American Academy of Child and Adolescent Psychiatry Conference*, Hawaii, Washington, DC: American Academy of Child and Adolescent Psychiatry, 2001, pp. 5–6.

Turnbull, H. *Correspondence of Isaac Newton*, Cambridge. Cambridge University Press, 1959.

van Krevelen, A.D. 'Early infantile autism and autistic psychopathy', *Journal of Autism and Childhood Schizophrenia*, 1971, 1(1): 84–5.

van Krevelen, A. and Kuipers, C. 'The psychopathology of autistic psychopathy', *Acta Paedopsychiatricia*, 1962, 29: 22–31.

von Wright, G.H. in collaboration with Heikki Nyman, *Culture and Value*, Oxford: Blackwell, 1980.

Wall, R. *Wittgenstein in Ireland* (trans. Martin Chalmers), London: Reaktion Books, 2000.

Warnock, M. *A Memoir*, London: Duckworth, 2000.

Weekes, D.J. and Ward, K. *Eccentrics: the Scientific Investigation*, Stirling: Stirling University Press, 1988.

Weininger, O. *Sex and Character*, London: Heinemann, 1906.

West, T. *In the Mind's Eye*, Buffalo, NY: Prometheus Books, 1991.

White, M. *Isaac Newton – the Last Sorcerer*, London: Fourth Estate, 1997.

White, M. and Gribbin, J. *Darwin – a Life in Science*, London: Simon & Schuster, 1995.

Whyte, I.E. 'The perfect light bulb', *Times Literary Supplement*, 11 November 1994, 6.

Widger, T.A., Cadoret, R., Hare, R.D. and Robus, L. 'DSM-IV antisocial personality disorder field trial', *Journal of Abnormal Psychology*, 1996, 105: 3–16.

Wijdeveld, P. *Ludwig Wittgenstein, Architect*, London: Thames & Hudson, 1994.

Willerman, L., Schultz, R., Rutledge, J.N. and Bigler, N. 'In vivo brain size and intelligence', *Journal of Intelligence*, 1991, 15: 223–8.

Wing, L. 'Asperger's syndrome – a clinical account', *Psychological Medicine*, 1981, 11: 115–29.

Wing, L. 'Letter: Clarification on Asperger's syndrome', *Journal of Autism and Developmental Disorders*, 1986, 16: 513–15.

Wing, L. 'Asperger's syndrome and Kanner's autism', in U. Frith (ed.) *Autism and Asperger's Syndrome*, Cambridge: Cambridge University Press, 1991.

Wing, L. 'The relationship between Asperger's syndrome and Kanner's autism', in U. Frith (ed.) *Autism and Asperger's Syndrome*, Cambridge: Cambridge University Press, 1991.

Wing, L. *The Autistic Spectrum*, London: Constable, 1996.

Wing, L. 'Syndromes of autism and atypical development', in D. Cohen and F. Volkmar (eds) *Handbook of Autism and Pervasive Developmental Disorders*, New York: Wiley, 1997.

Wing, L. 'The history of Asperger's syndrome', in E. Schopler, G. Mesibov and L. Kunce (eds) *Asperger's Syndrome or High Functioning Autism?* New York: Plenum Press, 1998.

Wing, L. and Gould, J. 'Severe impairments of social interaction and associated abnormalities in children: epidemiology and classification', *Journal of Autism and Childhood Schizophrenia*, 1979, 9: 11–29.

Wittgenstein, L. *Vermischte Bemerkungen*, Frankfurt am main/Oxford: Suhrkamp/Blackwell, 1977/1978.

Wittgenstein, L. in G. Anscombe, R. Rhees and G.H. von Wright (eds) *Philosophical Investigations*, Oxford: Basil Blackwell, 1953.

Wittgenstein, L. in G.H. von Wright with Heikki Nyman (eds) *Culture and Value*, Oxford: Basil Blackwell, 1980.

Wolff, L. *The Journey not the Arrival Matters*, London: Hogarth Press, 1969.

Wolff, S. 'Schizoid personality in childhood: the links with schizophrenia spectrum disorders, Asperger's syndrome and elective mutism', in E. Schopler, G. Mesibov and L. Kunce (eds) *Asperger's Syndrome or High Functioning Autism*, New York: Plenum, 1988.

Wolff, S. *Loners: the Life Path of Unusual Children*, London: Routledge, 1995.

Wolff, S. and Barlow, A. 'Schizoid personality in childhood: a comparative study of schizoid, autistic and normal children', *Journal of Child Psychology and Psychiatry*, 1979, 19: 175–80.

World Health Organisation, *The ICD-10 Classification of Mental and Behavioural Disorders*, Geneva: WHO, 1992, pp. 255–9.

Yeats, J.B. in Joseph Hone (ed.) *Letters to His Son W.B. Yeats, 1869–1922*, London: Faber & Faber, 1944.

Yeats, M.B. *Cast a Cold Eye – Memories of a Poet's Son and Politician*, Dublin: Blackwater Press, 1999.

Yeung-Courchesne, R. and Courchesne, E. 'From impasse to insight in autism research', *Development and Psychopathology*, 1997, 9: 394.

Index